Macroeconomic Modelling in a
Changing World

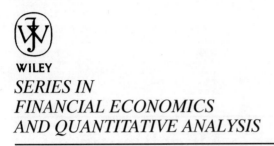

WILEY

SERIES IN
FINANCIAL ECONOMICS
AND QUANTITATIVE ANALYSIS

Series Editor: Stephen Hall, *London Business School, UK*

Editorial Board: Robert F. Engle, *University of California, USA*
John Flemming, *European Bank, UK*
Lawrence R. Klein, *University of Pennsylvania, USA*
Helmut Lütkepohl, *Humboldt University, Germany*

Macroeconomic Modelling in a Changing World

Towards a Common Approach

Edited by

Chris Allen and Stephen Hall

JOHN WILEY & SONS

Chichester • New York • Brisbane • Toronto • Singapore

Other Wiley Editorial Offices

John Wiley & Sons, Inc., 605 Third Avenue,
New York, NY 10158-0012, USA

Jacaranda Wiley Ltd, 33 Park Road, Milton,
Queensland 4064, Australia

John Wiley & Sons (Canada) Ltd, 22 Worcester Road,
Rexdale, Ontario M9W 1L1, Canada

John Wiley & Sons (Asia) Pte Ltd, 2 Clementi Loop #02 01,
Jin Xing Distripark, Singapore 129809

Library of Congress Cataloging-in-Publication Data

Macroeconomic modelling in a changing world : towards a common
approach / edited by Chris Allen and Stephen Hall.
p.   cm. — (Series in financial economics and quantitative
analysis)
Includes bibliographical references and index.
ISBN 0-471-95791-7 (hardback)
1. Great Britain — Economic conditions — 1945-1993 — Econometric
models. 2. Great Britain — Economic conditions — 1993- — Econometric
models. 3. Great Britain — Economic policy — 1945- — Econometric
models. 4. Macroeconomics — Mathematical models.   I. Allen, Chris.
II. Hall, Stephen, 1953- . III. Series.
HC256.6.M278 1996
339.5′0941 — dc20   96-22708
                                                     CIP

British Library Cataloguing in Publication Data

A catalogue record for this book is available from the British Library

ISBN 0-471-95791-7

Typeset in 10/12pt Times by Laser Words, Madras, India
Printed and bound in Great Britain by Biddles Ltd, Guildford
This book is printed on acid-free paper responsibly manufactured from sustainable forestation,
for which at least two trees are planted for each one used for paper production.

Contents

Contents ———————————————————————————— ix

List of Contributors

CHRIS ALLEN
Sussex University

HONG BAI
Centre for Economic Forecasting, London Business School

ANINDYA BANERJEE
Wadham College and I.E.S.

ANTHONY GARRATT
Bank of England

STEPHEN HALL
The Management School, Imperial College of Science and Technology

JAMES NIXON
Centre for Economic Forecasting, London Business School

ANDREW SENTANCE
Centre for Economic Forecasting, London Business School

RON SMITH
Birkbeck College

JOHN O'SULLIVAN
Centre for Economic Forecasting, London Business School

GIOVANNI URGA
Centre for Economic Forecasting, London Business School

JOHN WHITLEY
Bank of England

Acknowledgements

All the contributors to this volume wish to acknowledge the hard work and patience of Jane Wright and to thank her for her help in the completion of this project.

Series Preface

This series aims to publish books which give authoritative accounts of major new topics in financial economics and general quantitative analysis. The coverage of the series includes both macro and micro economics and its aim is to be of interest to practitioners and policy-makers as well as the wider academic community.

The development of new techniques and ideas in econometrics has been rapid in recent years and these developments are now being applied to a wide range of areas and markets. Our hope is that this series will provide a rapid and effective means of communicating these ideas to a wide international audience and that in turn this will contribute to the growth of knowledge, the exchange of scientific information and techniques and the development of cooperation in the field of economics.

Stephen Hall
London Business School, UK and
Imperial College, UK

INTRODUCTION
Macroeconomic Modelling: A Perspective

STEPHEN G. HALL

1 INTRODUCTION

The last 15 years have seen an enormous amount of detailed work on the large econometric models across a very broad research front, which has included such diverse areas as pure econometric methodology in the form of dynamic modelling and cointegration to pure theoretical developments in the development of the supply side. In this introduction I will try to stand back from this detailed work and attempt to paint the broad picture of the motivation and success of this research strategy. I hope it will serve as a useful introduction to the later chapters in this book which essentially attempt to implement and combine the research strands I will be discussing here.

Macroeconomic modelling is an area that has a long tradition and literature stemming from the pioneering work of Tinbergen (Tinbergen (1937)) and the Cowles commission (Klein (1950)). An extensive survey of the development of modelling may be found in Bodkin, Klein and Marwah (1991). It grew rapidly in importance during the late 1950s and 1960s, going on to achieve a very influential role in macroeconomic policy-making during the 1970s. Its failure to deliver the detailed economic control which it had seemed to promise then led to a barrage of attacks, ranging from disillusion and scepticism on the part of policy-makers to detailed and well argued academic criticism of the basic methodology of the approach.

Perhaps the most powerful and influential of these academic arguments came from Sims (1980) in his article 'Macroeconomics and Reality'. Sims argued, on

Macroeconomic Modelling in a Changing World. Edited by C. Allen and S. Hall
© 1997 John Wiley & Sons Ltd

three quite separate grounds, against the basic process of model identification that lies at the heart of the Cowles Commission methodology. First, that economic theory gives rise to identification restrictions that are typically more complex than those traditionally applied in macroeconometric models. In particular that theory normally implies complex cross-equation restrictions that require system estimation and which cannot be imposed on a single equation basis. Secondly, that traditional identification conditions are often met simply because of the presence of dynamics in the models. Sims argued that this identification is spurious and technically invalid, as purely dynamic terms cannot help in structural identification in the conventional sense. Finally, that the importance of expectations effects and the interaction of policy regimes and agents expectations make identification very difficult.

Sims argued that any one of these problems would form a challenging, but feasible, research agenda, but that 'Doing all of these at once would be a program which is so challenging as to be impossible in the short run'. He then proposed a methodology, based on vector autoregressive (VAR) models, which tried to avoid the identification problem as far as possible. This proposal has given rise to a major branch of empirical research literature. Other researchers have taken this cue to investigate alternative strategies, the most notable of which has been work undertaken on Computable General Equilibrium (CGE) models which now have an important role in the policy debate.

While parts of the academic community have been exploring these alternative strategies, the mainstream macroeconometric modellers have attempted a research agenda that directly confronts Sims' 'impossible' challenge. Because this approach is, by definition, diverse, and covers all the areas of difficulty mentioned above, it is generally not recognised as a single unified research program but rather it is discussed in isolated parts. This chapter attempts to bring together these research strands and to give an overview of the progress that has been made in macroeconometric modelling since the publication of Sims' paper. I will argue that considerable progress has been made in all three of the areas that Sims highlighted but that many questions and difficulties still remain. At the same time we have come to understand some of the limitations of the VAR and CGE paradigms, which leads me to the conclusion that structural macroeconometric modelling still remains the most promising approach to understanding macroeconomic behaviour generally, and is the most likely approach to provide a really powerful policy tool.

The 1980s and the first half of the 1990s have been a time of increasing disenchantment on the part of policy-makers and governments with large econometric models partly because of their perceived failure as a policy tool but mainly because of their failings in forecasting. I will argue that this is due partly to the developments that have been taking place in modelling itself. As we have experimented with the ideas and techniques that have grown up to confront the Sims arguments, the models themselves have gone from being relatively simple and robust (complex only by virtue of their size) constructs to highly sophisticated tools which include expectations mechanisms, system estimation, cointegration and long-run identification. While these developments are aimed at producing better models, there have clearly been phases of model development when new ideas were only partly understood or were still being developed. In fact, the more sophisticated models undoubtedly performed worse than their simpler predecessors, both as forecasting and policy analysis tools. Macroeconometric modelling is, however, a progressive strategy, in the sense that the use of formal econometric tools allows us to progressively rule out bad models. I believe we are approaching the point at which models are emerging that are both sophisticated and offer real insights into policy and forecasting problems.

The structure of this chapter is as follows. The next three sections outline the developments that have taken place in modelling to confront each of Sims' major criticisms; Section 5 outlines some of the main problems that have emerged in the area of CGE and VAR modelling; and finally Section 6 draws some general conclusions.

2 DYNAMICS, IDENTIFICATION AND THE LONG RUN

Perhaps the most cogent criticism of the identification of large macroeconometric models made by Sims was that the conventional formal conditions of identification were misinterpreted when the models contained a significant number of dynamic terms. His argument rested on Hatanaka (1975) which showed that if the maximum lag length of an equation, or the order of serial correlation of the error process, had to be estimated, then the lagged dependent variables could not be used in identification. So if we consider a model in vector error correction form the question of identification has to focus on the error correction terms themselves rather than exploiting the dynamic effects, although Sims did not express his conclusion in quite this way.

Developments in cointegration have led many of us to a very similar conclusion, though by a rather different route. The initial work in the area of cointegration (Granger (1983, 1986), Granger and Weiss (1983), Hall and Brooks (1985), Hall (1986), Engle and Granger (1987)) considered only the case of a single cointegrating vector. This was often interpreted as a structural identified relationship, although the formal theory made it clear that in a multivariate context it was a reduced-form equilibrium relationship of the whole system and a structural interpretation was not correct. It quickly became apparent that thinking about structural systems required the presence of a number of distinct cointegrating vectors. Johansen (1988) provided the estimation technology to deal with systems of multiple cointegrating vectors, in the sense that testing the number of significant cointegrating vectors and estimating the cointegrating space became feasible. But this did not solve the fundamental problem of identification that still existed within these systems. Johansen's (1988) maximum likelihood technique essentially estimates the cointegrating space of a reduced-form VAR system. The system itself is not identified and so none of the cointegrating vectors produced by the estimation technique can be given a structural interpretation.

The identification problem was first fully confronted by Davidson and Hall (1991) who showed how a structural set of 'target' relationships (in their terminology) would be recombined in the reduced-form VAR system. They also showed how they could be identified in a system only by full system estimation techniques that applied a set of cross-equation restrictions similar to the standard identification conditions except that they are applied only to the long-run relationships. This issue has been further studied in Phillips (1991) and Johansen (1992), and a full structural approach has been developed by Pesaran and Shin (1994) who provide a formal discussion of the conditions for identification and a testing procedure for the over-identifying restrictions.

This series of developments then arrived at a conclusion that broadly parallels that of Sims. The important aspect of a structural model is the long-run relationships that drive it and these need to be estimated and identified separately from the dynamics. This outcome is, however, much more positive than seemed to be likely following Sims' original article since we have also developed the means to estimate and test these structural relationships and over-identifying restrictions. So, far from being a serious problem, this line of research has led to a more powerful modelling strategy that has a clearer relationship with economic theory and which promises to provide better models from both a statistical and theoretical perspective (Hendry and Mizon (1993), Engle and Granger (1991).

3 EXPECTATIONS AND LEARNING

The problems posed by the importance of expectations effects in macroeconomics was another of the central difficulties of identification that Sims highlighted. At the time of his article expectations had already become a central issue in modelling following an explosion of theoretical research on this topic in the 1970s (Walters (1971), Lucas (1972a, b, 1973, 1975), Sargent (1973, 1976), Sargent and Wallace (1973, 1975, 1976), Barro (1976, 1977) and Kydland and Prescott (1977)). Even as Sims was writing, macroeconometric modellers were beginning to investigate the usefulness of these ideas in an empirical setting. The initial models (Sargent (1976) and Taylor (1979)) were essentially more elaborate versions of the simple theoretical models and not true econometric models. The first estimated macroeconometric models incorporating rational expectations (RE) were Anderson (1979) (which included only current dated expectations of current dated variables) and Fair (1979) (a fairly large model of 84 equations including expectations of future prices in the bond and stock markets). Introducing RE terms into the Fair model required the development of new model solution procedures, which had been discussed, but not carried out, in Anderson (1979). Macroeconometric modellers then embarked on a major research effort both to develop techniques and tools that were appropriate for the implementation of RE into these large non-linear models and to understand the full implications of RE for both policy analysis and forecasting.

Despite the path-breaking work carried out by Fair, the main focus of development switched from the United States to the United Kingdom with the publication in 1980 of the first results from the Liverpool model (see Minford *et al.* (1984)). From this point on subsequent developments in solution techniques and the analysis of non-linear models with rational expectations happened mainly in the United Kingdom. Holly and Corker (1984) reported the introduction of model consistent expectations into the exchange rate and financial sector of the London Business School model. Hall and Henry (1985, 1986) reported the introduction of RE into both the exchange rate sector and the real side of the National Institute model. Westaway and Whittaker (1986) discussed the introduction of RE into HM Treasury's model. The late 1980s saw the spread of RE more widely. Murphy (1989) introduced expectations effects into an Australian model and Lahti and Viren (1989) reported the introduction of RE into a model of the Finnish economy. Masson *et al.* (1988) discussed the first introduction of RE into an international model, the IMF Multimod, and Gurney (1990) introduced RE into the Global Econometric Model (GEM). A large amount of work then began in order to understand fully the implications of these changes for the models. Surveys of some of this work may be found in Fair (1984), Hall and Henry (1988), Fisher *et al.* (1988, 1989), Fisher (1990) and Currie and Hall (1993).

While the introduction of RE into these large models raised a number of difficult issues, some of a purely technical nature, others were more conceptual. A model solution was greatly complicated by the presence of RE, and new solution techniques were needed. The original Fair–Taylor algorithm was quickly supplemented by a range of alternatives. Hall (1985) proposed a more general algorithm and Fisher, Holly and Hughes-Hallett (1985) and Fisher and Hughes-Hallett (1988) developed a family of iteration schemes which are particularly efficient within the overall Hall framework. Holly and Zarrop (1979, 1983) proposed a variant of optimal control procedures as a solution technique and Lipton *et al.* (1982) proposed a variant of the multiple shooting technique used in the engineering literature. Much effort has also gone into the choice of appropriate terminal conditions for the RE model (see Fisher (1990) for a detailed discussion of this issue). A conceptually more difficult problem is the way information sets are used in policy analysis under RE where the modeller can no longer assume that future realisations of exogenous variables are known by agents. This greatly complicates the use of models in policy analysis, as Budd *et al.* (1989) show. A closely related problem to that of the appropriate information set is the time inconsistency problem first highlighted by Kydland and Prescott (1977). Calculating the time inconsistent policy is straightforward and is the result of standard control algorithms. However, calculating the optimal time consistent policy for a large non-linear model is more complex. This problem was addressed in Hall

(1986b), who proposed an algorithm which solved the optimal control problem for the time consistent solution, while Fisher (1990) developed a generalisation of this algorithm.

As Sims foresaw, dealing with expectations effects in econometric models has not been a simple matter. But it is probably true to say that the technical problems of implementing RE have now been overcome and we are in a position to assess how successful this branch of research has been. On the positive side, few model proprietors remain unconvinced as to the importance of expectations effects. Areas such as exchange rate modelling, as well as our understanding of both company and personal sector behaviour, have been improved considerably through the use of explicit models of expectations. Perhaps the most striking example of such an area of positive achievement is the exchange rate. The fact that exchange rates are almost impossible to model in a structural way has become a piece of received wisdom within the economics profession. However, our experience over the last decade has demonstrated that the exchange rate sector is one of the more obvious areas of convergence between the main large models that include rational expectations. The empirical evidence to support this emerging consensus is both strong and consistent across data sets. It rests on the use of a model based on an augmented uncovered arbitrage relationship to represent the fundamental behaviour of investors. If we relax the risk neutrality assumption, define Z_t as a risk premium and augment the model with a general lag structure, then stating the relationship in logs using obvious notation provides an equation of the following form:

$$e_t = \Phi_1(L)e_{t+1} + \Phi_2(L)(r_t - r_{tf}) + \Phi_3(L)z_t \qquad \ldots (1)$$

A series of papers have investigated structural models of this form with surprising success. The initial work was presented in Hall (1987) and subsequent studies have confirmed this general specification (Currie and Hall (1989), Gurney, Henry and Pesaran (1989), Fisher et al. (1991), Hall (1992) and Hall and Garratt (1992a)). Contrasting the success of this approach relative to that of the reduced-form approach normally used suggests strongly that expectations are a crucial factor in exchange rate determination and that the reduced-form treatment of expectations does not make adequate allowance for the instability in expectations formation.

However, this does not mean that the use of model consistent expectations is completely accepted. Simulation and policy exercises using RE often provide rich insights and yet it has not been general practice to use RE in a forecasting context. The reason for this is that the presence of RE tends to cause jumps in the initial period value of a range of variables, most notably the exchange rate, which are considered implausible by the forecasters. Indeed, model simulation properties are often dominated by large initial period jumps which many would find implausible. The reconciliation of these two views is, of course, that agents do not have full model consistent expectations and full information but take time to learn about regime changes and to assimilate new information. In other words expectations are important but rational expectations does not provide a good description of the short-run behaviour of real economic systems. In the short run many aspects of economic activity are much better characterised by either a failure of full credibility, or a learning process of some type, rather than the full RE assumption.

Learning models of expectations have received increasing attention in the theoretical literature over the last decade. The early theoretical literature, e.g. Friedman (1975), Townsend (1978, 1983), Bray (1983), Bray and Kreps (1984) or Frydman (1982), made the assumption that agents knew the true structural model. A slightly weaker informational assumption gives rise to the boundedly rational learning models. Here the general assumption is that agents use some 'reasonable' rule to form expectations and that the form of the rule remains constant over time and that agents 'learn' the parameters of this rule (see, for example, DeCanio (1979), Radner (1982), Bray and Savin (1986)). According to Marcet and Sargent (1988), who summarise the main results and the most recent developments in this literature, the concept of learning is characterised as a mapping of the parameters of the agents' expectations rule from one period to the next. A fixed point of this mapping is then a situation where the parameters of the expectations rule cease to change. Marcet and Sargent (1989a) demonstrate that this fixed point is also a full rational expectations equilibrium. Furthermore, Evans (1983, 1985, 1986), Woodford (1990) and Marcet and Sargent (1989a,b) demonstrate that the use of a simple least squares learning procedure actually rules out many of the undesirable rational equilibria which can arise in conventional rational expectations models.

These ideas have now been extended to the large econometric models. The basic approach is to follow the boundedly rational learning literature by specifying a relatively simple expectations rule and then allowing the parameters of this rule to vary in the light of the expectations errors made by that rule. Over time we would expect the expectations rule to adjust to the particular regime under which the model is operating and an RE solution will result. But in the short term, the learning rule will make mistakes and hopefully give a more plausible path to equilibrium. This approach to the treatment of expectations was first adopted in a large econometric model in the exchange rate sector of the London Business School model of the UK economy (Hall and Garratt (1992a,b)) and it has subsequently been applied to wage behaviour in three countries in the Global Econometric Model (GEM) (Barrell et al. (1992)). Hall and Symanski (1994) reported on some experiments that introduced this type of learning mechanism into the IMF's MULTIMOD.

Once again I would argue that the work that has grown out of Sims' challenge to expectations has resulted in an enormous increase in our understanding of how to model a complex system such as the macroeconomy where agents are themselves intelligent players in a complex game. This line of research has probably had some detrimental effects on the models as we came to learn both how to use RE and its limitations. But once again the models are emerging as a much richer, and hopefully more realistic, representation of reality. This line of investigation is still not complete, and a very serious outstanding question facing the learning approach is: How do we choose an appropriate expectations rule? This may be seen as just another version of Sims' identification problem and the search is still on for an appropriate set of selection criteria.

4 THEORY AND SYSTEMS

In his section on 'the genesis of a priori restrictions', Sims stresses that theory tells us about systems of equations rather than single relationships, such as the almost ideal demand system or the interrelated factor demand systems which come from a standard model of firm behaviour. Before Sims was writing, econometric models had almost uniformly been estimated as sets of individual, unrelated equations. Therefore the extent to which they could legitimately be said to draw on theory for identification was very limited. At most, theory was used to justify exclusion and sign restrictions and, as Sims argued, these restrictions were often highly implausible. This practice would have been justified on the pragmatic grounds that estimating one equation in the 1950s or 1960s was a computational feat and that estimating even a small model as a system was simply infeasible. Since the early 1970s, however, this excuse ceases to have any real force as the power and availability of computers have expanded. In fairness to the large model-builders the climate of academic thinking amongst the econometric community in the 1970s was orientated mainly towards single equation analysis (Davidson *et al.* (1978)). Since the early 1980s, however, there have been two quite distinct strands of development which have moved the models towards more complex system estimation. The first was the introduction of cointegration briefly detailed in Section 2 above, where the developments in multivariate cointegration analysis have inevitably led to the estimation of systems of equations. The second strand was a broad movement across the whole macroeconometric modelling community to make much more use of theory in the specification and estimation of models. This move has been spurred on by a number of quite different influences. Simple time-series econometrics did not seem to give sufficiently precise model estimates without some additional increase in efficiency from theory. The growth of CGE modelling and the illustration that much more could be drawn from theory provided a challenge for econometric modellers. And, perhaps most important, the need for a well-articulated supply side to most macroeconometric models required a quite sophisticated theory to allow the demand and supply sides to relate to each other in a reasonable way.

Developments in this direction have been numerous and I cannot provide anything approaching a full survey here. I shall instead mention just a few examples of system estimation as it has recently been implemented in the large models. In terms of estimation technology, perhaps the most important contribution has been made by Fair (1984) who outlined an algorithm which allows a complete model to be estimated simultaneously by a system instrumental variable technique. Fair applied this technique and contrasted it with standard single equation estimation strategies, although it is worth stressing that the models he used did not embody the complex cross-equation restrictions that might arise from economic theory.

In econometric modelling, theory has been largely used in one of two ways, either to impose restrictions on the dynamics of the model or to impose restrictions across whole subsectors of a model.

Early examples of the use of theory to restrict the dynamics of a model may be found in Henry and Wren-Lewis (1984) or Hall, Henry and Wren-Lewis (1986). These papers used a general quadratic adjustment cost model under rational expectations, following the work of Sargent (1978), to impose symmetric restrictions across both the lagged coefficients and the coefficients on the expectations terms. This type of model was implemented as part of the NIESR model for a range of company sector decision variables including stockbuilding and employment. Providing a direct example of the way the problem of dealing with unrestricted dynamics raised explicitly by Sims in his equations (1)–(5) may be overcome by the direct use of theory. Similar single-equation examples of the use of theory are the consumption functions based on intertemporal optimisation, the IMF's MULTIMOD, the Federal Reserve Board's MX3 and the Strathclyde model (Darby and Ireland (1993)).

One of the first attempts to build a large subsector of a macroeconometric model based around a well-specified theory was the Keating (1985) financial sector of the London Business School model. This model used the Brainard–Tobin mean–variance model of asset demand to estimate a large financial sector which was broadly consistent with economic theory. Courakis (1988) pointed out that this theory did not provide a sufficiently strong set of restrictions to ensure reasonable behaviour under all conditions. Subsequent work by Barr and Cuthbertson (1990) for the Bank of England econometric model used a more detailed theory based on the almost ideal demand system. In the context of that paper it is interesting that theory was being used to impose restrictions on the long-run relationships in a full multivariate cointegrating framework. Another notable use of theory and system estimation is the work of Wren-Lewis which introduced vintage production functions into large econometric models. This was first done with the NIESR model (see Wren-Lewis (1988)) and subsequently applied to the Strathclyde model (Wren-Lewis (1992a)).

A number of approaches to modelling the supply side of the economy have been used in the large models over the last 10 years and I will not attempt to document all these developments here. However, the current version of the London Business School model provides a good representation of current best practice in this area. The supply side of this model (a detailed account may be found in Allen (1994)) is built around an aggregate cost function which is a function of labour, energy, imported inputs and capital. This gives rise to a set of factor demand and price equations that embody the full set of restrictions implied by cost minimisation subject to the parametric form of the cost function. Many studies have used relatively simple functional forms for the basic form of the cost function which are not data admissible. This model avoids this problem by using a dynamic translog flexible functional form which is sufficiently complex to be a good representation of the data in estimation. The restricted cost function gives a measure of the shadow value of capital which may be used in a Tobin-Q style investment function. The rate of technical progress in the cost function also implies a rate of decline in the price-to-cost ratio in the price equation and this needs to be consistent with the long-run rate of increase in real wages in the wage equation. So the final estimated system comprises the translog cost function, all the factor demand equations, the price and wage equations and the investment function. This is estimated as a single system subject to all the cross-equation restrictions of the theory. The theory also implies a non-linear set of long-run relationships in each equation and these are tested for cointegration as part of the estimation and specification strategy. This is not of course the entire model, and so we have not yet reached the stage of being able to estimate the entire macroeconometric model simultaneously, but it does represent a very thorough use of economic theory. It might be argued that theory does not give such a strong set of cross-equation restrictions with respect to other sectors such as exports or consumption.

It is still not possible to estimate a large econometric model as a single system and pragmatic considerations force modellers to modify their estimation strategies. But it is now best practice to estimate the model in blocks of interrelated subsystems and to make as much use of theory in the specification of these blocks as possible. So here again we cannot claim to have completely overcome the problem outlined by Sims, but we can claim to have made substantial progress. Also, once again, I would claim this work has borne additional fruits in that, by confronting theory with econometric estimation, we are often able to rule out simple theories that still form the backbone of many, non-econometric, approaches. An obvious example here would be the use of a simple Cobb–Douglas production function as a relevant representation of the UK economy.

5 ALTERNATIVE APPROACHES: CGE AND VAR METHODOLOGY

Sims' criticisms of macroeconometric modelling were both effective and influential in stimulating much of the work mentioned above, but it is insufficient simply to criticise a methodology and not to propose some better alternative. Sims, of course, did this with his proposal for VARs; and another paradigm which was already under development and which has had great influence is the computable general equilibrium (CGE) modelling approach, perhaps best typified in the macroeconomic area by the work of McKibbin and Sachs (1991). In my view, experience with both of these areas over the last 10 years suggests that neither of them can replace the approach of structural modelling and the formal use of econometrics as the best tool for policy analysis at the macro level.

The great strength of the VAR modelling approach is the avoidance of the use of theory and therefore the elimination of the possibility of basing results on an incorrect theory. However, as a tool for policy analysis it has two main disadvantages. The first, rather ironically, is the identification problem. Before we can use a reduced-form VAR for any form of policy analysis we need to be able to identify the structural shocks in the system. This needs a set of identifying restrictions that gives rise to a range of complex issues (which are surveyed in detail by Robertson and Wickens (1994)).

Sims original suggestion was to perform a triangular orthogonalisation, although this amounts to assuming a recursive causal structure in the model. One problem is that the order of this causal ordering can have major consequences for the policy implications of the model. In the absence of some specific theory this ordering is arbitrary. Blanchard (1989) has augmented this approach to allow a certain degree of simultaneity in the system, but this requires even stronger a priori theory to justify these extra restrictions. The problem is further complicated by the presence of non-stationary variables and cointegration amongst the set of variables under consideration; the identification procedure then becomes much more complex (Robertson and Wickens (1994)). The second main problem that has emerged is a more pragmatic one. In any modelling exercise there is a balance to be struck between using theory to increase the efficiency of estimation and the danger of imposing an incorrect theory, which then produces biased results. Unconstrained VARs make no use of theory and much practical experience has led to the conclusion that they can give very poor forecasting performance simply because they are very inefficient estimates. This has led to the use of Bayesian VARs (Litterman (1986)) to constrain the parameters of the VAR to lie within a reasonable but often small range. This restriction on the VAR is imposing priors which often have less foundation than the original identification restrictions of the structural models. I would also emphasise that as we come to understand how to use VARs, as well as the full implications of cointegration for the long-run properties of a VAR, there is emerging a natural methodology of beginning from a general VAR and then moving towards a data-acceptable restricted version of it which exploits both theory and econometric testing to check the theory (Hendry and Mizon (1993)).

The CGE models began from an almost diametrically opposed view of modelling to the VAR approach. Here the paradigm proposes a well-specified theoretical model built on intertemporal market-clearing behaviour. This is then parameterised using calibration techniques rather than formal estimation (an excellent recent survey may be found in Willenbockel (1994)). In its simple form, CGE modelling has a number of drawbacks from an econometric point of view: the parameterisation, when it is done in a naive way, must be wrong; by focusing on the equilibrium state, little can be said about how long the adjustment to equilibrium may take or what the path to equilibrium may look like; and, perhaps most importantly, the policy implication flowing from these models is often built into them by construction. However, CGE models have grown in sophistication and bridges are being built between conventional econometrics and calibration (see the special issue of the *Journal of Applied Econometrics* on calibration techniques, December 1994). CGE models increasingly include disequilibrium effects so that they can analyse the path to equilibrium. Moreover, the link between econometrics and calibration is opening up the possibility of testing and choosing between theories. Thus, the most recent versions of the McKibbin model (McKibbin (1994)) has both dynamic effects and sophisticated calibration/estimation. However, by introducing these factors the clear distinction between CGE and econometric models is disappearing. I have already argued that econometric models draw increasingly on theory; as the CGE models increasingly incorporate dynamics and econometric techniques there is increasing convergence between the two methodologies.

6 CONCLUSION

I have argued that considerable progress has been made in dealing with Sims' three main criticisms of macroeconometric modelling advanced 15 years ago, namely systems, expectations and dynamics. Our understanding of these issues is still far from complete, but many of the developments over the last 15 years are leading towards a common approach to modelling. Cointegration has put much greater emphasis on sensible long-run properties and it has obliged us to think in terms of multivariate systems. Economic theory leads us towards system estimation and provides the kinds of identifying restrictions on those cointegrated systems that we need. VAR modelling presents a general encompassing framework for model assessment and it also provides a point of departure for any good modelling exercise. Finally, the CGE models have demonstrated what can be achieved in terms of using theory in large empirical systems. These developments all point to a convergence of methodology, with the emergence of a best practice model which starts from a general unrestricted dynamic specification and uses the full implications of theory to identify a data-acceptable, identified structural model. We have not reached the stage where this can be done for a large econometric system. But already practitioners are doing this for subsystems such as the LBS model supply side mentioned above. This is pointing the way towards a new generation of models which I believe will offer important practical insights into the assessment and management of both national and international economies.

7 ACKNOWLEDGEMENTS

This chapter is based largely on the paper 'Macroeconomics and a Bit More Reality', published in the *Economic Journal*, **105**, July 1995. I wish to thank Andrew Sentance, Ron Smith, David Currie, James Nixon, Giovani Urga, John Whitley and Robert Nairn for their helpful comments on this paper.

SECTION 1
Model Building

1
A Survey of Flexible Functional Forms Applied to Production Analysis

CHRIS ALLEN

1.1 INTRODUCTION

Theory, in its most general form, does not need to specify explicit functional forms. When we come to implement this theory in an empirical model, as recommended in the introduction to this book, we cannot avoid the use of some explicit function in specifying production, cost or utility functions. Many researchers have opted for relatively simple functional forms but the underlying modelling philosophy presented in this book is that models must both conform to a well-specified theory and be data admissible. That is to say, the model must embody sound theory but it must also be a good representation of the data as we observe it. Models that are based on simple functional forms often have the advantage of being easy to understand and implement, but in our experience they generally do not provide good representation of the data. This is not a criticism of the theory as such, but it is a criticism of the simple forms that have been assumed to implement the theory. However, empirical models that fit the data well are often 'ad hoc' and may, at worse, violate the basic requirement of consistency with theory, and at best not fully exploit the information offered by theory. We would argue that one compromise between these two extremes is to base a model around a well-specified theoretical framework which is implemented through a set of functional forms that are sophisticated enough to provide a good representation of the data. In the past this has been done partly through augmenting the models with

Macroeconomic Modelling in a Changing World. Edited by C. Allen and S. Hall
© 1997 John Wiley & Sons Ltd

rich dynamics but cointegration provides a requirement for the theory to be able to explain the long-run behaviour of the economy without recourse to dynamics. Therefore we need a range of functional forms so that we can search amongst them for a sufficiently general one so as to give a description of the data which meets the requirements of modern econometrics. This chapter surveys a range of functional forms which have been proposed in the literature and outlines some of the issues in implementing them in practice.

1.2 EARLY WORK ON FLEXIBLE PRODUCTION AND COST FUNCTIONS

The first widely used production function allowing substitution was that derived by Cobb and Douglas (1928) (see also Douglas (1948)). The function was arrived at by the observation that the share of labour in national income was a constant, at around 75%, despite wide fluctuations in the relative prices of labour and capital. Under constant returns to scale (homogeneous of degree one (HoD1) in factors) and the pricing of factors at their marginal products, the only function compatible with this observation was

$$y = A \cdot x_1^{\alpha} \cdot x_2^{\beta}, \quad \alpha + \beta = 1; A, \alpha, \beta > 0 \qquad \ldots (1)$$

The properties of the function can be trivially derived. The returns to scale of the function are given by $\alpha + \beta$, put equal to unity. The distributive shares are equal to the exponents of the factors and are constants (and hence 'consistent' with observation). The own elasticity is equal to 1 minus the factor share. The Hicks and Allen elasticities of substitution are identical and equal to unity.

The first major theoretical advance on the Cobb–Douglas production function was discovered independently by Arrow and Solow and published in Arrow *et al.* (1961). This introduced the constant elasticity of substitution production function. Again this was prompted by empirical observation: running regressions of labour productivity on real wages on an international cross-sectional data set resulted in an intermediate case between the unitary coefficient on the real wage (as would have been expected from a Cobb–Douglas production function) and the zero coefficient, which would have been expected from Leontief technology. Arrow *et al.* noted that such a property would be obtained from the derived demands from a production function which had the form of the mathematical function of a mean of order ρ:

$$y = \gamma \cdot [\delta \cdot x_1^{-\rho} + (1 - \delta) \cdot x_2^{-\rho}]^{-v/\rho} \qquad \ldots (2)$$

The resulting production function was called the constant elasticity of substitution (CES) production function. The returns to scale in this function is given by v (in Arrow *et al.*'s original work this was imposed as unity). The Hicks and Allen elasticities of substitution are once again identical, but here are equal to $1/(1+\rho)$.

Arrow *et al.* showed that the CES production function reduced to the Cobb–Douglas function when ρ was equal to zero, and to the Leontief as $\rho \to \infty$. The CES function could therefore be seen as a generalization of both. The authors also showed that maintaining positive linear homogeneity, any two-factor production function with a constant (Hicks or Allen) elasticity of substitution was either Cobb–Douglas or a CES function.

The two-factor CES function proved successful in that it allowed an arbitrary degree of substitutability between the two factors. It prompted research efforts to obtain an n-factor generalization with arbitrary constant elasticities. This search proved to be illusory. The first efforts were produced by Uzawa (1962) and McFadden (1963).

Uzawa (1962), exploiting duality methods, showed that for constant Allen elasticities of substitution the possible pattern of elasticities was very limited. Indeed, the Allen elasticities of substitution of a linearly homogeneous n-factor production function were constant if and only if the production function was a Cobb–Douglas function of CES or Cobb–Douglas aggregator functions. The CES function itself is an example of this when there is a single aggregator function.

Uzawa's proposed generalized form was

$$y = \prod_i \left[\left(\sum_j \beta_j \cdot x_j^{-\rho_i} \right)^{-1/\rho_i} \right]^{a_i} \qquad \sum_i a_i = 1 \qquad \dots (3)$$

where the Allen elasticities of substitution:

$$\sigma_{ij}^A = \begin{cases} \sigma_s = (1 - \rho_s)^{-1} & i, j \in G_s \\ 1 & i \in G_s, j \in G_t, s \neq t \end{cases} \qquad \dots (4)$$

McFadden (1963) likewise proved an 'impossibility' theorem for sets of arbitrary Hicks elasticities of substitution. He showed that the Hicks elasticities of substitution of a linearly homogeneous n-factor production function were constant if and only if the production function was a CES or Cobb–Douglas function of Cobb–Douglas aggregator functions. Again, the CES function itself is an example of this when the partition of all commodities results in a single commodity in each group.

Sato (1967) provided a further, restricted-elasticity nested form which has often been used (e.g. in Helliwell *et al.* (1985)). This is a CES function of CES aggregator functions:

$$y = \sum_s [\alpha_s \cdot z_s^{-\rho}]^{-1/\rho} \qquad \dots (5)$$

where z_s is defined as a CES aggregator function for each group of commodities:

$$z_s = \left[\sum_i \beta_i^s \cdot (x_i^s)^{-\rho_s} \right]^{-1/\rho_s}$$

The Allen elasticities of substitution are then

$$\sigma_{ij}^{A} = \begin{cases} \sigma + \sigma_s^{-1} \cdot (\sigma_s - \sigma) & i, j \in G_s \\ \sigma & i \in G_s, j \in G_t, s \neq t \end{cases} \qquad \ldots (6)$$

Powell and Gruen (1968) extended the single output production function to the two-output case. They defined the production frontier

$$[\alpha_1 \cdot y_1^{\rho_1} + \alpha_2 \cdot y_2^{\rho_1}]^{1/\rho_1} = [\beta_1 \cdot x_1^{\rho_2} + \beta_2 \cdot x_2^{\rho_2}]^{1/\rho_2} \qquad \ldots (7)$$

This is known as the constant elasticity of transformation–constant elasticity of substitution (CET/CES) production frontier.

The Cobb–Douglas and CES production functions together make up an important class of production function. Samuelson (1965), building on Bergson (1936), proved the following representation theorem in the consumer context. Any linearly homogeneous production function is strongly separable (or 'additive') if and only if it can be represented as either a Cobb–Douglas or CES production function. This proposition can easily be strengthened to apply to any homothetic production function.

Christensen *et al.* (1973) and Berndt and Christensen (1973b) generalized this to group-wise strongly separable, homogeneous production functions. They showed that a production function is homogeneous and strongly separable if and only if its representation is Cobb–Douglas or CES in homogeneous aggregator functions.

An important feature of strongly separable, linearly homogeneous production functions is that they are self-dual (Houthakker (1965)). If the production frontier is commodity-wise separable, then the price possibility frontier is commodity-wise additive and can be represented by the same class of strongly separable functional forms. If there is only one output, then the proposition says that the production function can be represented by a self-dual cost function. For example, a CES production function can be represented by a CES cost function, or a Cobb–Douglas production function by a Cobb–Douglas cost function.

1.3 FLEXIBLE FUNCTIONAL FORMS: DIEWERT'S GENERALIZED LEONTIEF FUNCTION

The conceptual breakthrough that allowed the derivation of true flexible functional forms for more than two variables came about as a result of the development of duality theory. The initiator of the research project to derive such functional forms was apparently Marc Nerlove. Nerlove himself used the dual cost function to a Cobb–Douglas production function to model non-constant returns to scale in electricity supply (Nerlove (1963)). He then directed his research assistant, Daniel McFadden, to examine the use of duality theory in production economics and the problem of generating flexible functional forms with more than two inputs, which were less restrictive than the Cobb–Douglas or CES functions. McFadden himself concentrated mainly on the theory and applications of duality theory itself. It was left to a student of McFadden, Edwin Diewert, to solve the problem of developing flexible functional forms with three or more inputs.

Diewert's PhD was submitted in 1969, and was summarized in his article 'An Application of the Shephard Duality Theorem: a Generalized Leontief Production Function' (1971). Diewert made use of two properties of duality theory, originally derived by Richard Shephard in a remarkable book published in 1953 (Shephard (1970)). The first was Shephard's duality theorem, which states that technology may be equivalently represented by a production function satisfying certain regularity conditions, or by a cost function satisfying a second set of regularity conditions. Secondly, he used what has become known as Shephard's lemma, namely if a cost function is at least once differentiable with respect to input prices, then the optimal factor demands are given by the derivative of the cost function with respect to own factor price.

Diewert explained the significance of these results as follows:

> The significance of the Shephard duality theorem … is that we need only exhibit a [cost] function $C(y; p)$ which satisfies [the regularity conditions], and we are assured that $C(y; p)$ may be interpreted as the total cost function of some underlying production function, even though we may not be able to express explicitly the production function in a neat and tidy form (Diewert, (1971, p. 497)).

We may therefore take an arbitrary differentiable cost function, which obeys a set of regularity conditions, and then use Shephard's lemma to straightforwardly derive a set of factor demand functions from it. Provided the cost function obeys the set of regularity conditions, we can then be assured that the resultant factor demand functions are in principle derivable from a cost minimization process, subject to a regular production function.

Diewert's regularity conditions for a cost function were the following:

1. $C(y; p)$ is a positive real valued function, defined and finite for all finite $y \geq 0$, $p \gg 0$.

2. $C(y; p)$ is a non-decreasing, left-continuous function in y and as $y \to \infty$, $C(y; p) \to \infty$, for $p \gg 0$.

3. $C(y; p)$ is a non-decreasing in p.

4. $C(y; p)$ is positively linearly homogeneous in p for all $y > 0$.

5. $C(y; p)$ is a concave function in p, for all $y > 0$.

Diewert illustrated the procedure for the case of what he called the generalized Leontief cost function:

$$C(y; p) = h(y) \cdot \sum_{i=1}^{n} \sum_{j=1}^{n} b_{ij} \cdot p_i^{1/2} \cdot p_j^{1/2}, \quad p_i, p_j \geq 0 \qquad \ldots (8)$$

where

(i) $h(y)$ is assumed to be a continuous, monotonic increasing function of y, with $h(0) = 0$ and $H(y) \to \infty$ as $y \to \infty$; and

(ii) $B = \{b_{ij}\}$ is a symmetric $n \times n$ matrix, with $\sum_{i=1}^{n} \sum_{j=1}^{n} b_{ij} = 1$ (which is required for linear homogeneity).

If all elements of B are non-negative, $C(y; p)$ straightforwardly fulfils the regularity conditions for any set of non-negative prices.[1] We may thus use this cost function to derive sets of factor demand equations.

Using Shephard's lemma, the factor demand equations from the cost function are as follows:

$$x_i = \frac{\partial C}{\partial p_i} = h(y) \cdot \sum_{j=1}^{n} b_{ij} \cdot (p_j / p_i)^{1/2} \qquad \ldots (9)$$

which is linear in the parameters b_{ij}, provided the function $h(y)$ is known.[2] The linearity greatly simplifies the estimation of the factor demand equations.

The Allen cross-price elasticities of substitution in this model are

$$\sigma_{ij}^{A} = C \cdot C_{ij}/C_i \cdot C_j = C^* \cdot \tfrac{1}{2} b_{ij} \cdot h(y) \cdot p_i^{-1/2} \cdot p_j^{-1/2}/x_i^* \cdot x_j^* \qquad \ldots (10)$$

For a given set of prices and output, there are potentially $n \cdot (n-1)/2$ independent Allen elasticities, exactly matched by $n \cdot (n-1)/2\, b_{ij}$ parameters $(i \neq j)$.[3] Note however that these elasticities will in general vary with prices: the Uzawa/McFadden impossibility theorems discussed above ensure that it is not possible to derive an arbitrary set of Allen elasticities that are independent of factor prices.

Diewert noted an important caveat on the use of flexible functional forms: the Shephard duality theorem requires that the postulated cost function must always obey the regularity conditions. For certain values of b_{ij}, the regularity conditions may depend on factor prices. Diewert derived the 'domain of application' of the cost function, i.e. the set of prices under which the cost function obeys the regularity conditions.

The regularity conditions are not satisfied for all prices if some of the b_{ij} are negative. For instance, $C(y; p)$ must be non-decreasing in p. This entails that

$$\frac{\partial C}{\partial p_i} = x_i = h(y) \cdot p_i^{-1/2} \cdot \sum_{j=1}^{n} b_{ij} \cdot p_j^{1/2} \geq 0 \qquad \ldots (11)$$

which requires that the price vector must satisfy

$$\sum_{j=1}^{n} b_{ij} \cdot p_{ij}^{1/2} \geq 0 \qquad \ldots (12)$$

For the concavity requirement to be fulfilled requires that $-C(y; p)$ is a convex function in p. Diewert derived a set of inequalities that will ensure that the matrix of second partial derivatives in p of this function is positive semi-definite.[4]

Diewert's paper does not contain any empirical application of his function. However, he notes that if some of the econometric estimates of the b_{ij} turn out to be negative, it would be necessary to check that the sample prices are within the domain of application. For sets of prices outside this domain, the regularity conditions do not hold, and we cannot appeal to the Shephard duality theorem. Conditions to ensure concavity became the focus of attention in the subsequent literature and are discussed in full below.

1.4 THE TRANSLOG PRODUCTION AND COST FUNCTION

Almost simultaneous with the work of Diewert, a second flexible functional form was proposed, namely the transcendental logarithmic or *translog*. This has become the workhorse of much subsequent empirical analysis. It had its origins in Kmenta's (1967) log-linearization of the CES production function which can be written in the form:

$$\log y = \log \gamma - \frac{\nu}{\rho} \log[\delta x_1^{-\rho} + (1 - \delta)x_2^{-\rho}] \qquad \ldots (13)$$

Kmenta used a second-order Taylor series to approximate the CES production function around $(\rho = 0)$ as a quadratic function of logarithms:

$$\log y = \log \gamma + \nu\delta \log x_1 + \nu(1 - \delta) \log x_2 - \tfrac{1}{2}\rho\nu\delta(1 - \delta)[\log(x_1/x_2)]^2 \quad \ldots (14)$$

The resulting function was linear in variables and could therefore be estimated by ordinary least squares (OLS). The parameters themselves could then be recovered directly, and their standard errors derived from an expansion of the variance–covariance matrix of parameters.[5]

An obvious generalization of Kmenta's work was to estimate a production function as a general, unrestricted quadratic function of logarithms. The same idea was used in three independent research projects, all published in 1971. Sargan (1971) directly estimated what he called the *log-quadratic* production function as part of a study of the role of qualified manpower in the UK electrical engineering industry. Griliches and Ringstad (1971) also estimated log-quadratic production functions in a study of elasticities of scale. Finally, Christensen, Jorgenson and Lau (1971, 1973) coined the term *translog* in a paper which used duality theory to propose alternative tests of the assumption of a Cobb–Douglas or CES functional form.[6]

Christensen, Jorgenson and Lau's paper is perhaps the most interesting. Its aim was to test the additivity (or strong separability) and homogeneity assumptions of the Cobb–Douglas and CES functional forms, including the strong separability between outputs and inputs implicit in the Powell and Gruen CET/CES production possibility frontier (see equation (7) above). They noted that under the hypothesis of strong separability and homogeneity the production frontier was self-dual with the price possibility frontier, and therefore these assumptions could be tested using either a flexible production frontier or its dual.

Their specific functional form used was a quadratic or *transcendental* function of the logarithms of the functions arguments. For instance, take the aggregate production frontier

$$F(C, I; L, K) = 0 \qquad \ldots (15)$$

where C and I are outputs of consumption and investment goods, respectively, and L and K are inputs of labour and capital. We can approximate the logarithm of the production frontier (plus unity) by a quadratic function of inputs and outputs:

$$
\begin{aligned}
\ln(F + 1) = {}& \alpha_0 + \alpha_c \cdot \ln C + \alpha_i \cdot \ln I + \alpha_l \cdot \ln L + \alpha_k \cdot \ln K \\
& + \ln C \cdot \left(\tfrac{1}{2} \cdot \beta_{cc} \cdot \ln C + \beta_{ci} \cdot \ln I + \beta_{cl} \cdot \ln L + \beta_{ck} \cdot \ln K \right) \\
& + \ln I \cdot \left(\tfrac{1}{2} \cdot \beta_{ii} \cdot \ln I + \beta_{il} \cdot \ln L + \beta_{ik} \cdot \ln K \right) \\
& + \ln L \cdot \left(\tfrac{1}{2} \cdot \beta_{ll} \cdot \ln L + \beta_{lk} \cdot \ln K \right) \\
& + \ln K \cdot \left(\tfrac{1}{2} \cdot \beta_{kk} \cdot \ln K \right) \qquad \ldots (16)
\end{aligned}
$$

Relative factor demands were derived from the condition that under profit maximization the relative price ratio is equal to the marginal rate of transformation between any two commodities:

$$
\begin{aligned}
\frac{p_l \cdot L}{p_k \cdot K} &= \frac{\partial \ln F / \partial \ln L}{\partial \ln F / \partial \ln K} \\
&= \frac{\alpha_1 + \beta_{cl} \cdot \ln C + \beta_{il} \cdot \ln I + \beta_{ll} \cdot \ln L + \beta_{kl} \cdot \ln K}{\alpha_k + \beta_{kc} \cdot \ln C + \beta_{ki} \cdot \ln I + \beta_{kl} \cdot \ln L + \beta_{kk} \cdot \ln K} \qquad \ldots (17)
\end{aligned}
$$

Likewise, an arbitrary profit function can be approximated by a quadratic function of input and output prices:

$$
\begin{aligned}
\ln(\Pi + 1) = {}& \alpha_0 + \alpha_c \cdot \ln P_c + \alpha_i \cdot \ln P_I + \alpha_l \cdot \ln P_L + \alpha_k \cdot \ln P_K \\
& + \ln P_c \cdot \left(\tfrac{1}{2} \cdot \beta_{cc} \cdot \ln P_c + \beta_{ci} \cdot \ln P_I + \beta_{cl} \cdot \ln P_L + \beta_{ck} \cdot \ln P_K \right) \\
& + \ln P_I \cdot \left(\tfrac{1}{2} \cdot \beta_{ii} \cdot \ln P_I + \beta_{il} \cdot \ln P_L + \beta_{ik} \cdot \ln P_K \right) \\
& + \ln P_L \cdot \left(\tfrac{1}{2} \cdot \beta_{ll} \cdot \ln P_L + \beta_{lk} \cdot \ln P_K \right) \\
& + \ln P_K \cdot \left(\tfrac{1}{2} \cdot \beta_{kk} \cdot \ln P_K \right) \qquad \ldots (18)
\end{aligned}
$$

Using Shephard's lemma the optimal relative factor demands and output supplies are given by equations of the form:

$$\frac{p_l \cdot L}{p_k \cdot K} = \frac{\partial \ln \Pi / \partial \ln L}{\partial \ln \Pi / \partial \ln K}$$

$$= \frac{\alpha_l + \beta_{cl} \cdot \ln P_c + \beta_{il} \cdot \ln P_I + \beta_{ll} \cdot \ln P_L + \beta_{kl} \cdot \ln P_K}{\alpha_k + \beta_{kc} \cdot \ln P_c + \beta_{ki} \cdot \ln P_I + \beta_{kl} \cdot \ln P_L + \beta_{kk} \cdot \ln P_K} \quad \ldots (19)$$

The model was applied to aggregate annual US data. Rather than estimate directly the production frontier and profit function, the authors used the equations for relative factor demands to derive indirect estimates of the parameters. This allowed testing of the 'assumptions' of the models, including homogeneity and symmetry. These restrictions were found to be true. However, both versions of the model were found to reject the assumption of additive separability, suggesting that neither a Cobb–Douglas nor a CES production function was adequate to describe the data.

1.5 ALTERNATIVE DEFINITIONS OF FLEXIBLE FUNCTIONAL FORMS

Diewert defined the notion of a flexible functional form in a survey paper published in 1974. His definition, given in the context of a production function, was as follows:

A 'flexible' functional form for [a production function] f could be defined as one which is capable of providing a second order approximation to an arbitrary production function which satisfies [the regularity] conditions [for a production function] (Diewert (1974, p. 112)).

Hence a twice continuously differentiable function $G(x)$ is a second-order approximation to a production function $F(x)$ at x_0 if and only if the function satisfies the following $l + n + n^2$ equations at x_0:

$$G(x_0) = F(x_0)$$

$$\left[\frac{\partial G}{\partial x_i}\right]_{x=x_0} = \left[\frac{\partial F}{\partial x_i}\right]_{x=x_0} \quad \ldots (20)$$

$$\left[\frac{\partial^2 G}{\partial x_i \partial x_j}\right]_{x=x_0} = \left[\frac{\partial^2 F}{\partial x_i \partial x_j}\right]_{x=x_0}$$

subject to the imposition of the $n \cdot (n-1)/2$ symmetry conditions on the second-order derivatives:

$$\left[\frac{\partial^2 F}{\partial x_i \partial x_j}\right]_{x=x_0} = \left[\frac{\partial^2 F}{\partial x_j \partial x_i}\right]_{x=x_0} \quad \ldots (21)$$

and additionally the property that the Hessian of the function was positive semi-definite. Thus overall the flexible function must satisfy $1 + n + n^2 - n \cdot (n-1)/2 =$

$(n + 1)(n + 2)/2$ equations, which requires that it has at least that number of free parameters.

Two distinct definitions of *flexible functional forms* have subsequently emerged in the literature. The first takes seriously the notion that a flexible functional is a Taylor approximation. The functional form is therefore only a second-order approximation to the true or *underlying* functional form at a given point of approximation. Lau (1974), commenting on Diewert (1974), suggested a rigorous definition of what he called *second-order flexibility*: $G(y_0) = F(y_0)$ and that the third- and successive order terms be negligible in the neighbourhood of y_0.

A second notion of the *flexible functional form* was put forward by Fuss, McFadden and Mundlak (1978) (on the basis of earlier work by Hanoch (1975)). They argued that Diewert's definition was equivalent to requiring that the flexible function must have enough free parameters to allow the representation of an arbitrary set of comparative statics effects. For a production function, for example, we would expect a functional form to be able to display an output level, returns to scale, distributive shares, own-price elasticities, and cross-price Allen elasticities of substitution. For a production function with n inputs, there are altogether $(n + 1)(n + 2)/2$ distinct economic effects. Since these effects can be quantified in terms of the production function itself and its first and second derivatives, it is therefore unsurprising that they can be adequately defined by a second-order Taylor expansion.

The differences between these two definitions is not immediately apparent. If the true production function is a quadratic function of prices, then a second-order approximation to it will describe it exactly. However, clearly not all second-order approximations will exactly describe any arbitrary production function. The difference between the two definitions becomes crucial when restrictions on the form of the function are being tested. On the approximation definition, the restrictions need only hold at the point of approximation; on the second definition, restrictions are required to hold globally. This latter assumption is much stronger: a practical demonstration of the differences in the consequences of the two definitions for the testing of weak separability is discussed in Section 1.9.

We can provide similar definitions of a flexible functional form for a cost function (Diewert and Wales (1987)). A twice continuously differentiable function $C(y; p)$ is a flexible representation of a given cost function $C^*(y; p)$ at a point $\{y_0; p_0\}$ if and only if it satisfies the following $1 + (n + 1) + (n + 1)^2$ equations at $z_0 = \{y_0; p_0\}$:

$$C(z_0) = C^*(z)$$

$$\left[\frac{\partial C}{\partial z_i}\right]_{z=z_0} = \left[\frac{\partial C^*}{\partial z_i}\right]_{z=z_0}$$

$$\left[\frac{\partial^2 C}{\partial z_i \partial z_j}\right]_{z=z_0} = \left[\frac{\partial^2 C^*}{\partial z_i \partial z_j}\right]_{z=z_0}$$

... (22)

subject to the imposition of the $(n+1) \cdot n/2$ symmetry conditions on the second-order derivatives:

$$\left[\frac{\partial^2 C}{\partial z_i \partial z_j}\right]_{z=z_0} = \left[\frac{\partial^2 C^*}{\partial z_j \partial z_i}\right]_{z=z_0} \qquad \ldots (23)$$

and additionally the imposition of linear homogeneity in factor prices, which imposes the following $n+2$ conditions:

$$\sum_i \left[p_i \frac{\partial C^*(y_0; p_0)}{\partial p_{i0}}\right]_{z=z_0} = C^*(y_0; p_i)$$

$$\sum_i \left[\frac{\partial C^*}{\partial p_i \partial y}\right]_{z=z_0} = \left[\frac{\partial C^*}{\partial y_i}\right]_{z=z_0} \qquad \ldots (24)$$

$$\sum_i \left[\frac{\partial^2 C^*}{\partial p_i \partial p_j}\right]_{z=z_0} = 0$$

In addition, we must also have that the Hessian of price derivatives must be negative semidefinite. Hence, overall the flexible cost function must satisfy $1 + (n+1) + (n+1)^2 - n \cdot (n-1)/2 - (n+2) = (n+1)(n+2)/2$ equations.

Hence, a flexible cost function must again have at least $(n+1)(n+2)/2$ free parameters. This is exactly what we would expect from the principle of duality: there must still be $(n+1)(n+2)/2$ independent economic effects. The extra degrees of freedom from there being $n+1$ variables in the cost function are reduced to $(n+1)(n+2)/2$ by the additional imposition of linear homogeneity in prices.

Denny and Fuss (1977) showed that a second-order approximation to an arbitrary production function could be represented by a translog function with symmetry imposed. Note that an arbitrary production can be written in the form:

$$\ln(Y) = \ln F(e^{\ln X_1}, \ldots, e^{\ln X_n}) = f(\ln X_1, \ldots, \ln X_n) \qquad \ldots (25)$$

Expanding around the expansion point $\{X^*\} : X_1 = X_2 = \ldots = X_n = 1$, we have

$$\ln \hat{Y} = f(\ln X_0) + \sum_i \left[\frac{\partial f}{\partial \ln X_i}\right]_{X=X_0} (\ln X_i - \ln X_i^*)$$

$$+ \frac{1}{2} \sum_i \sum_j \left[\frac{\partial^2 f}{\partial \ln X_i \partial \ln X_j}\right]_{X=X^*} (\ln X_i - \ln X_i^*)(\ln X_j - \ln X_j^*)$$

$$\ldots (26)$$

We can write the translog form as

$$\ln \hat{Y} = \alpha_0 + \sum_i \alpha_i \cdot \ln X_i + \frac{1}{2} \sum_i \sum_j \gamma_{ij} \cdot \ln X_i \cdot \ln X_j \qquad \ldots (27)$$

Hence, we can identify the parameters as follows:

$$\alpha_0 = f(X^*)$$

$$\alpha_i = \left[\frac{\partial f}{\partial \ln X_i}\right]_{X=X^*}$$

$$\gamma_{ij} = \left[\frac{\partial^2 f}{\partial \ln X_i \partial \ln X_j}\right]_{X=X^*} = \left[\frac{\partial^2 f}{\partial \ln X_j \partial \ln X_i}\right]_{X=X^*} = \gamma_{ji}$$

...(28)

since $\ln X^* = 0$ (Denny and Fuss (1977, proposition 2, p. 407)).

Denny and Fuss further show that a second-order approximation to a *linearly homogeneous* production function can be represented by a translog function with symmetry and linear homogeneity imposed (Denny and Fuss (1977, proposition 3)).[7]

Linear homogeneity therefore additionally implies that

$$\sum_i \alpha_i = \sum_i \left[\frac{\partial f}{\partial \ln X_i}\right]_{X=X^*} = 1$$

$$\sum_j \gamma_{ij} = \sum_j \left[\frac{\partial^2 f}{\partial \ln X_i \partial \ln X_j}\right]_{X=X^*} = 0$$

...(29)

1.6 IMPOSING CURVATURE CONDITIONS

A key regularity condition for the representation of a cost function is that the proposed function must be concave in factor prices. Likewise, many production functions require convexity to be well behaved. This was not an issue with early functional forms such as the Cobb–Douglas or CES which have these properties anyway; it is much more important in terms of flexible functional forms which may violate them.

It is well known that the curvature properties of twice differentiable functions can be characterized in terms of its Hessian or matrix of second-order derivatives (see, for example, Lau (1978)). Convexity requires that the Hessian be positive semi-definite, i.e. its principal minors are all non-negative, or alternatively its eigenvalues are all non-negative. Likewise, concavity requires that the Hessian be negative semi-definite, i.e. its principal minors alternate in sign (starting with a negative sign) or that its eigenvalues are all non-positive.

Diewert (1971), as described above, discussed the importance of concavity in the context of the estimation of cost functions and found a set of inequality restrictions that were sufficient to impose this within the generalized Leontief cost function. In general, however, it is difficult to actually impose his highly non-linear conditions. Similar problems occur for the translog flexible functional form: if all the quadratic terms are zero, then the translog reduces to the Cobb–Douglas form, which is straightforwardly concave. However, where the quadratic parameters are non-zero, Diewert (1974) despaired of finding a set of simple conditions for the translog function to be concave.

Lau (1974, 1978) suggested a straightforward method to test and impose curvature conditions. His method depends on the Cholesky factorization of semi-definite matrices. Lau (1978) demonstrated that a real symmetric matrix A has the following unique factorization:

$$A = L^{\mathrm{T}} \cdot D \cdot L \qquad \ldots (30)$$

where L is a unit lower triangular matrix and D is a diagonal matrix.

Thus in the 3×3 case:

$$L = \begin{bmatrix} 1 & 0 & 0 \\ \lambda_{21} & 1 & 0 \\ \lambda_{31} & \lambda_{32} & 1 \end{bmatrix}, \qquad D = \begin{bmatrix} \delta_1 & 0 & 0 \\ 0 & \delta_2 & 0 \\ 0 & 0 & \delta_3 \end{bmatrix} \qquad \ldots (31)$$

Hence,

$$A = \begin{bmatrix} \delta_1 & \delta_1\lambda_{21} & \delta_1\lambda_{31} \\ \delta_1\lambda_{21} & \delta_1\lambda_{21}^2 + \delta_2 & \delta_1\lambda_{21}\lambda_{31} + \delta_2\lambda_{32} \\ \delta_1\lambda_{31} & \delta_1\lambda_{21}\lambda_{31} + \delta_2\lambda_{32} & \delta_1\lambda_{32}^2 + \delta_2\lambda_{32}^2 + \delta_3 \end{bmatrix} \qquad \ldots (32)$$

Lau proved that A is positive semi-definite if and only if all elements of D, the Cholesky values, are non-negative. Likewise, A is negative semi-definite if and only if the Cholesky values are all non-positive.

Lau proposed that a test of the curvature conditions would be given by computing the δ_i's and using a likelihood ratio test of whether they are significantly different from zero. He pointed out that the method also allows the global imposition of curvature conditions by requiring the δ_i's to have the correct sign (for instance by replacing them with δ_i^2 or $-\delta_i^2$ as required).

Diewert and Wales (1987) suggested the use of an alternative simpler procedure for imposing curvature restrictions based on the work of Wiley, Schmidt and Bramble (1973), originally derived in the context of covariance matrices. They proved that a necessary and sufficient condition for a matrix A to be positive semi-definite is that it can be written in the form:

$$A = T \cdot T^{\mathrm{T}} \qquad \ldots (33)$$

where T is lower triangular (Diewert and Wales (1987, theorem 9)).

If A is a 3×3 matrix, then

$$T = \begin{bmatrix} \tau_{11} & 0 & 0 \\ \tau_{21} & \tau_{22} & 0 \\ \tau_{31} & \tau_{32} & \tau_{33} \end{bmatrix} \qquad \ldots (34)$$

and

$$A = \begin{bmatrix} \tau_{11}^2 & \tau_{11}\tau_{21} & \tau_{11}\tau_{31} \\ \tau_{11}\tau_{21} & \tau_{21}^2\tau_{22}^2 & \tau_{21}\tau_{31} + \tau_{22}\tau_{32} \\ \tau_{11}\tau_{31} & \tau_{21}\tau_{31} + \tau_{22}\tau_{32} & \tau_{31}^2 + \tau_{32}^2 + \tau_{33}^2 \end{bmatrix} \qquad \ldots (35)$$

Similarly a matrix is negative semi-definite if it can be written

$$A = -T \cdot T^T \qquad \qquad \dots (36)$$

In the case of some flexible functional forms, such as the generalized Leontief, the Lau or Wiley *et al.* conditions can be straightforwardly imposed onto the parameters of the model, since these correspond directly with the elements of the Hessian matrix. However, in the case of the translog, the situation is rather more complicated.

Jorgenson, Gollop and Fraumeni (1987) adapted Lau's technique to impose concavity on a translog cost function. They showed that the Hessian of the translog unit cost function can be characterized as

$$C^{-1} \cdot W \cdot H_{WW}(C) \cdot W = \Gamma + S \cdot S^T - \Sigma \qquad \qquad \dots (37)$$

where $H_{WW}(C)$ is the Hessian of the cost function, s is a vector of factor shares, Σ is a diagonal matrix with the share vector on its main diagonal, and W is a diagonal matrix with the vector of factor prices on its main diagonal.

Jorgenson and Fraumeni noted that a sufficient condition for the Hessian to be negative semi-definite is that Γ be negative semi-definite, since $S \cdot S^T - \Sigma$ is clearly negative semi-definite (all shares must be less than or equal to unity). They argued that this was also a *necessary* condition in order for the cost function to fulfil *global concavity* in the range of non-negative shares.[8]

Clearly, the Jorgenson and Fraumeni's requirement of global concavity of the cost function is a very strong requirement for a flexible functional form. Concavity of the function is imposed well outside the range of any region of empirical interest. Inevitably this will lead to possible distortions of the function within the empirical range. This was explored by Diewert and Wales (1987), who showed how the imposition of global concavity destroys the flexibility properties of the flexible functional form.

Diewert and Wales (1987) showed that the imposition of global concavity imposes a lower bound on the allowable own-price elasticities in the translog model. Note that the own-price elasticity can be written as

$$\eta_{ii} = -1 + S_i + \gamma_{ii}/S_i \qquad \qquad \dots (38)$$

Imposing Γ as negative semi-definite requires that $\gamma_{ii} \leq 0$. Hence, $\eta_{ii} \leq -1 + S_i$. Averaging over all inputs entails that at least one own-price elasticity must be greater than

$$-1 + 1/n$$

where n is the number of inputs. For instance, in the case of three inputs, not all of the elasticities can be less than $-2/3$. Since empirical elasticities are typically found to be small, the imposition of global concavity may severely distort the estimates of the elasticities of substitution.

Kohli (1991) suggested that it would be better not to impose concavity globally, but rather to test for it at every data point. If it is necessary to impose concavity, then it should be done at the worst offending data point. This is usually sufficient for the estimated function to satisfy the curvature conditions for all observations, although this cannot be guaranteed. However, it does seem a sensible solution, which is in keeping with the general philosophy of imposing the concavity conditions over a regional domain of observation.

1.7 REGIONAL DOMAINS OF THEORETICAL CONSISTENCY

Flexible functional forms are capable of providing a local second-order approximation which may attain arbitrary elasticities of substitution at a single point. However, the question remains: To what extent can an estimated flexible functional form represent cost-minimizing behaviour over a range or region of observations? Rational behaviour, for instance, implies that the cost function must obey monotonicity and quasi-concavity in prices. Many early empirical studies using flexible functional forms found that these conditions were violated over part of the domain of estimation.

One response to this problem is the global imposition of monotonicity and quasi-concavity. However, as we saw in the preceding section, this may not be a straightforward answer. Imposing these conditions globally considerably reduces the flexibility properties of a functional form. This led to the search for *more* flexible functional forms, as discussed in the next section.

An alternative response was to examine directly the domain over which various functional forms could be theoretically valid. Early work in this area was by Wales (1977) who examined empirically the properties of estimated translog and generalized Leontief indirect utility functions in approximating the demands given by a homothetic two-good CES direct utility function. Wales noted that the translog would fit exactly when the Allen elasticity of substitution was unity, since the CES function reduced to a Cobb–Douglas function; on the other hand, the generalized Leontief function would fit exactly when the underlying Allen elasticity of substitution was zero, since the underlying utility function would then reduce to a fixed-coefficients one. Wales found that the translog function performed poorly for low elasticities, $\sigma_A \leq 0$, over which range quasi-concavity was often violated. It performed much better for $0.5 \leq \sigma_A < 2$. For large values of σ_A, the translog function violated monotonicity. In contrast, the generalized Leontief function performed well for low σ_A, but was worse than the translog for $\sigma_A \geq 1$. Both functions performed poorly for $\sigma_A \geq 2$.

Caves and Christensen (1980) provided a more general comparison of the properties of the translog and generalized Leontief functions. They noted that a flexible functional form could achieve an arbitrary set of price elasticities at a given data point. This would be consistent with a unique set of parameters. Once this set of parameters is given, the pattern of price elasticities is given for all data points. By bounding the set of theoretically consistent elasticities, one can trace out the domain of theoretical consistency of the function in price space.

More formally, the *domain of theoretical consistency*[9] of a flexible functional form, conditional on a set of elasticities $\{\sigma^*\}$, is the set of prices $\{p\}$ such that

$$C(p; \alpha) \geq 0$$

$$C_p(p; \alpha) \geq 0 \qquad \qquad \qquad \text{...(39)}$$

$$C_{pp}(p; \alpha) \text{ is negative semi-definite}$$

where α is defined by the solution to

$$\{\sigma_A^*\} = C^{-1}(p_0; \alpha) \cdot C_p(p_0; \alpha) \cdot C_{pp}(p_0; \alpha) \cdot C_p^T(p_0; \alpha) \qquad \text{...(40)}$$

for a given base price vector p_0.

Caves and Christensen examined two- and three-good homothetic indirect utility functions and two-good, non-homothetic functions, normalized around unit price ratios. As might be expected, the generalized Leontief model had good regional properties when functions were homothetic and substitutability was low. In contrast, the translog function had a larger domain for near unit elasticities that were homothetic. In both cases the domains contracted sharply as elasticities were moved away from their optimal values and homotheticity was removed. Barnett and Lee (1985) provided further results examining the case of three-good, non-homothetic preferences.

Given the relative regularity properties of the translog and generalized Leontief functions, it would seem that a more general first-order function, which does not restrict the elasticity of substitution to one or zero, would be desirable. A possible candidate would be the CES/translog function introduced by Pollak, Sickles and Wales (1984). This function replaces the log-linear terms of the translog functional form with a CES function of variables. As we saw above, the CES functional form reduces to the Leontief form (if $\sigma = 0$) or the Cobb–Douglas form (if $\sigma = 1$). It thus encompasses both Cobb–Douglas and Leontief forms and could therefore be expected to have more favourable regional properties than either the translog or generalized Leontief functions. To my knowledge, this aspect of the CES/translog function has not been exploited in the literature.

Using a CES/translog function may ease the situation, but one cannot but agree with Lau's (1986) summing up of the debate on the regional properties of flexible functional forms. Lau noted that it was almost essential to accept a limitation in the domain of application of a functional form. He suggested that an investigator must compromise on the *extrapolative domain of applicability* by limiting the space of independent variables to a sufficiently large, compact subset of the entire domain. He further argued that the *interpolative domain of applicability* could also be profitably limited by restricting a priori the allowable set of elasticities again to a compact subset of values. With these restrictions a 'practical solution' to the problem of imposing curvature conditions could be found.

1.8 FURTHER FUNCTIONAL FORMS

The search for global satisfaction of monotonicity and concavity conditions led to the development of further flexible functional forms. Diewert and Wales (1987) discussed two of these forms and adapted them for use in the production context.

The first is the normalized quadratic (or symmetric generalized McFadden) cost function, based on a suggestion of McFadden (1978). Here the cost function has the following form:

$$C(y; P) = y \cdot \sum_i \sum_j b_{ij} p_i p_j \bigg/ \sum_i \bar{\theta}_i p_i$$

$$+ \sum_i b_i p_i + y \cdot \sum_i b_{iy} p_i + b_{yy} y^2 \cdot \left(\sum_i \bar{\gamma}_i p_i \right) \quad \ldots (41)$$

where $b_{ij} = b_{ji}$ and $\Sigma_i b_{ij} = 0$. The $\bar{\theta}_i (\Sigma_i \bar{\theta}_i \neq 0)$ and $\bar{\gamma}_i (\Sigma_i \bar{\gamma}_i \neq 0)$ are sets of predetermined parameters defining indices. Diewert and Wales suggested normalizing their sums to unity and deriving weights equal to sample average factor volume shares or else to $1/n$.

The cost function clearly is linearly homogeneous in factor prices and symmetric. It can be shown that it is additionally globally concave provided the matrix $\{b_{ii}\}$ is negative semi-definite. This can be straightforwardly imposed using the techniques discussed in Section 1.6. Furthermore, it can easily be shown that the cost function has $(n + 1)(n + 2)/2$ free parameters and can therefore be considered as a flexible functional form.

Factor demands are given by

$$x_k = b_k + b_{ky} \cdot y + b_{yy} \bar{\gamma}_k \cdot y^2$$

$$+ y \cdot \frac{\sum_i b_{ik} \cdot p_i}{\sum_i \bar{\theta}_i p_i} - y \cdot \bar{\theta}_k \frac{\frac{1}{2} \sum_i \sum_j b_{ij} \cdot p_i p_j}{\left(\sum_i \bar{\theta}_i \cdot p_i \right)^2} \quad \ldots (42)$$

These factors demand equations are linear in parameters. Each separate equation, however, contains a large number of parameters. System estimation therefore requires a large number of degrees of freedom. Diewert and Wales (1987) estimated such an unrestricted equation set.

In a later paper Diewert and Wales (1988) suggested a way of reducing the required degrees of freedom, whilst retaining the imposition of the curvature conditions. Degrees of freedom can be saved by reducing the rank of the Hessian matrix to $k < n$: the number of free parameters of the Hessian matrix can therefore be reduced by $(n - k)(n - k - 1)/2$ parameters. The authors called such a representation a *semi-flexible* functional form. They proved that such a reduced rank Hessian matrix can be represented by a k-column lower triangular decomposition (see the discussion in Section 1.6 above):

$$B = S \cdot S^T \qquad \ldots (43)$$

where S is an $n \times n$ lower triangular matrix, with zeros in its last $n - k$ columns. For instance, in the 3×3 case, with $k = l$, the S matrix takes the form

$$S = \begin{bmatrix} S_{11} & 0 & 0 \\ S_{21} & 0 & 0 \\ S_{31} & 0 & 0 \end{bmatrix} \qquad \ldots (44)$$

with only three parameters, and

$$B = \begin{bmatrix} S_{11}^2 & S_{11}S_{21} & S_{11}S_{31} \\ S_{11}S_{21} & S_{21}^2 & S_{21}S_{31} \\ S_{11}S_{31} & S_{21}S_{31} & S_{31}^2 \end{bmatrix} \qquad \ldots (45)$$

The original six parameters have therefore been reduced to only three. Likewise, if $k = 2$, we could represent the original six parameters by $(3 + 2 =)$ five parameters.

Diewert and Wales (1987) suggested a second possible flexible functional form based on the miniflex–Laurent demand system, introduced in a consumer demand context by Barnett (1983). The Laurent series is a generalization of the conventional Taylor series which takes account of negative as well as positive powers in its expansion. Barnett reasonably claims and documents (Barnett (1983) and Barnett and Lee (1985)) that a functional form based on a second-order Laurent series is likely to have a substantially larger regional domain of applicability than standard functional forms based on second-order Taylor series. The cost is in terms of a considerably more complex functional form.

The adaption of the miniflex form to the production case is not straightforward. Price homogeneity, which is easily imposed in the consumer demand case through normalization on income, is more difficult to impose within a cost function. Diewert and Wales suggest a number of possible functional forms, differing in their treatment of the numeraire. Their final suggested functional form, the symmetric generalized Barnett cost function, can be written as

$$C(y; P) = \left[\sum_{i=1}^{n} b_{ii} p_i + \sum_{i=1}^{n} \sum_{j=1, j \neq i}^{n} b_{ij} p_i^{-1/2} p_j^{-1/2} \right.$$

$$\left. - \sum_{i=1}^{n} \sum_{j=1, j \neq i}^{n} \sum_{k=1, k \neq i, k<j}^{n} f_{ijk} p_i^2 p_j^{-1/2} p_k^{-1/2} \right] \cdot h(y) \quad \ldots (46)$$

where we impose that b_{ij}, $f_{ijk} \geq 0$. The first two terms would be those of a standard generalized Leontief cost function (compare equation (8)) where the parameter non-negativity constraint is relaxed. The final price term adds the Laurent terms, normalized by the arbitrary p_i^2 term to preserve price homogeneity.

Using Shephard's lemma, the demand functions are

$$
x_i = \left[b_{ii} - \sum_{j=1, j \neq i}^{n} b_{ij} p_i^{-1/2} p_j^{1/2} \right.
$$

$$
- 2 \cdot \sum_{j=1, j \neq i}^{n} \sum_{k=1, k \neq i, k < j} f_{ijk} p_i p_j^{-1/2} p_k^{-1/2}
$$

$$
+ \tfrac{1}{2} \cdot \sum_{j=1, j \neq i} \sum_{k=1, k \neq j, k > i} f_{jik} p_j^2 p_k^{-1/2} p_i^{-3/2}
$$

$$
\left. + \tfrac{1}{2} \cdot \sum_{j=1, j \neq i} \sum_{k=1, k \neq i, k < i} f_{jki} p_j^2 p_k^{-1/2} p_i^{-3/2} \right] \cdot h(y) \qquad \ldots (47)
$$

Again the problem with this function is the excessive number of parameters that need to be estimated. The $n(n-1)/2 b_{ij}$ terms are themselves enough to define a flexible functional form; the additional $n(n-1)(n-2)/2$ non-negative f_{ijk} terms serve only to improve the functional structure and impose the symmetrical treatment of all variables. Estimation of this function is only feasible for relatively restricted sets of inputs.

Interestingly the function seems to be effective in extending the regional domain of applicability. Diewert and Wales (1987) found in their empirical application that the function preserved in-sample concavity, despite this being violated at every sample point by the generalized Leontief function.

Barnett (1985) suggested using a second-order Laurent log expansion to derive a miniflex–Laurent translog flexible functional form for the consumer demand case. It would be interesting to extend this to the cost function case.

1.9 WEAK SEPARABILITY AND THE INFLEXIBILITY OF FLEXIBLE FUNCTIONAL FORMS

In Section 1.2 we discussed the notion of *strong separability* or *additivity*, which we showed had major implications for functional structure. In particular, a production function that is strongly separable in a given partition of commodities must have a Cobb–Douglas or CES structure of functions of aggregates. If a function is *completely separable* or *commodity-wise additive*, then it must have a Cobb–Douglas or CES structure over commodities. Tests for strong separability are therefore equivalent to tests of flexible functional forms against restricted Cobb–Douglas or CES functions.

There is, however, a further, more subtle, notion of separability, which is important in its own right, but which does not impose such a drastic restriction on flexible functional structures. This is the notion of *weak separability*, which was originally introduced by Leontief (1965).

Weak separability is important because it is a necessary condition to enable aggregation, whether of inputs or outputs. Examples are the existence of a measure of value-added production (Arrow (1974)) or of the aggregate capital stock (Solow (1955)). These are often measured by various simple indices, the most general of which is a Divisia index.[10] For a Divisia index to be path independent requires that a consistent underlying price/quantity index must exist. This requires the production function/cost function to be homothetic and weakly separable.

Weak separability also forms the basis of two-stage budgeting. For instance, if imports as a class were separable from domestic goods, then we would be able to model the demand for aggregate import expenditures, conditional on an aggregate import price index, and then the demand for each sort of import conditional on this overall import expenditure (see, for example, Allen and Whitley (1994)).

A production function,[11] $F(X)$, is said to be *weakly separable* with respect to a partition of its inputs if the marginal rate of substitution between any two inputs, x_i and x_j, belonging to the same group, N^s, is independent of the quantities of inputs outside of N^s:

$$\frac{\partial}{\partial X_k}\left(\frac{F_i}{F_j}\right) = 0, \quad \forall i, j\varepsilon N^s, k \in N^t, S \neq t \qquad \ldots (48)$$

Strotz (1957) showed that such a function could be represented in the form:

$$F(X) = F(X^1, X^2, \ldots, X^r) \qquad \ldots (49)$$

where each of the X^s are functions only of the variables in the corresponding group N^s. Strotz described this as a [production] tree, in which each group could be thought of as a separate intermediate input. Alternatively, the X^s could be considered as a group quantity index.

Gorman (1959), in an extraordinary paper, effectively proved that provided the production function was homothetic, it could also be represented in the dual, cost function form:

$$C(P; y) = C(P^1, P^2, \ldots, P^r; y) \qquad \ldots (50)$$

where the P^s are functions only of the factor prices of the corresponding group N^s in the same partition.[12] The P^s can be considered as group input price indices.[13] Their existence allows the possibility of *two-stage budgeting*, in which the original expenditure on each group is initially decided upon, using this set of price indices; actual expenditures on each factor can then be determined by relative prices within the overall expenditure on the group.

Finally, Berndt and Christensen (1973b) showed that weak separability, combined with homotheticity, was necessary and sufficient for the equality of all Allen elasticities of substitution with respect to different subsets of the partition, i.e.

$$\sigma_{ik}^A = \sigma_{jk}^A, \quad \forall i, j \in N^s, k \in N^t, s \neq t \qquad \ldots (51)$$

The importance of weak separability clearly requires the availability of flexible functional forms that allow for both the testing of weak separability and the representation of it.

Berndt and Christensen (1973a) derived conditions for weak separability in the translog function, interpreted as a structural function. They showed that, taking the case of a translog production function of the form

$$\ln Y = \alpha_0 + \sum_k \alpha_k \cdot \ln X_k + \tfrac{1}{2} \cdot \sum_k \sum_l \gamma_{kl} \cdot \ln X_k \cdot \ln X_l \qquad \ldots (52)$$

the necessary conditions for separability are

$$(\gamma_{ik}\alpha_j - \gamma_{jk}\alpha_i) + \sum_m (\gamma_{ik}\gamma_{jm} - \gamma_{jk}\gamma_{im}) \ln X_m = 0, \quad \forall i, j \in N^s, k \in N^t, s \neq t$$
$$\ldots (53)$$

They showed that there were two possible sets of conditions under which these equations would be satisfied. First, a set of 'linear' restrictions:

$$\gamma_{ik} = \gamma_{jk} = 0, \quad \forall i, j \in N^s, k \in N^t, s \neq t \qquad \ldots (54)$$

An alternative set of 'non-linear' restrictions were as follows:

$$\frac{\alpha_i}{\alpha_j} = \frac{\gamma_{ik}}{\gamma_{jk}} = \frac{\gamma_{im}}{\gamma_{jm}} = 0, \quad \forall i, j \in N^s, k \in N^t, s \neq t; m = 1, \ldots, n \qquad \ldots (55)$$

Clearly, in either set of conditions there are too many equalities required, relative to the number of restrictions implied by weak separability. For instance, in the three-input case, weak separability of inputs one and two from input three requires only one restriction (equality of $\sigma_{13}^A = \sigma_{23}^A$), whereas linear separability will impose two restrictions, as will non-linear separability.

Blackorby, Primont and Russell (1977) showed that in fact for any 'generalized quadratic' functional form (which includes the translog as a special case), the restrictions required by weak separability placed very strong restrictions on the separable functional form. Indeed, they showed that Berndt and Christensen's 'linear restrictions' led to a functional form that was a Cobb–Douglas function of translog aggregator functions; the 'non-linear' restrictions, in contrast, resulted in a translog function of Cobb–Douglas aggregates. In the first case, the Cobb–Douglas assumption led to a unit elasticity of substitution between aggregator functions; in the second, it imposed a unit elasticity of substitution within an input group. Clearly, both are very strong assumptions. Blackorby *et al.* noted that the Berndt and Christensen tests of weak separability were in fact tests of the joint hypothesis of separability and the unit elasticity assumption.

Denny and Fuss (1977) suggested that the restrictiveness of the separability came about as a result of the requirement that the functional form was an exact representation of the underlying technology and therefore must be globally separable. They suggested that an alternative interpretation of flexible functional forms was as a second-order approximation to some unknown functional form. Under these conditions it was enough to test for separability around the point of expansion.

Assuming that the input indices are normalized around $X_i = 1$, the 'non-linear' separability restrictions reduce to

$$\frac{\alpha_i}{\alpha_j} = \frac{\gamma_{ik}}{\gamma_{jk}} = 0, \quad \forall i, j \in N^s, k \in N^t, s \neq t \qquad \ldots (56)$$

These are exactly the right number of restrictions required by separability. Denny and Fuss prove straightforwardly that under these separability conditions the restricted translog function continues to retain its flexibility.[14]

1.10 CONCLUSIONS AND SOME OUTSTANDING ISSUES

The development of flexible functional forms is an essential component in the structural econometric modelling of production. The pioneering work of Diewert (1971) showed how the alternative representation of technology in the form of a cost function could be exploited to generate flexible functional forms with easily derivable factor demand functions. Such a function has enough parameters to allow for an arbitrary set of elasticities of substitution, whilst embodying the regularity conditions imposed by economic theory. The constraints of economic theory could then be imposed directly on the cost function and on the derived factor demand functions.

Clearly flexible functional forms have limitations as well as advantages.

1. A major difficulty in using flexible functional forms is in imposing global concavity conditions. As we have seen, it is difficult to do this without seriously limiting the flexibility of the functional form. Imposing global concavity on generalized Leontief or translog functional forms severely limits their flexibility. Functional forms such as the normalized quadratic offer the possibility of being able to impose concavity, but at the cost of severely reducing the number of degrees of freedom.

2. Given the problems associated with imposing global concavity discussed above, it is important in practical applications of flexible functional forms to maximize the regional domain of theoretical consistency of the functional forms used. For relatively small elasticities of substitution the generalized Leontief cost

function is best; for almost unit elasticities, the translog dominates. The use of the generalized CES/translog function may offer a way forward here.

3. Finally, it should be noted that flexible functional forms are only a second-order approximation to an arbitrary cost function. They can therefore only characterize first- and second-order derivative properties, such as factor demands and elasticities of substitution. For some purposes, we may be interested in the third-order properties of the cost function (e.g. how elasticities of substitution change with factor shares).

In general, second-order flexible functional forms have very inflexible third-order properties. For instance, a globally concave translog cost function will always have a negative own-price third-order derivative. Hence, as a factor's price rises, its own-price elasticity of demand will always become more elastic. This is a property that was utilized in Allen (1993), who exploited the property of an AIDS consumer demand function (analogous to a producer translog cost function) that own-price elasticity of demand becomes more inelastic as market share increases.

This is clearly an issue worth exploring further: an obvious way forward would be to consider third-order Taylor expansions as super-flexible functional forms. Clearly, this would result in potentially a large number of additional parameters to be estimated. These are considerably reduced however by the constraints of economic theory. Work on this issue looks encouraging.

1.11 ACKNOWLEDGEMENTS

I am grateful to Stephen Hall and James Nixon for comments on earlier drafts of this paper. I alone am responsible for errors remaining. The work was carried out under ESRC grant W116251003.

1.12 ENDNOTES

1. Concavity in p in these circumstances is easily shown. Each of the functions $p_k^{1/2} \cdot p_1^{1/2}$ is concave (i.e. the 2×2 matrix of their second partial derivatives is negative semi-definite); hence since a non-negative sum of concave functions will itself be concave, the function $C(y; p)$ will itself be concave.
2. The name of the function is derived from the fact that if $b_{ij} = 0$, for all $i \neq j$, and $h(y) = y$, the factor demand function reduces to $x_i = y \cdot b_{ii}$, which are of course the factor demands from a Leontief production function.
3. Overall Diewert's model has $n \cdot (n-1)/2 + n - 1$ parameters, which is just enough for it to be a valid second-order approximation to an arbitrary cost function. Diewert alludes to this in his article (1971, p. 506), although his actual definition of a flexible functional form was not published until 1974! (Diewert (1974, p. 113)).
4. Other characterizations of this criterion are discussed below.

5. Note that in the two-factor case there are as many structural parameters in the CES as translog function. The CES specification is therefore only restrictive if the number of factors is greater than two.

6. Heady and Dillon's (1961) work on agricultural production functions is a very early anticipation of the use of quadratic functional forms.

7. These results straightforwardly generalize to the case of a translog cost function. Clearly, we require of the cost function that it is linearly homogeneous in factor prices and a concave function of those prices.

8. The extreme case is when $s \cdot s^T - \Sigma$ is zero, which occurs if one share is unity (all other shares must in this case be zero).

9. The term was coined by Lau (1986).

10. The Divisia index uses current value shares to aggregate components: it thus consists of shifting weights over time. Other commonly used indices such as the Lesperes or Pascche indices use fixed weights, and are thus only consistent with very restrictive cost or production functions.

11. We assume continuity and twice differentiability of the production function. Blackorby, Primout and Russell (1978) show that equivalent definitions are available which do not require differentiability.

12. Lau (1969) is credited with the full proof. The Strotz, Gorman, and Lau papers were all written in the consumer demand context. The generalization to production functions is trivial.

13. Of course, these will not be conventional additive price indices of the Lesperes or Pascche type, unless the function is strongly separable. The existence of the indices, however, is required for a flexible price index, such as a Divisia index, to be consistent.

14. Allen and Whitley (1994) suggest an extension of the Denny and Fuss result to test separability within the almost ideal demand system.

$$\boxed{\begin{array}{c} 2 \\ \text{Modelling Investment with} \\ \text{Adjustment Costs Using} \\ \text{Flexible Functional Forms} \\ \text{CHRIS ALLEN} \end{array}}$$

2.1 INTRODUCTION

In this chapter we propose, derive and estimate a new model of investment in the forward-looking neoclassical tradition. The model utilizes the translog flexible functional form and therefore relaxes many of the restrictive assumptions about elasticities of substitution often used in the investment literature. It also adopts a gross output formulation, allowing the influence of energy and raw materials prices on investment, thereby avoiding the usual assumption about the separability of value-added from other inputs commonly used in the existing literature.

Our model is explicitly linked with the Tobin Q model of investment. We directly derive the shadow value of the capital stock by estimating the parameters of the underlying technology of the economy. Using a restricted cost function, the shadow value of capital is measured by the impact of a marginal addition to the capital stock in reducing the total cost of production. We therefore have in principle a Tobin Q model of investment in which we can directly measure the shadow valuation of the capital stock through its role in reducing costs. In our theoretical work we explicitly derive this relationship.[1]

The empirical success of our formulation suggests that the well-documented poor performance of the Q model may be a result of the considerable mismeasurement problems that have plagued the conventional approach of testing it. Since Hayashi (1982), it has been understood that the identification of the stock market valuation of a company with the underlying theoretical concept of the

Macroeconomic Modelling in a Changing World. Edited by C. Allen and S. Hall
© 1997 John Wiley & Sons Ltd

shadow value of the capital stock is at best only valid under very restrictive conditions.[2] Recently, it has been realized that these problems are compounded by the likelihood that financial markets themselves systematically mismeasure the actual financial value of a firm (see Blanchard, Rhee and Summers (1993) and Leroy (1989)). Increasing empirical evidence is available of financial market imperfections, excess volatility, and the presence of asset market bubbles.

In the light of these measurement problems, the poor empirical performance of conventional Q models is hardly surprising. Unfortunately, their failure has cast doubt upon the adequacy of the forward-looking neoclassical investment theory itself. An example of this scepticism is in the recent paper by Blundell *et al.* (1992) (which adopts an eclectic approach) which, after noting the poor empirical performance of the Q model in both time-series and panel data models, suggest that cash flow variables, representing liquidity constraints, must also be added in addition to Q to obtain an adequate investment equation.[3]

In the current chapter our emphasis is on the estimation and testing of the forward-looking model. The forward-looking Euler equation is estimated and found to be reasonably well behaved. We then test for the addition of a cash-flow variable, namely the rate of profit, which is not found to be significant in our model. Finally, we examine an alternative model, that of a backward-looking error correction model. Here we find some limited evidence of a stable backward-looking equation, with some instability in the marginal processes generating the forcing variables. Unfortunately, this test lacks power.

We believe that the use of flexible functional forms in investment analysis is an important part of the emerging research agenda. Recent papers by Morrison (1986, 1988) and Peeters (1994) have used the generalized Leontief cost function and generalized quadratic cost functions, respectively. Unfortunately these flexible functional forms are not attractive for aggregate analysis owing to the difficulty in testing for and imposing the desirable property of a unit elasticity of substitution between labour and capital within that framework. Other work using the translog cost function is Pindyck and Rotemberg (1983a,b). Our work differs from these papers in that we use a restricted cost function and use a slight modification of adjustment costs, which makes the first-order conditions considerably simpler and more interpretable.

2.2 A MODEL OF INVESTMENT

The firm is assumed to minimize the expected present value of a stream of future costs in each period t, given the entire expected future paths of its input prices and output. The firm's minimand at an arbitrary base period 0 is therefore:

$$\min_{\{K_s\}} E_0 \left\{ \sum_{s=0}^{\infty} \left[\prod_{j=0}^{s} \beta_{s+j} \right] \left(\sum_i W_{is} \cdot X_{is} + V_s \cdot K_s \right) \right\} \qquad \ldots (1)$$

where β_t is discount factor of the ex ante required rate of return in period t, W_{it} is the price and X_{it} the quantity of the ith variable factor of production, V_t is the rental cost and K_t is the quantity of capital available in the tth period.

The firm's technology is described by a restricted variable cost function, which we shall write as $\Phi(W_t, Y_t, K_t, K_{t-1})$. The function includes the vector of variable factor prices W_t, the required level of output Y_t, and incorporates the quasi-fixed capital stock and the internal adjustment costs associated with changing the capital stock.

In our empirical work we shall assume that the internal adjustment costs are quadratic and additively separable in investment. The augmented restricted cost function can therefore be written in the following form:

$$\ln \Phi_t = \ln C(W_t, Y_t, K_t) + \frac{\gamma}{2}(k_t - k_{t-1} + \delta)^2 \qquad \ldots (2)$$

where $\ln C$ is a standard translog *static* restricted cost function. The final term represents adjustment costs. Lower case letters represent logarithms. The term δ represents the extent to which investment for replacement purposes incurs adjustment costs. Note that if δ is equal to the depreciation rate, then we have the approximation, $k_t - k_{t-1} + \delta \approx I_t/K_{t-1}$.

Variable factor demand shares are given by Shephard's lemma:

$$S_{it} = \frac{\partial \ln \Phi_t}{\partial \ln W_{it}} = \frac{\partial \ln C_t}{\partial \ln W_{it}} \qquad \ldots (3)$$

Variable factor shares are therefore unaffected by capital adjustment costs as a result of the separability assumption.

We define the shadow value of the capital stock relative to variable costs as

$$E_t\{S_{kt}\} = E_t \left\{ -\frac{\partial \ln C_t}{\partial \ln K_t} \right\} \qquad \ldots (4)$$

We can now derive the Euler equation for the optimal investment sequence as

$$\Phi_t \cdot \left[\frac{V_t \cdot K_t}{\Phi_t} - S_{kt} \right] + \Phi_t \cdot \gamma(k_t - k_{t-1} + \delta) - E_t\{\beta_t \cdot \Phi_{t+1} \cdot \gamma(k_{t+1} - k_t + \delta)\} = 0 \quad \ldots (5)$$

This Euler equation has a straightforward interpretation. Along the optimal investment sequence path the firm is indifferent between a marginal proportional increase in capital in period t, and a similar proportional decrease in capital in the following period. (The log formulation ensures that these are symmetric.)

The associated transversality condition is

$$\lim_{\tau \to \infty} E_0 \left\{ \left[\prod_{j=0}^{\tau} \beta_j \cdot \frac{\Phi_{j+1}}{\Phi_j} \right] \left(\frac{V_\tau \cdot K_\tau}{\Phi_\tau} - S_{k\tau} + \gamma(k_\tau - k_{\tau-1} + \delta) \right) \right\} = 0 \quad \ldots (6)$$

The transversality condition restricts the value of the firm and the value of the capital stock from exploding. Clearly, this requires that $\beta_j \cdot \Phi_{j+1}/\Phi_j < 1$, i.e. that the discount factor, β_j, is small enough.

Note that in the presence of adjustment costs, the conventional envelope theorem of duality theory will in general cease to hold. With zero adjustment costs the conventional envelope theorem entails that in equilibrium the shadow value of capital will equal its rental cost, i.e.

$$S_{kt} = \frac{V_t \cdot K_t}{\Phi_t} \qquad \ldots (7)$$

However, from the Euler equation it can be seen that the shadow value of capital will actually be greater than its rental value in a steady-state growth equilibrium in which the capital stock grows at the rate g. From the Euler equation we have

$$\frac{V_t \cdot K_t}{\Phi_t} - S_{kt} = \left[\beta_t \cdot \frac{\Phi_{t+1}}{\Phi_t} - 1\right] \cdot \gamma \cdot (g + \delta) < 0 \qquad \ldots (8)$$

Hence, in the presence of adjustment costs the degree of capital accumulation will be less then the static optimum. This is true even for *net* adjustment costs ($\delta = 0$) if the economy is experiencing steady-state growth. If adjustment costs are on *gross* investment ($\delta > 0$), then the envelope theorem will not even hold in a zero growth static steady state.

The use of the transversality condition allows us to derive the general solution to the set of Euler equations. Solving the set of Euler equations (5) forward, subject to the transversality condition (6), we derive the following decision rule:

$$\gamma(k_t - k_{t-1} + \delta) = E_t \left\{ (-1) \sum_{i=0}^{\infty} \left[\prod_{j=0}^{i} \beta_{t+j} \cdot \frac{\Phi_{t+j+1}}{\Phi_{t+j}} \right] \left(\frac{V_{t+i}K_{t+i}}{\Phi_{t+i}} - S_{k,t+i} \right) \right\}$$
$$\ldots (9)$$

Hence, current investment is related to the discounted sum of the future expected excess of the shadow value of the capital stock relative to the rental cost of capital.

It is straightforward to relate this decision rule to the marginal Q ratio of Tobin. We obtain the formula

$$P_t^i \cdot (Q_t - 1) \cdot \frac{K_t}{\Phi_t} = E_t \left\{ (-1) \sum_{i=0}^{\infty} \left[\prod_{j=0}^{i} \beta_{t+j} \cdot \frac{\Phi_{t+j+1}}{\Phi_{t+j}} \right] \left(\frac{V_{t+i}K_{t+i}}{\Phi_{t+i}} - S_{k,t+i} \right) \right\}$$
$$\ldots (10)$$

where P_t^i is the price of investment goods and Q_t is Tobin's marginal Q (see Hayashi (1982)).

2.3 THE EMPIRICAL MODEL

We parameterize the model using a static translog restricted cost function. We can write the restricted cost function in the form

$$\ln C_t = \alpha_0 + \sum_i \alpha_i w_{it} + \sum_r \alpha_r Z_{rt}$$

$$+ \frac{1}{2} \cdot \sum_i \sum_j \gamma_{ij} w_{it} w_{jt} + \frac{1}{2} \cdot \sum_i \sum_s \alpha_{is} w_{it} z_{st}$$

$$+ \frac{1}{2} \cdot \sum_r \sum_j \alpha_{rj} Z_{rt} w_{jt} + \frac{1}{2} \cdot \sum_r \sum_s \alpha_{rs} Z_{rt} Z_{st} \qquad \dots (11)$$

The subscripts i and j range over the domain of variable factor prices, whilst r and s have as domain the set $\{y_t, k_t, t\}$, {output, capital stock, technology trend}. All the variables are in natural logarithms.

We place the following restrictions on the parameters of the static cost function to impose the requirements of rationality and to reduce the parameter space required for estimation.

1. *Symmetry.*   Symmetry imposes the following restrictions on the parameters of the cost function:

$$\gamma_{ij} = \gamma_{ji}, \qquad \alpha_{is} = \alpha_{si}, \qquad \alpha_{rs} = \alpha_{sr}, \qquad \alpha_{rs} = \alpha_{sr} \qquad \dots (12)$$

where the domains of the subscripts remain as before.

2. *Linear homogeneity in factor prices.*   Cost functions are linearly homogeneous in variable factor prices. This requires

$$\sum_i \alpha_i = 1, \qquad \sum_j \gamma_{ij} = 0, \qquad \sum_i \alpha_{is} = 0, \qquad \sum_j \alpha_{rj} = 0 \qquad \dots (13)$$

Symmetry and linear homogeneity together ensure the so-called property of 'adding up' of factor demands. Adding up ensures that the sum of variable factor shares add up to unity.

3. *Concavity in factor prices.*   A sufficient condition for the cost function to be concave in factor prices is that the matrix of price coefficients, $\Gamma_{ij} = \{\gamma_{ij}\}$, should be negative semi-definite (see Jorgenson and Fraumeni (1981)). Imposing this restriction globally places very strong restrictions on the possible values of the elasticities of substitution (Diewert and Wales (1987)). Therefore we do not impose this restriction globally, but rather check the empirical estimates for conformity.

4. *Constant returns to scale.* Constant returns to scale is required for aggregation of individual firm cost functions. Constant returns to scale implies that the cost function is linearly homogeneous jointly in output and fixed factors. It therefore implies that

$$\alpha_y + \alpha_k = 1, \qquad \alpha_y > 1, \qquad \alpha_k < 0$$

$$\alpha_{yi} = -\alpha_{ki}, \qquad \alpha_{yt} = -\alpha_{kt} \qquad (14)$$

$$\alpha_{yy} + \alpha_{kk} + 2\alpha_{ky} = 0$$

The subscript i again ranges over the domain of factor prices.

The fully augmented restricted cost function can therefore be written in the following form:

$$\ln \Phi_t = \alpha_0 + \sum_i \alpha_i w_{it} + \sum_r \alpha_r z_{rt}$$

$$+ \frac{1}{2} \cdot \sum_i \sum_j \gamma_{ij} w_{it} w_{jt} + \frac{1}{2} \cdot \sum_i \sum_s \alpha_{is} w_{it} z_{st}$$

$$+ \frac{1}{2} \cdot \sum_r \sum_j \alpha_{rj} z_{rt} w_{jt} + \frac{1}{2} \cdot \sum_r \sum_s \alpha_{rs} z_{rt} z_{st}$$

$$+ \frac{\gamma}{2} \cdot (k_t - k_{t-1} + \delta) \qquad \dots (15)$$

Using Shephard's lemma we can derive the variable factor demand shares from the augmented cost function as

$$S_{it} = \frac{w_{it} \cdot x_{it}}{C_t} = \alpha_i + \sum_j \gamma_{ij} w_{jt} + \alpha_{yi} y_t + \alpha_{ki} k_t + \alpha_{ti} t \qquad \dots (16)$$

As noted above, these are independent of the capital adjustment costs.

We can also derive the equation for the shadow value of the capital stock (see equation (4)). This has the form

$$S_{kt} = - \left[\alpha_k + \sum_i \alpha_{ik} w_{it} + \alpha_{yk} y_t + \alpha_{kk} k_t + \alpha_{kt} t \right] \qquad \dots (17)$$

2.4 DERIVING AN EMPIRICAL INVESTMENT EQUATION

The fully stochastic control problem is highly non-linear and therefore is not susceptible to a closed-form solution.[4] We therefore cannot estimate the equations using a fully efficient maximum likelihood method, which would require the use of such a solution. Instead, we will need to use a limited information technique that will seek to estimate the first-order conditions or Euler equations alone.

Substituting the equation for the shadow cost of capital (17) into the Euler equation (5), we can derive the Euler equation for the optimal investment sequence in our parametric model:

$$\left[\frac{V_r \cdot K_t}{\Phi_t} + \alpha_k + \sum_i \alpha_{ik} w_{it} + \alpha_{yk} y_t + \alpha_{kk} k_t + \alpha_{tk} t \right]$$
$$+ \gamma(k_t - k_{t-1} + \delta) - E_t \left\{ \beta_t \cdot \frac{\Phi_{t+1}}{\Phi_t} \cdot \gamma(k_{t+1} - k_t + \delta) \right\} = 0 \quad \dots (18)$$

We shall estimate this equation using a generalized method of moments (GMM) estimator. The technique we shall use is the so-called errors in variables method for the estimation of rational expectations models. This technique involves replacing the expectation of a future variable by its realization and incorporating the resultant measurement (or innovation) error into the disturbance term.

It is straightforward to show that this substitution method will result in a moving average error of at least the order of the forward expectation. In fact, the error process may be in general of order greater than this depending on the precise dating of the expectation set and the length of the planning horizon. Our equations contain only single-period-ahead expectations, but planning horizons generally are typically at least six months to a year ahead, which may result in a moving average process of up to four quarters. The length of the moving average process is an empirical question, but it should be noted that its order is likely to be finite.

A further complication is provided by the fact that the data set contains principally non-stationary forcing variables. Investment, output and factor prices all are non-stationary variables.

Wickens (1993) suggests the use of the Wickens and Breusch (1988) transformation for the limited information estimation of Euler equations containing integrated variables. The Wickens–Breusch estimator is effectively a Bewley (1979) transformation of the original Euler equation, putting it into a form in which the only levels variables are those in the cointegrating regression, whilst all the other variables are in a differenced form.

Wickens (1993) shows that in a standard backward-looking dynamic equation the Bewley transform can be used to obtain consistent estimates of both the long- and short-run parameters of the original equation by a single-stage estimation. In the presence of cointegrated I(1) variables, the estimates of the long-run parameters will further be super-consistent and Wickens shows that estimators of the long-run parameters have an asymptotic mixed normal distribution.[5] He makes the reasonable conjecture, without demonstration, that this result will also carry over to analogous Bewley transformations of Euler equations with future expectations.

In what follows we make use of the Wickens conjecture to estimate our Euler equation. We can reformulate equation (18) using a quasi-Bewley transform as

$$\frac{V_t \cdot K_t}{\Phi_t} = - \left[\alpha_k + \sum_i \alpha_{ik} w_{it} + \alpha_{yk} y_t + \alpha_{kk} k_t + \alpha_{tk} t \right] - \gamma \cdot \Delta k_t$$

$$+ E_t \left(\beta_t \cdot \frac{\Phi_{t+1}}{\Phi_t} \cdot \gamma \cdot \Delta k_{t+1} \right) + \gamma \cdot \left(\beta_t \cdot \frac{\Phi_{t+1}}{\Phi_t} - 1 \right) \cdot \delta \quad \ldots (19)$$

In what follows we shall assume that $\beta_t \Phi_{t+1}/\Phi_t$, the real discount rate, is a constant, which can be estimated.

Clearly, not all of the parameters of (19) are identified. Only γ, the adjustment coefficient, $\beta_t \Phi_{t+1}/\Phi_t$ the discount rate, plus the long-run parameters are identified. Note that unless we have an independent estimate of α_k, then δ will also not be identified in equation (19). Gregory, Pagan and Smith (1993) argue that the discount rate also is likely to be non-identified in a standard linear-quadratic control problem. Their result does not immediately apply to our non-standard problem, but it is likely that the identification problem that they identify will affect our estimation here.

2.5 ECONOMETRIC CONSIDERATIONS

The presence of non-stationary data will cause us a variety of problems of non-standard inference. To reduce these to a minimum, we first test the data for cointegration. Conditional on such cointegration existing, we then proceed to estimate equation (19) using a GMM estimator.

Several methods exist for testing the hypothesis of cointegration. Here we employ the standard Engle–Granger and Johansen maximum likelihood canonical correlation estimator.

The Johansen estimator is normally considerably more powerful than the Engle–Granger estimator. However, in these circumstances, Gregory, Pagan and Smith (1993) have criticized the appropriateness of the procedure for tackling a problem in which there is likely to be moving average errors. The estimator requires the assumption that the data-generation process follows a finite-order vector autoregression (VAR) with white noise, which is clearly invalidated by the presence of a moving average error. Our use of the Johansen technique therefore must presume that empirically a finite-order VAR will prove an adequate proxy to a finite moving average process.

To estimate the final equation we have used a GMM estimator (Hansen (1982)).[6] GMM is robust to non-standard disturbances. Because our model clearly will have at least an MA(1) process in the error term, this makes GMM an attractive estimator. GMM allows us to correct for the moving average process in the final estimate of the parameter variance–covariance matrix and to utilize a consistent and efficient method of weighting the orthogonality conditions.

The GMM estimator is applied directly to the set of orthogonality conditions, implied by the application of rational expectations to the Euler equation (19).

Specifically, the moments are formed by using the realized values of the conditional future expectations in the Euler equations and utilizing as instruments a set of variables known at the time the expectation is formed. The parameter estimates are then derived by minimizing the weighted quadratic form of the moment conditions using as optimal weights the inverse of a consistent estimate of the variance–covariance matrix of the orthogonality conditions.

The resultant parameter estimates are then given by

$$\hat{\beta} = (X^\mathrm{T} Z \hat{\Omega}^{-1} Z^\mathrm{T} X)^{-1} X^\mathrm{T} Z \hat{\Omega}^{-1} Z^\mathrm{T} y \qquad \ldots (20)$$

where $\hat{\beta}$ is the $k \times 1$ vector of parameter estimates, y is the $T \times 1$ vector of the observations on the factor share, X is the $T \times k$ matrix of observations on the right-hand side variables (including 'realized' expectations), and Z is the $T \times j$ matrix of instrumental variables. Clearly, we require $j \geq k$. The $j \times j$ matrix, $\hat{\Omega}$, is a consistent estimator of the variance–covariance matrix of the orthogonality conditions.

The asymptotic covariance estimator of the parameters is then:

$$\mathrm{Var}(\hat{\beta}) = (X^\mathrm{T} Z \hat{\Omega}^{-1} Z^\mathrm{T} X)^{-1} \qquad \ldots (21)$$

The estimation of the $\hat{\Omega}$ matrix is done by iteration. Hansen (1982) showed that the inverse of a consistent estimator of the variance–covariance matrix of the orthogonality conditions provided the optimal weighting matrix of orthogonality conditions. In our work we have used a heteroscedasticity and autocorrelation consistent (HAC) covariance matrix estimator (Andrews (1991)). To guarantee the positive definiteness of our estimated covariance matrix, potentially compromised by the presence of the moving average error, we have used a Parzen kernel estimator (see Gallant (1987)). The expected finite order of the moving average process allows us to truncate this estimator at a relatively low order. Corrections for potential conditional heteroscedasticity were also made.

Under the hypothesis of stationarity in the stochastic processes generating the variables, Hansen (1982) showed that the GMM parameter estimator (equation (2)) provided a consistent estimator satisfying the central limit theorem. This allows us to derive a robust estimator of the variance–covariance matrix of parameter estimates. Using Johansen's theorem about inference in the presence of cointegration, we shall assume that Hansen's theorem will also hold in the presence of non-stationary variables, provided we have a valid cointegrating vector for all I(1) variables and that all other variables are I(0).

The great advantage of GMM, namely that it makes few assumptions about the distribution of the empirical moments, is also a source of difficulty when it comes to testing model adequacy. Hansen (1982) suggested the use of a portmanteau test of both model specification and instrument validity. The test is based on the quadratic form of the optimally weighted moment conditions. If the model is correctly specified (i.e. assuming we have a consistent estimator of the parameter vector) and the instruments are valid, then by the law of large numbers, each of the empirical moments should be close to zero in large samples. Provided we have more moment conditions than parameters, the empirical moment conditions will not all be identically zero, so that we can construct a test to show that the empirical moments are not too far from zero, after appropriately accounting for sampling error using asymptotic theory.[7] The proposed test is based on the objective function, which can be shown asymptotically to be distributed with a chi-squared distribution with degrees of freedom equal to the number of overidentifying restrictions. Unfortunately, Tauchen (1986) shows that the test sometimes lacks power in finite samples.

A key issue in our estimation will therefore be our choice of instruments. In principle, increasing the number of valid instruments will lead to a smaller asymptotic covariance matrix. However, Hansen (1985) proved that there is a lower bound to the asymptotic covariance matrix and evidence from Monte Carlo experiments on small samples suggests that increasing the number of instruments may result in increased bias (see Tauchen (1986) and Kocherlakota (1990)). Essentially what seems to be happening in small samples is that the distribution of the instrumental variable estimator as the number of instruments increases tends towards that of a biased OLS estimator (see Davidson and MacKinnon (1993, p. 604)). Hence, Tauchen (1986) suggests that the most credence should be placed on those estimates obtained with the smallest instrument set because their confidence intervals will be most reliable. In the work reported here, we have experimented with a number of instrument sets, each of which are proper subsets of each other.

2.6 STATIONARITY AND COINTEGRATION IN THE INVESTMENT EQUATION

In this section we consider the stationarity properties of the data used in the investment function and examine the cointegration properties of the investment equation itself. The stationarity properties of most of the data are examined in Allen (1994), in which all of the relevant factor-price series are found to be non-stationary I(1) series.

The principal remaining issue is the order of integration of the capital stock series. Since the primary focus in this chapter is on capital accumulation, we have re-derived the capital stock series on the basis of the gross investment series and used a depreciation rate in keeping with that used in our cost of capital measure.[8]

The stationarity properties of the capital stock are extensively discussed in Appendix 2 where, we conclude that the capital stock is likely to contain a single unit root, but with an additional root close to the unit circle.

To test for cointegration in the investment function, both the single-equation Engle–Granger and the VAR full information maximum likelihood (FIML) Johansen techniques were utilized. Table 2.1 reports the alternative estimates of the cointegrating vector for investment.[9] As in the case of the variable

Table 2.1 Alternative estimates of cointegrating vectors

	Engle–Granger	Johansen	GMM*	ECM†
α_{fy}	0.020	0.058	0.010	0.006
α_{yy}	0.057	0.154	0.204	2.03
α_{yt}	0.00007	n.a.	0.00010	0.00047
DMAN	−0.432	−0.889	−0.327	−1.324
Constant	−0.315	n.a.	−0.177	n.a.
DF	3.15	—	—	—
ADF(1)	4.41	—	—	—
ADF(2)	4.74*	—	—	—
ADF(3)	5.06*	—	—	—
ADF(4)	5.71*	—	—	—
Eigenvalue	—	32.50*	—	—
Trace	—	65.30*	—	—
$\hat{\alpha}$	—	−0.196	—	—

*Estimate of cointegrating vector from final forward-looking specification (from Table 2.2, equation (4)).

†Estimate of cointegrating vector from unrestricted error correction model (from Table 2.3).

factor demands (see Allen (1994)), it was found that an extra variable, the ratio of manufacturing output to total non-energy output, was required to obtain cointegration in the investment equation.

The first two columns of the table present the minimal set of cointegrating variables using Engle–Granger OLS. From the Engle–Granger Dickey–Fuller and augmented Dickey–Fuller tests, there is clear evidence of cointegration in investment. However, we know that the OLS procedure lacks power, especially against structural breaks (see Campos, Ericsson and Hendry (1993)).

The more powerful Johansen technique also finds a significant cointegrating vector for investment with a suitably large and significant equation loading weight. Perhaps reflecting the issue of moving average approximation, the Johansen procedure required a relatively long lag length of four quarters to deliver independent Gaussian residuals. The cointegrating vector clearly belongs to the investment equation, as the highly significant weighting shows.

2.7 ESTIMATION RESULTS FOR THE FORWARD-LOOKING MODEL

Conditional on cointegration existing in the long run between the variables in the investment equation, we can now estimate the fully dynamic Euler equation (19), using the quasi-Bewley transformation. As described in Section 2.5, we have used a GMM estimator and tested for alternative instrument sets.

Table 2.2 reports the results for the estimation of the single-equation, forward-looking model. Four equations are given, the first three with increasing instrument sets; the final equation is the estimates of a model with a restricted time preference rate. The Hansen test is both a test of the overidentifying restrictions on the instrument set and acts as a quasi-likelihood ratio test.

The first three equations present results for a monotonically increasing instrument set. We expanded the instrument set from a minimal set without any lags on the forcing variables (equation (1)) to a single lag on each forcing variable (equation (2)) to both first and second lags on each variable. As expected, increasing the number of lags in the instrument set improved the precision of our estimates. The Hansen test of the overidentifying restrictions indicated the validity of the increased number of instruments. No more than two lags of the forcing variables were used in our final equation (equation (3)). Adding more than second-order lags to the instrument set made little difference in reducing the estimated parameter covariance matrix, suggesting that we may have reached an approximate lower bound. Further lagged instruments were not used in order to avoid possible biases. The parameter estimates of the third equation are similar to those given by the minimal instrument set.

Both the estimation of the parameter covariance matrix and the derivation of the optimal weighting matrix requires a truncation of the lag used in the

Table 2.2   GMM estimates of net investment equation

	(1)	(2)	(3)	(4)
α_{fy}	0.028	0.013	0.027	0.010
	(1.32)	(0.59)	(1.51)	(0.82)
α_{yy}	0.384	0.427	0.617	0.204
	(1.08)	(1.40)	(2.30)	(2.09)
α_{yt}	0.00022	0.00050	0.00073	0.00010
	(0.37)	(1.04)	(1.65)	(0.33)
DMAN	−0.349	−0.304	−0.330	−0.327
	(−3.45)	(−3.96)	(−3.98)	(−4.97)
Δk_{t+1}	19.90	10.17	21.46	10.71
	(1.17)	(0.74)	(1.90)	(1.44)
Δk_t	−16.76	−6.44	−15.85	—
	(−1.15)	(−0.57)	(−1.64)	—
Constant	−0.231	−0.162	−0.207	−0.177
	(−1.81)	(−1.58)	(−1.98)	(−2.19)
Dummy 1984Q4/1985Q1	−0.088	−0.047	−0.090	−0.056
	(−1.36)	(−0.94)	(−2.13)	(−1.87)
Hansen test (df)	0.104	4.344	4.793	7.469
	(1)	(4)	(9)	(10)

heteroscedasticity and autocorrelation consistent covariance matrix. Rather than make an a priori judgement or use an automatic bandwidth selector, we have made the choice on the basis of the estimated residuals. Examination of the residuals from the early estimates of the equations suggested evidence of an auto regression (AR) process as well as the expected moving average (MA) term in the error process. Consideration of the autocorrelation and partial autocorrelation plots suggests that a stationary ARMA (1,1) process might be an adequately parsimonious model for the error term. In the circumstances, a relatively long lag before truncation was used to estimate the HAC covariance matrix. The reported results use a truncation lag of six quarters: increasing this to eight quarters or reducing the lag to four quarters gave similar results.

Equation (3) represents our final unrestricted equation. All the parameters are significant and have the correct signs. From the transversality condition, however, we would expect that the coefficient on forward investment was less in absolute value than that on current investment. This does not hold for our point estimates of these two coefficients, although their respective values are within a single standard error of each other. We therefore restricted the real-time preference rate to a quarterly rate of 2%.

The restricted equation is reported as equation (4). It was estimated with the same instrument set as equation (3). The difference in the absolute values of the overidentification test can be used as a quasi-likelihood ratio test of the restriction. The restriction was easily accepted with the value $\chi^2(1) = 2.94$.

2.8 TESTING THE FORWARD-LOOKING MODEL AGAINST A BACKWARD-LOOKING MODEL

As we have already noted, the direct tests of our forward-looking Euler equation model lack power in small samples. To confirm our model as an adequate description of firm behaviour it is therefore helpful to test it against a well-specified alternative model. The most obvious alternative is a backward-looking error correction model. Such a model, widely used in the econometric literature, explains investment purely in terms of the constant-parameter representation of observed variables.

To derive the test we must derive a framework into which it is possible to nest the two alternative models. In fact, using our original model it turns out to be relatively easy to derive such a framework. By linearization it is possible to derive a backward-looking representation of the optimal choice sequence. Going back to the decision rule itself, note that we can write equation (9) in the form

$$\gamma(k_t - k_{t-1} + \delta) = \mathrm{E}_t \left\{ \sum_{i=0}^{\infty} \left[\prod_{j=0}^{i} \zeta_{t+j} \right] M_{t+i} \right\} \qquad \ldots (22)$$

where

$$\zeta_{t+j} = \beta_{t+j}\frac{\Phi_{t+j+1}}{\Phi_{t+j}}$$

and

$$M_{t+i} = S_{k,t+i} - \frac{V_{t+i}K_{t+i}}{\Phi_{t+i}}$$

Following Abel and Blanchard (1986),[10] using a first-order Taylor expansion, we may linearize the right-hand side expression around the sample means $\bar{\zeta}$ and $\bar{M}$:

$$\gamma(k_t - k_{t-1} + \delta) = \mathrm{E}_t \left\{ \frac{\bar{\zeta}\cdot\bar{M}}{1-\bar{\zeta}} + \frac{\bar{M}}{1-\bar{\zeta}} \cdot \sum_{i=0}^{\infty} \bar{\zeta}^i \cdot (\zeta_{t+i} - \bar{\zeta}) \right.$$

$$\left. + \sum_{i=0}^{\infty} \bar{\beta}^{i+1} \cdot (M_{t+i} - \bar{M}) \right\} \qquad \ldots (23)$$

This expression gives an equation for the current investment rate in terms of the expectations at t of the future sequences of ζ_{t+j} and M_{t+j}. In principle these can be derived using a standard k-step Wiener–Kolmogorov predictor based on the set of observed variables (see Hansen and Sargent (1980) and Sargent (1987, Chapter 11). In principle, therefore, we would be able to use this closed-form linearized solution to estimate the forward-looking investment sequence in a fully efficient way: equation (23) could be estimated by FIML, jointly with the data-generation processes of the exogenous variables. Although attractive, we will not pursue this course in the present chapter.

Instead, we shall use the equation to generate a backward-looking representation of the investment equation. On condition that there exists a stable data-generation process for each of the exogenous variables, we may substitute out the expectations using the Wiener–Kolmogorov formulae to derive an investment equation that depends purely on variables dated at t or earlier. This is the backward-looking representation of the model.

This backward-looking representation is theoretically extremely fragile since it is derived under a specific set of prediction formulae. The parameters of the backward-looking representation therefore depend directly on the parameters of the data-generation process of the forcing variables. Under the null of the forward-looking model, these parameters will change every time the marginal processes generating the exogenous variables are subject to structural change.

Using this framework, Hendry (1988) and Favero and Hendry (1992) suggest an encompassing test of the two models. There are four possible outcomes.

First, it is well known that if both marginal processes and error correction representations are stable, then the forward-looking Euler equation and a backward-looking error correction representation are observationally equivalent and cannot be distinguished (Sargent (1976)).

Secondly, if the marginal processes are found to be unstable, whilst a stable error correction representation can be found, then Hendry argues that this is strong evidence in favour of a backward-looking model (Hendry (1988)). Unfortunately, as Cuthbertson (1991) notes, in finite samples Hendry's test cannot rule out that there is in fact an expectations generating process that is indeed stable, but which is as yet undiscovered by the econometrician. The obvious example of this would be that the instability is caused by a variable omitted from the equations generating the expectations.

Alternatively, if the marginal processes and error correction representation are unstable, then whilst an Euler equation performs reasonably well, this is evidence in favour of the forward-looking model.

The final case is the unlikely result in which we have stable marginal processes together with an unstable error correction representation. This case merely suggests some misspecification of the error correction model.

2.9 EVIDENCE FROM BACKWARD-LOOKING MODELS

2.9.1 The Error Correction Model

We first estimated the backward-looking model for investment itself. Our procedure was first to estimate a parsimonious statistical model in order to maximize the power of our stability tests and then to subject the model to a battery of stability tests.

The backward-looking model was estimated in an error correction formulation. Two alternative models of the error correction model were estimated. The first was derived from a general AR distributed lag model with unrestricted levels terms. The second was estimated using the same cointegrating vector derived by the Johansen procedure as was used in the forward-looking model above. This vector was placed into a general autoregressive distributed lag model in difference form. This latter model provides a check on our specification.

Both error correction models were originally estimated in an unrestricted form with a fourth-order lag on each variable. We then used a standard data-based reduction procedure to achieve a final congruent and parsimonious model.

The final stage in each reduction process is reported in Table 2.3. Each model was found to have a similar basic dynamic specification. In each case the likelihood ratio tests of the model reduction reported in the last row of the table show that the final equations parsimoniously encompass the generalized original model. The final models also appear to provide an adequate description of the data: Lagrange multiplier tests on the residuals show the absence of significant serial correlation, non-linearity, heteroscedasticity, or significant divergences from normality.

The cointegrating vector from the Johansen procedure is significant in the first equation. The relatively small coefficient is a result of the relative scaling of

Table 2.3 Error correction models

	Unrestricted cointegrating vector	Using Johansen vector
$\Delta LK(-1)$	0.838 (10.70)	0.955 (12.76)
$\Delta LK(-2)$	0.174 (2.04)	0.185 (2.10)
$\Delta LK(-4)$	−0.167 (−2.61)	−0.173 (−3.15)
ΔLY	0.0226 (3.73)	0.0234 (3.74)
$\Delta KSHARE(-1)$	−0.0123 (−2.32)	— —
$\Delta Vector(-1)$	—	−0.00909 (−2.09)
Error correction parameter	−0.00623 (−2.20)	−0.00541 (−2.04)
α_{fy}	−0.006* (−0.10)	−0.05[†]
α_{yy}	−2.035* (−1.69)	−0.155[†]
α_{yt}	0.00047* (0.30)	n.a.[†]
DMAN	−1.324* (−2.49)	−0.889[†]
LM(4)	3.00	0.79
Functional form (1)	1.15	0.11
Normality (2)	1.14	0.00
Heteroscedasticity (1)	0.70	2.75
Overidentifying restrictions (df)	14.22 (14)	26.29 (17)

*Long-run parameters derived from parameters of original equation. Standard errors derived from Wald's expansion of the original parameter variance–covariance matrix.
[†]Long-run parameters from Johansen canonical correlations.

the endogenous variable. The coefficient on the lagged share in the unrestricted auto-regressive distributed lag (ADL) equation is marginally insignificant (with a p-value of 6.6%) and has a similar coefficient to that of the other equation.

The equations were then tested for stability. An issue of particular importance here was how to account for dummy variables in the stability tests. Dummy variables represent a temporary breakdown in the underlying relationship and are normally excluded when computing stability tests. However, in the present context it is not clear whether some allowance should be made for their presence. One–zero dummy variables merely represent temporary influences. Moreover, if dummy variables are excluded, then it is possible that the resulting higher equation variance may actually serve to conceal some real structural break. Alternatively, it can be argued that many of the dummies represent pre-announcements and that it is only in periods involving such changes in the expectation generation process that the forward-looking approach can prove its worth.

We therefore have computed the stability tests both with and without accounting for dummies. When dummies are allowed for, we have set the recursive residuals used for computing the tests to zero in the dummied out periods. We then proceeded to use the dummy variables in the regression equation to explain subsequent periods.

Predictive Chow tests were used to test for stability in the equations, with and without dummy variables. The standard critical values for Chow tests are strictly conditional on a given, known, break-point. These values therefore are not valid in tests for an unknown break-point. Hansen (1992) and Andrews (1993) have proposed alternative tests and critical values under these conditions (see Appendix 2 for a discussion).

An examination of the sequence of predictive Chow tests scaled by the conventional 5% critical value for a known break-point shows no sign of structural instability. Similar results apply to the model with the error correction model restricted by the Johansen cointegrating vector. Broadly, the models appear to be stable, although it is clear that the Lawson announcement in the United Kingdom

Table 2.4 Stability tests on ECMs and marginal processes

	SupChow (π)	MeanChow
ECM without dummies	1.661 (0.65)	1.011
ECM with dummies	0.952 (0.71)	0.685
Wages	1.013 (0.25)	0.502
Energy prices	0.381 (0.22)	0.137
Materials prices	1.605 (0.21)	0.418
Cost of capital	0.915 (0.18)	0.233
Output	1.3435 (0.67)	1.005

π is the proportion of the sample at which the SupChow value occurs (see Andrews (1993)).

in the March 1994 Budget of a further tranche of tax changes for the subsequent Budget causes problems for the equation.

Table 2.4 reports the results of the SupChow and MeanChow portmanteau tests for stability with an unknown break-point suggested by Andrews (1993) and Hansen (1992). The tests indicate that the instability is insignificant.

2.9.2 Models for the Marginal Processes

We then proceeded to derive models for the marginal processes of our forcing variables, in this case the cost of capital, wages, fuel prices, materials import prices, and output.

Our modelling technique is to estimate a vector error correction model (VECM) (see, for example, Robertson and Wickens (1994)). This is equivalent to a VAR for the log differences of the five variables, conditional on the set of cointegrating vectors amongst them. We are therefore able to keep inferences within an I(0) space, making possible the use of conventional significance and stability tests. To optimize the power of our stability tests, we reduced each component equation of the VAR to its most data-congruent, parsimonious representation.

Initial cointegration analysis using the Johansen procedure found two cointe-grating vectors, giving us a system with three stochastic trends. The results are reported in Appendix 3.

The cointegrating vectors were then included in the VECM for the marginal processes in first difference form. Each of the equations was then tested down to provide a parsimonious, but congruent model. The final equations, including encompassing tests, are again reported in Appendix 3.

Predictive Chow tests were again used to test for stability. None of the equations was found to be unstable, conditional on a given, known, break-point.

The portmanteau tests for stability with unknown break-point are reported in Table 2.4. These confirm that there is no indication of instability in the dynamics of any of the equations.

2.9.3 Encompassing Tests

Our results indicate that the models for the forcing variables are broadly stable. Under these conditions we would expect to find that the backward-looking investment equation is stable.

The Lawson tax changes of 1984 clearly cause problems for the backward-looking equation. This is almost a paradigmatic incident of the Lucas critique. In the circumstances, it is perhaps reasonable to assume that we are testing for a *known* structural break. The predictive Chow test indicates that this would be significant in 1985 quarters 1 and 2.

The results of our investigation into a well-specified, backward-looking model therefore broadly supports the use of a forward-looking model.

Further work would test the forward-looking model itself for evidence of structural change (see Andrews and Fair (1988) and Ghysels and Hall (1990)). In addition, it would be interesting to implement a direct encompassing test between the forward- and backward-looking models, such as that suggested by Smith (1992).

2.10 CONCLUSIONS

In this chapter we have proposed, derived and estimated a new model of investment in the forward-looking neoclassical tradition. The model allows for a more general set of elasticities of substitution than allowed for in much of the investment literature, in particular allowing for the influence of energy and raw materials prices on investment.

Using an explicit restricted cost function, we have been able to avoid the usual mismeasurement problems associated with the Q approach to investment. We were able therefore to test the forward-looking model of investment separately from the usual joint assumption that the stock market accurately measures the shadow value of capital.

Our results are broadly favourable to the forward-looking model. Direct estimation of the Euler equation resulted in well-determined equations, with parameters that were significant and had the correct signs. In contrast, explicit estimation of an alternative backward-looking model revealed evidence of parameter instability.

Clearly, this chapter has concentrated on the estimation of the investment function alone. In principle further efficiency could be obtained by the simultaneous estimation of the investment function along with the underlying cost function and other factor share equations. Some further work along these lines is reported in Allen (1994).

2.11 ACKNOWLEDGEMENTS

I am grateful to Andrew Burrell, Stephen Hall, James Nixon and Peter Smith for help and comments. I am solely responsible for any errors and omissions that remain. The work was carried out under ESRC grant W116251003.

2.12 ENDNOTES

1. The explicit relationship is derived in equation (10).
2. Hayashi's identification is of average with marginal Q. He showed that this requires perfect competition in both product and factor markets and the linear homogeneity of both production technology and adjustment costs.
3. The dismal performance of standard Q models is further documented in the survey of investment modelling by Chirinko (1993).

4. Although a linearized solution does exist, which we have derived in Section 2.8.
5. Note that strictly, as pointed out by Banerjee *et al.* (1993, pp. 152–53), the Wickens–Breusch estimator will only result in a consistent estimator of the cointegrating *space*, rather than unique estimates of the cointegrating parameters, if the number of cointegrating vectors is non-unique.
6. Our estimator differs from the linear two-step, two-stage estimator of Cumby, Huizinga and Obstfeld (1983) in that we iterate on the parameter vector until convergence is achieved, instead of using a single iteration. Asymptotically the Cumby *et al.* estimator should have the same distribution as GMM, although use of GMM ensures that the final estimates are invariant to the initial weighting matrix (which may be influenced by the scaling of the variables) (see Hamilton (1994, p. 413)). An alternative estimator would be the Hayashi and Sims (1983) instrumental variable estimator.
7. If the model is only just identified (i.e. the number of empirical moments is just equal to the number of parameters), then the use of the first-order conditions will set each of the empirical moments to zero and no test is available.
8. See Appendix 1 for details of the derivation. Lynde and Richmond (1993) make a similar adjustment.
9. In this section we consider only the first three columns of Table 2.1. The other estimates are presented only for convenience.
10. Abel and Blanchard also experimented with a second-order expansion, but found that a first-order expansion was in fact adequate.
11. See Harvey (1981, Section 5.7). This formulation considerably reduces the computational burden of the recursive Chow tests. The recursive Chow tests were derived from this formula using a set of recursive residuals derived from Microfit.

APPENDIX 1: TESTING FOR THE ORDER OF INTEGRATION OF THE CAPITAL STOCK

Dickey and Pantula (1987) propose the following sequential test procedure for the determination of the number of unit roots in an AR time series.

Given, for example, a third-order autoregression of the form

$$y_t = \sum_{j=1}^{3} \alpha_j y_{t-j} + e_t \qquad \ldots (24)$$

we can write the model's characteristic equation in the form

$$m^3 + \alpha_1 m^2 + \alpha_2 m + \alpha_3 = 0 \qquad \ldots (25)$$

Denote the roots of this equation by m_1, m_2, and m_3, where the roots are ordered in reducing absolute size $1 \geq |m_1| \geq |m_2| \geq |m_3|$.

Dickey and Pantula show that tests on these roots can most easily be performed by estimating a reparameterization of (24):

$$\Delta^3 y_t = \theta_1 y_{t-1} + \theta_2 \Delta y_{t-1} + \theta_3 \Delta^2 y_{t-1} + e_t \qquad \ldots (26)$$

where the parameters can be explicitly identified with functions of the underlying roots of the characteristic equation:

$$\theta_1 = -(1 - m_1)(1 - m_2)(1 - m_3)$$

$$\theta_2 = -2\theta_1 - (1 - m_1)(1 - m_2) - (1 - m_1)(1 - m_3) - (1 - m_2)(1 - m_3) \quad \dots (27)$$

$$\theta_3 = m_1 m_2 m_3 - 1$$

We can now clearly identify the restrictions imposed by a given number of unit roots with restrictions on the reparameterized parameter vector. On the hypothesis of three unit roots H_3, we have

$$H_3 : \ \theta_1 = \theta_2 = \theta_3 = 0 \qquad \qquad \dots (28)$$

Likewise, on the hypothesis of two, one, and zero unit roots, we have, respectively,

$$H_2 : \theta_1 = \theta_2 = 0 \text{ and } \theta_3 < 0$$

$$H_1 : \theta_1 = 0, \theta_2 < 0, \text{ and } -2 < \theta_3 < 0 \qquad \dots (29)$$

$$H_0 : \theta_1 < 0, \text{ and other restrictions}$$

The conventional Dickey–Fuller test is a test for the presence of a single unit root against the alternative of stationarity. In a Monte Carlo study, however, Dickey and Pantula found that the Dickey–Fuller statistic rejected the hypothesis of a single unit root in favour of stationarity considerably more than the 5% critical level, when more than one unit root was in fact present. Dickey and Pantula show, relying on unpublished work by Pantula, that this is explicable in theoretical terms, since t-tests only have the Dickey–Fuller distribution under the hypothesis of at least the correct number of unit roots.

The authors therefore suggest an alternative unit root testing procedure for the general case in which the number of unit roots is unknown a priori. First test for the hypothesis of n unit roots against the alternative of $n - 1$ unit roots, where n is the largest reasonable (?) number of unit roots. The authors appear to think this is in the region of 3 or 4 roots.

The test proceeds using the reparameterization outlined above. For example, the test for three against two unit roots has maximum power when carried out under the null of two unit roots. Hence the test is carried out on the equation

$$\Delta^3 y_t = \theta_3 \Delta^2 y_{t-1} + e_t \qquad \qquad \dots (30)$$

The test is for the hypothesis that $\theta_3 < 0$. Inference is based on a standard Dickey–Fuller distribution. Conditional on the rejection of a hypothesis of three unit roots, the equation can then be augmented to

$$\Delta^3 y_t = \theta_2 \Delta y_{t-1} + \theta_3 \Delta^2 y_{t-1} + e_t \qquad \qquad \dots (31)$$

where the test for two against one unit root will now be based on a test that the parameter $\theta_2 < 0$. Dickey and Pantula counsel the addition of a constant to the testing equations in order to allow for a non-zero mean in the general data-generating process: in this case the Dickey–Fuller distribution in the presence of a intercept should be used. Unfortunately, the Monte Carlo results presented by Dickey and Pantula show that this test procedure has only relatively weak power properties.

We have implemented the Dickey and Pantula testing procedure to examine the order of integration of the capital stock series. Initial investigation of the series using conventional augmented Dickey–Fuller tests showed that both the investment–capital stock ratio and the change in the log of the capital stock both tested as non-stationary series, whilst paradoxically the log of the capital stock itself appears to be trend stationary. This result would be unsurprising in the presence of two unit roots given the Dickey and Pantula finding of over-acceptance of stationarity in these conditions.

The results of the Dickey and Pantula sequential hypothesis testing procedure (with and without an intercept) are reported in Table A1. The log of the capital stock was tested for up to three unit roots. The tests of the hypothesis of two versus three unit roots are shown in the first two columns of the table. The relevant t-style statistics (-11.54 and -11.58 for the with and without intercept cases, respectively) decisively rejected the null of three unit roots. The subsequent test for two versus one unit root shown in the next two columns, however, could not reject the null of two unit roots. The final columns show that this result is robust to the inclusion of the lagged level term.

What can we conclude from this investigation? Clearly what has been ruled out by using the Dickey and Pantula test is that the capital stock is a stationary process. The investment series is clearly a non-stationary I(1) process; hence, it would be absurd for the capital stock to in fact be I(0).

However, there may be reasons to doubt the result that the capital stock in fact contains two unit roots as suggested by the Dickey–Pantula test. In fact, it is more likely that what we really have is a process with one unit root and a second root close to, but smaller than, unity. A simple example will make this clear. Assume that investment (in unlogged levels) is a random walk:

$$\Delta I_t = \varepsilon_t$$

The capital stock is then defined (again in unlogged levels) as

$$K_t = (1 - \delta) \cdot K_{t-1} + I_t$$

where δ is the depreciation rate. δ is of course both positive and extremely small, here 0.0175 at a quarterly rate. Hence K_t is a process with two roots, one of unity and one of 0.9825, extremely close to the unit circle. It seems likely that this will also be the case with a more general process-generating investment.

Dickey and Pantula's Monte Carlo simulations clearly show that their test lacks the power to discriminate between unit root and near unit root processes. For example, for a sample size of 50, with a data-generating process containing two non-zero roots, one a unit root and a second of 0.9, the false hypothesis of two unit roots is only rejected 14% of the time. We therefore can plausibly maintain that the capital stock is likely to contain a single unit root, but with an additional root close to the unit circle.

Table A1 Dickey–Pantula tests on capital stock

	(ia)	(ib)	(iia)	(iib)	(iiia)	(iiib)
			Dependent variable: $\Delta^3 Lk_t$			
Constant	-0.00003	—	0.00045	—	0.00684	—
	(-0.27)		(1.39)		(1.19)	
$\Delta^2 Lk_{t-1}$	-1.109	-1.108	-1.076	-1.104	-1.090	-1.076
	(-11.53)	(-11.58)	(-11.02)	(-11.51)	(-11.08)	(-10.99)
ΔLk_{t-1}	—	—	-0.059	-0.010	-0.054	-0.057
			(-1.57)	(-0.79)	(-1.43)	(-1.51)
Lk_{t-1}	—	—	—	—	-0.0005	0.00003
					(-1.11)	(1.32)
LM(4)	8.04	7.98	12.62*	8.72	11.13*	12.73*

*Significant at the 5% level.

APPENDIX 2: TESTS OF MODEL STABILITY

This appendix outlines briefly the model stability tests used in Section 2.9. The tests are based on the series of recursive residuals.

The series of recursive residuals is defined as the series of scaled one-step prediction errors:

$$v_t = \frac{y_t - \hat{y}_{t|t-1}}{f_t^{1/2}} \qquad \ldots (32)$$

where $\hat{y}_{t|t-1}$ is the prediction of y_t, using only the first $t - 1$ observations. The scaling factor takes account of parameter uncertainty:

$$f_t = 1 + x_t^{T}(X_{t-1}^{T}X_{t-1})^{-1}x_t \qquad \ldots (33)$$

The cumulative sum of squares of the recursive residuals (CUSUMSQ) test was suggested by Brown, Durbin and Evans (1975) as a test of model stability. It can be written as

$$\text{CUSUMSQ}(s) = \frac{\sum\limits_{t=k+1}^{s} v_t^2}{\sum\limits_{t=k+1}^{T} v_t^2} \qquad \ldots (34)$$

where T is the overall size of the sample and k is the number of estimated parameters. When the model is correctly specified the statistic has a beta distribution with mean $(s - k)/(T - k)$. The test can be performed for the $T - k$ observations in the sample and is therefore usually presented graphically, plotted against its two-sided confidence intervals.

An alternative stability test is the standard predictive Chow test which can be shown to also be definable in terms of the series of one-step recursive residuals:[11]

$$\zeta^*(l) = \frac{\sum\limits_{j=1}^{l} v_{t+j}^2/l}{\sum\limits_{t=k+1}^{T-l} v_t^2/(T - l - k)} \qquad \ldots (35)$$

where l is the length of the forecast horizon. Against a given known break-point, this test has an asymptotic F distribution.

Since we want to test for an arbitrary break-point, we shall also employ the predictive Chow test as a recursive test. Unfortunately, the problem of testing for structural change with an unknown break-point does not fit into a standard testing framework and standard asymptotic distributions cannot be straightforwardly used. Hansen (1992) and Andrews (1993) have proposed and evaluated, using simulation methods, the MeanChow and SupChow statistics, respectively. The MeanChow statistic uses the mean of the Chow statistics over the central part of the sample, omitting the first and last 15% of the observations to avoid end-point problems. The SupChow statistic is based on the highest recursive Chow test result (again omitting end-points). The critical values of these statistics are given in the respective papers.

As suggested by Hansen (1992), we have carried out our stability tests conditional on the existence of a stable long-run cointegrating vector. We do this for two reasons.

First, the principal difference between the forward-looking and backward-looking models is in their dynamics; therefore, conditioning on a common stable cointegrating vector increases the power of our tests. Secondly, as noted by Hansen (1992), the presence of non-stationary variables affects the properties of standard stability tests.

APPENDIX 3: EQUATIONS FOR MARGINAL PROCESSES

A3.1 Equation for Cost of Capital

```
                    Ordinary Least Squares Estimation
*******************************************************************************
Dependent variable is DLCICC
103 observations used for estimation from 1967Q2 to 1992Q4
*******************************************************************************
Regressor       Coefficient      Standard Error     T-Ratio[Prob]
DLCICC(-1)         .34194           .068442          4.9960[.000]
DLCICC(-4)         .18842           .074851          2.5172[.014]
DLPF(-2)          -.15241           .073621         -2.0702[.041]
DLPF(-3)           .18899           .076296          2.4771[.015]
DLPF(-4)          -.46414           .074194         -6.2558[.000]
DDLPNF             .77760           .24436           3.1821[.002]
DLPNF(-4)         -.81679           .27553          -2.9645[.004]
RES1(-1)          -.11899           .028914         -4.1152[.000]
RES2(-1)          -.16894           .028851         -5.8557[.000]
CNST              2.0182            .70241           2.8733[.005]
T                 -.0098158         .0017881        -5.4895[.000]
*******************************************************************************
R-Squared                  .64282   F-statistic F(10, 92)    16.5576[.000]
R-Bar-Squared              .60400   S.E. of Regression              .057609
Residual Sum of Squares    .30533   Mean of Dependent Variable      .6729E-3
S.D. of Dependent Variable .091547  Maximum of Log-likelihood    153.6358
DW-statistic              1.9784
*******************************************************************************
                          Diagnostic Tests
*******************************************************************************
*  Test Statistics    *   LM Version    *    F Version
*******************************************************************************
A:Serial Correlation *CHI-SQ( 4)=  7.6067[.107]*F( 4, 88)= 1.7543[.145]*
B:Functional Form    *CHI-SQ( 1)= .22968[.632]*F( 1, 91)= .20338[.653]*
C:Normality   *CHI-SQ( 2)= 5.1499[.076]*  Not applicable
D:Heteroscedasticity*CHI-SQ(1)= 2.3287[.127]*F(1, 101)= 2.3363[.130]*
E:Encompassing *CHI- SQ( 13)= 4.054 [>.95]*
*******************************************************************************
A: Lagrange multiplier test of residual serial correlation
B: Ramsey's RESET test using the square of the fitted values
C: Based on a test of skewness and kurtosis of residuals
D: Based on the regression of squared residuals on squared fitted values
E: Likelihood ratio test of overidentifying restrictions
```

A3.2 Equation for Fuel Prices

```
                    Ordinary Least Squares Estimation
*******************************************************************************
Dependent variable is DLPF
107 observations used for estimation from 1966Q2 to 1992Q4
*******************************************************************************
Regressor       Coefficient      Standard Error       T-Ratio[Prob]
DLPF(-1)          .29079              .081328          3.5755[.001]
DLPF(-2)          .11472              .083120          1.3801[.171]
DLPF(-4)          .40050              .085914          4.6616[.000]
DLW(-3)          1.7166               .41173           4.1693[.000]
DLY(-4)          1.9606               .51131           3.8344[.000]
RES1(-1)          .15259              .030375          5.0234[.000]
CNST             1.6377               .32743           5.0018[.000]
T                -.8614E-3            .2659E-3        -3.2399[.002]
*******************************************************************************
R-Squared                   .40405  F-statistic F( 7, 99)       9.5889[.000]
R-Bar-Squared               .36191  S.E. of Regression              .071635
Residual Sum of Squares     .50802  Mean of Dependent Variable      .029385
S.D. of Dependent Variable .089678  Maximum of Log-likelihood    134.4016
DW-statistic               2.1095
*******************************************************************************
                            Diagnostic Tests
*******************************************************************************
*     Test Statistics       *       LM Version        *      F Version
*******************************************************************************
A: Serial Correlation*CHI-SQ( 4)= 2.6211[.623]*F( 4, 95)= .59640[.666]*
B: Functional Form  *CHI-SQ( 1)= 60.1011[.000]*F( 1, 98)= 125.5871[.000]*
C: Normality        *CHI-SQ( 2)= 931.9399[.000]*   Not applicable
D: Heteroscedasticity*CHI-SQ( 1)= 88.9771[.000]*F( 1, 105) = 518.3750[.000]*
E: Encompassing     *CHI-SQ( 8)= 5.7144 [>.65]*
*******************************************************************************
A: Lagrange multiplier test of residual serial correlation
B: Ramsey's RESET test using the square of the fitted values
C: Based on a test of skewness and kurtosis of residuals
D: Based on the regression of squared residuals on squared fitted values
E: Likelihood ratio test of overidentifying restrictions
```

A3.3 Equation for Imported Raw Material Prices

```
                    Ordinary Least Squares Estimation
*******************************************************************************
Dependent variable is DLPNF
105 observations used for estimation from 1966Q4 to 1992Q4
*******************************************************************************
Regressor        Coefficient     Standard Error      T-Ratio[Prob]
DLCICC(-2)          .065688           .024093         2.7265[.008]
DLPNF(-1)           .49069            .082249         5.9659[.000]
RES1(-1)           -.015590           .0063360       -2.4606[.016]
CNST               -.15504            .066460        -2.3328[.022]
*******************************************************************************
R-Squared                 .36859   F-statistic F(3, 101)    19.6531[.000]
R-Bar-Squared             .34983   S.E. of Regression          .021148
Residual Sum of Squares   .045169  Mean of Dependent Variable  .017061
S.D. of Dependent Variable .026227 Maximum of Log-likelihood  257.9544
DW-statistic             1.9966    Durbin's h-statistic         .031908[.975]
*******************************************************************************
                            Diagnostic Tests
*******************************************************************************
*      Test Statistics     *      LM Version      *       F Version
*******************************************************************************
A: Serial Correlation*CHI-SQ(4)= 2.4347[.656]*F(4, 97)=  .57565[.681]*
B: Functional Form *CHI-SQ(1)= 1.9724[.160]*F(1, 100)=   1.9144[.170]*
C: Normality       *CHI-SQ(2)= 16.9892[.000]*   Not applicable
D: Heteroscedasticity*CHI-SQ(1)=  .49592[.481]*F(1, 103)=  .48878[.486]*
E: Encompassing    *CHI-SQ(20)= 5.7084 [>.95]*
*******************************************************************************
A: Lagrange multiplier test of residual serial correlation
B: Ramsey's RESET test using the square of the fitted values
C: Based on a test of skewness and kurtosis of residuals
D: Based on the regression of squared residuals on squared fitted values
E: Likelihood ratio test of overidentifying restrictions
```

A3.4 Equation for Wages

Ordinary Least Squares Estimation

****

Dependent variable is DLW

103 observations used for estimation from 1967Q2 to 1992Q4

****

Regressor	Coefficient	Standard Error	T-Ratio[Prob]
DLCICC(-1)	−.044327	.015618	−2.8381[.006]
DLPF(-4)	.10680	.016770	6.3687[.000]
DLW(-2)	.29943	.076340	3.9224[.000]
DLW(-3)	.18357	.073607	2.4940[.014]
DLY(-4)	.29819	.10543	2.8284[.006]
CNST	.0093350	.0029832	3.1292[.002]

****

R-Squared	.51349	F-statistic F(5, 97)	20.4755[.000]
R-Bar-Squared	.48841	S.E. of Regression	.014203
Residual Sum of Squares	.019567	Mean of Dependent Variable	.027512
S.D. of Dependent Variable	.019857	Maximum of Log-likelihood	295.1337
DW-statistic	2.0336		

****

Diagnostic Tests

****

*	Test Statistics	*	LM Version	*	F Version

****

A: Serial Correlation*CHI-SQ(4)= 3.8615[.425]*F(4, 93)= .90559[.464]*

B: Functional Form *CHI-SQ(1)= 2.0713[.150]*F(1, 96)= 1.9701[.164]*

C: Normality *CHI-SQ(2)= 4.9592[.084]* Not applicable

D: Heteroscedasticity*CHI-SQ(1)= .075265[.784]*F(1, 101)= .073857[.786]*

E: Encompassing *CHI-SQ(18)= 16.4368 [>.50]*

****

A: Lagrange multiplier test of residual serial correlation

B: Ramsey's RESET test using the square of the fitted values

C: Based on a test of skewness and kurtosis of residuals

D: Based on the regression of squared residuals on squared fitted values

E: Likelihood ratio test of overidentifying restrictions

A3.5 Equation for Output

```
                    Ordinary Least Squares Estimation
*******************************************************************************
Dependent variable is DLY
103 observations used for estimation from 1967Q2 to 1992Q4
*******************************************************************************
Regressor      Coefficient      Standard Error     T-Ratio[Prob]
DLPF(-4)       −.029469             .014745         −1.9986[.048]
DLW(-3)        −.15157              .067488         −2.2460[.027]
CNST            .010862             .0023143         4.6935[.000]
*******************************************************************************
R-Squared                  .086771  F-statistic F(2, 100)      4.7508[.011]
R-Bar-Squared              .068506  S.E. of Regression             .013582
Residual Sum of Squares    .018447  Mean of Dependent Variable    .0058039
S.D. of Dependent Variable .014073  Maximum of Log-likelihood   298.1688
DW-statistic              2.0610
*******************************************************************************
                            Diagnostic Tests
*******************************************************************************
A: Serial Correlation*CHI-SQ(4)= 2.6432[.619]*F(4, 96)=  .63211[.641]*
B: Functional Form *CHI-SQ(1)= .0024955[.960]*F(1, 99)=  .0023987[.961]*
C: Normality       *CHI-SQ(2)= 20.1401[.000]   Not applicable
D: Heteroscedasticity*CHI-SQ(1)=  .76596[.381]*F(1, 101)=  .75671[.386]*
E: Encompassing    *CHI-SQ(21)= 29.2492 [>.05]*
*******************************************************************************
A: Lagrange multiplier test of residual serial correlation
B: Ramsey's RESET test using the square of the fitted values
C: Based on a test of skewness and kurtosis of residuals
D: Based on the regression of squared residuals on squared fitted values
E: Likelihood ratio test of overidentifying restrictions
```

3
Forward-Looking Consumption and Financial Liberalisation in the United Kingdom

HONG BAI AND JOHN WHITLEY

3.1 A REVIEW OF RESEARCH ON AGGREGATE CONSUMER EXPENDITURE

The consumption equation has always been at the heart of macroeconometric models. The most common approach in the late 1970s was to treat consumers as constrained in their purchase decisions by current income, very much in the spirit of Keynes. The early models tended to imply a marginal propensity to consume of around 0.8. Other influences on consumption were largely absent except for the effect of changes in hire purchase regulations.

The mid-1970s saw a breakdown of this form of equation which with its implied constancy of the saving ratio could not explain its rise. This forecast failure resulted in the familiar paradox of thrift and caused the models to over-predict the level of overall economic activity and to miss the 1975 recession. This sequence of events created fresh academic interest in the consumption equation in the United Kingdom and Davidson *et al.* (1978) found econometric support for the presence of an inflation term in the equation, and also concluded that the rise in inflation in the 1970s was the factor behind the rising savings ratio. Their article was not only important in reviving the consumption equation but was also highly influential in introducing the error correction approach to econometrics.

The traditional simple consumption function took the (log-linear) form

$$C_t = a + bY_t + cC_{t-1}$$

Macroeconomic Modelling in a Changing World. Edited by C. Allen and S. Hall
© 1997 John Wiley & Sons Ltd

The new form was

$$\Delta_4 C_t = \alpha_0 + \alpha_1 \Delta_4 Y_t + \alpha_2 \Delta P_t + \alpha_3 (C_{t-4} - Y_{t-4})$$

This 'error correction' model was derived as a 'parsimonious' reparameterisation and restriction from a general dynamic model of the form

$$C_t = \beta_0 + \sum_{i=1}^{n} \beta_i C_{t-i} + \sum_{i=0}^{n} \gamma_i Y_{t-i} + \sum_{i=0}^{n} \delta_i P_{t-i}$$

If the model is stable, then the general dynamic model has a long-run solution $C = k + y$ in the steady state when $y_t = y_{t-i}$ for all i, where k is a constant, i.e. $C = kY$, the proportional relationship as in Friedman's permanent income theory. Note that when expressed in log-linear form k represents a constant elasticity.

The economic rationale for the inclusion of inflation was as a proxy for the inflation loss on liquid assets, although Deaton (1987) suggested an alternative explanation in that variable inflation created uncertainty, and hence a decision to postpone consumption. Subsequent work by Hendry and von Ungern-Sternberg (1981) specifically included a liquid assets term and argued that the inflation loss on this variable should be deducted from the income variable. The existing treatment had often provided a positive effect on consumption from higher inflation since higher nominal interest rates (which adjusted to the higher level of inflation) increased nominal interest receipts by the personal sector. Deflation by the (higher) price index could not actually reduce consumption. Hendry and von Ungern-Sternberg argued that the income variable itself needed to be adjusted, and a similar approach was proposed by Pesaran and Evans (1984).

The second main challenge to the consumption equation came a decade later in the mid-1980s, when this time the models failed to explain the sharp fall in the savings ratio. This proved to be a key reason in the failure to forecast the boom of 1988.

Modellers reacted to the impact of the forecast failures in the late 1980s by assuming that financial deregulation had increased the liquidity of physical assets held by the personal sector. Deregulation resulted in the personal sector increasing its debt-to-income ratio. At the same time this boost to demand stimulated a rise in asset prices (especially house prices) but the ratio of debt to assets rose in spite of the asset appreciation. Physical wealth began to appear in consumption equations. The equations then began to appear more like the life-cycle models of consumption rather than the original Keynesian form.

However, these models of consumption behaviour in turn failed to explain the rise in the savings ratio that occurred in 1990–91 and research began to focus on the forward-looking behaviour of consumers, going back to the original life-cycle model adjusted for forward-looking behaviour by Hall (1978) and subsequently adapted by Hayashi (1982) to deal with liquidity constraints.

The life-cycle approach can be summarised as follows: Households are assumed to maximise the discounted utility of current and future consumption subject to the constraint that the present value of consumption does not exceed initial wealth. The stock of wealth is defined as the sum of the real value of assets held by households plus the present value of the flow of disposable labour income ('human wealth'). Because households face a constant probability of death, λ, and the total population is growing at a rate n, not all future labour income accrues to households. The rate of discount used is then the real interest rate plus $\lambda + n$. Human wealth, WH, can then be defined as

$$WH = \int_{t=0}^{\infty} (Y_t - T_t) e^{-(r+\lambda+n)t} \, dt$$

where $(Y - T)$ is the flow of disposable income. Total wealth is the sum of human and asset wealth (A):

$$W = H + A$$

The optimization of utility gives the determination of current consumption in terms of the real interest rate, r, the degree of relative risk aversion, σ, the rate of time preference, δ, and the probability of death, λ.

$$C = \alpha(r, \sigma, \delta, \lambda)W$$

Human wealth, H, is forward looking, being the discounted value of future income plus the initial stock. The degree of risk aversion and the death rate are typically ignored or assigned 'plausible' values. The original life-cycle model then expresses consumption as homogeneous of degree one in total wealth with the long-run consumption–wealth ratio dependent on the real interest rate:

$$C_t = \frac{W_t}{\kappa}$$

where

$$\kappa = 1 + 1/(1 + r)$$

and r is the real rate of interest which, in the original Hall paper, is equal to the subjective discount rate of households.

This can be described as a 'solved out' consumption equation (Muellbauer (1994)). The original Hall (1978) paper used the first-order condition for consumers maximising utility under rational expectations to derive the Euler equation which implied that consumption was a random walk and was not forecastable.

The Hall equation can be written:

$$c_t = c_{t+1} + \varepsilon_t$$

Hayashi (1982) extended the Hall approach and, by allowing for the discount rate of consumers to be different from the real interest rate, the resulting equation includes terms in lagged asset stocks, so that lagged information matters. Blanchard (1985) shows that dropping the infinite life assumption justifies household discount rates higher than the aggregate interest rate, although the spirit of the Hayashi paper is in terms of imperfect capital markets. We then have:

$$c_t = \beta[A_{t-1} + H_{t-1}]$$

The problem then lies in ways of treating the unobserved human wealth variable, which is the discounted sum of future income. The so-called backward-looking approach is to substitute current and lagged income as a proxy for human wealth. Under the specific form of adaptive expectations the familiar error correction mechanism (ECM) form of the consumption function can be derived. Another way would be to use forward expectations of income. The Hayashi approach is to use quasi-differencing to remove the infinite sum, leaving consumption determined by asset stocks and innovations to labour income:

$$c_t = (1 + \mu)c_{t-1} + \beta[A_{t-1} - y_{t-1} - (1 + \mu)A_{t-2}] + \beta\gamma y_t^*$$

where μ is the discount factor, and is greater than the market rate of interest, and y^* is the innovation to income.

Muellbauer (1994) argues that the Hayashi equation is not a Euler equation since it is not the first-order condition for intertemporal optimisation.

The next extension is to allow for liquidity constraints, first introduced by Hall and Mishkin (1982) and tested by Hayashi (1982) and Campbell and Mankiw (1991). The basic idea is that many households have small initial values of assets and are unwilling or unable to borrow. Hence their current consumption is constrained by current income. Aggregate consumption is then given by the behaviour of both unconstrained and constrained households:

$$c_t = (1 - \pi)c^u + \pi c^c$$

where π is the proportion of consumers who are credit constrained. Financial liberalisation is assumed to have reduced this proportion. In addition, financial deregulation may have reduced the size of the mark-up between the discount rate and the real market rate of interest.

The following sections describe research on consumption behaviour which applies the forward-looking model to UK aggregate consumption expenditure, and which allows for financial liberalisation to change the proportion of credit-constrained consumers, π. By using non-nested tests it is then possible to test between the forward-looking approach and the hitherto conventional backward-looking explanation.

3.2 AN AGGREGATE FORWARD-LOOKING CONSUMPTION MODEL

Approaches using the permanent income and life-cycle income hypotheses together with the assumption of forward-looking agents have argued that aggregate consumption should be smooth. This smoothness has been attributed to the smoothness of permanent income. However, the literature on liquidity constraints on consumption have suggested that aggregate consumption responds to changes in both permanent and current income. In the spirit of the framework outlined above, this is equivalent to distinguishing between forward-looking consumers (the wealth constrained) who smooth their consumption according to the basic life-cycle hypothesis and backward-looking or credit-constrained consumers (liquidity constrained) whose consumption is restricted by their current incomes. The major goal of this chapter is to encompass the two extreme positions by allowing for current and permanent income effects and for the fact that financial liberalisation may have changed the relative proportions of the two different groups of agents. The relaxation of borrowing constraints has allowed previously liquidity-constrained consumers to borrow, thus increasing their consumption of both goods and housing. The housing market has been an area where these changes have been particularly important, both legal constraints on building society behaviour and the conventions of day-to-day operations in building societies have changed enormously over the decade. These developments are particularly significant since 'in all developed economies the prices of an average house is several times average annual disposable income' (Miles (1992)).

Miles develops an aggregate consumption model that stresses the effects of financial deregulation on the proportion of income received by credit-constrained and unconstrained consumers. A range of different potential measures of financial deregulation are assessed within the context of the model. The conclusion drawn is that aggregate consumption has been smooth during the last 20 years and that the consumption share of credit-constrained consumers has been declining from the mid-1980s to the early 1990s with financial liberalisation.

The plan of the chapter is as follows. In this section we outline the basic model of consumption to be investigated. Section 3.3 discusses some details of the estimation strategy and presents a range of estimates for different measures of financial liberalisation. Section 3.4 allows for a small generalisation of the theoretical model. Section 3.5 makes some comparisons of the forward- and backward-looking models and our general conclusions are offered in Section 3.6.

The importance of liquidity constraints in consumption behaviour has been widely recognised, recent important empirical implementations of this idea include Abel (1988), Campbell and Mankiw (1989), Darby and Ireland (1993) and Campbell and Deaton (1989). They assume that some consumers can borrow or lend at an exogenous rate of interest while others, who would like to increase their current borrowing in order to increase current consumption, are unable to do so because of liquidity constraints. This basic insight provides the foundation for a model that behaves quite differently in the two groups of consumers.

The model presented here is based on this theoretical analysis. It assumes forward-looking consumers and credit-constrained consumers, i.e. wealth-constrained consumers and liquidity-constrained consumers. These two distinct groups of consumers are postulated to behave in quite different ways. We discuss each form of behaviour in turn.

3.2.1 The Consumption of Forward-Looking Consumers

The basic premise of the permanent income hypothesis is that consumers set their current consumption equal to the present discounted value of their present and future wealth, with wealth consisting of both non-human and human wealth. The consumption equation for permanent income consumers is

$$C_{1t} = \beta(A_{ft} + H_{ft}) \qquad \ldots (1)$$

where C_{1t} is the consumption of forward-looking consumers, A_{ft} is net financial and physical wealth (real non-human wealth) at time t, and H_{ft} is human wealth at time t for forward-looking consumers.

Forward-looking consumers are assumed to use rational expectations when forecasting future labour income. So the consumption function for unconstrained consumers can be written as the present discounted value of current and future labour income, using quasi-differencing to substitute for unobserved human wealth. Here we differ from the original Hayashi formulation by using forward quasi-differencing rather than backward differencing, following Darby and Ireland (1993):

$$C_{1t} = \mu(C_{t+1} - YD_{2t+1}) + \beta(A_{ft-1} - \mu A_{ft} + YD_{1t}) \qquad \ldots (2)$$

where YD_{1t} is post-tax labour income received by forward-looking consumers, YD_{2t} is post-tax labour income received by credit-constrained consumers, and μ is the discount rate of labour income, $\mu = 1/(1 + r + m)$.

Because this applies to a highly uncertain income stream, μ should be much higher than the rate of interest, r; m is a financial deregulation mark-up. One simple way to model m in terms of financial liberalisation is by a linear relationship: we assume that the mark-up falls as financial deregulation decreases the proportion of credit-constrained consumers, π. Thus $m = a_0 + a_1 \pi_t$.

This model allows the discount rate, μ, to vary over time, giving the fact that the discount rate is higher than the real rate of interest the Hayashi rather than Blanchard interpretation.

3.2.2 The Consumption of Credit-Constrained Consumers

We assume (following Darby and Ireland (1993)) that this group uses its current income to finance its expenditure and that its housing assets are exactly offset by its mortgage debts. So the group's consumption is equal to its disposable non-property income, assuming that all current grant recipients are credit-constrained:

$$C_{2t} = YD_{2t}$$
$$= CG_t + \pi_t(YD_t - EC_t - IP_t) \qquad \ldots (3)$$

where C_{2t} is the consumption of credit-constrained consumers, CG_t is current grants, YD_t is total post-tax labour income, EC_t is employers' contributions to pension funds, and IP_t is the interest payment on existing debt.

Aggregate consumption is then a linear function of total wealth of the two types of consumers:

$$C_t = C_{1t} + C_{2t}$$

$$C_t = \beta(A_{ft} + H_{ft}) + YD_{2t} + u_t$$

where C_t is the aggregate consumption for two groups, and u_t is an independently distributed random error term. Estimation requires a particular functional form for the relationship between the series for financial deregulation, FLIB, and the proportion of labour income received by credit constrained consumers, π. This relationship must map any allowable value for the variable measuring financial liberalisation into the unit interval. We follow Darby and Ireland (1993) in assuming the following simple formulation:

$$\pi_t = e^{-(b_0 + b_1 * FLIB)}$$

where $b_0 > 0$, $b_1 > 0$, and $0 < \pi_t < 1$, which implies that when FLIB is zero the proportion of income received by constrained consumers is defined by b_0 and, as FLIB increases, π falls at an ever decreasing rate towards zero.

The key variable in this model then is FLIB itself. This is, by definition, an unobserved variable and so we must find some way to proxy this effect. The key developments in the mortgage market were the changes in the legal status of building societies during the early 1980s, the opening up of the market to a wider range of institutions, the development of the second mortgage market which allowed the high degrees of equity extraction that occurred during the 1980s and perhaps, most importantly, the increasingly competitive nature of the mortgage market itself. (Further details of these changes may be found in Bank of England (1985, 1989, 1991, 1992).) All of these combined to lead progressively to a lowering of the stringent requirements for the granting of mortgages which is illustrated by the rise in the average mortgage to income ratio that took place steadily over this period. We will consider five possible measures of FLIB:

(a) The first is given by Muellbauer and Murphy (1991). They derived FLIB from the residuals from a regression of the mortgage advance to income for first-time buyers on interest rates and the house price to income ratio. Where the regression is carried out over the period 1975–81 the residuals are defined outside this period. By construction within the estimation period the variable is set to zero. Figure 3.1 shows the series of FLIB1 over the period of 1972–91, obtained from this procedure. It starts at a high point in 1972–74 and then falls sharply, is zero by definition between 1975 and 1982 and then rises strongly in the early 1980s. The behaviour of this series in the early 1970s implies declining financial

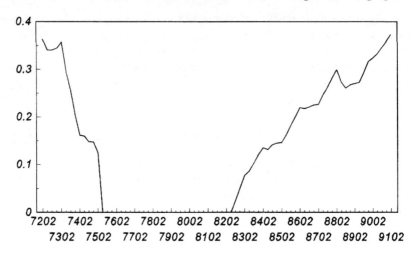

Figure 3.1 *FLIB1*

liberalisation. This is difficult to interpret in terms of structural changes during the period which were, if anything, in the direction of increased liberalisation.

(b) Secondly, we regress the ratio of mortgage advance to income for all house purchases on interest rates and the house price to income ratio. *FLIB2* is the residual of this regression and is plotted in Figure 3.2. This shows an implied trend in financial liberalisation with some cyclical behaviour.

(c) The third measure *(FLIB3)* is simply given a non-linear relationship using the ratio of mortgage advances to income for first-time buyers. The liberalisation

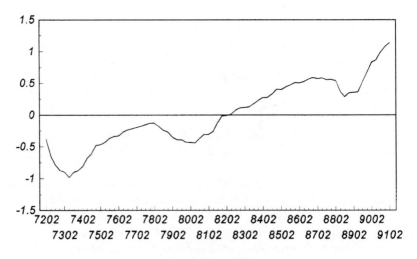

Figure 3.2 *FLIB2*

measure takes the value of this ratio when it is above its value in 1974, otherwise it is set to zero. The resultant series is shown in Figure 3.3. *FLIB3* has the same broad pattern as *FLIB1* and shows that the Muellbauer–Murphy measure was dominated by the movements in the mortgage to income ratio despite the apparent sophistication of its construction.

(d) The fourth measure *(FLIB4)* uses the Darby and Ireland (1993) measure and is shown in Figure 3.4.

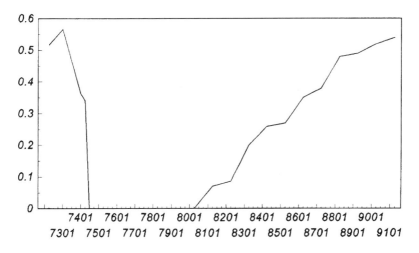

Figure 3.3   *FLIB3*

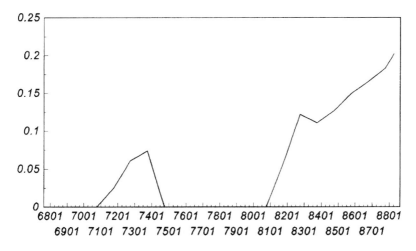

Figure 3.4   *FLIB4*

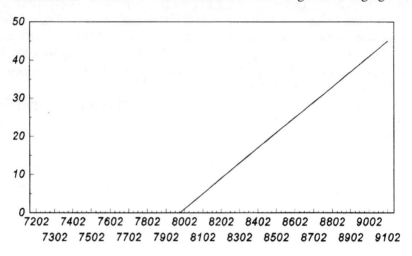

50

40

30

20

10

0
7202 7402 7602 7802 8002 8202 8402 8602 8802 9002
   7302 7502 7702 7902 8102 8302 8502 8702 8902 9102

Figure 3.5 *FLIB5*

(e) The fifth and final measure assumes that financial liberalisation is proxied by a simple split time trend which takes the value zero until 1980Q1. This is shown as *FLIB5* in Figure 3.5.

3.3 ESTIMATION AND RESULTS

From equations (2), (3) and (4) the aggregate consumption function to be estimated is in a linear form:

$$C_t = \mu_t(C_{t+1} - CG_{t+1} - \pi_t(YD_{t+1} - EC_{t+1} - IP_{t+1}))$$
$$+ \beta(A_{t-1} + \pi_t DB_{t-1} - \mu_t(A_t + \pi_{t+1}*DB - (1 - \pi_t)*YD_t))$$
$$+ CG_t + \pi_t(Y_t - EC_t - IP_t) + b_2 DUM + e_t \qquad \ldots (5)$$

where

$$\pi_t = e^{-(b_0 + b_1 * FLIB)}$$

$$\mu_t = 1/(1 + r_t + m_t)$$

$$m_t = a_0 + a_1 \pi_t$$

$$e_t = -\mu u_{t+1} + u_t + \varepsilon_t$$

A_t is real non-human wealth and DB_t is personal sector non-mortgage debt.

This is a non-linear model with expectations of future variables. The appropriate estimation strategy is an errors-in-variable method under the assumption of rational expectations. This amounts to replacing the future expected variables with their realisations which then creates an errors-in-variable problem and induces a correlation between the error term in the estimated equation and the realisation of the expected variable. It also produces the possibility of a moving average (MA) error process. A number of strategies have been proposed for dealing with such problems; see Cuthbertson, Hall and Taylor (1991) for a survey. Darby and Ireland (1993) estimate the model using generalized method of moments (GMM) with a correction for the MA error process. A GMM estimator of the true parameter vector is obtained by finding the element of the parameter space that sets linear combinations of the sample of cross products as close to zero as possible. These population orthogonality conditions equate the expected products of instruments and serially independent disturbances to zero. GMM applies a correction to the standard covariance matrix and should achieve asymptotic efficiency. The instrument set is chosen in a conservative way to ensure the independence of the instruments and the MA error process. However, GMM is not a robust method when there is a near unit root in the equation and, instead we use a non-linear two-stage least squares method in MICROFIT. We include a dummy variable in 1979Q2 to allow for the anticipated effects of the change in value-added tax (VAT). Table 3.1 shows the estimates using the various alternative measures of the financial liberalisation variables. The data used are quarterly, seasonally adjusted, and in per capita terms. They are described fully in Section 3.7. Non-human wealth includes both financial and physical assets and the clearing bank base rate adjusted for inflation is used as a measure of real market interest rates.

The model is estimated using data from 1972Q1 through to 1988Q2, which is the longest, common sample period for the financial liberalisation variables. However, subsequent tests are carried out over a period extending to 1991Q1. The variables chosen to instrument components of forward consumption are lagged values of the independent variables together with government expenditure, dollar world oil prices and world GNP. Since there is a MA(1) process the instruments are lagged at least twice. Apart from the dummy variable and constant term there are four parameters to be estimated; β, a_1, b_0, and b_1.

Table 3.1 Estimation method: 2SLS; estimation period: 1972Q2–1988Q2

Parameter	FLIB1		FLIB2		FLIB4		FLIB5	
a_1	0.15	(1.65)	0.22	(1.90)	0.19	(1.91)	0.16	(2.56)
b_0	1.77	(3.99)	2.19	(4.99)	1.81	(4.32)	1.40	(3.57)
b_1	0.63	(0.94)	0.77	(2.25)	4.09	(2.09)	0.042	(2.20)
β	0.01	(3.00)	0.01	(2.91)	0.01	(3.70)	0.011	(4.69)
b_2	0.048	(3.26)	0.058	(3.83)	0.051	(3.67)	0.053	(3.43)
R^2	0.99		0.99		0.99		0.99	
D.W. statistic	2.28		2.27		2.39		2.19	
Res. sum of squares	0.012		0.10		0.011		0.015	
S.E. of regression	0.015		0.14		0.014		0.015	

t-statistics in parentheses.

The proportion of post-tax labour income received by credit-constrained consumers is determined by b_0 and b_1 and varies over the sample period.

The four sets of parameter estimates are based on the constructed financial innovation variables FLIB1, FLIB2, FLIB4 and FLIB5. The results using FLIB3 are not shown since these are almost identical to FLIB1. The results using different measures of FLIB are all quite similar and there is little to choose between them. The financial deregulation effects are correctly signed but are not always significant. The model using the split time trend (FLIB5) performs at least as well as the more sophisticated alternatives and we adopt this as our preferred equation on these grounds.

A possible extension of the model is to allow credit-constrained consumers either to make some precautionary saving or to borrow to a limited extent in excess of their current income. This amounts to relaxing the assumption that the marginal propensity to consumer of credit-constrained consumers is equal to unity. The generalized model then takes the form:

$$C_t = \mu_t(C_{t+1} - CG_{t+1} - \pi_t(YD_{t+1} - EC_{t+1} - IP_{t+1}))$$
$$+ \beta(A_{t-1} + \pi_t DB_{t-1} - \mu_t(A_t + \pi_{t+1}DB - (1 - \pi_t)*YD_t))$$
$$+ b_3(CG_t + \pi_t(Y_t - EC_t - IP_t)) + b_2 DUM + e_t \qquad (6)$$

with $b_3 \geq 0$.

The results from estimating this extended model using FLIB5 as a financial liberalisation proxy are shown in Table 3.2 with the results from FLIB4 shown for comparison. Figure 3.6 plots the residuals for the preferred consumption function. The results show that the unit restriction is easily satisfied.

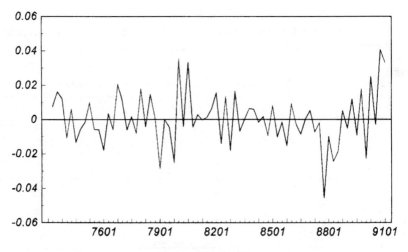

Figure 3.6 RES1

Table 3.2 The estimates of models using FLIB4 and FLIB5
Estimation methods: 2SLS; estimation period: 1972Q2–1991Q1

Parameter	Model with *FLIB4*		Model with *FLIB5*	
a_1	0.20	(1.55)	0.080	(1.87)
b_0	1.89	(3.34)	1.10	(1.89)
b_1	3.83	(1.81)	0.039	(2.10)
b_3	1.09	(2.74)	0.94	(2.13)
β	0.010	(3.38)	0.0059	(1.68)
b_2	0.050	(3.47)	0.055	(3.80)
R^2	0.99		0.99	
D.W. statistic	2.40		2.56	
Res. sum of squares	0.010		0.01	
S.E. of regression	0.014		0.013	

t-statistics in parentheses.

The estimated parameters can be used to calculate the impact of financial liberalisation on the proportion of credit-constrained consumers and the size of the mark-up on the discount rate. Our preferred equation, based on *FLIB5*, implies that the proportion of credit-constrained consumers has fallen from 33% before 1980 to just 6% by 1991 (Table 3.3). This suggests that by 1991 the majority of consumers are forward-looking and are able to borrow without obvious liquidity constraints. The estimates from Table 3.2 imply a mark-up on the discount rate of forward-looking consumers of 2.7 percentage points under regulation, falling to just 0.5 percentage points by 1991. Table 3.3 also decomposes the calculated values of consumption into contributions from the different income and asset components. The share of income received by different groups changes dramatically after financial liberalisation, even though the growth of aggregate consumption is smooth. Current and future discounted income received by forward-looking consumers more than doubles by 1991 over its value in 1973, with most of this increase occurring after 1980. In contrast, income received by credit-constrained consumers falls by over 20% as the proportion of income-constrained consumers falls.

3.4 COMPARISON BETWEEN FORWARD-LOOKING AND BACKWARD-LOOKING CONSUMPTION MODELS

3.4.1 Non-Nested Tests

Within our overall modelling work for the UK economy we have a more conventional model of aggregate consumption based around the ECM approach. This model has been recently estimated using standard dynamic modelling techniques and represents, in our view, a good example of this approach to modelling consumption. Consequently we have two consumption models: one that is wholly backward-looking based on the ECM approach and fully documented in the

Table 3.3 Estimates of mark-up and credit constraints (the model with *FLIB5*)

	1973Q2	1981Q2	1991Q1
Mark-up (percentage points)	2.66	2.19	0.47
Proportion credit-constrained	0.33	0.27	0.060
Income from forward-looking consumers	0.539	0.644	1.173
Income from credit-constrained consumers	0.403	0.454	0.314

Income from forward-looking consumers = $(\mu(C_{t+1} - YD_{t+1}) + \beta(A_{t-1} - \mu A_t + YD_{1t})$.
Income from credit constrained consumers = YD_{2t}.

Model Manual for the London Business School's UK model (see Appendix 1); and the other given by the forward-looking model of Section 3.4. The question then naturally arises: Which, if either, of these two models may be considered superior? The standard approach to testing this question would be to nest one model within the other and then perform econometric tests of the restrictions implied by the smaller model. However, in this case one model cannot be obtained from the other, they contain quite different sets of explanatory variables, the functional forms are quite different, and even the dependent variables are not exactly the same (in the ECM model the log of consumption is used while above we use the level of consumption). We therefore need to use a set of techniques that fall under the general heading of non-nested tests. There are many different ways to construct these tests. Three tests will be introduced briefly as follows:

1. The J-test. Assume two models

$$M1 : y = aX_{1t} + u_t \qquad \ldots (7a)$$

and

$$M2 : y = bX_{2t} + u_t \qquad \ldots (7b)$$

where X_{1t} and X_{2t} are different sets of explanatory variables. If M2 is the null hypothesis, then we may construct the forecast from model 1 using the estimated value of a from the model. The J-test of Davidson and Mackinnon is based on the t-ratio of the coefficient of this forecast $(\hat{y}_1)$ when it is included in M2, i.e.

$$y = bX_{2t} + \alpha \hat{y}_1 + u_t \qquad \ldots (8)$$

2. The JA-test (Fisher–McAleer–Atkinson). This takes account of the stochastic nature of the forecast from M1 by using its expectation under M2. Thus we regress X_2 on X_1 and then use this to form the fitted value for M1 $(\hat{y}_3)$,

and then replace $\hat{y}_2$ in the J-test equation. Thus the JA-test equation will be

$$y = aX_{2t} + \alpha\hat{y}_3 + u_t \qquad \ldots (9)$$

In the absence of stochastic regressors this yields an exact t-test, in contrast to the J-test which rests on asymptotic distribution theory.

3. The parameter-encompassing test (F-test). This proceeds by the construction of a composite alternative hypothesis written as:

$$Mc : y = aX1_t + bX2_t \ldots + u_t \qquad \ldots (10)$$

where $b = 0$ if M1 cannot be rejected by another model.

All these tests can be carried out either under the null that M1 or M2 is the true model. This emphasises the importance of clearly stating the hypothesis being tested. It is of course possible that M1 will reject M2 and M2 will reject M1, or conversely that both models will fail to reject each other. It is also worth stressing that these tests do not strictly allow for the degree of divergence that is apparent between our two models. In particular, they do not properly allow for different dependent variables, different estimation techniques (OLS in the case of the ECM model and 2SLS in the case of the forward-looking model) or the very important difference of future expectations being explicit in one of the two variables. However, we feel that these tests are worth pursuing in this context because they may be viewed simply as ways of assessing the added informational (or forecasting) content of one model over another.

3.4.2 Results of the Non-Nested Test on the Two Consumption Models

Let model 1 (M1) be the backward-looking model (ECM) and let model 2 (M2) be the forward-looking model. Table 3.4 sets up the null hypothesis that M1 is the true model and Table 3.5 sets up the null that M2 is the true model, both tables report the J-test and JA-test results for the two models.

The results in Table 3.4 suggest that fitted values from M2 of both $\hat{y}_2$ and $\hat{y}_3$ are significant in the J-test and JA-test based on the α value and t-ratio. So M1 is rejected by M2. On the other hand, in Table 3.5 we obtain that the negative fitted values from M1 are not significant in M2 and hence M2 cannot be rejected by M1. The results therefore support M2 rather than M1.

However, both the J-test and the JA-test may be misleading in this case both because of the form of the dependent variable and the presence of the future consumption variable in the forward-looking model which may unduly favour this model.

Table 3.6 gives the results of the parameter-encompassing test from the composite equation. M1 is a linear function estimated by OLS estimation but M2 is a non-linear equation and is estimated by 2SLS. So we need to use the same method (2SLS) to estimate the composite models. (The estimation results for the two models estimated separately are in parentheses.)

Table 3.4   Results of the non-nested test with M2 against M1

Dependent variable is LC; 75 observations from 72Q3 to 91Q1
Regressors for M1 in J-test: C, $LC(-1)$, $DLRPDI$, $DLRPDI(-1)$, $DLHTU$, $DLPY(-1)$, $CECM(-1)$, $\hat{y}_2$
Regressors for M1 in JA-test: C, $LC(-1)$, $DLRPDI$, $DLRPDI(-1)$, $DLHTU$, $DLPY(-1)$, $CECM(-1)$, $\hat{y}_3$

Test statistic	M2 against M1	
J-test ($\hat{y}_2$)	α: 0.29	t-ratio: 4.47
JA-test ($\hat{y}_3$)	α: 0.24	t-ratio: 3.52

	In J-test	In JA-test
Std. dev. of dependent variable	0.15	0.15
Sum of squared residuals	0.039	0.033
SE of regression	0.079	0.074
R^2	0.99	0.99
D.W. statistic	1.71	2.08
Log of likelihood	251.10	257.17

Where $LC = \log(C)$
$DLRPDI = \log(RPDI) - \log(RPDI(-1))$
$DLPY = \log(PHAS(-1)/YEM(-1)) - \log(PHAS(-2)/YEM(-2))$

Table 3.5   Results of the non-nested test with M1 against M2

Dependent variable is LC; 75 observations from 72Q3 to 91Q1
Parameters for M2 in J-test: C, a_1, b_0, b_1, b_2, β, $\hat{y}_2$
Parameters for M2 in JA-test: C, a_1, b_0, b_1, b_2, β, $\hat{y}_3$

Test statistic	M1 against M2	
J-test ($\hat{y}_2$)	α: -0.00054	t-ratio: 1.51
JA-test ($\hat{y}_3$)	α: -0.00056	t-ratio: 1.52

	In J-test	In JA-test
Std. dev. of dependent variable	0.15	0.15
Sum of squared residuals	0.011	0.011
SE of regression	0.013	0.013
R^2	0.99	0.99
D.W. statistic	2.36	2.38

The results from our non-nested test suggest that the forward-looking model rejects the backward-looking model, in particular we would note that:

1. The composite model has counter-intuitive signs on many of the variables in the backward-looking model, e.g. LC(−1), DLRPDI, and DLPY(−1). However, the parameters for our forward-looking model remain plausible.

2. The key variables in the backward-looking model, e.g. DLRPDI(−1), DLHTU and the error term, become less statistically significant.

Table 3.6   Results of the parameter-encompassing test

Dependent variable: LC; Current sample: 72Q3 to 91Q1; Number of observations: 75

Parameter	Estimate		t-statistic	
a_1	3.04	(0.14)	1.68	(1.87)
b_0	0.67	(1.38)	1.81	(3.04)
b_1	0.02	(0.038)	4.68	(3.13)
b_3	0.76	(0.96)	2.17	(3.07)
β	0.0046	(0.010)	1.80	(9.85)
$LC(-1)$	−0.22	(1.007)	−3.27	(153.16)
$DLRPDI$	−0.45	(0.29)	−3.34	(4.89)
$DLRPDI(-1)$	0.0146	(0.12)	0.37	(1.87)
$DLHTU$	−0.039	(0.048)	−1.19	(3.68)
$DLPY(-1)$	−0.015	(0.063)	−0.37	(3.39)
$CECM(-1)$	−0.11	(0.27)	−0.57	(2.84)
Constant	2.71	(0.08)	3.64	(1.12)

Std. dev. of dependent variable = 0.15
Sum of squared residuals = 0.0086
SE of regression = 0.012
$R^2 = 0.99$
D.W. statistic = 2.06
Original estimation in parentheses.

This test essentially suggests that the forward-looking model is the better one and has something to offer in terms of a statistical explanation of consumption. However, the encompassing model cannot be seen as a satisfactory explanation in its own right because it clearly violates many of our prior expectations. Thus it is still not very clear which is the better model. We judge that it is worth pursing the situation a little further with some less formal diagnostics for the two models.

3.4.3 Other Comparison Approaches

There are other, less rigorous, methods available for nesting alternative models within a more general framework. We investigate a range of these mainly by using the fitted values instead of the set of working variables in our regressions to avoid the weakness of the above tests. We denote:

$C(T)$ = the true value of consumption

$C(F)$ = the fitted value from the forward-looking model

$C(B)$ = the fitted value from the backward-looking model

where these variables are defined in logarithmic form.

First we compute the regression

$$C(T) = \alpha C(F) + \beta C(B)$$

where $\alpha + \beta = 1$.

We can then test the alternative hypotheses:

$$H0 : \alpha = 1, \beta = 0$$

which implies that M2 explains the observed consumption and nothing is added from the information in M1; or the alternative hypothesis

$$H1 : \alpha \neq 0, \beta \neq 0$$

which implies that both models contribute to the explanation of actual consumption and hence M1 and M2 cannot reject each other.

The OLS estimation results show that both the fitted values of M1 and M2 are significant as $\alpha = 0.41$, $\beta = 0.59$, both parameters being statistically significant. We reject the null hypothesis in favour of H1 which implies that M1 and M2 cannot reject each other (although the estimate of β is slightly greater than α).

Alternatively we can regress the difference between the true value and the fitted value from M2 (or M1) on the fitted value from M1 (or M2). This measures the proportion of the residuals from one model explained by the other model. The null hypothesis is then that the errors from M2 (alternatively M1) cannot be explained by the fitted values from M1 (M2) and that the estimated coefficient is not significantly different from zero. The results are as follows:

$$C(T) - C(F) = -0.69\text{E-}5 \ C(B) \qquad \dots (6a)$$

standard error: 0.0013; t-statistic: 0.052

$$C(T) - C(B) = 0.80\text{E-}6 \ C(F) \qquad \dots (7a)$$

standard error: 0.0011; t-statistic: 0.071

The results suggest neither of the fitted values from one model can explain the forecast error from the other.

The results from this series of tests show that it is difficult to choose between the rival models. On balance we prefer the forward-looking model marginally, given the results of the parameter-encompassing test. This relative preference for the forward-looking model may, to some extent, reflect the fact that the forward-looking model includes some backward elements through the allowance for credit-constrained behaviour.

3.5 CONCLUSION

In this chapter we have explored the idea that the permanent income, rational expectations approach to consumption may be used as a fruitful basis for an empirical model. Given recent work and our institutional understanding of events in the United Kingdom over the last decade we have placed great emphasis on modelling the process of financial innovation and this has proved to be a crucial part of successfully implementing such a model. A range of measures of financial liberalisation have been tried and, somewhat surprisingly, we found that the model based on a simple split time trend performs at least as well as more sophisticated alternatives. This suggests that proxy variables for financial liberalisation that have both economic rationale and statistical support have yet to be developed. The model of forward-looking behaviour we have developed is to be well determined and has broadly sensible properties. It suggests that the degree of credit constraint in the economy declined dramatically between 1980 and 1990 from around 30% of the population to below 10%. A comparison of the forward-looking approach with the backward-looking alternatives found a marginal preference for the former, but there is little to choose between them.

3.6 ACKNOWLEDGEMENTS

We are grateful to Stephen Hall and James Nixon for their comments. Financial support from ESRC grant no. W116251003 is gratefully acknowledged.

3.7 DATA SOURCES AND DEFINITIONS

C (Aggregate consumption per person): $= CN/POPWA$

CG (Current grants per person): $= ((YJG*100)/PC)POPWA$

EC (Employers' contributions to pension funds per person):
$= ((YEC*100)/PC)POPWA$

YD (Post-tax labour income per person): $= ((YDN*100)/PC)/POPWA$

A (Net financial and physical wealth per person):
$= ((NFWP+ALLU)*100)/PC)/POPWA$

DB (Personal sector non-mortgage debt per person):
$= ((TFL*100)/PC)/POPWA$

IP (Interest payment on existing debt per person):
$= ((RMG*LHP)/PC)/POPWA$

1. The data below are from the LBS data bank:

CN: Aggregate consumption

YJG: Total current grants

YEC: Total employers' contributions to pension funds

YDN: Total post-tax labour income

$NFWP$: Net financial assets of the personal sector in current prices

TFL: Personal sector non-mortgage debt

RLB: Nominal interest rate; the real rate is the nominal rate less consumer price inflation

PC: Consumer expenditure deflator

2. The data below are from the CSO:

ALLU: Personal sector total tangible assets

RMG: Average mortgage rate

LHP: Personal sector mortgage debt

POPWA: Population of working age

APPENDIX 1: MODEL 1
(BACKWARD-LOOKING MODEL)

The long-run equation

$$CECM = \log(C(-1)/RPDI(-1)) - 1.148 - 0.108*DUMHP$$
$$-0.221*\log(PHAS(-1)/YEM(-1))*DUMHP$$
$$-0.015*\log(NFWP(-1)/YEM(-1))$$
$$+0.0024*RLB(-1) + 0.114*\log(RPDI(-1))$$

OLS estimation:

104 observations	Sample: 1968Q1 to 1993Q4
DF = −7.2	ADF = −4.6

$$C = \exp(\log(C(-1)/RPDI(-1)) + \log(RPDI) - 0.001$$
$$(0.52)$$
$$+0.16*\log(C(-4)/RPDI(-4)) - \log(C9-5)/RPDI(-5))$$
$$(2.05)$$
$$+0.21*\log(RPDI(-1)/RPDI(-2)) - 0.14*\log(RPDI(-2)/RPDI(-3))$$
$$(2.37) \qquad\qquad\qquad (1.71)$$
$$-0.40*CECM + 0.058*D7902 - 0.03*D7902(-1)$$
$$(3.46) \qquad (3.25) \qquad\qquad (1.8)$$

where

$RPDI$ = real disposable income

$PHAS$ = house price

YEM = income from employment

RLB = interest rate

$NFWP$ = net financial wealth in the personal sector

$DUMHP$ = dummy variable

OLS estimation:

96 observations	Sample: 1969Q2 to 1993Q1	
$\overline{R}^2$: 0.37	SE regression:	0.014
Serial correlation:	$\chi^2(4)$:	3.05
Function form	$\chi^2(1)$:	8.36
Normality	$\chi^2(2)$:	1.13
Heteroscedasticity (ARCH)	$\chi^2(1)$:	0.54

4

Stockbuilding, Risk and the Forward-Looking Behaviour of the Firm

HONG BAI, STEPHEN G. HALL
AND JOHN WHITLEY

4.1 INTRODUCTION

Stock movements have long been recognised as crucial in cyclical movements in the economy. Movements in the level of aggregate output in the United Kingdom since 1980 have often been associated with large movements in the level of stocks. Changes in the level of stocks accounted for around one-quarter of the increase in growth during the economic recovery of 1981–82 and about the same proportion of the decline in output during the recession of 1991. The traditional approach to modelling stockbuilding has been to derive models based on the concept of adjustment to a desired level of stocks. Costs of adjustment are then introduced to give a dynamic relationship for stockbuilding. The determination of stockbuilding has typically been based on a similar approach to that used for fixed capital. These models initially used a backward looking formulation which has not been adequate in explaining either the fact that stockbuilding tends to lead rather than lag the economic cycle, or that observed movements in stocks are often far larger in magnitude than models based on smooth adjustment imply. Unlike models of fixed investment, however, the foundations of the model tend not to be neoclassical. Rather, models of stockbuilding emphasise the transactions, precautionary and speculative motives. The transactions motive relates to lags between production and delivery. Trend declines in the aggregate stock–output ratio over time are often associated with improvements in the efficiency of the

Macroeconomic Modelling in a Changing World. Edited by C. Allen and S. Hall
© 1997 John Wiley & Sons Ltd

transactions demand for stocks, such as through new methods of organisation like 'just-in-time'. The precautionary motive is concerned with the use of buffer stocks as insurance against unexpected changes in demand, whereas speculation is concerned with motives for holding stocks when their prices are expected to change markedly. Some models distinguish between different forms of stocks, usually raw materials, work in progress, and finished goods. A major complication in the analysis of stockbuilding concerns the quality of the data. There is a tendency for national account statisticians to allocate a high proportion of the residual error between a measure of GDP output and expenditure to stockbuilding. These adjustments can be substantial and could, for example, completely change the direction and size of stockbuilding movements. Furthermore, the fact that the residual adjustment tends to be revised over time makes the measure of stockbuilding highly vulnerable to the vintage of the data employed.

The traditional form of the model can be written as

$$S_t^* = f(Y^e, r, \Delta p^e, Z)$$

where Y^e is a measure of expected sales or output, r is the interest rate, Δp^e is the expected change in prices and Z is a vector of other influences such as business confidence or liquidity. The appropriate measure of the cost of holding stocks, r, is properly defined in terms of the expected rate with an allowance for the tax treatment of stocks. Before 1974 inflationary gains from holding stocks were subject to a corporation tax. A variety of schemes followed until 1984 when capital gains were exempt from tax.

Since costs are assumed to be associated with stock adjustment, the actual level of stocks is assumed to adjust in relation to the deviation of stocks from their desired level. Thus

$$S_t - S_{t-1} = \lambda(S_t^* - S_{t-1})$$

Substituting for the determinants of desired stocks, S^*, gives an estimating equation of the form

$$\Delta S_t = a_0 + a_1 \lambda Y^e + a_2 \lambda r + a_3 \lambda \Delta p^e + a_4 Z - \lambda S_{t-1} + e_t \qquad \ldots (1)$$

where the expected level of output or sales is replaced by a distributed lag on past values. Unanticipated stock changes may occur from unanticipated changes in production or sales, but this element is not captured if the error term in this equation is treated as purely random.

This model can be derived more formally from a cost of adjustment model where

$$C_t = a(S_t - S_t^*)^2 + b(S_t - S_{t-1})^2$$

where the first component of this expression relates to the cost of disequilibrium, and the second to the costs of adjusting production.

Models of the form of (1) have been used extensively, but their empirical performance has been less than satisfactory. Hall, Henry and Wren-Lewis (1986) show the poor system performance that these models had over the early 1980s and Wallis *et al.* (1987), in a survey of stockbuilding equations used in the main UK macroeconometric models, demonstrate their poor within-sample predictive power.

The two main extensions to this basic model have been to introduce the explicit treatment of expectations and to allow the variance of output or sales to influence the desired level of stocks. The implicit treatment of expectations in the basic model of stockbuilding (1) assumes that expected output or demand can be proxied by past movements in these series. This denies a role for unexpected or unanticipated stockbuilding and assumes that all stockbuilding is planned. Yet it has long been recognised that stocks and liquidity can play an important buffer role between sales and production. Firms will increase their inventory investment to smooth out expected fluctuations in production as a result of expected changes in future sales. There are two distinct types of inventory investment, anticipated and unanticipated, and these can have opposite effects on aggregate demand, i.e. the accumulation of inventories could be associated with either an unexpected decline in sales or an expected increase in future sales.

Expectations can be more formally introduced by generalising the costs of adjustment formulation, following Blanchard (1985). Here the firm engages in intertemporal cost minimisation:

$$\min \mathrm{E} \left[\sum_{i=1}^{N} \delta^t a(S_t - S_t^*)^2 + b(S_t - S_{t-1})^2 + c(\Delta S_t - \Delta S_{t-1})^2 | \Omega_0 \right]$$

where Ω refers to the information set at time t.

The solution to this problem can be written as

$$S_t = \lambda_1 S_{t-1} + \lambda_2 S_{t-2} + (1 - \lambda_1 - \lambda_2)^2 \sum_{i=0}^{\infty} \gamma_i S_{t+i}^*$$

so that stockbuilding now depends on the infinite progression of the expected values of the determinants of the desired level of stocks. An allowance for unanticipated stockbuilding can now be introduced simply by adding the term

$$\beta[\mathrm{E}(Y_t) - Y_t]$$

to represent involuntary stockbuilding.

There remains the problem of measuring the unobserved future values of the determinants of desired stocks. The usual approaches (see Hall, Henry and Wren-Lewis (1986)) are to use either a time-series model, a vector autoregression, or direct measures of expectations available from surveys, etc.

Although this extension deals with the dynamic nature of the stockbuilding decision by making expectations explicit, the second extension to the basic model notes that stocks are typically non-cointegrated with the level of output in the

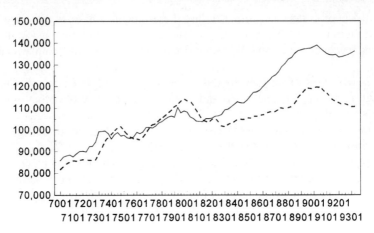

Figure 4.1 The comparison of the level of output (——) and stocks (- - -) from 1970 to 1993

United Kingdom. This reflects the declining stock–output ratio (see Figure 4.1) which the standard models do not capture unless through the addition of a time trend.

Callen and Henry (1989) have suggested that it is necessary to use financial variables as well as the cost of stockbuilding and output variables to obtain a reasonable explanation of stock levels. Callen, Hall and Henry (1990) have further shown that the lack of cointegration can be explained by the implicit assumption that the conditional variance of output or demand is constant. By deriving a measure of this conditional variance using a generalised ARCH process (GARCH) they are then able to improve the cointegration properties of stock-building relationships for the United Kingdom.

This chapter describes how this extended stockbuilding model can be estimated, and contrasts its empirical performance with the more traditional backward-looking explanation of stockbuilding. The latter is represented by the current stockbuilding equation in the London Business School's econometric model.

The plan of the chapter is as follows. In Section 4.2 we outline the basic model of stockbuilding to be investigated and describe the GARCH process briefly. Section 4.3 discusses some details of the estimation strategy and presents results. Section 4.4 compares the forward-looking and backward-looking models. Our general conclusions are offered in Section 4.5.

4.2 AN AGGREGATE MODEL OF STOCKBUILDING

In equilibrium the firm desires to hold positive levels of stocks because the level of sales in the future is uncertain and it is costly to face a 'stockout', i.e. the inability to meet desired sales because stocks have reached zero and so potential sales are lost. Following Callen, Hall and Henry (1990) we assume that the expected costs of a stockout are a function of the variance of sales, the level of production and the level of stocks. If there were no costs associated with holding stocks, then firms would naturally hold infinitely large levels of stocks. However, there are other costs in the form of both forgone interest on the wealth tied up in the stocks and the direct cost of holding stocks in the form of storage and other factors. So the overall desired equilibrium stock level, S^*, is a function of the variance of sales, the level of output and the cost of holding stocks. The dynamic path for stocks is assumed to be given by the solution to a cost-minimisation problem which sees costs of both being away from the desired stock level and in adjusting the stock level too quickly:

$$\min E \left\{ \sum [a(S_t - S_t^*)^2 + b(S_t - S_{t-1})^2 + c(\Delta S_t - \Delta S_{t-1})^2] | \Omega_t \right\} \quad \ldots (2)$$

where Ω_t is the current information set. The first-order condition for this optimisation can be stated as

$$B(L)S_t = aS_t^* \quad \ldots (3)$$

where $B(L)$ is a polynomial in the lag operator L, or

$$S_t = \alpha(S_{t+1} + S_{t-1}) + \beta(S_{t+2} + S_{t-2}) + S_t^* \quad \ldots (4)$$

Assuming that the discount factor is constant and $\alpha = -(b + 4c)/(a + 2b + 6c)$, $\beta = c/(a + 2b + 6c)$ and using $\lim S_T = S$ as the transversality condition, (4) can be arranged as

$$S_t = \lambda_1 S_{t-1} + \lambda_2 S_{t-2} + (1 - \lambda_1 - \lambda_2)^2 \sum \gamma_i S_{t+i}^* \quad \ldots (5)$$

This then defines the dynamic model to be estimated, but we also need to derive the underlying equilibrium relationship. The standard techniques associated with cointegration allow us to do this in the usual case, but here we have the unusual problem of wishing to focus on the conditional variance of sales. We therefore need to build a model that allows us to do this, and we have chosen to use the ARCH or GARCH approach to modelling heteroscedasticity. Engle, Lilien and Robins (1987) suggest an extension of Engle's (1982) ARCH model whereby the conditional first moment of a time series itself becomes a function of the conditional second moment, which follows an ARCH process:

$$y_t = \alpha' x_t + \delta h_t^2 + \varepsilon_t$$
$$\varepsilon_t | \Omega_{t-1} \sim N(0, h_t^2) \quad \ldots (6)$$

$$h_t^2 = \gamma_0 + \sum_{i=1}^{n} \gamma_i \varepsilon_{t-i}^2 \quad \ldots (7)$$

where x_t is a vector of conditioning variables, weakly exogenous for all parameters in (2) and (7). Thus h_t^2 is the conditional variance of ε_t formed at period t based on the information set (σ-field) of all information up to period $t-1$, and by the assumption that h_t^2 is non-stochastic.

A further extension has been suggested by Bollerslev (1986). In Bollerslev's GARCH formulation the conditional second moments are functions of their own lagged values as well as the squares and cross-products of lagged forecast errors. The GARCH-M (n, p) formulation of the above model would consist of (7) and

$$h_t^2 = A_0 + \sum_{i=1}^{n} A_i \varepsilon_{t-i}^2 + \sum_{i=1}^{p} B_i h_{t-i}^2 \qquad \ldots (8)$$

where B_i and A_i are coefficients.

Stacking all the parameters of the system into a single vector:

$$\mu = (\alpha, \delta, A_0, A_1, \ldots, A_n, B_1, \ldots, B_p) \qquad \ldots (9)$$

and applying Schweppe's (1965) prediction error decomposition form of the likelihood function, the log-likelihood for a sample of T observations (conditional on initial values) is proportional to

$$L(\mu) = \sum_{t=1}^{T} (-\log |h_t^2| - \varepsilon_t^2 / h_t^2) \qquad \ldots (10)$$

(where we have assumed normality of the forecast errors).

Although the analytic derivatives of (10) can be computed (see Engle, Lilien and Robins (1987)) variable-metric algorithms that employ numerical derivatives are simpler to use and easily allow changes in specification. Under suitable regularity conditions (Crowder (1976)), maximisation of (10) will yield maximum likelihood estimates with the usual properties.

Our proposed modelling strategy is then to begin by applying the GARCH-M model to the data for aggregate sales. This will provide an actual measure of the variance of sales which we can then use in a cointegration analysis along with the level of output and stocks and the cost of stockholding to derive a suitable cointegrating vector for stocks. Finally, we will use this cointegrating vector in the dynamic forward-looking model for stocks.

4.3 ESTIMATION AND RESULTS

The first stage of our estimation is to build the GARCH-M model of sales. We take GDP to be a proxy for sales and so we postulate a simple autoregression of the following form:

$$LGDP_t = \alpha LGDP_{t-i} + \delta VAR_t + \varepsilon_t$$

$$VAR = \sum \beta VAR_{t-i} + \sum \gamma_i \varepsilon_{t-i}^2 + \mu$$

Table 4.1 GARCH parameters (1970Q1–1993Q2)

Parameter	Estimate			
Constant	0.001	(1.36)		
β	0.66	(7.61)		
γ	0.10	(1.52)		
δ	0.004	(0.30)		
α_{11}	1.07	(3114.3)		
α_{12}	0.13	(5.65)		
Mean of residuals	−0.01			
Variance of the equation	2.31			
Standard deviation	0.01			
Skewness	0.45			
Kurtosis	1.63			
B.J. normality test	13.24			
	Lag 1	4	7	9
Box Pierce test	0.02	2.67	7.77	12.50
LeJong Box test	0.02	2.85	8.48	13.83

The results of the maximum likelihood estimation of this model are given in Table 4.1.

This model is reasonably well behaved but with a strong autoregressive variance process the lagged variance effect is significant as $\delta > 0$ and the sum of β and γ is 0.77, which is close to unity, suggesting that the model may be close to being integrated in variance (Engle (1987)). The small coefficients of skewness and kurtosis indicate that it is not a normal distribution and the B.J. normality test also rejects the null. With the significant values of the Dickey–Fuller (DF) test (−9.21) and augmented Dickey–Fuller (ADF) test (−8.25), the data-generation process is stationary. However, the values for the B.P. test and the L.B. test are not strong enough to reject serial correlation at the 5% level, especially in the lower lags. Figure 4.2 presents our measure of the conditional variance of output. This clearly emphasises the much greater volatility of output during the 1970s and early 1980s compared with most of the 1980s.

We now begin the cointegration exercise by checking the orders of integration of the four variables in our potential model, i.e. the log of GDP (*LGDP*), the cost of stock holding (*CSKEL*), our measure of the conditional variance (*VAR*) and the log of the stock level itself (*LS*). Table 4.2 then reports standard statistics for stationarity tests for these variables.

The conclusion from Table 4.2 is quite clear: GDP, the cost of holding stocks and stocks are all clearly I(1) processes, and the variance term is probably stationary (which accords with our estimates of the GARCH model) but it is highly persistent.

We then proceed to investigate the potential cointegration of this set of variables both by ordinary least squares (OLS) estimation and Johansen maximum likelihood procedures.

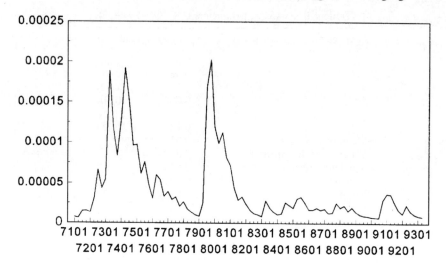

Figure 4.2   The conditional variance of sales from 1970 to 1993

Table 4.2   The time-series properties of
the data (1970Q1–1992Q1)

	Level		Difference	
	DF	ADF	DF	ADF
LGDP	−1.6	−1.7		−8.8
CSKEL	−2.0	−2.5	−6.1	−4.8
VAR	−3.7	−3.9	−3.6	−3.8
LS	−1.4	−2.5		−4.4

The cointegrating regression by OLS is

$$LS = \underset{(6.72)}{2.6} + \underset{(23.03)}{0.77*LGDP} - \underset{(6.57)}{0.004*CSKEL} + \underset{(12.00)}{309*VAR} \quad \dots (11)$$

Phillips test $= -9.2$; ADF test $= -2.97$

The same relationship estimated by maximum likelihood procedures for a *VAR* lag length equal to 5 finds there is only one significant cointegrating relationship:

$$LS = 0.98*LGDP - 0.007*CSKEL + 1579*VAR \qquad \dots (12)$$

All the parameter values in these two equations are plausible and statistically significant. Figure 4.3 shows the residuals from both methods. It is not easy to state the properties of both sets of estimates. We investigate these further below.

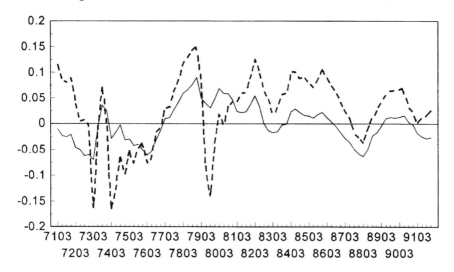

Figure 4.3 The residuals from two cointerating regressions (- - -) and one from OLS estimation

4.3.1 Estimation of the Forward-Looking Dynamic Equation

We base our estimation of the dynamic model around the Euler equation form of the dynamic model summarised in (5). From (5) we can state:

$$LS_t = g*LS_t^* + h*(LS_{t+1} + LS_{t-1}) - i*(LS_{t+2} + LS_{t-2}) \qquad \ldots (13)$$

or

$$DLS_t = g*LS_t^* + h*LS_{t+1} + (h - 1)*LS_{t-1} - i*(LS_{t+2} + LS_{t-2}) \qquad \ldots (14)$$

where g, h and i are positive and where $g + 2h - 2i = 1$ should be unity, which implies $i = h + 0.5g - 0.5$ according to the theoretical model in Section 4.2.

The model contains a term in the expected value of future stocks which we treat in estimation by using the errors in variables approach to estimation under rational estimation (we actually use a system estimation technique based on three-stage least squares). This estimate is consistent and asymptotically normal. Under certain conditions it is asymptotically more efficient than single-equation estimates. If the model is linear in the parameters and variables, then three-stage least squares estimates are asymptotically equivalent to maximum likelihood estimates. The instrument set is chosen conservatively to avoid any simultaneous equation bias. The estimation results are shown in Table 4.3 and Table 4.4 for each of the two cointegrating vectors based on OLS and ML estimation procedures.

Table 4.3 and Table 4.4 show reasonably similar sets of results, both closely obey our priors on the restriction on the parameters. On purely statistical grounds

Table 4.3 (S^* = fitted value in the OLS estimation) ML estimates for dynamic stockbuilding model (1970Q1–1992Q3)

Parameter	Estimate	Standard error	t-statistic
g	0.045	0.026	1.72
h	0.89	0.46	19.27
i	0.52	0.13	39.80

$R^2 = 0.70$
Variance of residuals = 0.05E-4
D.W. statistic = 2.25

Table 4.4 (S^* = fitted value in the Johansen procedure) ML estimates for dynamic stockbuilding model (1970Q1–1992Q3)

Parameter	Estimate	Standard error	t-statistic
g	0.003	0.007	0.42
h	0.67	0.07	8.91
i	0.17	0.05	3.44

$R^2 = 0.87$
Variance of residuals = 0.2E-4
D.W. statistic = 3.28

the OLS model is marginally better than the ML based model, but both are satisfactory.

4.4 COMPARISON BETWEEN FORWARD-LOOKING AND BACKWARD-LOOKING MODELS

We now have two alternative stockbuilding models: the first is a backward-looking model currently used in the LBS model based around an error correction approach to modelling stocks (see Appendix 1), which is the best backward-looking model that we could find. The second is the more sophisticated model outlined in the preceding sections. Both models have the same data base and instrument variables. The question now arises as to which of the two models is superior. However, one model cannot be obtained from the others because of their very different assumptions about functional form and estimation techniques. We propose the use of non-nested tests to attempt to decide if one model clearly dominates the other. There are many different ways to construct such tests. The tests used are described in full in Chapter 3 and will only be briefly described here.

4.4.1 Non-Nested Tests

We use the following tests.

1. The J-test, which tests whether the forecast of model 1 can improve the explanation of model 2, and vice versa.

2. The JA-test, which uses the expected value from model 1 in model 2 and vice versa.

3. The parameter-encompassing test (F-test), which is based on testing the individual models against the composite alternative.

In addition there are a range of tests that essentially evaluate information criteria to compare the explanatory powers of two models. These include the Cox test (N), the adjusted Cox test (NT) and the Wald tests between the two models (W).

All these tests can be carried out either under the null that M1 or M2 is the true model. This emphasises the importance of clearly stating the hypothesis being tested. It is of course possible that M1 will reject M2 and M2 will reject M1, or conversely that both models will fail to reject each other. It is also worth emphasising that these tests do not strictly allow for the degree of divergence that is apparent between our two models. In particular they do not properly allow for different estimation techniques (OLS in the case of the ECM model and IV in the case of the forward-looking model) or the very important difference of future expectations being explicitly in one of the two variables. However, we feel that these tests are worth pursuing in this context because they may be viewed simply as ways of assessing the added informational (or forecasting) content of one model over another.

4.4.2 The Non-Nested Tests for the Stockbuilding Model

We assume

M1: $\Delta LSt = \text{const} + d\Delta LS_{t-1} + eSECM$

M2: $\Delta LS_t = gLS_t^* + hLS_{t+1} + (h-1)LS_{t-1} - iS2$

where $S2 = LS_{t+2} + LS_{t-2}$.

Table 4.5 reports the non-nested test results for these two models. All the regressions are estimated by OLS estimation over the same sample period.

M2 can reject M1 since all the tests in the first column are significant when M1 has M2 included in it, but none of them is significant for M2 against M1. We also report the coefficient, standard error and t-ratio of the composite model in Table 4.6 (the coefficient estimates from the original models are given in parentheses, treated in turn as the null hypothesis). We can examine the change in coefficients between the null hypotheses and the composite alternative.

M2 is more stable in the parameter-encompassing equation; neither the signs nor the t-ratio change vary much in the composite model. However, M1 changes a lot with low t-ratios and less important coefficients. The F-test also confirms this. When the null is M1, the F-test is 66.34 (M1 against M2) and 0.06 (M2 against M1). The composite model is well specified statistically with an absence of serial correlation.

All the tests suggest that M2 rejects M1. However, as noted above, these tests may overstate the case because they are not designed to cope with the divergence

Table 4.5 Alternative test for the non-nested regression model

Dependent variable is ΔLS;   85 observation used from 1971Q2–1992Q2
Regressors for model M1:   Const $\Delta LS(-1)SECM$
Regressors for model M2: $LS^*LS(+1)LS(-1)S2$

Test statistic	M1 against M2	M2 against M1
N-test	−23.62	−0.17
NT-test	−21.77	−0.12
W-test	−10.42	−0.12
J-test	16.58	0.16
JA-test	7.59	0.16
Encompassing	$F(4, 77)86.87$	$F(3, 77)0.058$

Model M1: D.W. = 1.92; $\bar{R}^2 = 0.47$;   Log-likelihood = 280.19
Model M2: D.W. = 3.28; $\bar{R}^2 = 0.88$;   Log-likelihood = 343.08
Model M1 + M2: D.W. = 3.29; $\bar{R}^2 = 0.87$;   Log-likelihood = 343.17
Akaike's information criterion of M1 versus M2 = −61.88 favours M2
Schwarz's Bayesian information criterion of M1 versus M2 = −60.66 favours M2

Table 4.6 The parameter-encompassing test

Dependent variable: ΔLS

Variable	Coefficient		Standard error	t-statistic	
Constant	−0.023	(0.14)	0.074	−0.31	(2.61)
$DLS(-1)$	0.005	(−0.65)	0.075	0.072	(8.44)
$SECM$	−0.23	(−0.002)	0.0057	−0.41	(−2.59)
$LS(+1)$	0.67	(0.89)	0.072	9.30	(19.26)
$LS(-1)$	−0.32	(−0.11)	0.043	−7.36	(−19.26)
$S2$	−0.18	(−0.52)	0.051	−3.51	(−39.27)
LS^*	0.002	(0.045)	0.018	0.12	(1.71)

of functional forms between our two models. So we confirm these results with some less formal diagnostics.

$LS(T)$ = the true stock value (in logs)

$LS(F)$ = the stock value estimated by the forward-looking model (in logs)

$LS(B)$ = the stock value estimated by the backward-looking model (in logs)

We assume $LS(T) = \alpha^*LS(F) + \beta^*LS(B)$, where $\alpha + \beta = 1$.

$H_0 : \alpha = 1$ if M2 is better than M1.

This can be estimated by OLS to give

$$LS(T) = 1.00^*LS(F) - 0.0063^*LS(B)$$
$$(16.19)(-0.10)$$

It is clear that for stockbuilding, a forward-looking model can outperform the traditional ECM in terms of the criteria we have used.

4.5 CONCLUSION

We have estimated a forward-looking model for stock behaviour which makes explicit allowance for the uncertainty of future sales. This forward-looking stockbuilding model is a better approximation to the data-generation process than conventional backward-looking models judging by a statistical comparison of two models. The difference between M1 and M2 is not only the effect of the expectation of future variables but also the conditional variance of output in the long-run solution in our forward-looking stockbuilding model.

Only one earlier paper has found this risk effect to be important: 'The main effect now seems to be the conditional variance of output and the cost of stockbuilding' (Callen, Hall and Henry (1990)). Our results support this point: stockbuilding responds strongly to the variance in output and this may have an important impact on economic fluctuations. However, the level of output itself also plays an important role in inventory behaviour in these results.

4.6 DATA SOURCES AND DEFINITIONS

Source: CSO databank

$CSKEL$: Cost of holding inventories:

$$CSKEL = (PS/PGDP)*(((1 - TC)*(RLB + 2)$$
$$- QDOT)*(1 + ((1)*TCT)) + (1)*TC*(QDOT/(1 - TC)))$$

where

$$QDOT = 100*\log(PS/PS(-4))$$

$$TC = TRYC/100$$

$$TCT = (TRYC/100)/(1 - TRYC/100)$$

GDP = Gross domestic product: output (1990 prices)

$PGDP$ = price of GDP at factor cost (index 1990 = 100)

PS = Price of level of stocks (index 1990 = 100)

S = stock level (1990 prices)

$TRYC$ = corporation tax rate (%)

APPENDIX 1: THE ERROR CORRECTION MODEL FOR STOCKS (BACKWARD-LOOKING)

The long-run equation:

$$SECM = 23.44*LS_{t-1} - 17.20*LGDP_{t-1} + 0.18*CSKEL_{t-1} \quad \text{(Johansen procedure)} \quad \text{(2a)}$$

98 observations; sample: 1968Q1 to 1993Q2

DF $= -9.31$; ADF $= -3.42$

$r = 1$ and a *VAR* system of maximum lag $= 4$

The dynamic model:

$$\Delta LSt = \underset{(2.61)}{0.14} - \underset{(8.44)}{0.65\Delta LS_{t-1}} - \underset{(2.59)}{0.002SECM} \quad \text{(estimated by OLS)} \quad \text{(3a)}$$

5
UK Fiscal Policy Over the Medium Term

STEPHEN HALL, JOHN O'SULLIVAN AND ANDREW SENTANCE

5.1 INTRODUCTION

A medium-term approach to fiscal policy has been a major theme of UK government policy since 1979. The Conservative government that came to power in that year launched a Medium Term Financial Strategy (MTFS), the objective of which was to reduce both inflation and the public sector deficit. In the original formulation of the MTFS, these objectives were directly linked, with the reduction in the contribution to monetary growth from public borrowing identified as a key mechanism through which inflation would be curtailed. As the 1980s progressed, the government's faith in this mechanistic link between public borrowing, the money supply and inflation faded. However, the medium-term framework for fiscal policy that the UK government currently uses is still based on broadly the same principles as in 1979: tight control of public expenditure and prudent medium-term objectives for government borrowing.

Over the 1980s the UK government seemed to make good progress towards achieving these objectives. Public borrowing was contained during the early 1980s recession and public spending began to fall as a share of national output as the recovery proceeded. By the late 1980s, the Public Sector Borrowing Requirement (PSBR) had been eliminated and public sector debt was being repaid. However, all this progress came unstuck in the early 1990s as the combined impact of tax cuts made in the late 1980s, a relaxation in the control of public

Macroeconomic Modelling in a Changing World. Edited by C. Allen and S. Hall
© 1997 John Wiley & Sons Ltd

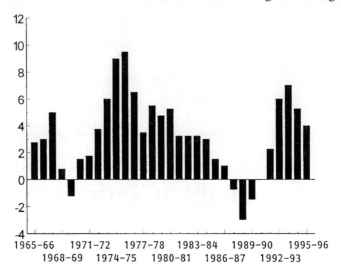

Figure 5.1 Public sector borrowing requirement (percentage of GDP)

spending and the recession combined to push the PSBR to a peak of over £45bn (7.1% of GDP), as Figure 5.1 shows.

One fact apparent from this chain of events is how vulnerable public finances were to the state of the cycle. Government expenditure is pushed up by recessions, whereas tax receipts fall, causing the deficit to rise in periods when economic activity is weak and fall when the economy is growing strongly. Recent estimates by the Treasury suggest that the PSBR/GDP ratio will fall/rise by around 0.8% of GDP for every 1% by which output is above/below trend (Virley and Hirst (1995)). But while we can explain away the short-term volatility of the deficit in terms of the boom–bust cycle, this still leaves unanswered a very important question: Why has progress in controlling public finances over the last 15 years been so disappointing over a period when government policy has been so firmly committed in this direction?

In this chapter we seek to answer this question with the aid of a new model of UK public finances which has been developed as part of the re-estimation and re-specification of the London Business School's SLEEC model. The model has two particular features that make it particularly suitable for analysing public finances over the medium term. First, it aims to capture in a systematic way the process by which current government policy seeks to control public expenditure in the face of a variety of political and economic constraints. Secondly, it models tax revenues within a cointegration framework, providing more satisfactory estimates of the evolution of government receipts over a number of years.

The chapter is organised as follows. Section 5.2 outlines the main principles of our approach to modelling public expenditure and the tax system. In Section 5.3

we present the main equations which make up our public finances model. In Section 5.4 we draw out the implications from our model for UK fiscal policy over the medium term, both as an aid to understanding fiscal policy developments since the late 1970s and as a means of analysing current plans for reducing the PSBR.

5.2 MODELLING PUBLIC FINANCES

In order to answer questions relating to fiscal policy over the medium term, we need a model of public finances with sensible medium-term properties. In relation to this requirement, previous versions of the London Business School (LBS) model of the UK economy (Budd et al. (1984) and Dinenis et al. (1989)) were unsatisfactory in two respects. First, public expenditure was built up from a set of assumptions about the behaviour of its key components, which were either exogenously imposed or which depended very heavily on other exogenous variables (such as the number of pensioners, or families drawing Child Benefit). These assumptions were not obviously informed by any clear model of government behaviour, or based on the observed response of fiscal policy to changing economic circumstances.

The second unsatisfactory aspect of previous versions of the LBS model was in their treatment of the tax system. Tax revenues were based on a set of working rules that effectively determined the growth of tax receipts, taking as their starting point revenues in recent quarters. This system had the unfortunate property of making estimates of receipts over the medium term sensitive to recent data, which in turn was affected by random shocks and changes in the timing of payments.

Our approach has been to re-estimate the key equations affecting public finances within a cointegration framework. To do this we have developed a stylised model of the way in which public expenditure and tax revenues are determined. Equations based on this model are then estimated using cointegration techniques.

5.2.1 Public Expenditure

The natural reference point for analysing trends in public expenditure is its share of GDP. The size of national income determines the ability to finance government spending and also affects the demand for public services. As a society becomes better off, it would be normal for the demand for services provided within the public sector to rise, as well as private expenditures. Over the years, various theories have been advanced to explain the way in which public spending is related to national income. As early as 1890, the German economist Wagner noted the tendency for public spending to rise faster than national output (Wagner (1890)) — subsequently described as 'Wagner's Law' — implying that the public spending share of GDP would rise over time. Wagner's analysis was based on the idea that in a more industrialised society the State would need to have a greater role in providing a supporting infrastructure. Others have since suggested that there would be a 'relative price effect' as a result of slower productivity growth in service activities, where government spending is concentrated (see Baumol (1967)).

A different line of explanation is provided by Peacock and Wiseman (1961), who noted that big shifts in the public spending share of GDP tended to take place in wartime. They argued that large social disturbances, which occurred in wartime, created a 'displacement' effect, by which government activity as a share of national output is ratcheted up. This occurred both because of influences on the demand for public services — wars required the mobilisation of the population as a whole and focused attention on social problems for which higher government spending was seen as the solution — as well as acclimatising people to paying higher taxes, thereby paving the way for the acceptance of higher tax levels in peacetime.

A third line of explanation for trends in public spending is provided by economists of the 'public choice' school, such as Downs (1956, 1967) and Buchanan and Tullock (1962). According to this line of analysis, public spending decisions are seen as the outcome of a complex set of interactions between voters, politicians and bureaucrats. In particular, politicians and bureaucrats are seen as vulnerable to the actions of pressure groups, which see public expenditure as a mechanism by which the community as a whole is obliged to finance activities that are of benefit to only one group. On these grounds, Buchanan and Tullock argue that the practical operation of the democratic process will lead to over-provision of public services. Another view is that political pressures lead to a process of 'incrementalism', whereby government is encouraged to take on new responsibilities without withdrawing from other roles it inherited from past periods. A further suggestion is that democratic processes lead to a 'political business cycle' (Nordhaus, (1975)) with governments scaling up spending in the run-up to elections to win popular support and then attempting (not necessarily successfully) to rein back expenditure in post-election periods to avoid a permanent and politically unpopular increase in the tax burden.

A common theme of all these views is an attempt to explain the tendency of public spending to rise as a share of national income and output over time. However, this is clearly unsustainable in the medium term because it implies continually rising levels of taxation and/or borrowing. Recent experience has confirmed this view. Figure 5.2 shows that there was indeed a rise in the public spending/GDP ratio over the 1960s and early 1970s. But since the mid-1970s, the public spending share has shown, if anything, a slight downward trend. It has fluctuated strongly in response to the cycle, with a high public expenditure share in recessions (mid-1970s, early 1980s and early 1990s) and a low share in the boom period of the late 1980s.

A more detailed examination of trends in public spending shows that this pattern is, in fact, a product of three separate influences. First, since the

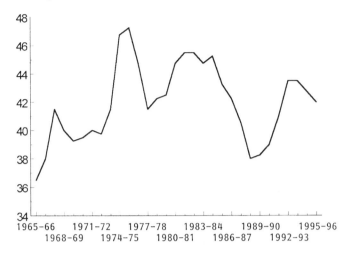

Figure 5.2 Government spending as a percentage of GDP $(GGE(X))$ — excluding privatisation proceeds and other adjustments)

mid-1970s the main elements of public spending — government consumption of goods and services and grants to the personal sector (mainly social security payments) — have been stable as a share of GDP, once allowance is made for the fact that the higher level of unemployment in the 1980s has pushed up social security payments. Together these two categories account for almost 90% of government expenditure, excluding privatisation proceeds and debt interest, so this property of long-run stability is a useful starting point for our medium-term analysis. Our sub-model of public expenditure variables is therefore based on a long-run cointegrating relationship between these components of government spending and GDP, allowing for unemployment in the case of personal sector grants.

We see this stability in the share of output taken by the key elements of public spending as the result of two offsetting pressures that have characterised the period over which UK governments have taken the control of public spending seriously — since the mid-1970s and, in particular, the financial crisis of 1976 that led to the IMF loan. For the various reasons discussed above, there is pressure to increase public spending at least as fast as living standards generally. However, the government faces a budget constraint over the longer term and is now reluctant to significantly increase the tax burden — unlike the 1960s (though it is worth noting that Roy Jenkins' decision to push up taxes in the run-up to the 1970 election contributed to Labour losing that election). The outcome of these twin pressures appears to be broad stability in the share of government current spending as a share of GDP over the longer term.

However, this stability is not apparent in the short term and there are pronounced swings in the ratio of government spending to GDP over the cycle, as Figure 5.2 shows. This anti-cyclical fluctuation occurs for two reasons: (i) government spending on unemployment-related benefits are pushed up directly in downturns; and (ii) discretionary government spending is not affected by the same cyclical pressures as private expenditures. The pattern of demand for public services such as health and education is relatively stable (growing over time) and there can be political influences for governments to offset a downturn in private expenditures by increasing its own spending through fiscal policy.

The third feature of our model of public expenditure explains how government spending has fallen slightly as a share of GDP over the last 20 years. This reduction has been achieved mainly by squeezing public sector investment — both directly and by reducing the government contribution to the financing of investment by nationalised industries (Sentance (1994)). As the CBI noted in 1988: 'When pressure is put on spending totals, capital spending can appear easiest to cut: few sewers will collapse if replacement is put off; buildings will not fall down; and roads will remain, albeit with growing potholes' (Confederation of British Industry (1988)). Figure 5.3 illustrates this point. The bulk of the 3.5 percentage point reduction in public spending as a share of GDP between the mid-1970s and the early 1990s (both similar points in the cycle) can be accounted for by a fall in the share of national output devoted to public capital expenditure.

This fact means that in our model of the determination of public spending overall, it is capital spending that 'takes the strain'. Periods when public spending is restrained — such as the mid-1970s, the early 1980s and the mid-1990s — have seen significant real cuts in capital spending. Our model suggests that any

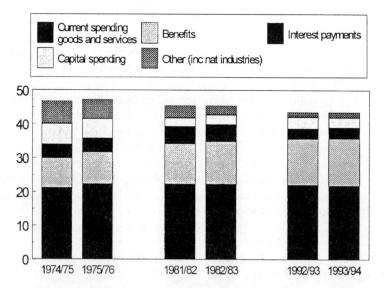

Figure 5.3 Government spending by category (percentage of GDP, at similar points in the economic cycle)

government that wishes to cut public spending as a share of GDP over the longer term must find ways to sustain a lower level of public sector capital expenditure. It could be argued that the current Conservative government has done precisely that, by moving the financing of investment 'off balance sheet' through the Private Finance Initiative.

It could be argued that our approach to modelling spending in this way rules out the possibility that major shifts in the boundaries of the public sector will change the parameters of our model and bring about either a resumption of the upward trend in spending or a marked downward trend. This is possible, though it is worth noting that even a Conservative government committed to 'rolling back the frontiers of the State' has achieved very little fundamental change in the areas for which the government is responsible. With the exception of the privatisation of the nationalised industries, most public sector reform has focused on different ways of providing services rather than changes in the boundaries of the public sector. A resumption of the upward trend in the public spending share of GDP is possible under a future Labour Government, but seems less likely in view of recent policy changes under the leadership of Tony Blair. So broad stability in the government current expenditure ratio seems a reasonable 'stylised fact' to underpin our analysis.

5.2.2 Tax Receipts

Turning to the revenue side of the account, the approach to take is more straightforward — in principle at least. In the absence of tax avoidance, variations in the timing of tax payments due and complicated tax rules relating to tax allowances, modelling tax receipts would require only a simple accounting identity. Tax receipts would be equal to the tax rate multiplied by the tax base. The reality is that the tax system is more complex than this, not least because of the multiplicity of rates and the complexity of the system of allowances.

A good economic model seeks to capture the essential ingredients of economic relationships. It follows from this that detail that captures every nuance of the relationship between variables is sacrificed for simplicity and clarity. Our approach to modelling tax receipts is to identify sensible long-run properties, based on the simple identity (receipts = base × rate) outlined above. The main allowances (for corporate and personal income tax) are incorporated into our measure of the relevant tax base. Once we have established a long-run cointegrating relationship between receipts, base and tax rates, we build a dynamic model around this to capture short-term movements in tax revenues.

We estimate five equations for taxes which make up in total close to 90% of public sector receipts: corporate taxation; personal income tax; VAT; national insurance; and excise duties. The exact specification of each equation is discussed in the next section. However, it is worth pointing out at this stage an important property of our equations. If the tax base we identify rises in line with money GDP, then we would expect tax revenue to rise at the same rate as GDP and the share of taxation in national income to remain broadly constant. It is possible that shifts in the composition of GDP will cause tax revenues to rise more rapidly or more slowly than national income in some periods. But if we set this possibility aside, there are only three ways in which a government can deliver a sustained reduction in tax rates over the medium term: (i) an increase in taxes elsewhere; (ii) a restriction of allowances, boosting the tax base; or (iii) cuts in public expenditure as a share of GDP. If, as we have argued, there is no underlying tendency of public spending to fall as a percentage of GDP, this casts a rather sceptical light on political promises to use the proceeds of economic growth to make sustained cuts in the burden of taxation!

5.3 ESTIMATION

Our technique of estimating our models of both public spending and taxation is to transform our dependent variables into ratios which we hypothesise to be stationary variables. This hypothesis is tested and, where appropriate, additional variables are included in the model to achieve stationarity. In our models of public expenditure the dependent variable is the ratio of the spending variable to GDP, implicitly imposing a unit coefficient on the spending variable with respect to GDP. In the model for government consumption, we expect GR (the ratio of current expenditure on goods and services to GDP) to be stationary allowing for the effect of the cycle, captured by GAP (the difference between the log of GDP and its trend). It is necessary to allow for the cycle because whilst we expect government spending to rise with GDP in the long run, it is much more stable than national output in the short run.

To explain government grants to the personal sector — the bulk of which is accounted for by social security payments — we construct a variable SSR which expresses social security as a percentage of GDP. In the social security expenditure model, we expect SSR to be stationary, allowing for the cycle (GAP) and the unemployment rate (U). We also include PH, the ratio of the retail price index to $RPIX$, the retail price index excluding mortgage payments. PH reflects the housing cost component of inflation in the government's indexation formula for social security payments, which is an important source of volatility relative to underlying measures of inflation.

In estimating models for these two key expenditure variables, we test for cointegration using the Johansen procedure. This requires starting from a very general vector autoregressive (VAR) model, and reducing to a more parsimonious model with fewer lags, using appropriate model selection criteria. Given that this is an investigation into government spending, it is likely that the effects of discretionary policy shifts will require the use of dummy variables, particularly around the time of general elections.

Our methodology for modelling tax receipts is similar to the one adopted on the expenditure side. First, we create a variable Y so that

$Y = \log(RECEIPTS/(BASE*RATE))$. This represents the expected long-run relationship we wish to incorporate in our dynamic model, and implicitly imposes the assumption that there are unit coefficients on the tax base and the tax rate (in logs) in relation to tax receipts. This ensures that our equation embodies the notion that a given percentage change in the rate or tax base will be reflected in the same percentage change in receipts. (For our purposes it is not necessary to have an exact measure of the tax base. Because we are working in logs, all we require is that the variable we identify moves proportionately with the 'true' base.) The constructed ratio is tested for stationarity using the standard Dickey–Fuller (DF) test. If it is not a stationary variable, then we seek to explain the trend movement in this ratio so as to establish a cointegrating vector. Where this is the case, we use the Johansen maximum likelihood procedure to test for and identify any cointegrating vectors.

The remainder of this section is devoted to describing the estimation of the seven key behavioural equations that make up our model of public finances. For detailed descriptions of variable definitions, see Appendix 1. The time-series properties of all variables used are summarised in Appendix 2. All variables are in logs unless otherwise stated.

5.3.1 Government Consumption

Our model of government consumption of goods and services explains current consumption, deflated by the GDP deflator (G), in terms of GDP, and trend GDP. Our procedure was to test for cointegration between the ratio of G to real GDP (GR) and the difference between actual and trend GDP (constructed by regressing log GDP on a linear trend over the period 1975Q1–1994Q3, giving a trend growth rate of 2.14% per annum) using the Johansen procedure. A lag length of two periods is chosen because this is the shortest lag length consistent with eliminating fourth-order serial correlation in the VAR. Dummy variables for outlying quarters (1976Q2, 1979Q2, 1979Q3 and 1985Q2) are included in the VAR as I(0) variables, and are set equal to one in the relevant quarter and zero in all remaining quarters in the sample period. The results of the Johansen maximum eigenvalue test are presented in Table 5.1.

The results strongly suggest the existence of one cointegrating vector. The Johansen procedure gives estimated values for this cointegrating vector, which are used to construct the error correction term, *GECM*. The estimated loading weight is -0.36804. Reparameterising the model and including the error correction term

Table 5.1

I(1) variables: *GR*, *GAP*
I(0) variables: *D76Q2*, *D79Q2*, *D79Q2*(−1), *D85Q2*

Null	Alternative	Statistic	95% critical value	90% critical value
$r = 0$	$r = 1$	23.3728	14.0690	12.0710
$r \leq 1$	$r = 2$	1.8548	3.7620	2.6870

derived from the Johansen estimation allows us to derive the final model, listed below together with the results from the standard misspecification tests. Standard t-tests for parameter significance are given in parentheses immediately below the relevant parameter:

$$\Delta G = \Delta GDP(-1) - 0.57 - 0.23*\Delta GR(-1) - 1.00*\Delta GAP(-1)$$
$$ (-4.7) \ (-1.9) (-4.7)$$
$$- 0.37*GECM(-2) + 0.055*D76Q2 - 0.029*D79Q2$$
$$(-4.7) (4.1) (-2.3)$$
$$- 0.28*D79Q2(-1) - 0.037*D85Q2$$
$$(-2.0) (-3.0)$$
$$GECM = GR + 1.0598*GAP$$

GR is the log of the ratio government consumption to GDP
GAP is the difference between (log)GDP and (log) trend GDP.

Sample (75 observations):		1976Q1–1994Q3
$\overline{R}^2$:		0.40812
SE regression:		0.01230
Serial correlation	$\chi^2(4)$:	5.0776
Functional form	$\chi^2(1)$:	0.8857
Normality	$\chi^2(2)$:	1.3723
Heteroscedasticity	$\chi^2(1)$:	0.2430

5.3.2 Government Grants to the Personal Sector

The structure of our equation to explain government grants is similar to that for spending on goods and services, though we include more dummies to capture political influences, as well as the effect of unemployment rate (U) and the difference between RPI inflation and underlying inflation (PH). We found two periods where social security spending deviated from its long-run relationship: 1978/79 and 1992/94. The first period (captured by the dummy variable $LABG$) represents a period during which public spending limits were relaxed in the run-up to an election, allowing some catch-up of benefit levels following a period of spending restraint. The new Conservative administration elected in 1979 took steps to limit the growth in unemployment-related benefits which reversed this upward shift.

The strong growth of social security payments in 1992/94 also accompanied a period of public spending relaxation. This expansion (captured by the dummy variable $INVB$) may also reflect some rise in 'hidden unemployment' because the invalidity benefit regime was relaxed and absorbed some of the long-term unemployed. Between 1979 and 1994, invalidity benefits nearly doubled as a proportion of total social security spending, with particularly strong growth in the early 1990s.

As with the government consumption model, we test for cointegration using the Johansen maximum likelihood procedure. A lag-length of three periods is

Table 5.2

I(1) variables: *SSR, GAP, U, PH*
I(0) variables: *LABG, INVB, D83Q1*

Null	Alternative	Statistic	95% critical value	90% critical value
$r = 0$	$r = 1$	36.1549	27.0670	24.7340
$r \leq 1$	$r = 2$	22.7686	20.9670	18.5980
$r \leq 2$	$r = 3$	8.9051	14.0690	12.0710
$r \leq 3$	$r = 4$	0.7073	3.7620	2.6870

chosen using the same model-selection criterion. An additional dummy for 83Q1 is added to the model to allow for the effects of pre-election manipulations of expenditure variables. The results are presented in Table 5.2.

SSR is the (log) ratio of social security payments (government grants to the personal sector) to GDP, *U* is the unemployment rate and *PH* is the (log) ratio of RPI to *RPIX*. Two cointegration vectors are identified by this test. The corresponding error correction terms are given here:

$$SSECM1 = 1.82*GAP - 0.027*U - 2.33*PH$$

$$SSECM2 = 0.24*GAP - 0.047*U + 0.80*PH$$

As with the model for government consumption the error correction terms are included in the reparameterised equation. Straightforward *t*-tests show that *SSECM2* and logged changes in *PH* are insignificant, and so are excluded from the final model listed below:

$$\Delta SS = \Delta GDP - 0.92 - 0.66\Delta SSR(-1) - 0.87*\Delta GAP(-1)$$
$$(-5.2) \ (-6.0) \qquad\qquad (-4.8)$$

$$+ 0.031*\Delta U(-1) - 0.40*SSECM1(-2) + 0.035*LABG$$
$$(5.1) \qquad\qquad (-5.3) \qquad\qquad (5.1)$$

$$- 0.052*D83Q1 + 0.024*INVB$$
$$(-3.9) \qquad\qquad (4.2)$$

Sample (75 observations):		1976Q1–1994Q3
$\bar{R}^2$:		0.64158
SE regression:		0.01297
Serial correlation	$\chi^2(4)$:	1.2424
Functional form	$\chi^2(1)$:	0.2182
Normality	$\chi^2(2)$:	0.1187
Heteroscedasticity	$\chi^2(1)$:	1.7978

5.3.3 Corporate Tax

Our approach to modelling corporate tax starts with the construction of a ratio, *CTR*, which represents the ratio of actual corporate tax receipts (*CT*) to the product of our measure of the corporate tax base (CTB) and CTT (the main corporate tax rate). Our measure of the tax base is described in detail in Appendix 1 and aims to take into account the shift in the system of investment tax allowances following the 1984 Budget. Table 5.3 shows the results of testing for stationarity of our tax ratio CTR, which in principle should be a stationery series. From these results, CTR is a non-stationary series. We believe the complexities of the corporate tax system allow for liabilities to be deferred for long periods, which makes adjustment to our stylised long-run equilibrium a lengthy process. For this reason, we believe that CTR is in fact a stationary series, and that this property could be satisfactorily established given a long enough sample period.

Consequently, we model corporation tax receipts as if CTR were a stationary variable, by making a one-period change in the log of CTR our dependent variable, and regressing it on one- and two-period lags of itself. CTR in log-level form is included as a regressor to act as an error correction term. The estimated parameters of this model and the associated t-statistics and specification tests are listed below:

$$\Delta CTR(-1) = -0.065 - 0.70*\Delta CTR(-1) - 0.50*\Delta CTR(-2)$$
$$(-1.7) \quad (-6.7) \qquad\qquad (-4.4)$$
$$-0.18*CTR(-3) + 0.59*D81Q3$$
$$(-2.0) \qquad\qquad (2.5)$$

Sample (83 observations):	1974Q2–1994Q4
$\overline{R}^2$:	0.42816
SE regression:	0.22110
Serial correlation $\chi^2(4)$:	2.6125
Functional form $\chi^2(1)$:	1.7892
Normality $\chi^2(2)$:	0.6761
Heteroscedasticity $\chi^2(1)$:	0.0019

While this model specification meets our requirement for sensible long-run properties, in the short run it has the undesirable simulation effect of adjusting immediately to a change in the corporation tax rate. Because there are considerable lags in corporation tax payments, we make a slight adjustment to this model by setting the effective tax rate in the model equal to a five-quarter moving average of the actual tax rate.

Table 5.3

Statistic	Sample	Without trend	With trend
DF	1973Q4 1995Q1	−4.70	−5.04
ADF(1)	1974Q1 1995Q1	−2.79	−2.90
ADF(2)	1974Q2 1995Q1	−1.88	−1.70
ADF(3)	1974Q3 1995Q1	−1.94	−1.83
ADF(4)	1974Q4 1995Q1	−1.76	−1.68

5.3.4 Personal Sector Income Tax

To model personal sector income tax payments we follow a similar methodology to that employed to estimate the model of corporate tax. We construct a tax ratio, YTR (receipts/rate*base), which will form the basis of our long-run model. This ratio is tested for stationarity; the results are summarised in Table 5.4.

The results suggest that YTR is a stationary series, and that there is a cointegrating relationship between YT (personal income tax receipts), YTB (tax base) and YTT (the standard income tax rate). Our estimated model uses YTR lagged by three periods as the error correction term in addition to some short-run dynamic terms. We impose a prior assumption on the model that in the short run around a 1% change in the tax rate produces a 0.8% change in tax receipts. The final model is listed below:

$$\Delta YT = -0.077 + 0.1*\Delta YTT + 0.3*\Delta YTT(-1) + 0.3*\Delta YTT(-2)$$
$$(-5.5)$$

$$+0.1*\Delta YTT(-3) + 0.28*\Delta YTB(-2) + 0.32*\Delta YTB(-3)$$
$$(4.3) \qquad\qquad (5.2)$$

$$-0.18*YTR(-4)$$
$$(-5.9)$$

Sample (79 observations):		1975Q2–1994Q4
$\overline{R}^2$:		0.62545
SE regression:		0.01368
Serial correlation	$\chi^2(4)$:	1.9619
Functional form	$\chi^2(1)$:	0.0433
Normality	$\chi^2(2)$:	0.4030
Heteroscedasticity	$\chi^2(1)$:	0.0049

5.3.5 VAT Receipts

To establish a cointegrating model of VAT receipts, we use a bi-variate model relating our tax ratio, VTR, constructed in a similar fashion to earlier tax ratios (see Appendix 1), to the savings ratio, SR. The savings ratio in this model is used in a similar way to GAP (output gap) in the two public expenditure equations

Table 5.4

Statistic	Sample	Without trend	With trend
DF	1975Q1 1995Q1	−3.70	−3.61
ADF(1)	1975Q1 1995Q1	−3.57	−3.47
ADF(2)	1975Q1 1995Q1	−3.54	−3.42
ADF(3)	1975Q2 1995Q1	−3.99	−3.68
ADF(4)	1975Q3 1995Q1	−4.52	−4.58

because it captures an important cyclical effect. In an economic upswing, the growth of consumer spending is above its long-run trend. In such periods there appears to be a shift in consumption away from goods and services that are exempt from VAT (e.g. 'necessities' like food and children's clothes) towards VAT-able goods which are more demand-elastic. In such periods VAT receipts are likely to rise relative to the increase in the tax base, with the result that $VRAT$ (the ratio of receipts to the tax base) trends upwards. However, by including the savings ratio SR in the cointegrating vector, we can explain this effect, because above-trend consumption growth is associated with falls in the savings ratio from its long-run equilibrium. This tendency was particularly noticeable in the 1980s consumer spending boom when the combination of financial liberalisation and rising asset prices led the personal sector to dis-save at an unprecedented rate.

To confirm the validity of this approach, a test for cointegration is carried out using the Johansen procedure. A lag-length of three periods in the VAR was selected because this is the most parsimonious model where there is no fourth-order serial correlation. Since the series VT (VAT receipts) is not seasonally adjusted, we use seasonal dummies in the VAR as well as a dummy variable $DLUX$, which proxies for the effect of the non-standard VAT rates. $DLUX$ is equal to 1 from 1976Q1 to 1979Q2 and zero from 1979Q2 to the end of the sample. The results from the Johansen test are presented in Table 5.5.

The results suggest that there is one cointegrating vector. The Johansen procedure gives estimated values for this cointegrating vector, which are used to construct the error correction term, $VTECM$. The estimated loading weight is -0.67104. In the final equation listed below, some terms (including, somewhat surprisingly, $DLUX$) drop out, which has the effect of altering the loading weight on the error correction model:

$$\Delta VT = \begin{array}{l} - 0.11 - 0.81*\Delta VT(-1) + 0.97*\Delta VTT(-1) + 2.22*\Delta C(-1) \\ \;\;(-2.7)\;\;(-8.5) \qquad\qquad (7.7) \qquad\qquad\quad (3.8) \end{array}$$

$$\begin{array}{l} - 0.47*\Delta VT(-2) + 0.74*\Delta VTT(-2) - 0.54*VTECM(-3) \\ \;\;(-4.3) \qquad\qquad (5.0) \qquad\qquad\quad (-4.8) \end{array}$$

$$\begin{array}{l} - 0.13*Q1(-1) - 0.10*Q1(-2) \\ \;\;(-6.3) \qquad\quad (-4.5) \end{array}$$

where $VTECM = VTR + 0.025697*SR$.

Table 5.5

I(1) variables: VTR, SR
I(0) variables: $Q1$, $Q2$, $Q3$, $DLUX$

Null	Alternative	Statistic	95% critical value	90% critical value
$r = 0$	$r = 1$	26.9048	14.0690	12.0710
$r \leq 1$	$r = 2$	1.9983	3.7620	2.6870

Sample (76 observations): 1976Q1–1994Q4
$\bar{R}^2$: 0.73550
SE regression: 0.06227
Serial correlation $\chi^2(4)$: 6.4545
Functional form $\chi^2(1)$: 1.9379
Normality $\chi^2(2)$: 3.5104
Heteroscedasticity $\chi^2(1)$: 0.8274

5.3.6 National Insurance Contributions

National insurance contributions (NI) are modelled on the basis that they will move proportionately with the wage and salary bill (NIB) in the absence of changes in the NI rate (NIR). However, in addition to this, our system of equations takes two other factors into account. First, there have been many structural changes in the NI system. DNI is a dummy variable that proxies for the effect of the reform of employee contributions in the March 1989 Budget (equal to 1 from 1978Q2 to 1989Q1 and equal to 0 otherwise). In addition, we include self-employment income as a ratio of the wage and salary bill (SE). Because the self-employed pay national insurance at a much reduced rate (which combines both the employee and employer element), a shift in employment pattern towards the self-employed will lower the NI take, for a given level of total employment.

A lag-length of four periods was selected as appropriate for the VAR. The results from the Johansen test are presented in Table 5.6.

The Johansen procedure gives estimated values for the cointegrating vector which are used to construct the error correction term, $NIECM$. The estimated loading weight is -0.74701. Again, because some terms prove insignificant in the final reparameterised model, the loading weight is slightly different to the one estimated by the Johansen method. The model is listed below along with its associated diagnostics:

$$\Delta NI = \Delta NIB(-1) + \Delta NIT(-1) - 0.17 - 0.63*\Delta NIR(-1)$$
$$(-5.9)(-5.0)$$
$$- 0.83*\Delta NIR(-2) + 0.36*\Delta SE(-2) - 0.70*\Delta NIR(-3)$$
$$(-6.7) \quad (2.3) \quad (-5.2)$$
$$- 0.67*NIECM(-4) + 0.079*DNI$$
$$(-5.2) \quad (5.5)$$

where $NIECM = NIR - 0.11*SE(-4)$.

Table 5.6

I(1) variables: NIR, SE
I(0) variables: DNI

Null	Alternative	Statistic	95% critical value	90% critical value
$r = 0$	$r = 1$	33.9573	14.0690	12.0710
$r \leq 1$	$r = 2$	0.0711	3.7620	2.6870

Sample (63 observations):   1979Q2–1994Q4
$\overline{R}^2$:   0.47836
SE regression: 0.02053
Serial correlation $\chi^2(4)$:   5.4565
Functional form $\chi^2(1)$:   6.2228
Normality $\chi^2(2)$:   2.0456
Heteroscedasticity $\chi^2(1)$:   3.5776

5.3.7 Excise Duties

ED is a variable for all taxes on consumption other than VAT. It mainly comprises excise duties. *ED* is a stationary series with a deterministic trend, which is likely to be that of consumer spending. We model this series by calculating an implicit excise duty rate from dividing receipts by consumer spending. Between 1975Q1 and 1988Q1 the series created fluctuates around a mean value of 0.109. From 1988Q2 onwards, there is a noticeable shift downwards and the mean implicit rate is 0.0976 between this date and the end of the sample period.

For forecasting purposes we extend this rate into the future, making the assumption that the government alters individual duties whilst aiming to keep the tax 'take' from this form of taxation constant in real terms. For example, in the November 1995 Budget, duties on wine and beer fell in real terms, while duties on petrol and tobacco rose in real terms. The net effect of these changes in duty was estimated by the Treasury to be broadly neutral, so that tax receipts from excise duties remain constant in real terms. This simple model of non-VAT consumption tax receipts is captured in the following equation, where *EDT* is the excise duty 'rate', and *CN* is consumers' expenditure in current prices:

$$ED = EDT*CN$$

5.3.8 Completing the Model

To complete our model of public finances, a number of other equations need to be added. On the expenditure side, one important missing link is a model of debt interest, which embodies the accumulation of debt and links interest payments to other interest rates in the model. Our approach to debt interest is in line with previous versions of the LBS model. A number of other miscellaneous items of public expenditure are modelled as a constant proportion of total public spending, including capital grants and net lending by government (which is affected by privatisation proceeds). Government investment is then determined as a residual, which is squeezed as government seeks to restrict its spending 'Control Total' below the trend implied by the other items.

On the receipts side, we have not modelled capital taxes and other miscellaneous items such as profits, rents, royalties and interest receipts. Some stylised equations are used to determine these elements in our forecasting model, but these do not change the essential features of our analysis of the medium-term evolution of public finances.

5.4 ANALYSING PUBLIC FINANCES

Our new model puts us in a much better position to analyse the performance of UK public finances over the medium term. In this concluding section we focus on three questions in particular. First, what insights does the model offer into the failure to make a sustained improvement in public finances over the period 1979–94? Secondly, how sensitive are public finances to the state of the cycle? Finally, what does our model suggest about the medium-term prospects for public finances and the realism of the Chancellor's 1995 Budget plans.

The system of equations described in this chapter so far provides a number of insights — both into past developments and future prospects for public finances. The difficulty in reducing public borrowing over the medium term becomes less of a puzzle once we recognise that current public spending has kept pace with the trend growth of GDP. Government expenditure as a share of national output falls in boom periods, but this apparent progress comes undone in recessions.

Some reduction in the public spending share of GDP has been achieved by cuts in government investment. These cuts in capital spending were used to help reduce public borrowing in the early and mid-1980s. But as cyclical forces led to a temporary improvement in public finances in the late 1980s, the government was encouraged to embark on an ambitious programme of tax reductions. Tax cuts went far beyond anything that was justified by the underlying control of public spending. And only by covertly clawing back the benefits of the tax giveaways of the late 1980s — in the form of reduced tax allowances, higher indirect taxes and higher national insurance contributions — has it been possible to restore some order to public finances during 1994 and 1995.

But there is a twist to this story. It is not just the fact that there was a boom in the late 1980s that caused such a dramatic improvement in public finances. It was the fact that this boom was led by consumer spending, which contributed to such a rapid reduction in the PSBR. Table 5.7 shows the effect of a cyclical rise in GDP on public finances arising from two sources: (i) a rise in consumption driven by a fall in the savings ratio, and (ii) a rise in exports, driven by higher world GDP. In each case the simulation has been conducted so as to generate an immediate and sustained 1% increase in GDP. The simulations are conducted with monetary policy set to keep inflation broadly steady, using the inflation control rules we have developed for the LBS model (see Chapter 9 by Stephen Hall and James Nixon in this volume). In both cases there is a fall in the share of government spending in GDP, reflecting the cyclical nature of the public spending/GDP ratio. (We are assuming that the trend growth of GDP and hence public spending have not changed.) But the effects through the tax system are very different in the two scenarios.

Higher consumer spending causes VAT and excise duties to rise, whereas there is no equivalent indirect tax boost from higher exports. Export-led growth does raise consumption as multiplier effects feed through, but much less significantly than in the other scenario. Indeed, as monetary policy is tightened to combat the inflationary impact of higher output, a strengthening exchange rate squeezes exports and boosts import volumes. As a result, a rise of over 2% in consumption is required to produce a one percentage point rise in real GDP. In addition, our system of equations indicates that a fall in the savings ratio (which generates the increase in consumer spending in our scenario) causes a disproportionate rise in VAT receipts as consumer spending on non-VATable items is much more stable than spending on goods and services liable to VAT.

Export-led growth causes a larger rise in corporation tax receipts than consumption-led growth. But the impact of this improvement in corporate tax revenues is modest by comparison with the increased VAT and other consumption taxes generated by strong consumer spending. As a consequence, the PSBR ratio falls by 0.4% of GDP more in response to a 1% rise in output driven by consumption, as opposed to export-driven growth.

As a reference point, Table 5.7 also shows recent Treasury estimates of the cyclical nature of public borrowing (Virley and Hirst (1995)). These estimates are in line with the figures produced by our simulations for the impact on the PSBR of a consumer-led cyclical rise in output. This is not surprising since the Treasury estimates were based on the 1980s experience, which was a strongly consumer-led cycle. However, in an expansion where recovery is more strongly export-led, as is the case in the current cycle, our simulations indicate that the improvement in public finances will be less dramatic. This is exactly what we are seeing over the current expansion phase of the economic cycle.

These findings suggest that simple estimates of the cyclical nature of public finances need to be treated with caution on two counts. First, if the cyclical impulse is overseas demand, the improvement in public finances is much less significant than if it is consumer-led. Secondly, a key component of the fall in the PSBR/GDP ratio stems from the failure of government spending to rise with GDP, causing a fall in the spending/GDP ratio, as Table 5.7 shows. If government

Table 5.7 Impact of a one percentage point 'cyclical' rise in GDP on public finances (cumulative effect as % of GDP)

	Government spending	Tax receipts	PSBR
LBS: Consumer-led			
Year 1	−0.36	+0.10	−0.46
Year 2	−0.34	+0.43	−0.77
Year 3	−0.48	+0.41	−0.89
LBS: Export-led			
Year 1	−0.36	−0.09	−0.27
Year 2	−0.41	−0.09	−0.32
Year 3	−0.48	—	−0.48
Treasury			
Year 1	−0.40	−0.10	−0.50
Year 2	−0.55	+0.25	−0.80

spending rises with GDP, then this element of the PSBR improvement will be wiped out. These two factors — together with other temporary influences, such as the impact of high privatisation proceeds and council house sales in 1988-89 — explain why the dramatic improvement in public finances in the late 1980s was not sustained. The fact that the cyclical recovery in the early 1990s was more strongly export-led also helps to explain why public finances have not improved as dramatically in recent years as the government and other forecasters expected.

So much for the past. What of the future? Government plans, laid out in the autumn 1995 Budget, envisaged a swing in government finances from an estimated deficit of around 4% of GDP in 1995-96 to a projected *surplus* of 1.5% of GDP in 2000-01. Underlying this projection is a very slight rise in the share of national income taken in taxes (from 38.25% to 39%). But the main contribution is expected to come from a projected fall in public spending from 42.5% of GDP in the current financial year to below 38% in 2000-01.

Our analysis suggests that this is unlikely to be achieved. Figure 5.4 compares the Treasury projection with our own forecast, which uses our model to determine current public expenditure alongside realistic estimates of government capital expenditure. Even though we see general government investment falling from around 2% of GDP to 1.3% over the next five years (reflecting the impact of the Private Finance Initiative, or its equivalent under a future Labour Government), we still find that this is not sufficient to generate a surplus on public finances by 2000-01. Our central projection does not suggest that public borrowing is running at an irresponsibly high level. Current public debt/GDP levels can be sustained with a deficit of just over 2% of GDP (assuming 5% money GDP growth). But there is clearly not much margin against an unforeseen downturn,

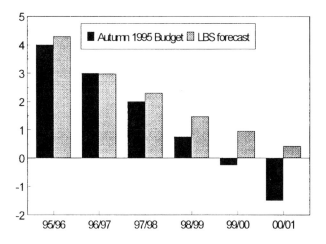

Figure 5.4 Public sector borrowing requirement (percentage of GDP)

and major tax giveaways could easily jeopardise the prospect of sustaining the improvement in public finances over the medium term.

The scenario is even more unfavourable if government plans to squeeze spending in a pre-election year come unstuck. The public spending plans confirmed in the Budget imply a fall of 0.9% in the real public spending control total in 1996–97 after a rise of just 0.2% in 1995–96. This compares with real increases in public spending of 2%–3% a year in real terms in previous pre-election periods (see Sentance and Nixon (1994)). Even a modest over-run, with spending allowed to rise by 2% in real terms over the next three years, instead of current plans for a standstill in real terms, would add a further £5bn (0.6% of GDP) to the PSBR by 1998–99.

5.5 CONCLUSION

Our analysis has highlighted the fact that two of the premises that have under-pinned the recent political debate on taxation are false. First, we have shown that the main elements of public spending have tended to rise with the trend in GDP and that the modest underlying fall in the public spending share of national output is the product of special factors and cuts in public investment. Looking to the future, tax cuts cannot be paid for from a natural tendency of public spending to fall as a share of GDP, even under Conservative governments. Secondly, the strong cyclical rebound in public finances in the late 1980s was the product of a consumer-led boom that was particularly favourable to tax receipts. The current recovery, which is more strongly export-led, is providing a much weaker revenue stream to the Exchequer.

In the light of this analysis, the medium-term outlook for UK public finances is much less rosy than that painted by the recent Budget forecasts — though we are not far from a sustainable Budget position. If UK public finances are to move towards broad balance, as measured by the PSBR, any 'tax cuts' over the next few years will more likely than not have to be paid for by tax increases elsewhere in the system. Given that this is the case, and we will therefore continue to have to raise close to 40% of GDP in tax revenues for the foreseeable future (to pay for spending of around 40% of GDP), the key issue then becomes how this sum can be raised as efficiently as possible, minimising distortions to economic behaviour. In other words, we should be having a much more active debate about tax reform. That debate is currently stifled by political posturing on taxation by both major parties. But it is long overdue.

APPENDIX 1: DATA SOURCES

1. All data used in the regressions referred to in this paper come from the Office for National Statistics (ONS), except for historical series for income tax rates and personal allowances which come from the Inland Revenue.

Table A1   Publications

ET	*Economic Trends* (ONS)
QA	*UK Economic Accounts*: A quarterly supplement to *Economic Trends* (ONS)
FS	*Financial Statistics* (ONS)
BB	*The Blue Book*: United Kingdom National Accounts 1994 (ONS)
AAS	*Annual Abstract of Statistics* (ONS)
IRS	*Inland Revenue Statistics*

2. The publications from which data are drawn are listed in Table A1. All series are seasonally adjusted by the ONS unless otherwise identified.

A.1 Public Expenditure

3. Table A2 lists the key data series used in our modelling of public expenditure, with their ONS identifiers.

4. Government consumption ($AAXV$) is the expenditure incurred by the day-to-day provision of public services, such as the National Health Service (NHS), national defence and education. It includes the government wage bill which is made up of payments to civil servants, NHS employees and teachers. The series $AAXV$ is a component of the general government current account, described in table 10.1D of *Financial Statistics*.

5. Personal sector current grants ($AIIS$) includes unemployment-related benefits, Income Support, Housing Benefit, Child Benefit and state retirement pensions. The series $AIIS$ is a component of personal sector current income, which is summarised in table A9 of the quarterly *Economic Accounts*. Note that the series differs from the current grants series in the expenditure section of the general government accounts (FS, Table 10.1D). This is because the latter series includes grants paid overseas, such as payments to the EC and foreign aid.

6. As Table A3 shows, G is derived using the GDP deflator (series $DJDT$), rather than the implicit price deflator of government consumption, for reasons of consistency. We are interested in the change in government consumption relative to the general price level, rather than the price of government consumption itself.

Table A2   Public expenditure raw data series

Description	ONS code	Publication and table
GDP at constant 1990 prices	*CAOO*	*QA*, A2
GDP deflator 1990 = 100	*DJDT*	*QA*, A1
Government consumption in current prices	*AAXV*	*FS*, 10.1D
Personal sector current grants from government	*AIIS*	*QA*, A9
Retail price index — all items 1987 = 100	*CHAW*	*ET*, 3.1
RPI excluding mortgage interest payments	*CHMK*	*ET*, 3.1
Unemployed as a percentage of total workforce	*BCJE*	*ET*, 4.2

Table A3 Public expenditure data definitions

Variable	Description	Transformation
G	Real government consumption	$\log(AAXV/DJDT)$
SS	Real social security expenditure	$\log(AIIS/DJDT)$
GDP	Real GDP	$\log(CAOO)$
U	Unemployment rate	BCJE
GR	Government consumption ratio	G-GDP
SSR	Social security expenditure ratio	SS-GDP
GAP	Output gap	$GDP - 11.0 - 0.00532*T$
PH	Housing costs	$\log(CHAW/CHMK)$

7. In the definition of *GAP*, *T* is a linear time trend where 1955Q1 = 1. *GAP* is defined as the residual, where log *GDP* is regressed on *T* over the period 1975Q1–1994Q3.

A.2 Public Sector Receipts

8. Table A4 lists the key data series used in our modelling of tax receipts, with their ONS identifiers. Table A5 lists the tax rates that we use in our analysis.

Table A4 Government revenue raw data series

Description (all variables are in £ millions current prices)	ONS code	Publication and table
Company sector gross trading profits	CIDE	QA, A10
Company sector stock appreciation	AIAP	QA, A10
Company sector rent and non-trading income	CICQ	QA, A10
Dividend payments	CIKI	QA, A10
Interest and miscellaneous payments	CIDW	QA, A10
Total taxes on company sector income	CIDO	QA, A10
Advanced corporation tax	CIDD	QA, A10
ICCs plant and machinery investment	GGAW	BB, 13.5
Financial companies plant and machinery investment	GGBS	BB, 13.5
Total taxes on personal sector income	AIIU	QA, A9
Personal sector wages and salaries	AIJB	QA, A9
Other personal sector income	AIIT	QA, A9
Personal sector savings ratio	AIIZ	QA, A9
Single person's income tax allowance (not CSO)	SPTA	IRS, A1
Employees in employment	BCAJ	ET, 4.1
Income from self-employment	CFAN	BB, 4.1
Consumers' expenditure	AIIX	QA, A2
Total taxes on expenditure	AAXP	FS, 10.1D
Value-added tax receipts (not seasonally adjusted)	ACDB	FS, 2.1D
Central government non-domestic rates distribution	CIPA	FS, 10.3A
Local authority rates receipts	ADBB	FS, 10.3A
National Insurance surcharge	ACEF	FS, 2.1E
Social security contributions	AIIV	QA, A9

Table A5   Tax rates

Variable	Description	Publication and table
YTTR	Standard personal income tax rate, %	*IRS*, A2
CTTR	Corporation tax rate, %	*IRS*, A4
NITR1	National Insurance — employers' standard rate, %	*AAS*, 3.14
NITR2	National Insurance — employees' standard rate, %	*AAS*, 3.14
NITR3	National Insurance surcharge rate, %	*AAS*, 3.14
VTTR	Standard VAT rate, %	*AAS*

9. In the equation for personal sector taxes, the standard tax rate (which was reduced to 24% in April 1996) is used as the key exogenous tax variable, although over the estimation period a varying number of tax rates have been in place. Currently there are the 20% and 40% rates in place in addition to the standard rate.

10. In our equation for National Insurance contributions there are two key rates — one each for employers and employee contributions. The employer rate is the standard rate from the beginning of the sample until 1986Q1, when the structure of contributions was changed. From 1986Q2 we use the rate paid on the top two of five income bands for non-contracted out employees. This is the same rate (10.45%) as the standard rate under the previous tax regime at the point of transition to the new regime. The contributions rate for employers includes the rate for National Insurance surcharge (in force from 1977Q2 to 1984Q3), the proceeds from which are included under expenditure taxes rather than National Insurance contributions. As a result, the National Insurance surcharge rate is subtracted from the sum of the two key rates, to give a total effective rate, *NIT* (see Table A6).

We follow a similar rule for employees' contributions. The rate is the standard rate for non-contracted out employees from the start of the sample until 1986Q1. In the period between 1986Q2 and 1990Q1 the rate paid by such employees varied with four income bands. Again, we use the rate for the top two income bands because this is the same as the standard rate from the previous regime at the point of transition to the new regime. From 1990Q2 a standard rate is reintroduced, which is identical to the top two rates under the banded income system of contributions.

11. The VAT rate used is this model is the standard rate (currently 17.5%). As with personal sector income tax (and to a certain extent corporation tax, with the small business rate), there are periods where multiple rates have been in force. Between 1973, when VAT was introduced, and the end of the Labour administration in 1979, there were three VAT rates with petrol and so-called 'luxury' goods taxed at a higher rate than standard VATable goods. In 1993, VAT was levied on domestic fuel bills at a rate of 8%. However, for simplicity and transparency we use the standard rate as the key tax variable in our equation, employing a dummy variable to proxy for the effect of multiple tax rates between 1973 and 1979.

12. For personal sector income tax, we multiply the single person's allowance (expressed in £million, as a quarterly average of the total figure) by the number of employees in employment. This figure is then excluded from the tax base (see the transformation for *YTB* in Table A6). Thus we make the implicit assumption that all employees take up their full tax allowance. Although this obviously is not the case, we feel that this is the best approximation that we can make to capture the effect of changes in allowances over the estimation period.

Table A6 Transformations

Variable	Description	Transformation
IFD	Corporate tax credit fund	$0.75*(IFD(-1) + (GGAW + GGBS))$
CTA	Corporate tax allowance	$0.25*(IFD(-1) + (GGAW + GGBS))$
CT	Corporate tax	$\log(CIDO - CIDD)$
CTB	Corporate tax base	$\log(CIDE + CICQ - AIAP - CIKI - CIDW - CTA)$
CTT	Corporate tax rate	$\log(CTTR/100)$
CTR	Corporation tax ratio	$CT - CTB - CTT$
YTA	Income tax allowance	$BCAJ*SPTA$
YT	Income tax	$\log(AIIU - CIDD)$
YTB	Net income tax base	$\log(AIJB + AIIT - YTA)$
YTT	Income tax rate	$\log(YTTR/100)$
YTR	Income tax ratio	$YT - YTB - YTT$
SR	Savings ratio	$\log(AIIZ)$
ED	Excise duties etc.	$AAXP - ACDB - CIPA - ADBB - ACEF$
C	Consumption (VAT base)	$\log(AIIX)$
VT	VAT receipts	$\log(ACDB)$
VTT	VAT rate	$\log(VATR/100)$
VTR	VAT receipts ratio	$VT - C - VTT$
SE	Self-employment income ratio	$\log(CFAN/AIJB)$
NI	National Insurance receipts	$\log(AIIV)$
NIB	Employment income	$\log(AIJB)$
NIT	Composite NI rate	$\log((NITR1 + NITR2 - NITR3)/100)$
NIR	NI contributions ratio	$NI - NIB - NIT$

13. The corporate tax allowance system is more complex, and we attempt to capture at least some of its main effects. Until fiscal year 1983–84, all investment on plant and machinery could be fully offset against corporate tax liability in the year in which the investment was made. Between 1984–85 and 1985–86, there was a transition to a system where such investment is offset against tax liability over a number of years on a sliding scale. So from 1986–87, capital expenditure on plant and machinery is offset against tax in the following way: 25% can be offset in the current year, with the residual being offset at a rate of 25% per year thereafter. The identities for IFD (store of tax credit) and CTA (corporate tax allowance) replicate this system in the data (see the transformations in Table A6).

14. Advanced corporation tax ($CIDD$) is included in both personal sector and corporate sector income tax receipts. $CIDD$ is the tax paid by companies on behalf of shareholders on dividend payments. Subsequently, $CIDD$ can be set against the tax liability of an individual company. To avoid double counting, $CIDD$ is subtracted from both series and the residual is then used as the dependent variable in regressions. $CIDD$ itself is treated separately in the LBS model.

15. The definition of YTB (income tax base) is slightly more complex than the description in Table A6. The actual transformation used is set out immediately below. This definition attempts to capture in the model the fact that self-employed workers pay tax a year in arrears. YTB is defined so that in any quarter in the current calendar year the base for taxing self-employment income is a quarterly average of $CFAN$ in the previous calendar year. For example, from 1995Q1 to 1995Q4, the self-employment tax base is the average

quarterly self-employment income for 1993–94. Note that $AIIT$ (other personal sector income) includes self-employment income, so $CFAN$ (self-employment income) is first subtracted before adding back in with the appropriate lag structure:

$$YTB = \log(AIJB + AIIT - YTA - CFAN$$
$$+ 0.25*(CFAN(-4) + CFAN(-5) + CFAN(-6) + CFAN(-7))*Q1$$
$$+ 0.25*(CFAN(-5) + CFAN(-6) + CFAN(-7) + CFAN(-8))*Q2$$
$$+ 0.25*(CFAN(-6) + CFAN(-7) + CFAN(-8) + CFAN(-9))*Q3$$
$$+ 0.25*(CFAN(-7) + CFAN(-8) + CFAN(-9) + CFAN(-10))*Q4)$$

16. The variable ED (excise duty receipts) is a residual after VAT receipts, local authority rates and National Insurance surcharge receipts are subtracted from total expenditure tax receipts. Local authority non-domestic rates and the National Insurance surcharge (which was levied between 1977 and 1984) are included under expenditure taxes in the national accounts. For the purposes of modelling public sector receipts, we treat local authority rates as largely pre-determined and concentrate on behavioural equations for VAT receipts (VT) and excise duties.

APPENDIX 2: TIME-SERIES PROPERTIES

All the series used in the public sector sub-model are first tested for stationarity for the sample period 1975Q1–1994Q2, using the standard Dickey–Fuller (DF) tests. Regressions as set out below are run producing a test-statistic for the significance of the parameter β_0.

DF test	$\Delta X_t = \alpha_0 + \beta_0 X_{t-1} + \varepsilon_t$
DF test with trend	$\Delta X_t = \alpha_0 + \alpha_1 T + \beta_0 X_{t-1} + \varepsilon_t$
ADF(i) test	$\Delta X_t = \alpha_0 + \beta_0 X_{t-1} + \Sigma \beta_i \Delta X_{t-i} + \varepsilon_t$
ADF(i) test with trend	$\Delta X_t = \alpha_0 + \alpha_1 T + \beta_0 X_{t-1} + \Sigma \beta_i \Delta X_{t-i} + \varepsilon_t$

If the test statistic falls within the critical range of the distributions derived by Dickey and Fuller (1981), then the series is non-stationary. Results from the Dickey–Fuller (DF) and augmented Dickey–Fuller (ADF) tests (with and without deterministic trends) are reported in the Table A7. The ADF test has four lags in the regression, i.e. $i = 4$. If the series in levels proves non-stationary, then it is differenced n times until it passes the test for non-stationarity. The order of integration $I(n)$ is given in the final column of Tables A7 and A8.

The results presented in Table A7 show that the principal tax rates used in the sub-model are all I(1) variables, i.e. stationary in first differences.

Table A7 Unit root tests (tax rates)

Variable	DF (no trend)	DF (with trend)	ADF(4) (no trend)	ADF(4) (with trend)	Order of integration
YTT	−1.78	−2.91	−1.99	−3.04	I(1)
CTT	0.68	−1.37	−1.12	−1.72	I(1)
VTT	−1.53	−1.81	−1.77	−2.08	I(1)
NIT	−1.77	−2.85	−2.04	−2.24	I(1)

Table A8 Unit root tests

Variable	DF (no trend)	DF (with trend)	ADF(4) (no trend)	ADF(4) (with trend)	Order of integration
G	0.24	−2.85	0.57	−2.27	I(1)
GDP	0.24	−0.24	−1.35	−2.63	I(1)
GAP	−1.35	−1.34	−2.84	−2.86	I(1)
SS	0.27	−0.37	−1.19	−2.70	I(1)
U	−2.04	−1.07	−2.24	−2.15	I(1)
PH	−0.95	−1.06	−1.41	−2.13	I(1)
CT	−2.38	−2.90	−1.47	−1.16	I(1)
CTB	−1.15	−2.33	−0.93	−1.73	I(1)
YT	−0.37	−1.13	0.10	−2.61	I(1)
YTB	1.84	−1.45	0.39	−2.11	I(1)
ED	−1.32	−9.00	−0.06	−4.81	I(0)
C	3.63	−2.05	1.02	−1.98	I(2)
VT	−0.34	−5.38	1.15	−3.02	I(1)
SR	−3.34	−3.39	−1.93	−1.99	I(0)
SE	−1.02	−1.19	−0.82	−2.60	I(1)
NI	0.30	−2.35	0.19	−3.07	I(1)
NIB	1.87	−0.72	−1.78	−2.35	I(2)

The results summarised in Table A8 show that most of the series tested are I(1). U (unemployment rate) is non-stationary over the sample period when differenced once, but over a longer sample (1965Q2–1994q2), the series is I(1). SR (the savings ratio) has a DF statistic slightly below the critical value, but is assumed to be an I(1) series. ED (excise duty receipts) is stationary with a deterministic trend, likely to be the upward trend in consumers' expenditure. Two of the nominal variables (C and NIB) are I(2), although when deflated by the consumers' expenditure deflated these series are I(1).

6
Two Concepts of the NAIRU

CHRIS ALLEN AND JAMES NIXON

6.1 INTRODUCTION

The impact of interest rates on unemployment has been somewhat neglected in the literature. In part this is an historical precedent; the work of Bruno and Sachs (1985) in the last decade, for example, reflected the general concern at the time with the impact of high oil prices. In some ways it is not surprising that a number of authors, most notably Phelps (1994), should begin to turn their attention to the impact of interest rates now that most central banks in the industrialised nations use this as the prime, and in some cases exclusive, instrument of macroeconomic control. We therefore see real interest rates and therefore the cost of capital as essentially exogenous. Our contention is that while this mainly achieves its objectives through the control of aggregate demand, interest rates also have an impact on aggregate supply that is typically ignored in the policy regimes alluded to above. Our task therefore is to develop a theoretical and, later, an empirical framework for analysing the impact of interest rates on aggregate supply.

We believe that many of the existing models of the supply side are unsuitable for this task since they typically assume that the capital stock is fixed (for example, Layard, Nickell and Jackman (1991)) and ignore the impact of relative factor prices between 'fixed' and variable factors. Because interest rates clearly affect the cost of capital, we need to consider both substitution between factors and the rate of capital accumulation. We address this by making the standard distinction between the short run, where capital is fixed, and the long run, where capital *has* adjusted optimally. Consequently we derive two concepts of the non-accelerating inflation rate of unemployment (NAIRU) consistent with this. This in effect makes explicit the structural relationships behind the long-

Macroeconomic Modelling in a Changing World. Edited by C. Allen and S. Hall
© 1997 John Wiley & Sons Ltd

and short-run NAIRUs estimated by Turner and Rauffet (1994). Critically, we think this distinction is important because it is the short-run NAIRU, i.e. before firms have a chance to bring on stream new capacity, that dictates where prices begin to accelerate and therefore it is the short-run NAIRU that acts as the overall 'supply constraint'. Our interest in the NAIRU is therefore not so much as to whether it is an equilibrium to which the economy will tend, but that it is the point that will prompt the monetary authorities to apply the brakes.

Of course, the short-run NAIRU is something of a misnomer, since capital is not fixed. Rather, interest rates and aggregate demand will influence the rate of capital accumulation, which in the presence of lags means that the transition to the long-run NAIRU will not be instantaneous. In reality, the economy will always be somewhere between what we have defined as the short- and long-run NAIRU. It is therefore possible to envisage a level of interest rates that implies a rate of capital accumulation that is not consistent with wage demands in the labour market. Such an economy may therefore not reach the long-run NAIRU but instead be stuck in a dynamic equilibrium between the rate of capital accumulation and the rate of growth of wages. This in effect would be a third dynamic concept of the NAIRU.

6.2 A FEW STYLISED FACTS

The concept of a 'natural rate' for unemployment dates back to the work of Friedman (1968) and Phelps (1967) a generation ago. The essential idea is that an expansion of aggregate demand may push unemployment below this rate, but only at the cost of increasing inflation. Similarly, a reduction in aggregate demand may push unemployment above the natural rate, but this will lead to decreasing inflation. Given a policy environment that avoids explosive inflation or deflation, the economy cannot then remain *persistently* above, or below, the natural rate of unemployment, although it may fluctuate around that level. The word 'natural', used in this context, is loaded with political ideology since it implies that this equilibrium is somehow ground out by structural factors not easily under the control of policy-makers and that this equilibrium is unique. 'Natural' makes it easier for us all to live with unemployment.

Some authors have questioned the validity of an equilibrium that takes many years or even decades to reach, arguing that if unemployment is more often *not* at the natural rate, then what use is the concept. For us, however, we believe that this rather misses the point. The natural rate is important because it marks the point at which inflation begins to pick up in an unsustainable manner. In that sense, the equilibrium level of unemployment represents a supply constraint on the growth of the economy. We wish to continue to use the concept of the natural rate, primarily because it is so well established in the literature, but also because it is this inflation propensity of the equilibrium level of unemployment that is important in the current policy regime. However, we note that a number of authors regard this as an absolute anathema (see, for example, Jenkinson (1988)) and it is really their contention that the natural rate or NAIRU can be affected by policy and aggregate demand that we wish to take up.

The starting point for our analysis is the observation that the key feature of unemployment in the United Kingdom that we seek to explain, is its persistence. Even in the most diehard of Keynesian models with significant degrees of wage and price rigidity, in the absence of continued shocks the economy would settle down with unemployment returning to its equilibrium, albeit after a protracted lag. It is hard to believe that rigidities associated with fixed-length contracts or the costs of adjusting prices or quantities can account for rising unemployment that persists over a decade or more. It is hard to escape the conclusion that it is the equilibrium itself that has risen (Blanchard and Summers (1986)).

Secondly, we need to explain the contrast between the British experience, and for that matter, the rest of the European Union, and the United States, where equilibrium unemployment has remained broadly stable. Figure 6.1 shows how inflation rates and unemployment rates have varied with time in the United States and in the United Kingdom. The United States and the United Kingdom now enjoy similar rates of inflation, even if the initial supply shocks of the 1970s generated much higher inflation in the United Kingdom. Equally, the disinflation process in both countries was at the cost of broadly comparable rates of

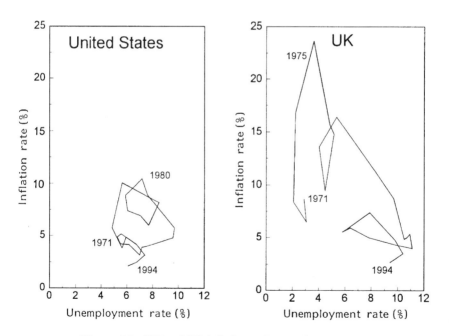

Figure 6.1 UK and US inflation and unemployment rates

unemployment. The key distinction, however, is that unemployment in the United Kingdom did not return to former levels once inflation was stabilised, again suggesting that the equilibrium rate of unemployment has risen (Bean (1994)).

How much of this experience can be laid at the door of an inflexible British labour market? The problem here, not withstanding the extensive supply-side reforms that have been made in the 1980s, is that Britain, and for that matter France and Belgium, maintained very low rates of unemployment in the 1950s and 1960s, lower than in the United States, for example. It seems hard to believe that the labour markets in these countries have become markedly more restrictive in the latter half of this century or that the welfare state has expanded in such a way that would explain the strong contrast between these periods and our current experience. We are therefore forced to argue that explanations of the rise in equilibrium unemployment that rely on these factors are essentially flawed. The answer must lie elsewhere.

Part of the answer clearly lies with more sophisticated models of the labour market. Models that highlight the costs associated with staff turnover in the spirit of Phelps (1976) or efficiency wage arguments such as introduced by Calvo (1979), make clear that an efficient market equilibrium may lie some distance from the neoclassical intersection of demand and supply. These models essentially offer a theory of involuntary equilibrium unemployment. But really, as Phelps (1994) notes, they do not allow for this equilibrium to shift sufficiently to explain the marked rise in equilibrium unemployment experienced by most European economies. We can go further if we view the labour market as segmented into groups of insiders and outsiders (Lindbeck and Snower (1989)), particularly if we think of insiders as having firm-specific capital, which improves their bargaining position, rather than just as union members (Pencavel (1985)). These models exhibit an asymmetric or ratchet effect on unemployment, where, as workers are laid off and become outsiders, their impact on wage negotiations becomes increasingly weak. Such models essentially imply that wage demands are unlikely to be moderated in the face of unemployment.

Figure 6.2 plots the interest rate for the United States and the United Kingdom. The key feature here is that interest rates in the 1980s have been markedly higher in the United Kingdom. We feel this is linked to the persistence of unemployment demonstrated in Figure 6.1. In a similar vein, Turner and Rauffet (1994) show econometrically that the rise in equilibrium unemployment is related to productivity. This is a feature that is not explained by the insider–outsider models.

We hope to put a theoretical structure on Turner and Rauffet's empirical findings and suggest that the NAIRU is dependent on the rate of capital accumulation and the cost of capital. In particular, the monetarist-style policy of using short-term interest rates to control inflation has a long-term effect on the supply side and has explicitly contributed to an increase in the NAIRU.

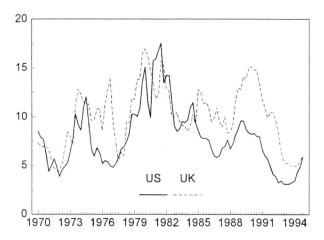

Figure 6.2   UK and US three-month interest rates

6.3 EXISTING MODELS OF THE NAIRU

Thus far we have used the terms natural rate, or NAIRU, or equilibrium rate
of unemployment interchangeably. We should, however, make some definitions
clear. The equilibrium rate of unemployment is strictly the Walrasian equilibrium where all markets clear. This may be distinct from the NAIRU, which is
the point at which prices begin to accelerate. In the NAIRU model expectations
are essentially adaptive, so if the economy is away from the NAIRU, then an
inconsistency develops between the expectations of firms and their employees
that begins a wage–price spiral. Below the NAIRU, inflation is never constant
but always increasing.[1] The natural rate refers to that equilibrium in the class
of models where expectations are rational. Periods of sustained inconsistency
between expectations are therefore ruled out and movements away from equilibrium can only come about through unanticipated shocks. We feel it is difficult to
reconcile the United Kingdom's experience of long periods away from equilibrium and extended wage price spirals with such a model. We therefore believe
that a model based on adaptive expectations continues to maintain significant
empirical relevance, and consequently prefer the term NAIRU to natural rate.

The now almost standard model for looking at the NAIRU is that set out
by Layard, Nickell and Jackman (1991). Stable inflation in this model requires
consistency (equality) between the mark-up of prices over wages ($p - w$) and
the mark-up of wages over prices ($w - p$). Only if the real wage desired by
wage-setters is the same as that desired by price-setters will inflation be stable.
Layard, Nickel and Jackman (LNJ hereafter) argue that the variable that brings
about this consistency is the level of unemployment, which in their model affects
both the wage mark-up and the price mark-up. Turning the model round the other

way, and this is particularly relevant to the United Kingdom at the moment; if the policy framework delivers stable inflation, then unemployment will adjust to its equilibrium level. It is probably also worth making the point at this stage that if dynamic homogeneity between wages and prices does not hold, then the equilibrium level of unemployment will depend on the level of inflation target chosen.[2]

The LNJ model is a very good point of departure because it has firm roots in microeconomic optimisation and because it articulates a system equilibrium rather than a partial one. We focus on the modelling of the firm's behaviour since this is where most of our own innovations lie. We also suppress the expectation terms in order to make the structure of the model more transparent.

Production is determined by constant-returns technology where the capital stock is taken as fixed. Thus in log form:

$$y - k = \alpha(l - k) \qquad \ldots (1)$$

where y is output, k is the capital stock and l is labour supply. The profit-maximising price for the imperfectly competitive firm, taking capital as fixed, is

$$p = \log[\eta/(\eta - 1)] + mc \qquad \ldots (2)$$

where marginal costs (mc) are

$$mc = w + b_2(y - k) + \text{const.} \qquad \ldots (3)$$

w is cost of labour per employee (including employer's taxes) and $\eta/(\eta - 1)$ is the standard mark-up on marginal cost. Additionally, LNJ argue that this mark-up may vary with the level of demand. Thus they have

$$\log[\eta/(\eta - 1)] = \text{const.} - b_1(y_d - \overline{y}) \qquad \ldots (4)$$

where $\overline{y}$ is potential output. Putting all this together and substituting the production function into the price equation gives

$$p - w = b_0 - b_1(y_d - \overline{y}) - b_2\alpha(k - l) \qquad \ldots (5)$$

Hence the mark-up depends on aggregate demand and on the capital–labour ratio.

The wage equation can similarly be derived from the firm's and employees' optimising behaviour in a bargaining framework.[3] This would be consistent with both efficiency wage and insider–outsider models of wage determination. The wage equation therefore takes the form

$$w - p = \gamma_0 - \gamma_1 u + b_2\alpha(k - l) + Z_w \qquad \ldots (6)$$

where the mark-up on prices depends on unemployment, the capital–labour ratio and exogenous wage pressure variables (Z_w) such as union and benefits effects and elements of the 'wedge' between producer and consumer prices.

Finally, the model is closed by setting actual output equal to aggregate demand (y_d), which can be thought of as being determined by a reduced form IS–LM system:

$$y_d = \sigma_1 x + \sigma_2(m - p) \qquad \ldots (7)$$

where x is a measure of fiscal stance and $m - p$ is the real money supply. This is a key part of the LNJ framework, since in a dynamic context one is forced to ask what mechanism restores the system to equilibrium if it is perturbed. Here the answer is effectively real balance effects with a fixed money supply. In reality, it is more likely to be the government responding to changes in inflation with appropriate changes in aggregate demand through monetary and fiscal policy. Given that the economy responds to changes in policy settings with long and variable lags, the dynamic transition path to equilibrium is likely to be far more protracted than suggested by the LNJ model.

The model is usually interpreted graphically by substituting labour demand into equation (5) for aggregate demand to give a direct relationship between the price mark-up and (un)employment. This slopes upwards because of the 'additional' dependence of the mark-up on marginal costs on activity. If the NAIRU is then defined as that point where the two mark-ups are equal ($p - w$ equal to $w - p$), then the system can be solved for a unique equilibrium level of unemployment, the NAIRU.

A number of points are worth making at this stage. First, as LNJ remark (p. 369), the model is fundamentally of the natural rate type, in that demand-side factors do not influence the equilibrium. Secondly, a large part of LNJ's explanation for the increase in the NAIRU over time is down to increases in the wedge, i.e. to relative import prices and changes in income, expenditure and employer's taxes. However, as LNJ themselves acknowledge (p. 33), there are strong arguments for believing that unemployment (or more specifically wages) should be neutral to changes in the level of the wedge in the long run (see, for example, Bean (1994) and Joyce (1990)). If this is the case, and it has to be said that the empirical evidence is mixed,[4] then the wedge is ruled out as a possible explanation for the increase in the NAIRU. By the same token, a question must hang over the union and benefit terms. Unions are generally perceived as having become significantly weaker since the mid-1980s but this has not been reflected in a significant reduction in unemployment. While it is true that a certain amount of today's unemployment in the United Kingdom, is cyclical, judging by the government's efforts to control inflation we believe most commentators would still put the NAIRU somewhere above 2 million. Equally, a similar story is true of benefits. Coulton and Cromb (1994, p. 19) note:

> a common feature is a decline in the replacement ratio since the early 1980s. This would appear to suggest that benefits cannot readily explain much of the increase in unemployment during the early 1980s.

The idea of a mismatch is much harder to dismiss, not least because it has a number of appealing intuitive features; namely that technological change (for example, Machin (1994)) or competition from the Third World (Wood (1994)) have significantly reduced the demand for unskilled labour. However, a number of recent papers (see, for example, Nickell and Bell (1994)) report that in the recent recession there has been a large rise in the unemployment rate of skilled labour in all countries except Japan. This evidence seems to be at odds with the mismatch argument.

It therefore appears that while a combination of supply and demand shocks may have brought about the rise in unemployment, the explanations described above cannot satisfactorily account for its persistence. The only models that do seem to offer some explanation of persistence are those that relate to the relative characteristics of either insiders or outsiders. In our view, an additional explanation for the persistent propagation of shocks over long periods of time might lie with that factor of production with the greatest longevity, namely the capital stock.

Clearly, there are a number of problems with such a line of argument. Bean (1989) probably puts it the most succinctly:

> capital intensity and productivity have been rising steadily since the Industrial Revolution. Yet the unemployment rate shows no discernible trend; consisting of a few minor wiggles at business cycle frequencies, plus the occasional major change of level. It does not require any formal statistical analysis to confirm that the unemployment rate and capital intensity cannot be related in the long run.

If we rule out the case of a vertical wage-setting schedule, then increases in capital intensity or technology reduce marginal costs and so shift the price setting line upwards. There must therefore be a 'sympathetic' shift up in the wage-setting line if unemployment is to remain unchanged. In other words, real wage aspirations tend to rise over time to exactly offset the effects of capital accumulation and technology.

Typically, this is usually imposed on the data by a cross-equation restriction on the capital–labour ratio in the price and wage equations. We believe that this obscures the fact that there are actually two processes taking place: capital accumulation and technological progress. Full neutrality would require two separate cross-equation restrictions as in Layard and Nickell (1985, 1986).[5] Statistically, this amounts to estimating the wage equation as a reduced-form cointegrating vector. While a relationship between productivity and wages may be true in the very long run, it is possibly not appropriate to use a reduced-form wage equation in a structural macro model.[6] It is also debatable whether this restriction should apply to the short run when the model treats capital as fixed. In reality the true relationship between the capital stock and wages probably comes about indirectly through profits and some target level of real wage growth. These, the latter especially, may not adjust 'automatically' to changes in productivity as the reduced form would imply. We feel to impose this cross-equation restriction may obscure some of the interesting issues a little prematurely. It is not clear, for example, whether the solution to a productivity slowdown should be a reduction

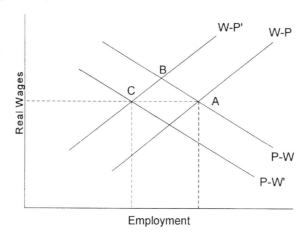

Figure 6.3 The determination of equilibrium employment

in the target real wage or a series of measures to promote investment; especially if high interest rates are actually to blame for the slowdown in productivity.

A number of authors appear to be thinking along similar lines. Within a vintage capital framework Bean (1989) considers a model where firms have a target level of capacity utilisation. Thus in Figure 6.3 an exogenous increase in wage pressure will shift the wage-setting schedule up and a new equilibrium will be established at B once wages and prices are consistent again. Now, at B, firms face higher real wages and experience a lower level of capacity utilisation than at A. Bean argues that as a consequence firms will cancel plans for new investment. This slower rate of capital accumulation will over time be reflected in the downward shift of the price-setting equilibrium until the target level of capacity utilisation is restored. One might describe the position at C as one of capital shortage, although that shortage is a reflection of past excessive wage pressure. To properly understand the nature of the new equilibrium one needs to consider the full range of possible factor substitutions, which we feel we are able to do in the model we present below. For now we note that the equilibrium at C describes a position where a slowdown in the rate of capital accumulation results in a reduction in the demand for labour and hence a corresponding increase in the NAIRU. Clearly, the effect would be the same if the rate of capital accumulation was sensitive to an increase in interest rates.

There is much here upon which we wish to build, while keeping the distinction between the short- and long-run models very clear. We begin with a simple two-factor model since this is useful for illustrative purposes. Later we generalise this with a view to implementing the framework empirically on the UK model at the London Business School. For now we abstract from wedge terms and the open economy but wish to bring these features back at a later stage.

6.4 TWO STYLISED MODELS

6.4.1 Two-Factor, Long-Run NAIRU

It is helpful to begin thinking about these issues in the simplest possible two-factor, closed-economy case. We start with the notion of the *long-run NAIRU*, where the optimal adjustment of all the factors of production, including capital, has taken place. Central to this is the concept of a *long-run cost function*.

We take a Cobb–Douglas production function with constant returns to scale which we can think of as a first-order approximation to any arbitrary production function. Thus

$$Y = L^{1-\alpha} K^{\alpha} \qquad \ldots (8)$$

The cost function is therefore

$$c(w, \rho, y) = A w^{1-\alpha} \rho^{\alpha} Y \qquad \ldots (9)$$

where $A = \alpha^{-\alpha}(1-\alpha)^{\alpha-1}$, w is the wage rate and ρ is the nominal cost of capital.

Long-run marginal costs are therefore

$$C_y = A w^{1-\alpha} \rho^{\alpha} \qquad \ldots (10)$$

Thus, by virtue of constant returns to scale, marginal costs are a constant function of factor prices and are independent of output, in the long run. Any 'upward' pressure on marginal costs from increases in output must come from a 'tightening' in the factor markets themselves, which will in turn be picked up by the wage and cost of capital equations.

Considering the behaviour of an imperfectly competitive firm faced with a constant elasticity of product demand, its prices will be given as a fixed mark-up over long-run marginal costs. We therefore have the following price mark-up equation (in logs):

$$p - w = \xi + \alpha(\rho - w) \qquad \ldots (11)$$

We can think of this equation as a distribution equation, giving us the relationship between achievable real wages and real rentals on capital. Such a relationship lies beneath any macro model, including those with a quasi-fixed capital stock.[7] The term in ξ, the mark-up, with free entry, will just be enough to cover the fixed costs of production, such as land rentals (Dixit and Stiglitz (1977)).

Using Shephard's lemma we can derive the labour demand function as

$$n = -\alpha(w - \rho) + y \qquad \ldots (12)$$

Wages are determined using a stylised wage equation that relates real wages to the rate of unemployment, u

$$w = p - \beta u \qquad \ldots (13)$$

Note that *unemployment* in this simple model is given by a transformation of employment:

$$u = l^s - n \qquad \ldots (14)$$

The real cost of capital is assumed fixed in real terms:

$$\rho = p + R \qquad \ldots (15)$$

where R is the real cost of capital.

To close the system, we add a reduced-form aggregate demand function, with m as the nominal money supply, as

$$y = \gamma(m - p) \qquad \ldots (16)$$

The solution of the system is recursive. Setting the price mark-up equal to the wage mark-up and substituting for the real cost of capital, we derive an expression for the long-run NAIRU:

$$u = \frac{\xi + \alpha R}{\beta(1 - \alpha)} \qquad \ldots (17)$$

The long-run NAIRU is therefore an increasing function of the real cost of capital and the mark-up. By virtue of constant returns to scale this definition of the NAIRU is independent of labour demand.

Output within this system is given by inverting the labour demand equation, subject to the warranted level of employment implied by the NAIRU:

$$y = l^s - \frac{(1 + \beta\alpha)}{\beta(1 - \alpha)}\xi - \frac{(2 + \beta\alpha)\alpha}{\beta(1 - \alpha)}R \qquad \ldots (18)$$

Hence we have a vertical long-run aggregate supply curve (as required by the theory of the NAIRU). The long-run price level is then given in monetarist fashion by inverting the aggregate demand curve.

The effects of an increase in the real cost of capital is illustrated in Figure 6.4. An increase in the cost of capital would require that a greater share of the overall product should go to capital and therefore that the real wage must decline. The increased cost of capital would also require that the real return on capital would have to rise. Given that there are diminishing returns to any individual factor, this requires a decumulation of capital to raise its return.

In terms of Figure 6.4, the upper left-hand corner diagram shows the labour market, where the upward-sloping wage equation is plotted together with the horizontal price (or distribution) equation. The required fall in the real wage is shown by the downward movement in the price line in the labour market diagram. These equations together determine employment and the NAIRU. The lower real wage must require higher unemployment and thus a lower level of employment.

The production function is shown in the lower right-hand quadrant and can be thought of as an optimal value function that relates the minimum cost level of

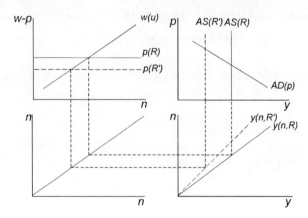

Figure 6.4

output to a given labour input and the cost of capital. Since capital decumulates, when the cost of capital rises, this function would shift up for an increase in the cost of capital, further magnifying the reduction in output.

Finally, the top right-hand quadrant of the diagram shows the implications of this for aggregate supply. Clearly, both employment and capital decumulation factors reinforce each other and aggregate supply declines.

6.4.2 Two-Factor, Short-Run NAIRU

In practice most macro models do not use a long-run cost function. Instead, they assume that capital is a quasi-fixed factor and describe the technology of the economy by a restricted cost function. (This is often implicit, as when price and employment equations use capacity utilisation.)

From the envelope theorem of duality theory we know that the two representations of the cost function describe identical technologies, and that alternative marginal costs and employment demand functions converge when the capital stock is at its optimum value. Clearly, divergences from this optimum capital stock can occur and may be persistent owing to adjustment costs or other, perhaps financial, constraints on investment.

We therefore investigate the properties of the NAIRU in the short run, i.e. that level of unemployment that would ensure the compatibility of the desired real wage with the determination of prices, conditional on a fixed, arbitrary capital stock.

When capital is fixed, the short-run cost function for the Cobb–Douglas technology that we discussed earlier is given by

$$c(w, \rho, y, k) = w(yk^{-\alpha})^{1/(1-\alpha)} + \rho k \qquad \ldots (19)$$

Again prices are set equal to a constant mark-up over short-run marginal costs resulting in the following short-run price equation in logs:

$$p = \xi + w + \gamma(y - k) \qquad \ldots (20)$$

where $\gamma = \alpha/(1 - \alpha)$.

A number of points of clarification are worth making at this stage. First, note that with the capital stock fixed, marginal costs are increasing in output. This is because we have lost constant returns to scale in the short run. An increase in output therefore will have to be produced from less than optimal combinations of capital and labour. An increase in output therefore will result in a required increase of prices over wages.[8]

Secondly, note that the long-run distribution equation is not entirely super-seded. From the envelope theorem, marginal costs and therefore prices will be the same in the short and long run provided the capital stock is at its optimum value. The real rate of return on capital in this case will be identical to the real cost of capital. Should the capital stock diverge from its optimum value, however, the rate of return on capital will differ from the cost of capital, and capital will tend to accumulate or decumulate.

The short-run labour demand function is given by

$$n = (1 + \gamma)y - \gamma k \qquad \ldots (21)$$

which again will be equal to long-run labour demand if the capital stock is at its optimum.

We can now combine the price and labour demand equations, eliminating output to derive a downward-sloping reduced-form labour demand schedule in real/employment space (see Figure 6.5).

The model is closed by adding wage, unemployment, and aggregate demand equations identical to those used in the previous section (equations (13), (14), and (16), respectively).

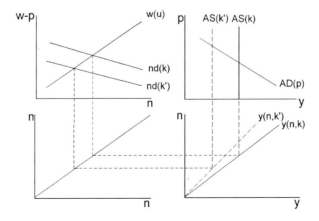

Figure 6.5 Response of the short-run NAIRU to a reduction in the capital stock

We can solve the model for the NAIRU:

$$u = \frac{\gamma l^s + (1 + \gamma)\xi - \gamma k}{\gamma + \beta(1 + \gamma)} \qquad \ldots (22)$$

Hence, the NAIRU is reduced by an increase in the capital stock and increasing in the mark-up over marginal costs.

A reduction in the capital stock is illustrated in Figure 6.5. This will lower the downward-sloping labour demand schedule, resulting in a lower real wage and reduced employment. Simultaneously the production function, in the lower right-hand quadrant, will move backwards as a result of the lower capital stock. The aggregate supply curve will move back, raising the price level for a fixed money stock.

How do the short- and long-run NAIRUs relate to each other? Suppose the cost of capital rises, with the capital stock quasi-fixed in the short run. The higher cost of capital would entail a lower optimal capital stock than is in existence and thus the exiting rate of return on capital will be lower than the cost of capital. Capital will therefore decumulate, with the results shown in Figure 6.5. Full long-run equilibrium will be restored when the capital stock has fallen back to its optimum, although this may take a prolonged period to occur. At this point the short-run labour demand, long-run price, and real wage functions will all coincide.

The behaviour of real wages during this process is interesting and instructive. In the short-run, real wages will be above their warranted long-run value; labour will take the same share of the product as prior to the shock. As capital decumulates, however, the marginal product of labour will decline and both employment and real wages will decline. The real wage after full adjustment has taken place will be compatible with the long-run distribution function (equation (11)).

6.5 GENERAL FRAMEWORK FOR THE SUPPLY SIDE

6.5.1 Production Technology

The previous section illustrated some of basic features of two different concepts of the NAIRU. We now turn to a general model with an eye to implementing this empirically on the UK model at the LBS. In particular, we have two modelling strategies available to us: (i) the restricted cost function approach of Allen (1994) or (ii) the unrestricted cost function estimated in Allen and Urga (1995). A restricted cost function approach, being conditioned on a given capital stock, lends itself very well to the two concepts of short and long run that we have used here. The main problem here is calculating the derived long-run price equation from the short-run price equation once capital stock is considered. This is done using the Le Chatelier–Samuelson principle, as in Appendix 2.

The unrestricted cost function, by contrast, estimates all factors (including capital) as flexible. Such an approach would give us the long-run price equation directly. However, the real benefit of the short-run conception of the NAIRU comes when one considers different rates of optimal adjustment for different factors (which was the chief innovation of Allen and Urga (1995)). Essentially, if demand increases faster than the rate of capital adjustment, then the increase in output will be met by using more of the faster adjusting factors. However, these will not be used at optimal scale and constant returns will no longer apply. Production will effectively climb the long-run average cost curve and be at an increasingly 'inefficient' scale. Hence, the mark-up over wages will rise. There will in effect now be a third dynamic concept of the NAIRU. The rate of capital accumulation will act as a speed limit on the economy. If demand expands faster than this speed limit, then inflation will begin to accelerate at a point above what we have described as the long-run NAIRU. In the Allen and Urga model this speed limit is a constant, equal to the error correction coefficient on the capital share equation. A full model would make the rate of capital accumulation endogenous.

For now we derive the two concepts the NAIRU consistent with the restricted and unrestricted cost function. In addition, since we are interested in what factors may shift the NAIRU, it is appropriate to express the analysis in terms of 'equations of change' in the spirit of Atkinson and Stiglitz (1980) and Jones (1965).

We describe the technology of the economy by a twice differentiable variable cost function, with constant returns to scale. We consider the case of four factor inputs: labour, capital, fuels and imported non-fuel commodities (including semi-manufactures). Additionally, we model the technological process by means of an exogenous time trend. The firm's price-setting decisions and factor demands can then all be derived from the cost function. We write the cost function as

$$C = C(w, p_r, p_e; y, k; t), \quad C_1, C_2, C_3, C_4 > 0; C_5, C_6 < 0 \qquad \ldots(23)$$

The cost function is homogeneous of degree one (HoD1) in variable factor prices: nominal wages (w), non-energy import prices (p_r), and energy prices (p_e). From the assumption of constant returns, it is also HoD1 jointly in output (y) and capital (k).

Assuming a constant product demand elasticity, output prices will be set as a mark-up (ξ) over marginal costs:

$$p = \xi \cdot C_y(w, p_r, p_e; y, k; t) \qquad \ldots(24)$$

Utilizing the homogeneity properties of the underlying cost function, we can write this equation as

$$1 = \xi \cdot C_y(w/p, p_r/p, p_e/p; y/k; t), \quad C_{y1}, C_{y2}, C_{y3} > 0; C_{y4}, C_y < 0$$
$$\ldots(25)$$

The price equation in this form is an implicit relationship between the real wage, real energy and raw materials prices, and the output–capital ratio.

Using Shephard's lemma, we can also derive the demand for labour, which can be written as

$$n = C_w(w, p_r, p_e; y, k; t) \qquad \ldots (26)$$

Employing the homogeneity properties of the cost function, this can be written in the form

$$n/y = C_w(w/p, p_r/p, p_e/p; y/k; t),$$
$$C_{w1} \leq 0, C_{w2}, C_{w3} \gtreqless 0; C_{w4} > 0, C_{w5} \gtreqless 0 \qquad \ldots (27)$$

The labour demand function is homogeneous of degree zero (HoD0) in factor prices and HoD1 jointly in output and capital. The elasticity of employment with respect to real wages is assumed non-positive and the *laws of demand* ensure that labour must be an Allen substitute for either or both energy and other input prices. The effect of technological progress is theoretically ambiguous, though in the case of Harrod-neutral technical progress will be negative.

Taking the capital stock as fixed in the *short run*, we can derive the following short-run price equation in terms of the output–capital ratio. This can be considered as a measure of short-run capacity utilisation. Given our assumption of constant returns to scale, an increase in the output–capital ratio will increase marginal costs and hence prices.

Differentiating the implicit price equation (21), we can write it in the rate of change form:

$$0 = \hat{\xi} + s_w^* \cdot (\hat{w} - \hat{p}) + s_r^* \cdot (\hat{p}_r - \hat{p}) + s_e^* \cdot (\hat{p}_e - \hat{p})$$
$$+ s_y^* \cdot (\hat{y} - \hat{k}) + s_t^* \cdot \hat{t} \qquad \ldots (28)$$

where the hats over the variables represent proportional derivatives. s_w^*, s_r^*, and s_e^* represent short-run quasi-factor shares of labour, non-fuel materials, and fuels, respectively. $s_y^* > 0$ is the elasticity of marginal costs with respect to the output–capital ratio. $s_t^* < 0$ is the elasticity of marginal costs with respect to technical progress. (See Appendix 1 for the full derivation.)

Likewise, we can totally differentiate the labour demand function to obtain it in rates of change form

$$(\hat{n} - \hat{y}) = \eta_{ww} \cdot (\hat{w} - \hat{p}) + \eta_{wr} \cdot (\hat{p}_r - \hat{p}) + \eta_{we} \cdot (\hat{p}_e - \hat{p})$$
$$+ (\eta_{wy} - 1) \cdot (\hat{y} - \hat{k}) + \eta_{wt} \cdot \hat{t} \qquad \ldots (29)$$

where η_{ww}, η_{we}, and η_{wr} are the elasticities of labour demand with respect to real wages, real energy prices, and real other input prices.[9] η_{wy} is the elasticity of labour demand with respect to output (assumed to be greater than unity), whilst η_{wt} is the elasticity of labour demand with respect to the index of technological progress.

In the *long run*, the output–capital ratio will be adjusted to the level compatible with full cost optimization. This ratio will reflect the real cost of capital as well as other factor prices and technological progress.

The long-run capital stock equilibrium condition is given by the envelope theorem as follows:

$$-C_5(w, p_r, p_e; y, k; t) = \rho \qquad \qquad \ldots (30)$$

where ρ is the user cost of capital. (Note that this equation will be slightly amended if there are adjustment costs on *gross* rather than *net* investment.) Again making use of the homogeneity properties of the underlying cost function, we can rewrite this expression as

$$-C_k(w/p, p_r/p, p_e/p; k/y; t) = \rho/p \qquad \qquad \ldots (31)$$

which we can rewrite as

$$y/k = \phi(w/p, p_r/p, p_e/p; \rho/p; t) \qquad \qquad \ldots (32)$$

This equation defines the long-run relationship between the output–capital ratio and relative factor prices.

We can write the long-run optimal output–capital ratio in the rate of change form as follows:

$$(\hat{y} - \hat{k}) = -[\varepsilon_{kk} \cdot (\hat{\rho} - \hat{p}) + \varepsilon_{kw} \cdot (\hat{w} - \hat{p})$$
$$+ \varepsilon_{kr} \cdot (\hat{p}_r - \hat{p}) + \varepsilon_{ke} \cdot (\hat{p}_e - \hat{p})] \qquad \qquad \ldots (33)$$

where ε_{kj} are the long-run elasticities of demand for capital with respect to the jth real factor price.

6.5.2 Wage Determination

We can write the typical wage equation as

$$w = \Phi(p_c; U; Z; t), \quad \Phi_1 > 0; \ \Phi_2 < 0; \ \Phi_3 > 0; \ \Phi_4 > 0 \qquad \ldots (34)$$

where p_c is the consumer price index, U is the unemployment rate, Z are wage shift factors (including inflation accelerations), and t represents increasing wage aspirations. We assume that wages are HoD1 in consumer prices.

We write the exact consumer price index as a linearly homogeneous combination of domestic prices (p) and consumer import prices (p_i):

$$p_c = H(p, p_i) \qquad \qquad \ldots (35)$$

Substituting (35) into (34) and making use of the homogeneity constraints, we can derive the following equation for real product wages:

$$w/p = \Phi(H(1, p_i/p); U; Z, t) \qquad \qquad \ldots (36)$$

Differentiating, we can write the real wage equation in the rate of change form as

$$(\hat{w} - \hat{p}) = e_i^w \cdot (\hat{p}_i - \hat{p}) + e_u^w \cdot \hat{u} + e_z^w \cdot \hat{z} + e_t^w \cdot \hat{t} \qquad \ldots (37)$$

where e_i^w is the real wage elasticity with respect to consumer import prices, e_u^w is the real wage elasticity with respect to unemployment, e_z^w is the real wage elasticity with respect to exogenous wage-push factors, and e_t^w represents the elasticity of real wage aspirations.

Finally, note that we can approximate the log of the unemployment rate by

$$\hat{u} = \hat{l}^s - \hat{n} \qquad \ldots (38)$$

6.5.3 Deriving the Short-Run NAIRU

The reduced form of the short-run labour demand schedule can be derived by substituting for output from the structural labour demand equation (27) into the price equation (25). We obtain:

$$1 = \xi \cdot C_y(w/p, p_r/p, p_e/p; \, y[C_w^{-1}(n; w/p, p_r/p, p_e/p; \cdot, k; t)]/k; t) \ldots (39)$$

The short-run NAIRU is then given by further substituting the real wage equation (36) into this equation.

It is straightforward now to derive the comparative statics of the short-run NAIRU case. They are given by the following equation in rate-of-change form:

$$
\begin{aligned}
\hat{u}^{SR} = 1 - \frac{1}{\Delta} \cdot [& e_z^w \cdot (s_w^* - s_y^* \cdot \eta_{ww} \cdot \eta_{wy}^{-1}) \cdot \hat{z} \\
& + e_i^w \cdot (s_w^* - s_y^* \cdot \eta_{ww} \cdot \eta_{wy}^{-1}) \cdot (\hat{p}_i - \hat{p}) + \hat{\xi} + s_y^* \cdot \eta_{wy}^{-1} \cdot \hat{l}^s \\
& + (s_r^* - s_y^* \cdot \eta_{wr} \cdot \eta_{wy}^{-1}) \cdot (\hat{p}_r - \hat{p}) \\
& + (s_e^* - s_y^* \cdot \eta_{wr} \cdot \eta_{wy}^{-1}) \cdot (\hat{p}_e - \hat{p}) - s_y^* \cdot \eta_{wy}^{-1} \cdot \hat{k} \\
& + [e_t^w s_w^* + s_t^* - s_y^* \cdot \eta_{wt} \cdot \eta_{wy}^{-1}] \cdot \hat{t}]
\end{aligned}
\qquad \ldots (40)
$$

where $\Delta = (s_w^* - s_y^* \cdot \eta_{ww} \cdot \eta_{wy}^{-1}) \cdot e_u^w - s_y^* \cdot \eta_{wy}^{-1} < 0$, since $s_{ww}^* - s_y^* \cdot \eta_{ww} \cdot \eta_{wy}^{-1} > 0$ and hence $-\Delta_{-1} > 0$.

Thus the short-run NAIRU is an increasing function of wage-push factors (z) and relative consumer import prices (p_i/p). It is also increasing in mark-ups (ξ) and labour supply (l^s), and decreasing in the capital stock (k).

The role of real producer imported raw materials prices (p_r/p) and real energy prices (p_e/p) is more complex. From the *laws of demand*, we know that $\eta_{ww} \leq 0$ and that $\eta_{ww} + \eta_{wr} + \eta_{we} = 0$. Hence, provided that labour demand is own-price elastic, labour must be an Allen substitute for at least one of these factors, and possibly both of them. One of the terms $(s_j^* - s_y^* \cdot \eta_{wj} \cdot \eta_{wy}^{-1})\{j = e, r\}$ can therefore potentially be negative. This would require that s_j^* is small, i.e. the factor makes only a small contribution to overall costs, and that η_{wj} is large and positive, i.e. the factor is a strong Allen substitute for labour.

The final term of interest is the derivative of the NAIRU with respect to the technology index; we would normally expect the NAIRU to be independent of this. Independence requires that the derivatives representing technological progress and real wage aspirations should be compatible and cancel each other out. This condition has been imposed in our empirical work.

6.5.4 Deriving the Long-Run NAIRU

A second, perhaps more satisfactory, concept of a NAIRU can also be defined. This occurs in the longer term where the optimal adjustment of all the factors of production, including capital, is allowed. The NAIRU is therefore a function of the user cost of capital rather than the capital stock. Under constant returns to scale, the NAIRU is independent of output.

To derive the long-run NAIRU, we must first obtain the long-run price equation. This will again give us a warranted mark-up over wages. The NAIRU is then found by calculating the compatible real wage from the wage equation.

The *long-run price equation* is derived by substituting the optimal output–capital ratio (equation (32)) in the implicit price equation (equation (25)). The resultant equation is of the form

$$1 = \zeta \cdot C_Y(w/p, \, p_r/p, \, p_e/p; \, \phi(w/p, \, p_r/p, \, p_e/p; \, \rho/p; \, t); \, t) \qquad \ldots (41)$$

The implicit price equation now depends on the prices of both 'variable' and 'fixed' factors.

The derivation of the comparative statics of the long-run price equation is given in Appendix 2. In rates of change form, we have

$$0 = \hat{\xi} + s_w^{\mathrm{LR}} \cdot (\hat{w} - \hat{p}) + s_r^{\mathrm{LR}} \cdot (\hat{p}_r - \hat{p}) + s_e^{\mathrm{LR}} \cdot (\hat{p}_e - \hat{p})$$
$$+ s_k^{\mathrm{LR}} \cdot (\hat{\rho} - \hat{p}) + s_t^{\mathrm{LR}} \cdot \hat{t} \qquad \ldots (42)$$

where s_i^{LR} are factor shares in total long-run costs. From linear homogeneity in costs, the factor shares sum to unity. s_t^{LR} is the elasticity of total costs with respect to time.

Substituting the real wage equation into the long-run price equation, we can now solve for the long-run NAIRU. We have the following equation in rate-of-change form:

$$\hat{u}^{\mathrm{LR}} = -\frac{1}{e_u^w \cdot s_w^{\mathrm{LR}}} \cdot [e_z^w s_w^{\mathrm{LR}} \cdot \hat{z} + e_i^w s_w^{\mathrm{LR}} \cdot (\hat{p}_i - \hat{p})$$
$$+ \hat{\xi} + s_r^{\mathrm{LR}} \cdot (\hat{p}_r - \hat{p}) + s_e^{\mathrm{LR}} \cdot (\hat{p}_e - \hat{p})$$
$$+ s_k^{\mathrm{LR}} \cdot (\hat{\rho} - \hat{p}) + [e_t^w s_w^{\mathrm{LR}} + s_t^{\mathrm{LR}} \cdot \hat{t}] \qquad \ldots (43)$$

Noting that $e_u^w < 0$, the long-run NAIRU multiplier is again positive.

The impact of the wage-push variables and real consumer import prices are again positive. They have exactly the same size as before since they have a direct effect on real wages.

The coefficient on price mark-ups (ξ) is positive and probably greater than before (since almost certainly $s_w^{LR} < s_w^*$). Relative producer imported raw materials prices (p_r/p) and relative energy prices (p_e/p) will also increase the long-run NAIRU. Their effects will be identical to earlier, provided separability between the capital stock and output with variable factor prices holds. The impact of the real cost of capital is unequivocally positive as expected. With constant returns to scale, the long-run NAIRU is now independent of the level of output.

The final term in the equation again gives the derivative of the NAIRU with respect to time. For the long-run NAIRU to be independent of time requires that the derivatives representing technological progress (s_t^{LR}) and real wage aspirations ($e_t^w s_w^{LR}$) should be compatible and cancel each other out. For this condition to be compatible with that required for the short-run NAIRU, neutrality requires that

$$\frac{s_w^*}{s_t^*} = \frac{s_w^{LR}}{s_t^{LR}} \qquad \ldots (44)$$

which requires the separability of both variable factor prices and the technology trend from output and capital.

6.6 CONCLUSIONS

In this chapter we have introduced two distinct concepts of the NAIRU. In the absence of any adjustment costs, or any lags in adjusting the capital stock, these two concepts would be identical. However, when this is not the case it is the short-run NAIRU that determines at what point inflation starts to rise. This is not an equilibrium in the sense of being an unemployment rate to which the economy will revert but rather marks the point at which the monetary authorities will apply the breaks. We have shown that the NAIRU is a function of relative factor prices and of the rate of capital accumulation. There will therefore be no unique short-run NAIRU; rather, the level of interest rates and the rate of growth of aggregate demand will determine a whole locus of unemployment rates at which inflation is stable.

We believe this has significant implications for how policy is conducted. In particular, while a 'quasi-monetarist' policy of using short-term interest to control inflation may well be successful in the short run by reducing aggregate demand, it also has negative implications for supply, pulling in the economy's production frontier and raising (in the sense of bringing closer) the point where the economy again runs into inflationary problems. Raising interest rates may not be an inappropriate response to inflation. In practice, raising interest rates is probably the most flexible response to variations in aggregate demand; it is hard to see the basic rate of income tax being changed on a monthly basis in response to the latest activity data. However, the interest rate policy in itself is no panacea. It does have real side consequences in that it only delivers low inflation through low growth and high unemployment. Other measures to promote investment therefore have to be an integral part of the macroeconomic policy framework if the authorities are going to rely on interest rates to control aggregate demand and hence inflation.

6.7 ENDNOTES

1. It should be noted that it is prices that are accelerating and not necessarily inflation, as the term implies.
2. Nickell (1993) points out that if dynamic homogeneity does not hold, then we only have to stabilise inflation at the appropriate rate to eliminate unemployment, which is another way of saying that the long-run Phillips curve has to be vertical. We feel that the relationship is probably more non-linear than this so while it might indeed be unrealistic to use the implied unemployment-inflation trade-off to reduce unemployment, it might equally be true that the choice of inflation target affects the NAIRU. Ultimately, this is an empirical question but we note that dynamic homogeneity is not often accepted by the data and certainly most major macroeconomic models do not exhibit complete dynamic homogeneity in their wage-price systems (see Sefton and Wright (1994) for example).
3. See, for example, Darby and Wren Lewis (1993) for the best recent example of a 'core' theoretical model.
4. For empirical support for long-run neutrality, see Newell and Symons (1986) and for the opposite prospective, see Darby and Wren-Lewis (1993).
5. As far as we can see, these restrictions were imposed in their original work but do not appear to hold in the version discussed on p. 441. This would seem to imply that the NAIRU they estimate there is dependant on the capital stock and therefore trended over time!
6. Mabey and Nixon (1995), for example, consider the implications of a supply-side shock where productivity is included in the wage equation. An increase in oil prices, for example, that leads to a substitution into labour would reduce productivity. If productivity was, included in the wage equation, this would reduced wages, making labour cheaper and lead to a further round of substitution away from other factors and into labour. Thus the model might prove unstable.
7. The price relationship is well known as a distribution function and is widely used as such in international trade theory.
8. We therefore do not need the mark-up over marginal costs to itself (ξ) to vary with output, as it does in Layard, Nickell and Jackman, in order to get the price-setting schedule to slope downwards in $w - p$, employment space.
9. Note that the *laws of demand* require that

$$\eta_{ww} \leq 0$$

and that

$$\eta_{ww} + \eta_{we} + \eta_{wr} = 0$$

APPENDIX 1: DERIVATION OF THE SHORT-RUN PRICE EQUATION

To derive the short-run price equation in rate-of-change form, we totally differentiate equation (25) and then substitute the price equation into the resulting expression (i.e. $p = \xi C_y$)

$$0 = \hat{\xi} + s_w^* \cdot (\hat{w} - \hat{p}) + s_r^* \cdot (\hat{p}_r - \hat{p}) + s_e^* \cdot (\hat{p}_e - \hat{p})$$
$$+ s_y^* \cdot (\hat{y} - \hat{k}) + s_t^* \cdot \hat{t} \qquad \qquad \dots (45)$$

where

$$s_w^* = \frac{C_{yw} \cdot w}{C_y}$$

$$s_r^* = \frac{C_{yr} \cdot p_r}{C_y} \qquad \qquad \dots (46)$$

$$s_e^* = \frac{C_{ye} \cdot p_e}{C_y}$$

We have called these *short-run quasi-factor shares*. Only if the variable cost function exhibits separability between output and the capital stock with variable factor prices will these quasi-factor shares be equal to the actual short-run factor shares in variable costs. We also have that

$$s_y^* = \frac{C_{yy} \cdot y}{C_y} = -\frac{C_{yk} \cdot k}{C_y}$$

$$s_t^* = \frac{C_{yt} \cdot t}{C_y} \qquad \qquad \dots (47)$$

APPENDIX 2: DERIVATION OF THE LONG-RUN PRICE EQUATION

The derivation of the long-run NAIRU depends on the relationships between the restricted and unrestricted cost functions. We can derive these relationships from the following identity, which will hold when the capital stock is at its static equilibrium condition. (The results given here are extensions of the results of Brown and Christensen (1982).)

$$L(w, \rho, y, t) = C(w, y, k^*, t) + \rho \cdot k^* \qquad \qquad \dots (48)$$

where the function $L(w, \rho, Y, t)$ is the unrestricted *total* cost function, $C(w, y, k, t)$ is the restricted *variable* cost function, and $k^* = k(w, \rho, y, t)$ is the optimal capital stock. Differentiating L with respect to the cost of capital, we obtain:

$$L_\rho = k^* + (C_k + \rho)\frac{\partial k}{\partial \rho} = k^* \qquad \qquad \dots (49)$$

where the second equality follows from the envelope theorem.

Differentiating L_ρ with respect to its various arguments, we can now derive relation-ships between the second-order derivatives of the restricted cost function (i.e. holding k constant at its originally optimal value) and the derivatives of the unrestricted cost func-tion (which allows k to vary optimally). The following four relationships are important in what follows:

$$C_{kk} = \frac{-1}{L_{\rho\rho}}, \qquad C_{ky} = \frac{L_{\rho y}}{L_{\rho\rho}}$$

$$C_{kw} = \frac{L_{\rho w}}{L_{\rho\rho}}, \qquad C_{kt} = \frac{L_{\rho t}}{L_{\rho\rho}} \qquad \ldots(50)$$

Assuming constant returns to scale, we can derive the following further results from the Euler equation:

$$C_{yy} = \frac{-L_\rho}{y}\frac{L_{\rho y}}{L_{\rho\rho}}$$

$$C_{yw} = \left[\frac{L_w}{y} - \frac{L_\rho}{y}\frac{L_{\rho w}}{L_{\rho\rho}}\right] \qquad \ldots(51)$$

$$C_{kt} = \left[\frac{L_t}{y} - \frac{L_\rho}{y}\frac{L_{\rho t}}{L_{\rho\rho}}\right]$$

(Analogous results are available for a homothetic cost function with returns to scale of any arbitrary degree.)

The short-run price equation in rate-of-change form is given in equation (28). We can now define the elasticities in this equation in terms of the derivatives of the unrestricted cost function:

$$s_k^* = \frac{-L_\rho}{L_y}\frac{L_{\rho y}}{L_{\rho\rho}}$$

$$s_w^* = \frac{w}{L_y}\left[\frac{L_w}{y} - \frac{L_\rho}{y}\frac{L_{\rho w}}{L_{\rho\rho}}\right] \qquad \ldots(52)$$

$$s_t^* = \frac{t}{L_y}\left[\frac{L_t}{y} - \frac{L_\rho}{y}\frac{L_{\rho t}}{L_{\rho\rho}}\right]$$

The optimal output–capital ratio in rate-of-change form is given in equation (33). It is trivial to write the elasticities in this equation in terms of the derivatives of the unrestricted cost function:

$$\varepsilon_{kk} = \frac{L_{\rho\rho}\cdot\rho}{L_\rho}$$

$$\varepsilon_{kw} = \frac{L_{\rho w}\cdot w}{L_\rho} \qquad \ldots(53)$$

$$\varepsilon_{kt} = \frac{L_{\rho t}\cdot t}{L_\rho}$$

Substituting the output–capital ratio equation in the price equation, we obtain the long-run price equation. Substituting out the terms in the real wage, from the wage determination equation and renormalizing, we obtain the long-run price equation:

$$0 = \hat{\xi} + [s_w^* - s_k^* \cdot \varepsilon_{kw}] \cdot (\hat{w} - \hat{p}) + [s_r^* - s_k^* \varepsilon_{kr}] \cdot (\hat{p}_r - \hat{p})$$

$$+ [s_e^* - s_k^* \varepsilon_{ke}] \cdot (\hat{p}_e - \hat{p}) + [s_k^* \varepsilon_{kk}] \cdot (\hat{\rho} - \hat{p}) + [s_t^* - s_k^* \varepsilon_{kw}] \cdot \hat{t} \quad \ldots (54)$$

where we can show, using the identities above, that the terms in square brackets reduce to factor shares in long-run total costs.

The resultant equation is equation (29) in the main text. We should not be surprised that all substitution effects have been cancelled from this long-run price equation. All we consider in this rate of change formulation are *first-order* effects. The substitution effects will all be *second-order* effects. This does not mean that they are not of empirical significance: second-order effects are explicitly identified in our econometric model.

APPENDIX 3: COMPATIBILITY OF TECHNOLOGY TRENDS

For the long-run NAIRU to be independent of time requires that the derivatives representing technological progress (s_t^{LR}) and real wage aspirations ($e_t^w s_w^{LR}$) should be compatible and cancel each other out. For this condition to be compatible with that required for the short-run NAIRU, neutrality requires that

$$\frac{s_w^*}{s_t^*} = \frac{s_w^{LR}}{s_t^{LR}} \quad \ldots (55)$$

Substituting out for the short-run quasi-factor shares gives

$$\frac{s_w^*}{s_t^*} = \frac{C_{yw}}{C_{yt}} \quad \ldots (56)$$

Likewise, we can write the ratio of the long-run shares as

$$\frac{s_w^{LR}}{s_t^{LR}} = \frac{L_w}{L_t} = \frac{C_w + (C_k + \rho) \cdot \partial k/\partial w}{C_t + (C_k + \rho) \cdot \partial k/\partial t} = \frac{C_w}{C_t} \quad \ldots (57)$$

where the last equality follows from the envelope condition.

The variable cost function exhibits the property of the equality of

$$\frac{C_w}{C_t} = \frac{C_{yw}}{C_{yt}} \quad \ldots (58)$$

if and only if there is separability of both variable factor prices and the technology trend from output and capital.

7

Investigating Structural Breaks in UK Manufacturing Trade

ANINDYA BANERJEE AND GIOVANNI URGA

7.1 INTRODUCTION

Investigating the presence of structural breaks in UK trade equations has been a topic of live debate in numerous recent papers. In the main these papers have concentrated in particular on empirical investigations of the export equation in order to shed light on the moot issue of the 'income elasticity' of demand for UK exports. In many of the papers this value has been demonstrated to be significantly different from one and such a departure from unit elasticity has been attributed principally to the presence of structural breaks.

The subject-matter of our chapter draws inspiration from two distinct but related sources. First, our theoretical interest in dating structural breaks in cointegrated systems of equations, as developed in Banerjee and Urga (1995a,b), and secondly our empirical concern for developing structurally stable trade equations to be used as part of the London Business School (LBS) model of the UK economy. It is to the latter task that we devote our primary attention by comparing and contrasting the existing equations of the trade sector in the LBS model with those derived from a full investigation of the structural break dating issue.

7.1.1 Current Literature Survey

A common approach to explaining export performance involves estimating a relationship between a measure of exports, world trade and a measure of relative prices. Equations of this form, estimated for UK exports, require either that

---

Macroeconomic Modelling in a Changing World. Edited by C. Allen and S. Hall
© 1997 John Wiley & Sons Ltd

demand for UK exports be income inelastic or that a secular unexplained decline exists, usually proxied by a simple time trend.

More recently, the stabilisation of the UK export share has been interpreted as a structural shift in export behaviour. This has been represented in several different ways. Some investigators have allowed for shifts in behaviour through rolling regressions, recursive techniques and stochastic time trends (e.g. Landesmann and Snell (1989), Anderton (1992)). Others (e.g. Blake and Pain (1994)) have argued that export relationships have been mispecified and have suggested additional variables such as research and development expenditure, or cumulated investment as measures of non-price competitiveness. Research in this spirit has been carried out by Owen and Wren-Lewis (1993) and Allen and Whitley (1994). In particular, Blake and Pain (1994) argue in favour of a structural break in the export demand relationship during 1981 and suggest that the break is explainable by these regressors which act as proxies for non-competitive features in the export sector.

Yet another view, advanced by Holly and Wade (1991), points to a shift in supply-side factors as the cause of the structural shift. Holly and Wade reject the findings of Landesmann and Snell on shifts in the income elasticity of demand. In contrast they conclude that UK firms have priced more competitively in world markets. Using standard Chow tests and dummy variables they date the structural break around 1979.

Our analysis does not make use of a priori knowledge of the timing of the potential break-point, as in Holly and Wade (1991). We suppose, instead, that the timing of the break is unknown, as in Landesmann and Snell (1989), Anderton (1992) and Blake and Pain (1994). Also, in contrast to all the above papers, we allow for the possibility of operating within the framework of a system of equations where the system is characterised by (a) the conditional model, where the variable proxying for export demand is conditioned, linearly, on a set of explanatory variables of undetermined exogeneity status, and (b) the marginal models of the explanatory variables. Further potential generality is lent to the procedure by allowing for the possibility of structural breaks (at temporally distinct periods of time) in both the conditional and the marginal models. As we show below, various simplifications of the testing procedure are possible once the exogeneity status of the independent variables is determined and the search for the break(s) in the conditional model is made conditional upon the search for the break(s) in the marginal model but the procedures lend themselves to fairly general application.

The sequential structural break procedure is also utilised to study the relationship between a measure of imports, output/income and a measure of relative prices. Moreover, this equation is augmented with a variable capturing cyclical movements in imports, and a trend that represents a term for trend specialisation. With regard to the imports equation, most of the literature[1] deals with the issue of modelling the *structural trend specialisation* and *cyclical movement* in imports and their possible effect on the activity/demand unit-elasticity restriction. Almost no attention has been focused on looking for possible effects of breaks in mean (or trend) in the import equation, although this could be presumed from their description of the stylised facts. For instance, on the basis of some evidence in Anderton, Pesaran and Wren-Lewis (1992), Sedgley and Smith (1994) impose two mean changes in their multivariate Johansen cointegration analysis, both of which may be shown to be statistically insignificant.

7.1.2 Modelling using Sequential Methods

The problem addressed in Banerjee and Urga (1995a) was that of more than one structural break (in almost all our cases, two breaks in mean) in the system when the breaks are allowed to occur at *different* points in time. The problem relates to making accurate inferences about these break dates assuming of course that no a priori imposition is undertaken. In our testing methods we operated within the framework of sequential and recursive tests in order to develop reasonably robust and powerful procedures.

The distinction between 'sequential' and 'recursive' procedures is described in detail in Banerjee, Lumsdaine and Stock (1992). Recursive procedures involve estimation by considering estimates derived from partial samples and augmenting the sample with additional observations at each stage. Sequential methods use full-sample estimates with the location of a particular event being varied across the length of this sample. The distinction is made clear later in the chapter. Both procedures have trimming restrictions associated with them.

We choose to concentrate only on sequential methods for detecting breaks. This decision is based on our experience of recursive tests, confirmed by the simulation analyses in Banerjee and Urga (1995a,b) and in Banerjee, Lumsdaine and Stock (1992), having low power.

In contrast with earlier work, we operate wherever necessary within a systems framework and allow for the possibility of distinct structural breaks affecting different points of a system of equations at different points in time. The broader aim of the analysis in this chapter is therefore to model the export and import sectors of the economy to provide a framework and generalised principles within which the testing for structural breaks may be undertaken.

In Section 7.2 we consider the general case where the breaks in the conditional and marginal models occur distinctly. We introduce the procedure of estimating the break in the marginal process first and then impose this knowledge in some form when searching for the break in the conditional process. We start by considering the case of strong exogenous regressors. We present an application to the export sector of the trade equation system of the LBS model, where testing indicates that strong exogeneity is likely to be a valid assumption. Section 7.3 discusses the case where strong exogeneity is explicitly violated. The empirical relevance of this theoretical analysis is then demonstrated and extended in our modelling of the import sector. Both Section 7.2 and Section 7.3 present dynamic models based on the long-run equations estimated earlier. Section 7.4 concludes.

7.2 DATA-GENERATION PROCESS, METHODS AND MODELS: STRONGLY EXOGENOUS REGRESSORS

THE CASE OF EXPORTS

Consider the data-generation process (DGP) given by

DGP A

$$y_t = \beta x_t + \gamma_1 D_t^1 + u_{1t}$$
$$x_t = x_{t-1} + \gamma_2 D_t^2 + u_{2t}$$

where

$y_0 = x_0 = 0; \; D_t^1 = I(t > k_1); \; D_t^2 = I(t > k_2); \; k_1 \neq k_2$ (in general);

$I(\cdot)$ is the standard indicator function;

$$\begin{bmatrix} u_{1t} \\ u_{2t} \end{bmatrix} \sim IN \begin{bmatrix} \begin{bmatrix} 0 \\ 0 \end{bmatrix}, & \begin{bmatrix} \sigma_{11} & 0 \\ 0 & \sigma_{22} \end{bmatrix} \end{bmatrix}$$

The null hypothesis has $\gamma_1 = \gamma_2 = 0$, and under this specification the DGP therefore takes the form of a bivariate cointegrated system (since the variables are each I(1)). Under the alternative, the system is structurally broken. Here the variable $\{y_t\}$ depends on $\{x_t\}$, while $\{x_t\}$ depends only on its own past. Later in the chapter we consider relaxing this condition.

In Banerjee and Urga (1995a) we proposed at least two methods, first where we search for the pair of break-points unconditionally, i.e. consider estimating model A' for all possible pairs of locations of the dummy variables, computing the F-test for testing $\gamma_1 = \gamma_2 = 0$ and identifying as the points where the breaks occur the pair for which the F-statistic achieves its maximum. Critical values for this test were computed on this basis.

Unfortunately, this procedure is extremely intensive in terms of computer time, as searching has to be undertaken over $O(T^2)$ terms. We therefore propose an alternative method. To reduce the dimensionality of the inferential problem, we consider a two-stage strategy. At the first stage, sequential-testing procedures are employed on the marginal model to date the break in this model. This knowledge is then used to date the remaining break in the reduced form of the conditional model.

The testing procedures are described in detail in Banerjee and Urga (1995a) which looks at the case of a bivariate system. As we show below, when modelling the import sector the framework needs to be extended to allow for higher order (in this case three) systems of variables. The logic of our approach nevertheless goes through without alteration in this more general case. Returning to the DGP above, critical values are computed for the sequence of t-tests for γ_1 in the model

Model A

$$y_t = \beta x_t + \gamma_1 D_t^1 + u_{1t}$$

where the test-statistic used is

$$\tau_2 = t - \max = \text{argmax}\{t_{\gamma_1=0}(k)\}, \quad k = 2, T\text{-}2$$

Here the regression is estimated over the full sample each time but the location of the dummy variable is moved sequentially over the sample.

Model A$'$ constitutes the reduced-form versions of these models, given by substituting for x_t in the equation generating y_t. This amounts to replacing x_t by its lag and by the lag of the dependent variable y_t.

Note that a difficulty is likely to arise in dealing with the sequential test with the reduced form of the model in the case where $k_1 \neq k_2$. Writing the model out in a reduced form would give a term of the form $\gamma_1 D_t^1 + \beta \gamma_2 D_t^2$, which would not be proxied adequately by a single dummy variable. In the case where $k_1 = k_2$, this is not likely to cause a problem. However, in the more general case where proxying by a single dummy variable is clearly likely to be inadequate, some method needs to be discovered for dealing with two dummy variables.

We look first at the DGP–Model combination given by DGP A and Model A or A$'$. The critical values for searching for the break in the marginal model, using sequential methods, are given in Banerjee, Lumsdaine and Stock (1992). The procedure here would be to estimate a regression of x_t on its lags (plus a constant and trend if necessary) and a sequential dummy D_t^2, where the location of the dummy is changed from a value of, say, k_0 to T-k_0 (k_0 reflects trimming the sample) and the regression is estimated over the full sample of size T at each stage.

The critical values for the equivalent procedure for the conditional model, given by estimating Model A or A$'$ (when knowledge of the break date for D_t^2 is imposed), need to be computed and are given as Tables 1A and 1B in Banerjee and Urga (1995b).[2] An empirical application of this method is given below when modelling the export sector of the LBS trade model.

7.2.1 The LBS Export Equation

In this subsection we briefly introduce the core of the export equation employed by the new London Business School model (LBS, 1995) of the UK economy and illustrate our sequential procedure by applying it to the equation modelling the export sector.

The trade equations typically focus on two main explanatory variables: output/income and relative prices. The exports block of the LBS model is divided into exports of goods and services, and exports of fuel. Our equation makes use of the conventional approach of modelling the volume of trade by emphasising only the 'demand side'[3] of the trade volumes and identifying a long-run cointegrated relationship between exports demand, world income and competitiveness effects. No use is made of the world trade variable to include any activity effects.

The *export equation* models exports of goods and services as a function of world income (as a proxy for world demand) and relative competitiveness, where the imposition of a unit coefficient on world income growth is supported by the data. The inclusion of a competitiveness term means that an appreciation of the exchange rate will make world export prices lower, and hence UK exports less competitive, unless the price of UK exports falls proportionately.

The exports equation in the long run can then be expressed as follows:

$$lx - ly = f(lpx - lpw)$$

where

lx = log(exports of goods and services, pounds sterling 1990),

ly = log(GNP, major 6),

lpx = log(price of exports of goods+services, 1990 = 1),

lpw = log(price of world exports of manufactures, 1990 = 1).

A visual inspection of the series[4] suggests that they are very likely to be integrated of order 1 with breaks in mean and (or) trend. We next estimate sequential tests for the marginal model where we allow for a break in the mean of the series.[5]

First, we are interested in testing the claim that $(lpx - lpw)$ is strongly exogenous for the parameters of interest in the conditional model. This explains the presence of the lagged $(lx - ly)$ terms in the marginal model, which are found to be jointly insignificant. The full details of the marginal model are reported as EQ(1) below. The break in the marginal model is dated at 1984. IV (i.e. where the t-test on the step-dummy D_t^2 achieves its maximum), a period characterised by strong and sustained appreciation of the dollar, while the estimated coefficients on the lagged $(lx - ly)$ indicate that the series is integrated, although this finding may be sensitive to the extent to which the sample is trimmed.

Note that in our analysis we have chosen to trim the sample at both endpoints, by disregarding the first 28 observations of the series (thereby starting the analysis off in 1977. I) and the final eight observations. Although this trimming may appear overgenerous, it is necessary to avoid dealing with the possibility of multiple breaks (more than two) in the series and also to overcome the loss of power of tests when the break happens too near the end or the beginning of the sample (we are therefore, by the same token, unable to take account of the impact of the introduction of floating exchange rates around 1972 and again after the September 1992 crisis).

EQ(1) Modelling $(lpx - lpw_t)$ by OLS

Sample period: 1977. I–1991. III

$$lpx - lpw_t = 0.70 + \text{seq. dummy} + 1.06*(lpx - lpw)_{t-1}$$
$$(7.5)$$

$$- 0.27*(lpx - lpw)_{t-2} + 0.08*(lpx - lpw)_{t-3}$$
$$(1.3) \qquad\qquad (0.4)$$

$$- 0.07*(lpx - lpw)_{t-4} - 0.04*(lx - ly)_{t-1}$$
$$(0.5) \qquad\qquad (0.2)$$

$$- 0.12*(lx - ly)_{t-2} + 0.01*(lx - ly)_{t-3}$$
$$(0.7) \qquad\qquad (0.1)$$

$$- 0.15*(lx - ly)_{t-4}$$
$$(0.9)$$

Seq. dummy $= -0.04$ (2.62) occurring at $t = 32$ (1984. IV)

Notes: t-statistics (absolute values) are in parentheses.

Next, substituting the value of the break in the marginal process in the conditional model (in its reduced form version) in EQ(2) below, we find a break in the ninth period of the sample, corresponding to the dock strike of 1979. I.[6] It should be noted that this finding is quite robust to the amount of trimming chosen (unless the trimming is such so as to exclude the date on which the break occurs!).[7]

EQ(2) Modelling $(lx - ly)_t$ by OLS

Sample period: 1977. I–1991. III

$$(lx - ly)_t = 2.17 + 0.02*D_t^2 + \text{seq. dummy}$$
$$(7.18) \quad (4.13)$$

$$- 0.08*(lx - ly)_{t-1} - 0.16*(lpx - lpw)_{t-1}$$
$$(0.65) \qquad\qquad (3.75)$$

Seq. dummy $= 0.04$ (2.93) occurring at $t = 9$ (1979. I) and $D_t^2 = 32$

Notes: t-statistics (absolute values) are in parentheses.

The dynamic error-correction formulation is given by EQ(3) below.[8] There is no evidence of misspecification, and the model is structurally stable in the presence of appropriate dummies.

EQ(3) Modelling Dlx by OLS

Sample period: 1977. I–1991. III

Variable	Coefficient	Std. error	t-value
Constant	1.6709	0.33421	4.999
$Dlx - 1$	−0.044509	0.081946	−0.543
$Dl\,px - l\,pw$	−0.12554	0.076583	−1.639
$DLM6GNP$	0.60282	0.45363	1.329
$l\,px - l\,pw - 1$	−0.19848	0.057429	−3.456
$lx - ly - 1$	−0.71310	0.14120	−5.050
$s79p1$	−0.096667	0.018334	−5.272
$s79p2$	0.18792	0.025311	7.424
$s79p3$	−0.079247	0.023060	−3.437
$s84p4$	0.015843	0.0076627	2.068

$R^2 = 0.79$; $F(9, 49) = 20.017$ [0.0000]; $\sigma = 0.0164352$; DW $= 2.12$

AR 1–5 $F(5, 44)$ $= 2.2326$ [0.0678]
ARCH 4 $F(4, 41)$ $= 0.90372$ [0.4707]
Normality $\chi^2(2)$ $= 2.765$ [0.2510]
X^2 $F(14, 34)$ $= 0.67311$ [0.7833]
RESET $F(1, 48)$ $= 0.021369$ [0.8844]

Tests of parameter constancy over: 1989. IV–1991. III

Forecast $\chi^2(8) = 8.5545$ [0.3813]
Chow $F(8, 38) = 1.0132$ [0.4414]

7.2.2 Violation of Strong Exogeneity: The Case of Imports

Strong exogeneity may of course be violated in several ways. In the case most relevant to our investigations pertaining to the import sector of the LBS model, strong exogeneity is violated via the presence of lagged y terms in the model generating the x's since these imply feedback from the conditional into the marginal process. The extension of our framework to take account of such violations is straightforward, involving a simple recomputation of the relevant critical values to take account of this more general case. The modified critical values are reported as tables 4A, 5A, 6A and 7A in Banerjee and Urga (1995a). These critical values are used below to model the import sector.[9]

7.2.3 The LBS Import Equation

The import volumes are disaggregated into goods and services, with goods being disaggregated further into final manufactures, non-fuels and fuel. In this chapter we focus on the equation dealing with imports of final manufactures. The imports equation includes competitiveness terms and the domestic demand variable, plus a trend (or specialisation index), and an index that captures the slow cyclical response of the supply side. The latter term (eight-period moving average) allows us to reduce the very large elasticity on demand which then is not statistically different from unity. For the *imports equation*, in conformity with LBS aggregation conventions, we use imports of final manufactures. This equation also imposes a unit long-run elasticity on imports with respect to total final expenditure and can be expressed as follows:

$$(lm - ltfe) = f(lpm - lpy), \ (lpoil - lpy), \ trend, \ \log(tfe/tfema(8))$$

where

$\quad lm = \log(\text{import volume: finished manufactures, pounds sterling 1990})$

$\quad ltfe = \log(\text{total final expenditure, pounds sterling 1990})$

$\quad lpm = \log(\text{price of imports: finished manufactures, } 1990 = 1)$

$\quad lpoil = \log(\text{sterling price of world oil, pounds sterling 1990})$

$\quad lpy = \log(\text{total final expenditure deflator, } 1990 = 1).$

The variable $(ltfe - ltfema(8))$ ratio, with $ltfema(8)$ being the log of the eighth-order moving average of $ltfe$, captures the slow supply-side adjustments in imports, whilst the *trend* represents a term for trend specialisation (measured in the previous version of the LBS model by the ratio of world imports to world income).[10]

It is well known that the *trend* term may spuriously proxy the deterioration in the UK's comparative advantages in manufacturing, but it remains a variable that is fairly frequently used in this class of macroeconometric modelling in order to facilitate easier economic interpretation of the results.[11]

From a closer look at the share of imports in terms of total final expenditure,[12] we notice a marked cyclically around a strong upward trend. The expansion periods are apparent in the early and late 1970s and between 1987 and 1989, whilst the current recession is also apparent along with the one between 1974 and 1975.

We next turn to an investigation of the marginal processes for the import sector, using methods identical to those applied to the exports sector above. The integratedness of these series is also evident from a visual inspection as well as from the results of estimating ADF-type statistics (not reported here).

EQ(4) Modelling $l\,pm - l\,py$ by OLS

Sample period: 1977. I–1991. III.

$$(l\,pm - l\,py)_t = -0.17 + \text{seq. dummy} + 0.81*(l\,pm - l\,py)_{t-1}$$
$$(4.6)$$

$$- 0.16*(l\,pm - l\,py)_{t-2} + 0.08*(l\,pm - l\,py)_{t-3}$$
$$(0.7) \qquad\qquad\qquad (0.4)$$

$$+ - 0.03*(l\,pm - l\,py)_{t-4} - 0.20*(lm - ltfe)_{t-1}$$
$$(0.2) \qquad\qquad\qquad (1.3)$$

$$- 0.22*(lm - ltfe)_{t-2} + 0.21*(lm - ltfe)_{t-3}$$
$$(1.1) \qquad\qquad\qquad (1.0)$$

$$+ - 0.25*(lm - ltfe)_{t-4}$$
$$(1.8)$$

Seq. dummy $= -0.11$ (4.09) occurring at $t = 7$ (1978. III)

Notes: t-statistics (absolute values) are in parentheses.

EQ(5) Modelling $(l\,poi - l\,py)$ by OLS

Sample period: 1977. I–1991. III

$$(l\,poil - l\,py)_t = -0.93 + \text{seq. dummy} + 1.12*(l\,poil - l\,py)_{t-1}$$
$$(8.2)$$

$$- 0.43*(l\,poil - l\,py)_{t-2} + 0.17*(l\,poil - l\,py)_{t-3}$$
$$(2.1) \qquad\qquad\qquad (0.9)$$

$$+ - 0.01*(l\,poil - l\,py)_{t-4} + 0.41*(lm - ltfe)_{t-1}$$
$$(0.04) \qquad\qquad\qquad (1.1)$$

$$- 1.03*(lm - ltfe)_{t-2} + 0.97*(lm - ltfe)_{t-3}$$
$$(2.1) \qquad\qquad\qquad (2.0)$$

$$+ - 0.59*(lm - ltfe)_{t-4}$$
$$(1.5)$$

Seq. dummy $= -0.49$(4.44) occurring at $t = 33$ (1985. I)

Notes: t-statistics (absolute values) are in parentheses

The results in EQ(4) and EQ(5) confirm that $(l\,pm-l\,py)$ and $(l\,poil-l\,py)$ are not strongly exogenous for the parameters of interest in the $lm - ltfe$ equation because the feedback terms are significant. The breaks in the marginal processes of interest (given by $(l\,pm - l\,py)$ and $(l\,poil - l\,py)$, respectively) are given at 1978. III and 1985. I. For the conditional model (in its reduced-form version) the break is deduced to occur at 1985. III, as reported in EQ(6) below, a result clearly in accord with Sedgley and Smith (1994). In fact, almost all the break-points discovered by this sequential procedures find evidence of breaks at economically interpretable times.

EQ(6) Modelling $(lm - ltfe_t)$ by OLS (sequential dummy)
Sample period: 1977. I–1991. III

$$(lm - ltfe)_t = -0.63 + 0.08*D_t^2 - 0.13*D_t^3 + \text{seq. dummy}$$
$$(2.70)\quad(2.03)\qquad(2.64)$$
$$-0.85*(lm - ltfe)_{t-1} + 0.21*(lpm - lpy)_{t-1}$$
$$(11.2)\qquad\qquad(1.64)$$
$$-0.01*(lpoil - lpy)_{t-1}$$
$$(0.4)$$

Seq. dummy $= 0.23(4.71)$ occurring at $t = 35$ (1985. III) and $D_t^2 = 7$ and $D_t^3 = 33$

Notes: t-statistics (absolute values) are in parentheses.

It needs of course to be noted that we report on the single-equation OLS results for the conditional model when clearly, strictly speaking, given the likely failure of even weak exogeneity, systems-estimation methods may be required.

We therefore repeated the sequential exercise, within the context of our imports model, using maximum likelihood systems-estimation techniques. To confirm the robustness of the analysis, the results remain quantitatively and qualitative unchanged when systems-estimation methods are used, and in the process validate the weak-exogeneity assumption which led us to settle for single-equation methods in the first place. For our purposes it is also reassuring to note the robustness, not just in the face of a switch from single-to systems-estimation methods, but also to the choice of the truncation dates for the sample.

The dynamic error-correction formulation is given by EQ(7) below.[13] As for the previous conditional export equation, here also there is no evidence of misspecification, and the model presents a structurally stable relationship in the presence of appropriate dummies.

EQ(7) Modelling $Dlm - ltfe$ by OLS
Sample period: 1977. I–1991. III

Variable	Coefficient	Std.error	t-value
Constant	−2.3493	0.51908	−4.526
$Dlpm - lpe$	−0.73331	0.13353	−5.492
$Dltfe - lt$	1.4348	0.54420	2.636
$lpm - lpef - 1$	−0.36378	0.15771	−2.307
$lpoi - lpe - 1$	0.089334	0.026116	3.421
$ltfe - ltf - 1$	2.1274	0.56476	3.767
$lm - ltfe - 1$	−0.67963	0.15214	−4.467
$s78p3$	−0.041622	0.026775	−1.555
$s85p1$	−0.0070612	0.033219	−0.213
$s85p3$	−0.060563	0.034778	−1.741
$trend$	0.0099087	0.0030439	3.255
$s81p2$	0.062050	0.031032	2.000
$s82p1$	−0.086817	0.030240	−2.871

$R^2 = 0.782876$; $F(12, 38) = 11.418$ [0.0000]; $\sigma = 0.0357201$; DW $= 1.90$

AR 1–5	$F(5, 33)$	$= 0.7340$ [0.6032]
ARCH 4	$F(4, 30)$	$= 0.2961$ [0.8781]
Normality	$\chi^2(2)$	$= 0.0394$ [0.9805]
ξ^2	$F(19, 18)$	$= 0.8166$ [0.6678]
RESET	$F(1, 37)$	$= 1.5246$ [0.2247]

Tests of parameter constancy over: 1989 (IV) to 1991 (III)

Forecast $\chi^2(8) = 4.4335$ [0.8160]

Chow $F(8, 38) = 0.4693$ [0.8700]

7.3 CONCLUSIONS

In this chapter the presence of multiple structural breaks is investigated within the framework of endogenous sequential break dating procedures. The methods are first summarised and then applied to investigate the behaviour of UK exports and imports.

We believe that our methods add to the understanding of the behaviour of the UK trade sector. In particular, we are able to identify genuine breaks at economically interpretable times. For the exports equation we find an indication of a break in the conditional model in 1979: I, in line with the findings of Landesmann and Snell (1989). Our results are in contrast with those of Anderton (1992) and Blake and Pain (1994) who find breaks in the mid-1980s and in 1981: III, respectively. For the imports equation, the main break occurs at 1985: III: this result is in accord with the description in Sedgley and Smith (1994) who do not attempt to look for a break but impose two mean changes in their cointegration analysis, both statistically insignificant.

The timing of the breaks is also fairly robust, as indicated in the results of some sensitivity analyses. In fact, and with regard to the exports behaviour, the conclusion of this chapter is supported by a companion work by Hall, Urga and Whitley (1995). They show that, although there is some support for a supply-side interpretation in that there have been changes in the behaviour of prices, there has also been a shift in the underlying demand for UK exports. This is in contrast, for instance, to theories that provide a role for cumulated investment as a proxy for changes in the quality of UK exports or other supply-side variables. These variables do have some empirical support but do not eliminate the case for the presence of a structural break in export behaviour. As we showed in the empirical exercise, several changes have taken place in both the volume of exports and its main determinants over the past two decades.

The shifts in imports is also evident, in contrast to the findings of the existing empirical literature which tends to disregard the issue completely. Therefore, on the basis of the results of this chapter, we can conclude that the behaviour of UK exports and imports has altered systematically and substantially over the period under investigation.

7.4 ACKNOWLEDGEMENTS

We are grateful to the ESRC for funding this project under various grants held at the Institute of Economics and Statistics, Oxford, and the Centre for Economic Forecasting (London Business School). The authors also wish to thank Steve Hall for his comments and helpful suggestions. The usual disclaimer applies.

7.5 ENDNOTES

1. See, *inter alia*, Anderton, Pesaran and Wren-Lewis (1992) and Sedgley and Smith (1994). The latter paper summarises the main characteristics of the NIESR and HMT models.
2. The power calculations reported in Banerjee and Urga (1995b) show that the sequential reduced-form tests pick up the break in the conditional model with high frequency and are remarkably good at dating the break in the conditional model. In particular, for the reduced form, the break date shows a strong central tendency around the true break date.
3. Recently Holly and Wade (1991) and Hall, Urga and Whitley (1995) have used an explicit supply and demand formulation.
4. The graphs, levels and first differences, are reported in figures 1–4 in Banerjee and Urga (1995b).
5. Results of estimating ADF-type statistics are not reported here but are available from the authors on request.
6. A single break may be taken to proxy for the existence of two or three shifts in the mean in quick succession. Thus, while 1979. I is the main period of instability, successful empirical modelling may require us to allow for fine-tuning around 1979. I along the lines discussed below. The sequential method provides us with the main information in this regard.
7. It is possible to repeat the exercise in one stage by estimating the unconditional model and to search over a larger subset of pairs of possible break-points. It turns out, as the simulation results indicate, that this is an inefficient and time-consuming procedure. Perhaps it is for this reason that the corresponding breaks, if this method is used, are found in 1979. I and 1979. III, respectively. This is simply a reflection of the scale of changes occurring in that period but possibly it is no help in providing information to pin down the break precisely. The power calculations from the simulations lead us to believe that the conditional procedure does rather better.
8. The sample period is the same as the one that we used for the conditional model.
9. It should be noted, *en passant*, that the framework is generalisable further to encompass the case where both strong and weak exogeneity are violated either by the presence of non-zero covariances or by the process of *conditioning* the search for the break in the conditional model on that of the marginal model. The method adopted in this case is to use sequential estimation in systems (described in Banerjee and

Urga (1995a) and Anderson and Mizon (1984) with the corresponding critical values given in tables 8A and 9A of Banerjee and Urga (1995a).

10. It is worth noting that alternative measures of cyclical and trend effects could be, as for instance in Anderton, Pesaran and Wven-Lewis (1992) and Sedgley and Smith (1994), a capacity utilisation variable and a specialisation index, respectively.

11. In the absence of such a trend, the unit-elasticity restriction is not accepted (see Allen and Whitley (1994)).

12. Figures 5–12 in Banerjee and Urga (1995b) report the graphs (levels and first differences) of the relevant series.

13. The sample period is the same as the one that we used for the conditional model.

8

A Supply-Side Model of the UK Economy: An Application of Non-Linear Cointegration

CHRIS ALLEN

8.1 INTRODUCTION

Since the work of Bruno and Sachs (1985) the modelling of the 'supply-side', i.e. the firms that make up the production sector of the economy, has been increasingly recognized as an essential part of an econometric model. Firms' pricing and factor demand decisions have a major role in the determination of aggregate output. It is essential to model them properly in order to assess the short-term macroeconomic implications of shocks to energy and raw materials prices or of changes in employer taxes. In the long term, firms' decisions ultimately determine the rate of growth of the economy and the warranted real wage.

This chapter examines the specification and estimation of a consistent model of producer behaviour for the non-energy business sector of the UK economy. The model forms the basis of the aggregate supply block of the London Business School macroeconomic model of the UK economy.

The model is based around a dynamic aggregate restricted cost function, which captures the economically relevant information contained in the underlying aggregate production function. The use of the dual representation of technology greatly simplifies the derivation of a consistent set of price and factor demand equations. We have derived and jointly estimated the parameters of the cost function, together with the output price and factor demand equations. The imposition of parameter restrictions between these equations allows improved efficiency

Macroeconomic Modelling in a Changing World. Edited by C. Allen and S. Hall
© 1997 John Wiley & Sons Ltd

of estimation and ensures the consistency of the behaviour of the production sector.

We have used an insight of Henri Theil's to derive a dynamic translog flexible functional form to represent the cost function. Dynamically, the cost function behaves like a cross between a translog and a Leontief cost function, with an equilibrium which is a standard translog. Factor shares adopt an error-correction representation. The flexibility of an equilibrium translog functional form allows us to estimate empirically an unrestricted set of elasticities of substitution between the factors of production. We therefore avoid the common pitfall of constraining a priori these elasticities to be unity, as with Cobb–Douglas, or to be all fixed at a common constant, as with a constant elasticity of substitution (CES) functional form. From the translog restricted cost function, both short- and long-run elasticities of substitution can be computed; the factor-bias of returns to scale and technological progress can also be assessed.

Previous work in this area has focused directly on the production function and used more restrictive functional forms. Prominent work in this area includes the work of Layard and Nickell (summarized in Layard, Nickell and Jackman (1991)), that of Helliwell *et al.* (1985) in the context of the OECD international model, Young's (1988) small supply model for H.M. Treasury, and Wren-Lewis's (1992a) work on vintage production functions.[1]

Our framework bears comparison with that of the so-called *GNP function* approach to modelling import demands. On the basis of production theory, import and other factor demands are derived from an underlying economy-wide cost or profit function. Previous work in this area includes Burgess (1974), Kohli (1978, 1990, 1993), and Diewert and Morrison (1988). Unlike our work, those models are static and assume perfect competition.[2]

An important aspect of this chapter is the attention given to the estimation of non-linear flexible functional forms in the presence of non-stationary data.[3] The translog cost function contains terms in quadratic functions of its arguments. Recently doubt has been thrown on the applicability of conventional techniques to deal with this problem. An example of this scepticism is the recent paper by Lynde and Richmond (1993) who argue:

> Although it is the case that in the last few years much progress has been made concerning the statistical analysis of linear models for non-stationary time-series, the complexity of the nonlinear interactions among variables that occurs in cost functions of flexible functional form is still largely *terra incognita* as far as statistical analysis is concerned (p. 882).

For this reason, the authors estimate only factor demand share equations and not the cost function itself. Hence, they are unable to estimate all the relevant parameters of the cost function and, in particular, the degree of returns to scale.

In contrast, we have employed recent developments in the theory of non-linear cointegration in order to derive direct estimates of the parameters of the quadratic translog cost function. The theory requires that a non-linear combination of the non-stationary variables must map into a variable that is stationary or I(0). To make use of the theory requires consideration of the properties of quadratic functions of non-stationary or I(1) variables.

A range of methods of testing for non-linear cointegration have been proposed recently by Granger and co-authors (see Granger (1993) and Granger and Terasvirta (1993)). We have used and compared a number of these in this chapter.

8.2 AN EMPIRICAL MODEL OF PRICING AND FACTOR DEMANDS

8.2.1 The Theoretical Framework and Aggregation Issues

We consider a standard model of an economy with a given number of monopolistic competitor firms.[4] Each firm produces and sells its own differentiated commodity. In product markets, firms play a Nash game in price strategies. In factor markets, they face given input prices; in the short run, adjustment costs prevent the instant adjustment of the capital stock.

The economy consists of n monopolistic competitors, each of which produces and sells its own slightly differentiated product. The system of aggregate customer demands for each product is described by an indirect utility function. We assume that the indirect utility function is symmetric and homothetic. The function can be written as

$$E(p_1, \ldots, p_n, Y) \qquad \ldots (1)$$

where p_i is the price of the ith firm's good, and Y is an exact index of aggregate *real* expenditure.

Associated with this indirect utility function is also an exact aggregate price index:

$$P = \chi(p_1, \ldots, p_n) \qquad \ldots (2)$$

which is linearly homogeneous in $\{p_i\}$.

Using Roy's Identity, we can derive the demand function for each firm's product from the aggregate indirect utility function. The ith firm's product demand function thus takes the form:

$$y_i = d_i(p_1, \ldots, p_n) \cdot Y \qquad \ldots (3)$$

where y_i is the output demand of the ith firm.

Firms compete in Nash price strategies. Each firm simultaneously and independently chooses its price to maximize its own profits, conditional on the set of competitor prices.

We describe the firm's production technology by a variable cost function, conditioned on its given capital stock. We can therefore write the ith firm's *restricted* variable cost function in the form:

$$c_i = c_i(w, k_i, y_i, t_i) = \min_{\{x_i\}}[w^T x_i : x_i \in L(y_i, k_i, t_i)] \qquad \ldots(4)$$

where c_i is ith firm's variable costs, x_i is a vector of its quantities of variable factor inputs, k_i is its predetermined capital stock, y_i is its output, and t_i is a trend representing technical progress. $L_i(y_i, k_i, t_i)$ is the ith firm's input requirement set, conditional on its predetermined capital stock. w is the vector of variable factor prices, assumed common to all firms.

The function $c_i(\cdot)$ is linearly homogeneous and concave in variable factor prices, non-decreasing in output, and non-increasing in the fixed factor. We further assume that the cost function has constant returns to scale, i.e. that it is linearly homogeneous jointly in output and the capital stock. We also assume twice differentiability with respect to each of its arguments.

The ith firm's profit-maximization problem can therefore be written as

$$\max_{\{p_i\}} \pi_i = p_i \cdot y_i - c_i(w, y_i, k_i, t_i) - r \cdot k_i \qquad \ldots(5)$$

where r is the user cost of capital.

The first-order conditions for this problem are well known to result in a price function of the form:

$$p_i = \zeta_i \cdot c'_{i,y_i}(w, d_i(p_1, \ldots, p_n) \cdot Y, k_i, t_i) \qquad \ldots(6)$$

where $\zeta_i = 1 - (1/\eta_{ii})$, and η_{ii} is the elasticity of demand. The function $c'_{i,y_i}(\cdot, \cdot)$ is the marginal cost function. It is linearly homogeneous in w and homogeneous of degree *zero* in $\{y_i, k_i\}$.

The ith firm's variable factor demand functions are straightforwardly derived from its restricted cost function, using Shephard's Lemma:

$$x_{i,j} = \frac{\partial c_i}{\partial w_j} = c'_{i,w_j}(w, y_i, k_i, t_i) \qquad \ldots(7)$$

Finally, we can also derive straightforwardly the cost of the firm's capital stock constraint. From the envelope theorem, the shadow price of a fixed factor is precisely the reduction in variable costs that would result from a marginal increase in that factor. Hence, differentiating the variable cost function with respect to the input of capital, we obtain the shadow price of capital:

$$\rho_i = -c'_{i,k_i}(w, y_i, k_i, t_i) \qquad \ldots(8)$$

where ρ_i is the shadow price of the fixed factor.

We now consider the required aggregation. We have assumed symmetric demand functions and that all firms have identical technology and equal capital stocks. The assumption of constant returns to scale ensures that the short-run cost function is strictly convex in output and hence that marginal costs are continuously increasing. This is sufficient to ensure equal outputs by each firm.[5]

We can now write down the set of aggregate variables: $Y = n \cdot y_i$, $K = n \cdot k_i$, and $X_j = n \cdot x_{i,j}$. From the linear homogeneity of (2), the aggregate price level $P = p_i$.

We can then characterize the economy-wide technology by an aggregate restricted cost function:

$$C = C(w, K, Y, t) = \min_{\{x\}}[w^T x : x \in L(Y, K, t)] \qquad \ldots (9)$$

The aggregate price equation can now be written in terms of aggregate observables:

$$P = \zeta \cdot C'_Y(w, Y, K, t) \qquad \ldots (10)$$

where C'_Y is the derivative of the aggregate cost function with respect to aggregate demand (= aggregate output).

Similarly, the firm-level variable factor demand functions represented in equation (7) can be aggregated to give aggregate factor demand functions of the form:

$$X_j = C'_j(w, Y, K, t) \qquad \ldots (11)$$

in terms of aggregate variables.

Finally, the shadow price of capital in the aggregate is

$$\rho = -C'_K(w, Y, K, t) \qquad \ldots (12)$$

where ρ is the shadow price of the fixed factor.

We do not discuss further the shadow price of capital in this chapter, although this was explored in Chapter 2. In general, it will not be equal to the actual user cost of capital unless there is an absence of market imperfections and adjustment costs. Studies have generally shown adjustment costs to be substantial (see Bernstein and Mohnen (1991)).[6]

8.2.2 The Equilibrium Translog Model

Our empirical work makes use of a dynamic translog restricted variable cost function. In the long run this function behaves as a standard static translog cost function. In this subsection we discuss these equilibrium properties. The dynamic context of the cost function is discussed in Subsection 8.2.4.

The translog is a flexible functional form which can be interpreted as a second-order approximation to any arbitrary cost function (see Denny and Fuss (1977)). It has enough parameters to allow us to estimate empirically an unrestricted set of elasticities of substitution between the different factors of production. We therefore are not constrained to restrict all of the elasticities of substitution to be unity a priori, as with the Cobb–Douglas production function. However, the translog cost function encompasses the Cobb–Douglas function; it therefore allows us to directly test the imposition of a unitary elasticity of substitution, as seems plausible between labour and capital.

The restricted cost function is a complete description of the economically relevant part of the firm's technology. From the translog restricted cost function, both short- and long-run elasticities of substitution can be computed; the factor-bias of returns to scale and technological progress can also be assessed.

We can write the equilibrium translog or *quadratic* restricted cost function in the form:

$$\ln C = \alpha_0 + \sum_i \alpha_i w_i + \sum_r \alpha_r z_r$$

$$+ \frac{1}{2} \cdot \sum_i \sum_j \gamma_{ij} w_i w_j + \frac{1}{2} \cdot \sum_i \sum_s \alpha_{is} w_i z_s$$

$$+ \frac{1}{2} \cdot \sum_r \sum_j \alpha_{rj} z_r w_j + \frac{1}{2} \cdot \sum_r \sum_s \alpha_{rs} z_r z_s \qquad \dots (13)$$

The subscripts i and j range over the domain of factor prices, whilst r and s have as domain the set {output, capital stock, technology trend}. All of the variables are in natural logarithms. The requirements of rationality and the properties of the Taylor approximation place a number of restrictions on the parameters of the cost function. These enable us to reduce the parameter space required for estimation.

Symmetry

Symmetry of the cost function is required both by rationality and by the requirements of the Taylor expansion. This imposes the following restrictions on the parameters of the cost function:

$$\gamma_{ij} = \gamma_{ji}, \quad \alpha_{is} = \alpha_{si}, \quad \alpha_{rs} = \alpha_{sr}, \quad \alpha_{rs} = \alpha_{sr} \qquad \dots (14)$$

where the domains of the subscripts remain as before.

Linear Homogeneity in Factor Prices

Cost functions are linearly homogeneous in factor prices. This further requires:

$$\sum_i \alpha_i = 1, \quad \sum_j \gamma_{ij} = 0, \quad \sum_i \alpha_{is} = 0, \sum_j \alpha_{rj} = 0 \qquad \dots (15)$$

Symmetry and linear homogeneity together ensure the so-called property of 'adding up' of factor demands. Adding up ensures that the sum of factor shares adds up to unity and therefore will exhaust the product.[7]

Concavity in Factor Prices

A sufficient condition for the cost function to be concave in factor prices is that the matrix of price coefficients, $\Gamma_{ij} = \{\gamma_{ij}\}$, should be negative semi-definite (see Jorgenson and Fraumeni (1981)). Imposing this restriction globally places very strong restrictions on the possible values of the elasticities of substitution (Diewert and Wales (1987)). We therefore do not impose this restriction globally, but rather check the empirical estimates for conformity.

Constant Returns to Scale

Constant returns to scale is required for the aggregation of the individual firm's cost functions. Its imposition allows us to further sensibly restrict the parameter space. Constant returns to scale implies that the cost function is linearly homogeneous jointly in output and fixed factors. It therefore implies that

$$\alpha_y + \alpha_k = 1, \quad \alpha_y > 1, \quad \alpha_k < 0$$

$$\alpha_{yi} = -\alpha_{ki}, \quad \alpha_{yt} = -\alpha_{kt} \qquad \ldots (16)$$

$$\alpha_{yy} + \alpha_{kk} + 2\alpha_{ky} = 0$$

The subscript i again ranges over the domain of factor prices.

In our estimation, we have imposed constant returns to scale and the requirement of rationality as maintained hypotheses. This differs from the standard treatment of a consumer demand system, where these are normally tested for. In the consumer demand case, utility is an unobservable, and it is necessary to ensure that the consumer demands integrate to a possible (non-estimated) indirect utility function. In the current cost function case, however, the cost function itself is estimated simultaneously with the factor demand and price equations. In these circumstances it would hardly make sense to test for symmetry and linear homogeneity because these are requirements for the existence of the cost function itself, and must be imposed before derivations can take place.

From the cost function in equation (13), we can now derive the equilibrium price and factor demand equations.

The price function is derived from marginal cost as described in equation (9). With a translog cost function, the equation is most easily expressed in the form of the ratio of sales to marginal costs:

$$\frac{PY}{C} = \zeta \cdot MC \cdot \frac{Y}{C} = \zeta \cdot \left[\alpha_y + \sum_i \alpha_{iy} w_i + \alpha_{yy} y + \alpha_{yk} k + \alpha_{yt} t \right] \qquad \ldots (17)$$

Using Shephard's lemma, we can also derive the factor demand shares for the translog cost function as

$$s_i = \frac{w_i \cdot x_i}{C} = \alpha_i + \sum_j \gamma_{ij} w_j + \alpha_{yi} y + \alpha_{ki} k + \alpha_{ti} t, \quad i \in w \qquad \ldots (18)$$

We will estimate consistently the cost function equations, along with the factor demand functions, and price mark-up equation.[8]

8.2.3 Elasticities of Substitution and Technical Progress

The variable cost function is a full description of the representative firm's technology. From it, we can describe the substitution possibilities between factors both in the short run, when the capital stock is a constant, and also in the long run, when the capital stock is optimally adjusted.

The Allen elasticity of substitution (Allen (1938)) is the traditional measure of substitutability of factors. It is essentially a non-normalized measure of own- or cross-price substitutability; it has an equivalent sign to that of the compensated cross-derivative between two factors.

The *short-run* elasticities of substitution are computed on the basis of optimal adjustment of all variable factors, whilst the capital stock remains fixed. It is straightforward to derive these elasticities. The own factor-price Allen elasticities of substitution are

$$\sigma_{ii}^{SR} = \frac{1}{s_i^2}[\gamma_{ii} - s_i \cdot (1 - s_i)] \qquad \ldots (19)$$

whilst the cross-price elasticities of substitution are

$$\sigma_{ij}^{SR} = \frac{1}{s_i \cdot s_j}[\gamma_{ij} + s_i \cdot s_j] \qquad \ldots (20)$$

From the variable cost function it is also possible to derive the long-run elasticities of substitution.[9] These are defined on the basis of optimal adjustment of all factors, including capital.

The long-run own-elasticities of substitution are as follows:

$$\sigma_{ii}^{LR} = (1 + s_k) \cdot \left[\sigma_{ii}^{SR} - \frac{1}{s_i^2} \cdot \left(\frac{(\alpha_{ik} - s_i \cdot s_k)^2}{s_k^2 + s_k - \alpha_{kk}}\right)\right] \qquad \ldots (21)$$

From the envelope theorem, the own-price elasticities of substitution must be at least as large in the long run as the short run. It can be easily confirmed that this is the case.

The cross-price elasticities of substitution between the variable factors can be shown to be

$$\sigma_{ij}^{LR} = (1 + s_k) \cdot \left[\sigma_{ij}^{SR} - \frac{1}{s_i \cdot s_j} \cdot \left(\frac{(\alpha_{ik} - s_i \cdot s_k)(\alpha_{jk} - s_j \cdot s_k)}{s_k^2 + s_k - \alpha_{kk}}\right)\right] \qquad \ldots (22)$$

Finally, we can derive the elasticities of substitution between variable and fixed factors as

$$\sigma_{ik}^{LR} = -\frac{1 + s_k}{s_i} \cdot \left[\frac{\alpha_{ik} - s_i \cdot s_k}{s_k^2 + S_k - \alpha_{kk}}\right] \qquad \ldots (23)$$

Blackorby and Russell (1989) contested the usefulness of the Allen measure of the elasticity of substitution. They point out that when there are more than two factors it is not a measure of the 'ease' of substitution or curvature of the isoquant between two factors. Such a measure should not in general be symmetric. They propose instead the use of the Morishima elasticity of substitution:

$$\sigma_{ij}^{\mathrm{M}} = \frac{\partial \ln(x_i/x_j)}{\partial \ln(w_j)} = \varepsilon_{ij} - \varepsilon_{jj}.$$

The derivative of the log of relative factor proportions with respect to a factor price is an exact measure of the curvature of the isoquant between two factors.

From the cost function we can also derive the factor bias of technological progress. The total rate of diminution of variable costs is

$$\frac{\partial \ln C}{\partial t} = \alpha_t + \sum_i \alpha_{ti} w_i + \alpha_{yt} y + \alpha_{kt} k + \alpha_{tt} t \qquad \ldots (24)$$

The α_{it} give the factor biases of technical progress: in particular, $\alpha_{lt} < 0$ represents labour-augmenting technical progress. If all of the α_{it} are zero, then the cost function exhibits 'cost-neutral' technical change. If in addition it is homothetic, then technological progress is Hicks neutral.

Finally, we can derive an implicit equation for the shadow cost of capital. This has the form:

$$-\frac{\rho K}{C} = \alpha_k + \sum_i \alpha_{ik} w_i + \alpha_{yk} y + \alpha_{kk} k + \alpha_{kt} t \qquad \ldots (25)$$

8.2.4 A Dynamic Model

Subsection 8.2.2 determined the equilibrium cost function and factor demands. To implement the model empirically requires a model of disequilibrium adjustment. The solution to this problem in the consumer case is well known. Examples are Anderson and Blundell (1982), and Barr and Cuthbertson (1991).

As Theil (1977) noted, however, there are substantive differences between the consumer and producer cases. The consumer demand problem is essentially an allocative one: the overall level of consumer expenditure is given, and the decision is merely how to allocate this expenditure over the set of commodities, given the set of their prices. In the producer case, however, the firm does *not* take its total input expenditure as a given; its objective rather is to *minimize* its costs. This is quite a different problem.

Our solution is to use an insight of Theil's to derive a dynamic cost function which results in an error correction formulation of the factor shares equations. Following most consumption studies, we have restricted attention to diagonalized adjustment matrices that impose the symmetric adjustment of variable factor shares.

Two assumptions are made about the behaviour of firms with regard to disequilibrium factor shares. First, that they are able to make an immediate partial proportional adjustment of factor shares to changes in factor prices (by the proportion $\alpha < 1$). Secondly, subsequent adjustments to equilibrium are made (at the rate γ), with an information lag of one period.

We show in Appendix 1 that the resulting dynamic cost function is of the form:

$$\Delta c_t = \alpha \cdot \Delta c_t^* + (1 - \alpha) \cdot \sum_j s_{j,t-1} \Delta w_{j,t} + (1 - \alpha) \kappa \cdot \Delta y$$

$$+ \gamma \cdot (c_{t-1}^* - c_{t-1}) + \gamma \cdot \sum_j (s_{j,t-1}^* - s_{j,t-1}) \Delta w_{j,t} \qquad \ldots (26)$$

Although dynamic, this cost function can be shown to obey all the properties of a standard flexible functional form.[10] We can therefore employ it as a conventional cost function.

Factor shares are therefore given by straightforward application of Shephard's lemma:

$$\Delta s_{i,t} = \alpha \cdot \Delta s_{i,t}^* + (\alpha + \gamma)(s_{i,t-1}^* - s_{i,t-1}), \quad i = 1, \ldots, n \qquad \ldots (27)$$

Marginal costs are given by differentiation of the dynamic cost function with respect to output. In principle, we could assume that firms use this measure of marginal cost as the basis of short-run pricing behaviour. However, other issues, such as price adjustment costs, need to be taken into account as well when determining pricing behaviour. We therefore did not put further restrictions on the form of the pricing equation.

8.3 EMPIRICAL RESULTS

The dynamic translog restricted cost function, factor demand functions, and price equations were estimated for the non-energy sector of the UK economy. The data used are seasonally adjusted, quarterly from 1965, quarter I, to 1992, quarter IV. We consider three variable inputs, labour (L), energy and fuels (F), and imported inputs into production (both raw materials and semi-manufactured goods) (NF), together with one fixed input, the non-energy business sector capital stock (K). Output is measured as the gross output of the non-energy sector (VGO), which is a series derived from a Divisa index of value-added output and inputs of fuels and imported inputs. Full details are in the data appendix.

8.3.1 Tests of the Order of Integration of the Data

One issue that must be confronted when assessing the order of integration of our data set is the order of integration of the nominal factor share terms. The factor shares are bounded variables, although they can still be non-stationary — imagine a series with a structural break. They may also be described as standard I(1) variables provided they are non-stationary, whilst their differences are stationary. Our problem comes in using tests for non-stationarity that employ the null hypothesis of a random walk. Clearly, we cannot use a random walk to describe the behaviour of a non-stationary bounded variable. Asymptotically, standard unit root tests on the levels of a bounded variable will always reject the null of a unit root. In small samples, the results are likely to be biased towards rejection of the null.

A solution to this problem is to consider instead a logistic representation of the share:

$$s_i = \frac{1}{1 - e^{-\phi_i}}$$

The variable ϕ_i is an unbounded variable equal to the log of the odds ratio of shares:

$$\phi_i = \log\left(\frac{s_i}{1 - s_i}\right)$$

Using this logit transformation of the share will not change the order of integration of the underlying series. However, it does result in an unbounded variable, which is more amenable to unit root testing.[11] It therefore provides a better framework for the employment of unit root tests. In our tests we have computed unit root tests on both the original shares and the logit transformation of the shares.

We have used and reported augmented Dickey–Fuller (ADF) unit root tests rather than alternative non-parametric tests since the former are more likely to be powerful against a general autoregressive data-generation process. Kiviet and Phillips (1992) suggest that Dickey–Fuller (DF) t-type tests augmented by trend and other particular regressor terms provide *exact similar* tests, which are robust to nuisance parameters of the data-generation process.

The results of the tests on the original and transformed shares and on the logs of the other variables are presented in Table 8.1. As expected, we find evidence that each of these series is non-stationary, except for the share of imported inputs that appears to be borderline I(0). Differencing the variables once was found to be enough to achieve stationarity. Each of these variables thus can be described as being integrated of order one, or I(1).

The estimation of the translog flexible functional form requires that we also assess the distribution of quadratic functions of the logarithms of factor prices, output and the capital stock. Since the original variables are themselves non-stationary, these quadratic functions introduce new problems into the analysis.

We hence need to analyse the properties of quadratic functions of I(1) variables. To understand the nature of the problem, in Table 8.2 we have computed some theoretical moment statistics for both the levels and differences of a squared function of a simple random walk with no drift.[12] The distribution of the levels

Table 8.1 Tests of the order of integration of the data

Variable	Levels: ADF(2) with trend	Differences:ADF(2) with trend
Level SL	−1.94	−5.59*
Level SF	−1.09	−5.57*
Level SNF	−3.60*	−3.61*
Φ_{SL}	−1.88	−5.52*
Φ_{SF}	−1.16	−5.58*
Φ_{SNF}	−3.53*	−4.91*
PYC	−1.64	−6.02*
$LW - LPNF$	−3.14	−4.78*
$LPF - LPNF$	−1.01	−5.86*
$LY - LK$	−1.89	−4.91*
LY	−1.94	−4.99*

*Significant at the 95% level.

Table 8.2 Theoretical properties of the squared function of a random walk

	x_t^2	Δx_t^2
Unconditional mean	$\sigma^2 \cdot t$	σ^2
Unconditional variance	$2\sigma^4 \cdot t.(t-1)$	$4\sigma^4 \cdot (t-1)$
Covariance $(t, T - \tau)$	$2\sigma^4 \cdot (t - \tau - 1) \cdot (t - \tau)$	0
Autocorrelation coefficient $(t, T - \tau)$	$\left[\dfrac{(t - \tau - 1) \cdot (t - \tau)}{t \cdot (t - 1)} \right]^{1/2} \approx \left[1 - \dfrac{\tau}{t} \right]^{1/2}$	0

Random walk:

$$x_t = x_{t-1} + \varepsilon_t, \quad \varepsilon_t \sim IN(0, \sigma^2)$$

$$x_0 = 0$$

of the square is clearly non-stationary, with a highly explosive variance. The autocorrelation function for a given lag tends to unity as the size of the sample increases, as with a standard I(1) series.

The series of differences of the quadratic variable cannot be described as stationary, since its variance is explosive. However, this series does share some of the properties of a stationary series. In particular, the series has a zero auto-covariance, and hence no permanence in memory.

This property of temporary memory, combined with other properties of non-stationarity, has prompted Granger (1993) to suggest that a wider notion of stationarity is appropriate to non-linear transformations of series. Granger calls a series short memory in mean (SMM) if and only if its autocovariance tends to zero as the horizon increases. His formal definition is that a series (X_t) is SMM if and only if its conditional forecast given a dated information set tends, as the horizon increases, to the series' unconditional mean:

$$\lim_{h \to \infty} E[X_{t+h}|I_t] = E[X_{t+h}]$$

where h is the forecast horizon and I_t is the information set at period t.

Granger calls a series which is SMM, but not stationary, an *extended* I(0) series. A series without this property is called an extended memory in mean (EMM). A series that is EMM, but which becomes SMM after being differenced d times, is called an extended I(d) series.

Tests for short-memory in mean are somewhat underdeveloped. The distribution of test statistics will be clearly non-standard. Granger and Hallman (1991), using Monte Carlo, found that the results from standard Dickey–Fuller and augmented Dickey–Fuller tests were potentially misleading.

Granger and Hallman suggested instead a non-parametric test, based on the ranking of the data. The use of a standard Dickey–Fuller test on the ordinal ranks of data was found to be more robust and have greater power than the conventional tests. These tests are particularly attractive in our case because they remove the problem of the explosive variance which would otherwise create heteroscedasticity in the residuals.

Table 8.3 shows the results for the rank Dickey–Fuller statistic performed on the levels and first differences of each of the combinations of the quadratic variables. Using Monte Carlo, Granger and Hallman found that the empirical 95% critical value was 4.22. Using this criterion of significance, most of the variables appear to be extended I(1). The principal exceptions are those variables containing terms in either the time trend or the capital stock. In rank terms, the capital stock has almost identical properties to a time trend. This result may suggest that the test lacks power in this case.

Table 8.3 Rank Dickey–Fuller statistics for quadratic terms

Levels	LW	LPF	LPNF	LY	LK
LW	−2.40				
LPF	−1.60	−1.49			
LPNF	−2.04	−1.49	−1.78		
LY	−1.26	−1.42	−1.69	−1.16	
LK	−1.84	−1.71	−1.90	−0.96	−1.09
T	−0.19	−1.04	−0.91	−0.12	−0.86

Differences	LW	LPF	LPNF	LY	LK
LW	−4.60				
LPF	−5.17	−6.55			
LPNF	−4.55	−5.95	−5.63		
LY	−6.73	−8.32	−7.12	−7.99	
LK	−1.81	−4.30	−2.84	−4.40	−0.92
T	−2.06	−4.83	−3.88	−4.52	−0.93

8.3.2 Direct Estimation of the Cost Function

In this subsection we make a preliminary attempt to estimate the parameters of the
cost function by direct estimation of the cointegrating vector of the cost function
itself. We also compare the results from using the translog cost function with the
simpler linear Cobb–Douglas cost function. We do this for two reasons. First,
because it allows us to assess the validity of the Cobb–Douglas form that has been
used in most previous studies. Secondly, because the Cobb–Douglas function is
straightforwardly nested within the translog form and gives us a baseline simple
functional form without the complexities of the quadratic terms of the translog.

The Cobb–Douglas cost function is a first-order flexible functional form. It
can be written as

$$c_t = \beta^T \cdot x_t + \varepsilon_{0t} \qquad \qquad \ldots (28)$$

The translog function adds in quadratic terms:

$$c_t = \beta^T \cdot x_t + x_t^T \cdot B \cdot x_t + \varepsilon_{1t} \qquad \qquad \ldots (29)$$

Since each of these vectors represents a cost function, we have imposed the a
priori restrictions implied by a constant returns to scale technology on the parameters of the cointegrating vectors of each of these functions. Linear homogeneity
in factor prices and constant returns to scale are the principal restrictions.

To preserve degrees of freedom and concentrate the power of the cointegration
tests, we have added in only quadratic terms in factor prices in the estimation
of the translog function. Clearly, these are the most important terms; if they are
required, then the cost function must be translog.

We first test for cointegration using Engle–Granger ordinary least squares
(OLS) cointegrating regression. The results are reported in Table 8.4.[13] Neither
linear nor quadratic forms strictly cointegrate. The respective cointegrating
vectors were plotted and the quadratic residuals looked more promising. This
is confirmed by the substantial improvement in the Dickey–Fuller statistic as a
result of the addition of the quadratic terms. Analysis of the residuals of the
quadratic Dickey–Fuller test show that these are white noise, and hence the
Dickey–Fuller statistic maximizes the power of the test. This is not the case
with the linear model: two differenced lags are required to obtain white noise
residuals; comparison therefore should be made between the Dickey–Fuller test
for the quadratic model and the ADF(2) test for the linear model.

Ideally, we would like a direct test that the quadratic terms in the translog
function are statistically significant. Unfortunately, as noted by Granger (1993),
a conventional LM test is going to work poorly in the context of the presence of
I(1) variables. The conventional test would be

$$\varepsilon_{0t} = \beta^T \cdot x_t + x_t^T \cdot B \cdot x_t + e_t \qquad \qquad \ldots (30)$$

where the hypothesis to be tested is that B is a null matrix (see Pagan
(1984)). Unfortunately, if the maintained hypothesis is true, then ε_{0t} is I(0) and

Table 8.4 Cointegration in the cost function

	Engle–Granger OLS		Johansen FIML	
	Cobb–Douglas	Translog	Cobb–Douglas	Translog
AL	0.828	0.808	0.753	0.665
AF	0.098	0.209	0.062	0.029
GLL	—	0.698	—	0.186
GFF	—	0.264	—	0.018
GLF	—	−0.173	—	−0.008
AY	1.060	1.109	1.148	1.601
AT	−0.0068	−0.0063	−0.006	−0.005
DF	−2.77	−4.51	—	—
ADF(1)	−2.23	−3.39		
ADF(2)	−2.37	−3.07		
$\lambda_{\max}(r \geq 1)$	—	—	32.1 [44.0]	74.4 [−]
$\lambda_{\max}(r \geq 2)$			30.4 [37.5]	62.9 [72.7]
$\lambda_{\max}(r \geq 3)$			24.5 [31.5]	55.5 [66.2]
$\chi^2(\mathrm{df})$			2.24 (2)	6.44 (5)
α	−0.070	−0.121	−0.288	−0.351
(t-stat)	(1.95)	(2.03)	(4.50)	(3.41)

equation (26) is unbalanced; alternatively, if it is false, then the residual is EMM and the standard errors in equation (28) do not have a standard distribution.

As an alternative test, Granger suggests that the significance of each of the cointegrating vectors as an error correction term is tested in the following equation:

$$\Delta c_t = \gamma^{\mathrm{T}} \cdot \Delta x_t + \delta \cdot res_{t-1} + \varepsilon_{3t} \qquad \ldots (31)$$

In this equation, under the hypothesis of cointegration, all of the terms are I(1) or SMM. We can therefore use standard t-statistics to test for the significance of the error correction terms. The coefficients on the error correction terms, together with their t-statistics, are reported at the bottom of Table 8.4. Both tests are borderline; the translog coefficient is just significant.

It is well known that in the absence of common factors, Engle–Granger static regression is an inefficient technique for estimating cointegrating vectors (Gonzalo (1994)). Far more powerful is the Johansen maximum likelihood canonical correlation estimator. This technique first partials out the effects of short-run dynamics from a set of variables, before deriving the long-run cointegrating vectors between them by computing the principal canonical correlations amongst the adjusted variables. Johansen showed that the likelihood function is proportional to a transformation of the corresponding eigenvalues of this problem (see Johansen (1988, 1991) and Johansen and Juselius (1990)). Reimers (1991) found that the Johansen procedure over-rejected when the null was true in small samples and suggested a small sample adjustment, which we have adopted here.

Our methodology was to estimate an unrestricted model and to derive the set of significant eigenvectors, as described above. We then imposed the restrictions of theory on this set of significant (or least insignificant) vectors.

Johansen (1991) shows that the maximum likelihood estimator of the β vector under a restriction of the form $\beta = H\phi$ is given by the solution to the generalized eigenvalue problem:

$$|\lambda^* H^T S_{kk} H - H^T S_{k0} S_{00}^{-1} S_{0k} H| = 0 \qquad \dots (32)$$

subject to the normalization $\hat{V}^T (H^T S_{kk} H) \hat{V} = I$.

The S_{ij} are the second-moment product matrices of the residuals and $\hat{V}$ is the matrix of concatenated ordered eigenvectors. H is an $n \times s$ matrix of restrictions. The form of H for the two cases is given in Appendix 2.

The log-likelihood function is proportional to a transformation of the ordered eigenvalues. A likelihood ratio test of the restrictions is then given by

$$\zeta_r = T \cdot \sum_{i=1}^{r} \ln[(1 - \lambda_i^*)/(1 - \lambda_i)] \qquad \dots (33)$$

which is asymptotically distributed as $\chi^2(r \cdot [n - s])$.

Since the Johansen technique is maximum likelihood, it is clearly important that the model is correctly specified and that the errors are independently normally distributed. Too short lag lengths, in particular, can lead to autocorrelation and make the maximum likelihood estimator no longer optimal; a too long lag length can lead to inefficiency. From examination of the residuals of various lengths of unrestricted vector autoregression (VAR), a lag length of 3 was found to be sufficient for approximate independent normality.

The results are reported in the last two columns of Table 8.4. The Cobb–Douglas cost function is a slightly non-standard case. The cointegrating vector contains six variables plus a restricted time trend. Osterwald-Lenum (1992) provides the asymptotic distribution of the test statistics in this case. Both maximum eigenvalue and trace tests rejected the hypothesis of a cointegrating vector. Our theory imposes two restrictions: (i) linear homogeneity in factor prices and (ii) constant returns to scale. The parameter estimates of the restricted vector with the largest eigenvalue are reported in Table 8.4. It is similar to that given by the Engle–Granger static regression; the loading matrix shows that in principle it belongs in the cost function.

We further tested for the cointegration in the translog cost function. This involves adding additional quadratic terms into the VAR. Once again these were restricted to quadratic terms in factor prices to preserve degrees of freedom. The problem here is even greater than with Engle–Granger: even adding the quadratic terms in the three factor prices adds another six variables. We now are testing for cointegrating vectors with 12 variables plus a restricted time trend.[14]

A potential problem in adding quadratic terms to the VAR is the risk of obtaining spurious cointegrating vectors between the quadratic terms. In practice this did not appear to happen. Canonical correlations provide only *linear* combinations of the variables. The *non-linearity* of the relationships between the quadratic variables was apparently enough to avoid the problem.

Again we evaluated the cointegrating vectors using the Osterwald-Lenum tables.[15] The results showed a vector of borderline significance at the 95% quantile. Theory now places five restrictions on this cointegrating vector (see Appendix 2). These were acccptable on the principal eigenvector. Again, the parameters of the restricted vector are reported in Table 8.4. The loading matrix showed that the vector belonged to the cost function. The resulting cointegrating vector again looks similar to that obtained by the Engle–Granger OLS procedure.

The results of this subsection give some support to the hypothesis that a translog function describes the data. The Johansen procedure is a maximum likelihood estimator, but does not use all the resources of our economic theory. Our theoretical results from the first part of the chapter show that both factor demand functions and product demand equations are intimately linked to the cost function. To achieve full efficiency in estimation, we should use the information from a full structural estimation of the cost function system. It is to this we turn in the next subsection.

8.3.3 Cointegration Properties of the Price Equation and Factor Demands

In this subsection we consider the cointegration properties of the factor demand equations and the price equation. These provide independent estimates of the parameters of the underlying cost function, which will indicate whether estimation of the full set of structural equations is feasible. Again we have utilized both single-equation Engle–Granger and full information maximum likelihood (FIML) Johansen techniques.

Table 8.5 shows two different sets of estimates of the cointegrating vectors in the labour demand, fuel demand, and price mark-up equations.[16] It was found that an extra variable, the ratio of manufacturing output to total non-energy output, was required to obtain cointegration in the fuel equation. It is not surprising that such a variable was required here owing to the very different fuel intensities of the manufacturing and non-manufacturing sectors.

The first columns of Table 8.5 present the minimal set of cointegrating variables using Engle–Granger OLS. From the Engle–Granger DF and ADF tests, there is clear evidence of cointegration in both the labour and fuel demand equations. Evidence for cointegration in the price mark-up equation is weaker; however, we know that the OLS procedure lacks power, especially against structural breaks (see Campos, Ericsson and Hendry (1993)).

The more powerful Johansen technique finds significant cointegrating vectors in each equation, with suitably large and significant equation loading weights.

Table 8.5 Cointegration in factor demand and price mark-up equations

	Engle–Granger OLS			Johansen FIML		
	Labour demand	Fuels demand	Price mark-up	Labour demand	Fuels demand	Price mark-up
GLL	0.191	—	—	0.185	—	—
GFF	—	0.067	—	—	0.067	—
GLF	−0.057	−0.069	—	−0.058	−0.065	—
ALT	−0.0014	—	—	n.a.	—	—
AFT	—	0	—	—	0	—
ALY	0	—	0	0	—	0
AFY	—	−0.116	−0.095	—	−0.117	−0.030
AYT	—	—	0.0015	—	—	$n.a$
AYY	—	—	0.206	—	—	0.116
LMGDP	—	0.066	—	—	0.083	—
DF	−7.89*	−5.15*	−3.89	—	—	—
ADF(1)	−4.36*	−4.62*	−3.34			
ADF(2)	−3.32	−4.30	−3.22			
$\lambda_{max} r \geq 1$	—	—	—	67.1*	35.73*	27.17*
$\lambda_{max} r \geq 2$				7.01	17.54	9.95
$\lambda_{max} r \geq 3$				1.48	14.54	9.06
α				−0.139	−0.513	−0.133

*Significant at the 95% level.

In contrast to the cost function equations, a VAR length of 2 was found to be adequate to deliver independent Gaussian residuals.

The parameter estimates from the two different estimation procedures are remarkably similar. Relative factor prices have effects on both labour and fuel demand shares. The labour share is negatively related to the time trend, suggesting Harrod-neutral technical progress, but appears unaffected by the output–capital ratio. Conversely, the fuel share is strongly influenced by the output–capital ratio, but not by the time trend. The implicit non-fuel share will thus be a function of both time trend and output–capital ratio. The price mark-up ratio is negatively related to relative fuel prices and is increasing in the output–capital ratio.

The similarity of the separate estimates of the parameters of the underlying cost function from the factor share and mark-up equations is very encouraging. The effects of relative fuel/non-fuel prices on labour and fuel demand shares (the parameter GLF) are approximately equal. Also, the effects of the output–capital ratio on factor demands should be equal to the (scaled) effects of relative factor prices on the price mark-up. These effects, expressed by the parameters ALY and AFY, are again similar.[17]

8.3.4 Estimation of the Full Set of Equations

We come now to the structural estimation of the full set of equations for the cost function itself, factor demands and the price equation. In principle, recent work by Johansen (1993) on identifying restrictions of linear equations within a simultaneous equation framework might be modified to give us a fully optimal systems estimator. However, as we saw in Subsection 8.3.2, our problem is rather too large to make this solution feasible.

Instead, we utilize two complementary methods of estimation of the parameters of the full cost function system. Their combined use allows us to solve the problem of inference in non-stationary systems.

The first method involves estimating by Iterative SURE (ISURE) the full set of equations in level form, omitting the dynamics. This can be considered as a multi-equation extension of the Engle–Granger OLS single equation cointegration technique. We test for cointegration in each of the equations separately, using conventional DF and ADF tests. On the hypothesis of cointegration, the non-stationary nature of the data will give us super-consistent estimates of the parameters of the cost function. The t-statistics, however, will not have a standard distribution.

The second method consists in estimating the parameters from estimation of the full set of dynamic equations as discussed in Subsection 8.2.4. We have used three-stage least squares (3SLS) for this in order to take account of the non-exogeneity of factor prices and output.[18] Under the hypothesis of cointegration, the coefficient estimates will be symmetrically distributed and median unbiased, and hypothesis tests may be conducted using standard asymptotic t- and χ^2-tests.

The employment of two complementary methods of estimation allows us to consistently test restrictions on the long-run parameters of our model. The method consists in first estimating the set of static equations under the restriction by ISURE to test for cointegration. If the hypothesis of cointegration under the restriction is accepted, then we can use conventional quasi-likelihood ratio tests to test the restriction within the full dynamic system.

Using tests on the 3SLS estimates, we tested down the original unrestricted cost function. At each stage of reduction we tested the corresponding ISURE equations to ensure cointegration. The χ^2-test of the over-identifying restrictions was $\chi^2(3) = 3.04$, well within the 95% critical value of 7.81.

The final long-run parameter estimates are presented in Table 8.6. The results for both estimators are remarkably similar, suggesting that the sample is large enough for the super-consistent properties of the ISURE estimator to be effective. All of the coefficients are well determined. From the 3SLS estimates, we can also derive estimates of the dynamic coefficients with t-statistics:

$$\alpha = 0.160(3.29)$$

$$\gamma = 0.144(2.50)$$

Examination of the negativity conditions showed that this generally held, except for a brief period during the 1960s, a period of extremely low real energy prices.

ADF tests on the residuals from the four equations estimated by ISURE strongly suggest cointegration in each of the equations. Note that the conventional

Table 8.6 SURE and 3SLS results

| | SURE | 3SLS | |
	Estimates	Estimates	t-statistics
AL	0.808	0.796	121.37
AF	0.213	0.232	11.77
GLL	0.186	0.159	11.22
GFF	0.067	0.071	19.20
GLF	−0.060	−0.060	−19.63
ALT	−0.0012	−0.0010	−6.17
AFY	−0.119	−0.099	−5.45
AY	0.615	0.879	5.16
AT	−0.0079	−0.0062	−6.40
AYT	0.00137	0.00097	1.47
ATT	0.00004	0.00002	2.05
EL	1.031	1.324	5.14
A0	10.759	10.858	53.41
MGDP	0.129	0.235	1.38

Cointegration tests of the SURE equations

	DF	ADF(1)	ADF(2)	ADF(3)	ADF(4)
SL	−5.01	−4.97	−4.04	−3.96	−3.31
SF	−4.57	−4.06	−3.66	−2.85	−2.86
PYC	−4.10	−3.71	−3.38	−3.24	−2.80
VCOST	−3.32	−2.85	−3.15	−2.78	−2.94

3SLS Equation diagnostics

	R^2	S.E.	$Q(1)$	$Q(2)$	$Q(3)$	$Q(4)$	ARCH(1)
SL	0.991	0.0030	1.27	1.38	5.09	5.11	0.94
SF	0.995	0.0021	0.21	1.42	1.46	3.09	0.26
PYC	0.958	0.0136	0.93	1.61	1.73	1.95	0.00
VCOST	0.999	0.0082	0.11	1.21	1.88	1.92	3.11

*Significant at the 5% level (none in table).
$Q(n)$ is Box–Pierce portmanteau test distributed $\chi^2(n)$.
ARCH (1) is $Q(1)$ performed on squares of residuals.

degrees of freedom of these tests have been substantially increased by the presence of cross-equation restrictions.

The diagnostics for the residuals of the four dynamic equations estimated by 3SLS are satisfactory. We have tested for up to fourth-order autocorrelation using Box–Pierce portmanteau statistics and for first-order ARCH processes.

8.3.5 Interpreting the Estimates

From the 3SLS parameter estimates we can derive estimates of the underlying elasticities of substitution between the different factors of production in the short

Table 8.7 Elasticities of substitution

Allen elasticities of substitution (σ_{ij}^A)

Col(i) wrt row(j)	Labour	Fuels	Raw materials
Labour	−0.037		
Fuels	0.103	−1.123	
Raw materials	0.128	0.127	−0.727

Morishima elasticities of substitution (σ_{ij}^M):

Col(i) wrt row(j)	Labour	Fuels	Raw materials
Labour	—	0.107	0.128
Fuels	0.107	—	0.128
Raw materials	0.125	0.109	—

Factor-price elasticities (ε_{ij})

Col(i) wrt row(j)	Labour	Fuels	Raw materials
Labour	−0.028	0.009	0.019
Fuels	0.079	−0.098	0.019
Raw materials	0.097	0.011	−0.109

Table 8.8 Long-run elasticities of substitution

Allen elasticities of substitution (σ_{ij}^A)

Col(i) wrt row(j)	Labour	Fuels	Raw materials	Capital
Labour	−0.349			
Fuels	1.201	−5.261		
Raw materials	−0.932	4.076	−4.969	
Capital	1.000	3.559	3.662	−4.387

Factor price elasticities (ε_{ij})

Col(i) wrt row(j)	Labour	Fuels	Raw materials	Capital
Labour	−0.205	0.080	−0.107	0.230
Fuels	0.706	−0.352	0.469	−0.823
Raw materials	−0.548	0.273	−0.571	0.842
Capital	0.588	0.238	0.421	−1.009

Formulae for Allen elasticities of substitution:

$$\sigma_{ii}^{LR} = (1+s_k) \cdot \left[\sigma_{ii}^{SR} - \frac{1}{s_i^2} \cdot \left(\frac{(\alpha_{ik} - s_i.s_k)^2}{s_k^2 + s_k - \alpha_{kk}} \right) \right] \qquad \ldots (a)$$

$$\sigma_{ij}^{LR} = (1+s_k) \cdot \left[\sigma_{ij}^{SR} - \frac{1}{s_i.s_j} \cdot \left(\frac{(\alpha_{ik} - s_i.s_k)(\alpha_{jk} - s_j.s_k)}{s_k^2 + s_k - \alpha_{kk}} \right) \right] \qquad \ldots (b)$$

$$\sigma_{ik}^{LR} = -\frac{1+s_k}{s_i} \cdot \left[\frac{\alpha_{ik} - s_i.s_k}{s_k^2 + s_k - \alpha_{kk}} \right] \qquad \ldots (c)$$

and long run. These are presented in Tables 8.7 and 8.8. We have evaluated all elasticities at sample means.

The short-run elasticities of substitution are presented in Table 8.7. They are computed at sample means. They show that the variable factors are all Allen substitutes. They are also Morishima substitutes, showing that their isoquants have a conventional shape.

Short-run elasticities measure the substitutability of the variable factors against each other, holding both the capital stock and gross output constant. They are therefore relatively small, since they do not allow for substitution between the variable factors and capital.

The own-price elasticities of fuels and raw materials are about 0.1, with that of labour only 0.03. Fuel and raw material demands are relatively sensitive to the cost of labour, whilst the other cross-price elasticities are relatively small.

Estimates of the long-run elasticities of substitution are given in Table 8.8. Here we allow for full substitutability between variable factors and the capital stock. Again, these have been evaluated at the sample average factor shares. We have assumed that the average capital share is optimal, on the basis that adjustment costs are only a short-run phenomenon.

Again our calculations are conditional on constant output. The full effect of (say) a rise in the real energy price may be considerably greater than these long-run effects. The full effect would include an impact on aggregate demand, and hence output.

The results show very much higher own- and cross-price elasticities. Capital is an Allen complement for fuel and labour is an Allen complement for raw materials. All the other combinations of factors are substitutes.

An interesting result in Table 8.8 is the unit long-run elasticity of substitution between labour and capital. This may explain the success of Cobb–Douglas value-added production functions prior to the oil shock of the 1970s. Clearly, if energy and raw materials prices were constant in real terms, than the long-run cost function would exhibit constant labour and capital shares. Unfortunately, such neglect of energy and raw materials inputs is no longer possible with the more volatile behaviour of these prices experienced since 1973.

The factor bias of technological progress revealed in our estimates also repays some close attention.

The highly significant negative term on the product of the wage and the technology trend is an indication of Harrod-neutral or pro-labour bias in technological progress. We can use this information to determine the *warranted* increase in the real wage. Assume the warranted increase in the real wage is that which would just keep the labour share constant. This is equal to the ratio of the rate of growth of Harrod-neutral technical progress to the share price elasticity of labour (*ALT/GLL*). Evaluated at an annual rate, this comes out at just over 2% real wage growth per year.

There is also a positive trend on *AYT*, which is the term in the output–capital ratio. An increase in capital relative to output therefore also progressively reduces costs. Hence there is also some evidence of capital-augmenting capital progress.

Finally, the terms *AT* and *ATT* provide an estimate of residual total factor productivity. The basic trend is large and negative, as expected, showing a steady decline in costs over time. However, the quadratic term (*ATT*) has a small positive parameter, which suggests that the rate of technological progress has been slowing. Obviously, technological progress is variable over time and is itself endogenous. Future work clearly needs to focus on the determination of technological progress.

8.4 CONCLUSIONS

In this chapter we have made use of recent developments in the theory of non-linear cointegration to estimate the parameters of a dynamic translog cost function, output price and factor demand equations for the non-energy sector of the UK economy.

The dynamic cost function allows for some inertia in variable factor demands. Dynamically it behaves like a cross between a translog and a Leontief cost function, with an equilibrium which is a standard translog. Factor shares adopt an error correction representation. Output prices are based on equilibrium marginal costs. The estimation of the full system of equations enables greatly improved efficiency of estimation and ensures consistency of the behaviour of the production sector as a whole.

In our empirical work we have confronted the problem of the estimation of flexible functional forms in the presence of non-stationary data. Tests for the order of integration of factor shares, factor prices, and capital–output ratios showed that these were clearly integrated series. Non-parametric tests of quadratic functions of these series showed that they could broadly be described as extended I(1) series.

Direct estimation of the cost function was made using Johansen's maximum likelihood estimator using the set of theoretical restrictions. The potential problem of obtaining spurious cointegrating vectors between the quadratic terms did not arise in practice. The non-linearity of the relations between the quadratic variables was apparently enough to avoid this problem. The estimation results gave support to the hypothesis that a translog cost function was adequate to describe the data.

The full system of cost function, output price, and variable factor demand equations was estimated using an iterative procedure involving the estimation of a set of static cointegrating regressions using ISURE and the set of full dynamic equations using 3SLS. Tests of this have been done both within a set of static equations estimated by ISURE and a set of dynamic equations estimated by

3SLS. The method of reduction used was first to compute cointegration tests under a restriction based on the static ISURE estimates and then, conditional on the existence of cointegration, to compute a standard (quasi-)likelihood χ^2-test for the restriction within the dynamic system.

Our results are of interest from an econometric point of view. The near-equivalence of the estimates of the long-run parameters of the cost function from static ISURE and dynamic 3SLS estimation is important. It shows that the ISURE static method does indeed provide super-consistent and efficient estimation on this data set and thus can be used to test for cointegration.

The parameters of the resulting cost function are well determined. The short-run, capital-fixed elasticities of substitution are all very small, but these become considerably larger when substitution with capital is taken into account. Labour is found to be a long-run complement with raw materials, and capital a complement to fuels. All the other combinations of factors are substitutes.

We found evidence of labour- and capital-augmenting technical progress. There is also some evidence of a productivity slowdown over the sample period. Future work will inevitably be focused on endogenizing technical progress in order to find an explanation for this phenomenon.

Our results finally allow us to reassess the methodology of previous authors. Conventional estimation techniques have followed Berndt and Wood (1975) in simultaneously estimating a set of static factor share equations together with the cost function.[19] Estimation techniques used ranged from iterative seemingly unrelated regression estimators (ISURE), to three-stage least squares (3SLS), and FIML on a set of static cost and factor share equations. In the presence of non-stationary data, conditional on the presence of cointegration, these methods can be seen as resulting in super-consistent, if potentially inefficient, estimates of the parameters.

The dynamic specification of such models was criticized by Anderson and Blundell (1982) in the context of tests for consumer rationality. They proposed the use of a dynamic error correction representation for the estimation of a set of factor share equations. From the Granger representation theorem (Engle and Granger (1987)), we can interpret such an equation system as an efficient estimation procedure of long-run parameters, conditional on the presence of cointegration. In this case, under cointegration the coefficient estimates will be symmetrically distributed and median unbiased, so that hypothesis tests may be conducted using asymptotic t- and χ^2-tests.

8.5 ACKNOWLEDGEMENTS

I am grateful for help and comments to Andrew Burrell, Stephen Hall, David Hendry, James Nixon and Peter Smith and to participants at H.M. Treasury's Academic Panel and the Warwick Macromodelling Conference, 1994. I am solely responsible for errors and omissions remaining. The work was carried out under ESRC grant W116251003.

8.6 ENDNOTES

1. Earlier work at the London Business School has been done within this framework. Allen and Robertson (1990) use a Cobb–Douglas cost function to estimate consistent price and factor demand functions in a multi-country study. Dinenis and Holly (1989) adopted a cost function approach to pricing in domestic and export markets for the manufacturing and non-manufacturing sectors, although these equations did not impose constraints on factor demand functions. Holly and Smith (1989) adopted a translog cost function approach to factor share determination.

2. Our approach makes two further innovations on previous work in the GNP functional framework. First, we explicitly disaggregate imports used as production inputs from final demand imports. Grinols (1988) noted that Diewert and Morrison's assumption that all imports entered into domestic production rather than directly into consumption was very strong. Secondly, our model explicitly identifies the gross output of the non-energy sector and therefore enables us to account for the large structural changes in the UK energy industry caused by the exploitation of North Sea oil and to model the impact of the large changes in relative energy prices on the UK economy.

3. Previous work on testing systems of equations in the presence of non-stationary data are Bewley and Elliott (1991) and Chambers (1991). Since these are applications in a consumer demand setting, the problem of non-linear, non-stationary variables is not encountered.

4. The number of firms is limited in the long run by arbitrary set-up costs and a zero excess profit condition. This is a standard model discussed by Blanchard and Kiyotaki (1987) and Layard and Nickell (1986).

5. See Baumol and Fischer (1978). Other weaker assumptions are possible. The assumption of constant returns to scale, however, is essential.

6. The advantage of our approach is that it allows us to abstract from the problem of the determination of investment; the formulation allows us to postulate a different form of capital adjustment costs from those of other factors. The approach is fully compatible with the neoclassical or q theory of investment. We explore this issue further in more recent work.

7. Adding up is a property of the data set itself, since the data on the shares must of course add up to total variable costs. The equation system is therefore singular and we can delete one of the factor demand equations as redundant. The parameters of the deleted equation can be trivially derived from the restrictions on the system after estimation.

8. Note that we have the following cross-equation restrictions between the factor demand and the mark-up equation as a result of their derivation from a single underlying cost function:

$$\alpha_{yi} = \alpha_{iy} \, i \in W$$

9. We have derived these by adaptation of the methodology of Brown and Christensen (1981).

10. It can be considered effectively as a convex combination of a translog and Leontief cost functions.

11. I am grateful to David Hendry for suggesting this transformation.

12. Little theoretical work in this area exists. Granger and Newbold (1976), in a remarkable early paper, revisited in Ermini and Granger (1993), used a Hermite polynomial expansion to examine analytically the distribution of a squared function of a random walk. Granger and Hallman (1988) also discuss the distribution of a squared function of a random walk.

13. The notation used to represent parameters is obvious: AL refers to the coefficient α_L, GLL to γ_{LL}, etc. See equation (13), and also equations (17) and (18).
14. Estimation was carried out using a (slightly) modified version of Hendrik Hansen's 'Cointegration Analysis of Time Series' RATS programme.
15. In fact, using an extrapolation of them, since they only consider up to 11 cointegrating vectors.
16. Note that owing to the adding up properties of demands, the system of demands is singular, and therefore the third (imported input) demand equation is redundant.
17. We cannot exactly identify the coefficients in the price mark-up equation owing to the presence of the elasticity term in the price equation (see equation (17)). However, we have a strong prior that this term is likely to be just over unity.
18. The instrument set included lags of factor prices and output.
19. Jorgenson (1986) presents a broad survey of this work.

8.7 DATA APPENDIX

The United Kingdom does not produce straightforward gross output accounts for the non-energy sector. Our data therefore have had to be derived from various published sources. Quarterly data on the following series is available from 1965: 1 to 1992: 4. All data are seasonally adjusted. I am grateful to Andrew Burrell for assistance in deriving the data.

The key to published sources is *ET, Economic Trends; MDS, Monthly Digest of Statistics; QA, Quarterly National Economic Accounts; MDTS, Monthly Digest of Trade Statistics.*

8.7.1 Energy Input into Industry
Volume:

$$VFUEL = 22348*(0.25*76462*(FDAH/FDAH_0) - CCCG)/52608$$

where $VFUEL$ is in £million 1990 prices. $FDAH$ is inland energy consumption (originally in million tonnes coal equivalent), rebased to $1990 = 1$ (*ET*, 5.10). $CCCG$ is consumer expenditure on energy products in £million 1990 prices (*ET*, 2.6), where the weights are taken from the 1990 Input–Output table.
Price:

$$PFUEL \text{ is the producer price index for inputs of fuel}$$
$$(\text{index } 1990 = 100).MDS, 18.6.$$

Value:

$$VALFUEL = VFUEL*PFUEL/100, \text{ in £million 1990 prices.}$$

8.7.2 Imported Inputs into Industry
Value:

$$VALNF = VALBM + VALFDT + VALSMAN$$

where $VALNF$ is in £million and:

$$VALBM = (5526/4)*VMBM/100*PMBM/100$$

$$VALFDT = (11606/4)*VMFDT/100*PMFDT/100$$

$$VALSMAN = (31555/4)*VMSMAN/100*PMSMAN/100$$

$VMBM$, $VMFDT$, $VMSMAN$ and $PMBM$, $PMFDT$, $PMSMAN$ are the volume and price indices, respectively, of basic materials, food drink and tobacco, and semi-manufactures imports (original 1985 price base) ($MDTS$, Tables 15.1, 15.8, 15.9). Pre-1970 data have been constructed from LBS model database.
Price:

$$PNF = (VALBM*PMBM + VALFDT*PFDT$$
$$+ VALSMAN*PSMAN)/VALNF$$

where PNF is a Divisia index (1990 = 100).
Volume:

$$VNF = (VALNF/PNF)*100, \text{ in £million 1990 prices.}$$

8.7.3 Labour
Value:
NWB is in £million, derived from total income from employment (QA, A3) minus the government wage bill in £million (national accounts data from H.M. Treasury).

Volume:
EMP is hours adjusted non-government employment (in thousands) (LBS model construct).

Price:

$$AWB = NWB/EMP, \text{ in £million per thousand hours.}$$

8.7.4 Capital
Volume:
KNE is derived from a quadratic interpolation of the non-energy UK capital stock (£million 1990) (National Accounts *Blue Book*).

8.7.5 Value-Added Output in Non-Energy Industries
Volume of value-added (£million 1990):

$$VANEI = GDPO - VAEI - GGWS$$

where $VANEI$ is in £million 1990 prices, $GDPO$ is GDP output measure, $GGWS$ is the government wage bill (both £million 1990 prices) and $VAEI$ is value-added in energy industries defined as

$$VAEI = ((7965/4)*YOIL + (2155/4)*YCOAL$$
$$+ (3097/4)*YNUC + (10583/4)*YENG)/100$$

where $YOIL$ is the value-added output index of the oil industry, $YCOAL$ that of the coal industry, $YNUC$ that of the nuclear industry, and $YENG$ that of electricity and gas (all 1990 = 100). *MDS*, 7.1.

Value of value-added:

$$VALVA = VANEI*PGDP/100$$

where $VALVA$ is in £million and $PGDP$ is the GDP deflator (1990 = 100).

8.7.6 Gross Output of Non-Energy Industries

Value of gross output:

$$VALGO = VALVA + VALFUEL + VALNF$$

where $VALGO$ is in £million.
Gross output price:

$$PGO = (VALVA*PGDP + VALFUEL*PFUEL + VALNF*PNF)/VALGO$$

where PGO is a Divisia price index 1990 = 100.
Gross output volume:

$$VGO = 100*VALGO/PGO$$

where VGO is in £million 1990 prices.

APPENDIX 1: DERIVATION OF THE DYNAMIC COST FUNCTION

Our derivation makes use of the following relationships. First, we write the definition of variable costs as

$$C_t = \sum_i W_{i,t} \cdot X_{i,t} \qquad \ldots (34)$$

Theil (1977) shows that, taking the differential of C_t and dividing the result through by C_t, we obtain the following approximation to the change in the log of costs:

$$\Delta c_t = \sum_j s_{j,t-1} \cdot \Delta w_{j,t} + \sum_j s_{j,t-1} \cdot \Delta x_{j,t} \qquad \ldots (35)$$

where lower case letters denote the logs of the corresponding variables.
Our dynamic cost function makes use of the following further relationship. If there is no change in relative factor proportions, then the change in costs between two periods will be the same as that resulting from a Leontief, fixed proportions technology:

$$\Delta \hat{c}_t = \sum_j s_{j,t-1} \cdot \Delta w_{j,t} + \kappa \cdot \Delta y \qquad \ldots (36)$$

where κ is the elasticity of factor demands with respect to output. The change is denoted by $\hat{c}_t$.

To derive the cost function, we make two assumptions about the behaviour of firms to disequilibrium factor shares. First, that they make an immediate proportional adjustment of factor shares to changes in factor prices (by the proportion α). Secondly, that they adjust the remainder of the disequilibrium (at the rate γ), with a lag of one period.

We can thus write the resulting cost function in the form:

$$\Delta c_t = \alpha \cdot \Delta c_t^* + (1 - \alpha) \cdot \Delta \hat{c}_t + \gamma \cdot (\hat{c}_{t-1}^* - \hat{c}_{t-1}) \qquad \ldots (37)$$

where c_t is the log of costs at t, c_t^* is optimal costs at t, and the hats represent costs based on the previous period's factor proportions.

Substituting from the fixed factor proportions formula (35) given above, we derive the cost function given in the text:

$$\Delta c_t = \alpha \cdot \Delta c_t^* + (1 - \alpha) \cdot \sum_j s_{j,t-1} \Delta w_{j,t} + (1 - \alpha)\kappa \cdot \Delta y$$

$$+ \gamma \cdot (c_{t-1}^* - c_{t-1}) + \gamma \cdot \sum_j (s_{j,t-1}^* - s_{j,t-1}) \Delta w_{j,t} \qquad \ldots (38)$$

APPENDIX 2 RESTRICTIONS ON THE COINTEGRATING VECTOR

The ordering of the variables in the VAR of the Cobb–Douglas cost function were as follows: $LVCOST$, LW, LPF, $LPNF$, LY, LYK, and $TIME$. The restrictions of linear homogeneity and constant returns to scale therefore imposed two restrictions on the cointegrating vectors. The form of the resultant restriction matrix was therefore:

$$H = \begin{bmatrix} -1 & -1 & -1 & 0 & 0 \\ 1 & 0 & 0 & 0 & 0 \\ 0 & 1 & 0 & 0 & 0 \\ 0 & 0 & 1 & 0 & 0 \\ 1 & 1 & 1 & 0 & 0 \\ 0 & 0 & 0 & 1 & 0 \\ 0 & 0 & 0 & 0 & 1 \end{bmatrix} \qquad \ldots (39)$$

The translog cost function, including only quadratic terms in factor prices, added the following six variables: LW^2, LPF^2, $LW \cdot LPF$, $LPNF^2$, $LW \cdot LPNF$, and $LPF \cdot LPNF$.

The form of the H matrix is then as follows:

$$H = \begin{bmatrix} -1 & -1 & -1 & 0 & 0 & | & 0 & 0 & 0 \\ 1 & 0 & 0 & 0 & 0 & | & 0 & 0 & 0 \\ 0 & 1 & 0 & 0 & 0 & | & 0 & 0 & 0 \\ 0 & 0 & 1 & 0 & 0 & | & 0 & 0 & 0 \\ 1 & 1 & 1 & 0 & 0 & | & 0 & 0 & 0 \\ 0 & 0 & 0 & 1 & 0 & | & 0 & 0 & 0 \\ 0 & 0 & 0 & 0 & 1 & | & 0 & 0 & 0 \\ - & - & - & - & - & | & - & - & - \\ 0 & 0 & 0 & 0 & 0 & | & .5 & 0 & 0 \\ 0 & 0 & 0 & 0 & 0 & | & 0 & .5 & 0 \\ 0 & 0 & 0 & 0 & 0 & | & 0 & 0 & 1 \\ 0 & 0 & 0 & 0 & 0 & | & .5 & .5 & 1 \\ 0 & 0 & 0 & 0 & 0 & | & -1 & -1 & 0 \\ 0 & 0 & 0 & 0 & 0 & | & 0 & -1 & -1 \end{bmatrix} \qquad \ldots (40)$$

which can be written in the form:

$$H = \begin{bmatrix} \Delta & | & 0 \\ -- & - & -- \\ 0 & | & \Gamma \end{bmatrix} \qquad \ldots (41)$$

where Δ is the Cobb–Douglas restriction matrix defined above.

SECTION 2
Using Models

9

Controlling Inflation: Modelling Monetary Policy in the 1990s

STEPHEN HALL AND JAMES NIXON

9.1 INTRODUCTION

At the heart of economic policy-making lies the task of specifying a set of objectives and trying to meet those objectives as closely as possible. To do this invariably needs a model of the economic universe we live in, even if the model is that the economy is unaffected by policy. To this end, large-scale macro models have become central to the policy work of many national and international agencies. Such models are often complex in size and highly non-linear. One is invariably drawn to the formal framework of optimal control as a method not only of characterising the policy process but also of making specific policy recommendations (see, for example, Chow (1975) or Fair (1984), who summarise much of the work in this area). The obvious attraction of this is something that has, in the past, been closely examined by various policy-making authorities. In the United Kingdom, for example, in 1978, a House of Commons Select Committee was commissioned to 'consider the present state of development of optimal control techniques as applied to economic policy'. This committee (known as the Ball Report) identified three main objections to optimal control in macroeconomics: (i) the uncertainty that exists as to the correct specification of an economic model; (ii) the problem of identifying a suitable objective function; and (iii) the difficulty in formulating policy when agents are forward looking. So large have been these objections, that optimal control has never been taken up by policy-makers, who have preferred instead to steer their economies using their own discretion.

Macroeconomic Modelling in a Changing World. Edited by C. Allen and S. Hall
© 1997 John Wiley & Sons Ltd

Recent years have, however, seen a gradual shift in economic policy towards explicit inflation targeting.[1] This removes a great deal of the uncertainty surrounding the policy-maker's objective function. On the basis of the proposition that, in the long run, the real level of activity is invariant to monetary policy, it is now widely held that price stability should be the primary focus of monetary policy (Haldane (1995)). For example, in the United Kingdom, since September 1992, when it was forced to 'suspend' Sterling's membership of the Exchange Rate Mechanism (ERM), monetary policy has focused on targeting the rate of inflation directly. The UK government's Medium Term Financial Strategy (MTFS) perhaps best articulates how policy-makers see this type of regime operating in practice:

> It is the role of monetary policy to deliver low inflation. The aim is to keep under-lying inflation in the range of 1 to 4 per cent. ... However, monetary policy influences inflation with a lag. Interest rate decisions are therefore based on an assessment of the prospects for underlying inflation in one or two years time (H.M. Treasury (1993, p. 15)).

Critically, this paragraph commits interest rates as the prime instrument of main-taining low inflation and suggests that interest rates will be set on the basis of 'predictive control', in that the government's forecast for inflation will determine when and by how much interest rates are changed. Given that the forecasts of inflation have to some extent be model-based,[2] and we now have a fairly well-defined objective function, we are drawn afresh to the techniques of optimal control.

This chapter therefore considers how monetary policy, operated in the manner set out above, might be expected to perform in practice and asks whether there are ways in which its performance could be enhanced by optimal control. These observations on the current monetary regime aside, a second, related objective of this chapter is the empirical modelling of the government's behaviour. This issue is important in a technical sense, in that suitable government reaction func-tions for both monetary and fiscal policy need to be specified to ensure adequate closure of an empirical macro model. But it is also important from a forecasting point of view, in that we need to gauge the size of interest rate movements and predict the likely future course of policy. For a given government objective function, this is also an issue we can tackle using control techniques.

A wide variety of feedback rules may, in principle, be considered. In this chapter we restrict attention to rules for monetary policy that seek to stabilise the rate of inflation: the motivation for such rules is that they correspond in broad terms to the current use of monetary policy to keep inflation within a defined range irrespective of the shocks hitting the economy.[3] Broadly the literature is divided between two alternative approaches. On the one hand, there are fully optimal control solutions that draw on the full information set. On the other hand, there are simple feedback rules that draw on some subset of the full information set. The main focus of this chapter is therefore to consider the relative merits of the two types of control rule.

9.2 OPTIMAL POLICY RULES

An important feature of any model is the set of policy rules that are used to complete or close the model, specifying the reaction of monetary and fiscal policy to developments in the economy. It is not always fully appreciated that the properties of a model, especially the dynamic features, can depend rather crucially on the policy rules that are used to specify the response of policy and thereby close the model.

It is common to specify the rule for monetary policy in terms of fixed nominal interest rates. However, this is a highly unsatisfactory closure rule for monetary policy, for reasons that have been familiar ever since work of Wicksell nearly a century ago. This is because in a wide class of models a fixed nominal interest rate is unstable. An upward impulse to inflation from any source, including an expansion of demand from fiscal policy, results in a fall in real short-term interest rates if short-term nominal interest rates are held constant. The fall in real rates fuels a further rise in demand and inflation, which further lowers the real rate of interest. This process can continue, resulting in continually rising inflation and eventually a hyperinflationary collapse of the economy. It is true that, in some classes of models, wealth effects can help to stabilise the system; but this is not true in general.

An alternative assumption is that of fixed short-term real interest rates. This approach avoids the worst instability of the fixed nominal interest rate rule, since a rise in the inflation rate, for whatever reason, is matched by a rise in the nominal interest rate. However, it has other disadvantages. Like the fixed nominal interest rate rule, the fixed real interest rate rule is an open loop rule that is likely to be rather poor at stabilising a model. It may lead to instability if the model uses uncovered interest parity to explain the exchange rate, as the London Business School (LBS) model does. With real interest rates fixed exogenously, this equation has a unit root if it is expressed in real terms. In the LBS model, the feedback of the real exchange rate onto the rest of the model modifies this unit root and leads to stability under a fixed real interest rate. But this need not happen, and if it does not, the model is unstable under this policy rule.

A further possible difficulty with a constant real interest rate policy rule is that it may not be feasible for the authorities to maintain a fixed real interest rate in the long run. Thus, for example, a fiscal expansion may alter the savings/investment balance and the relative supply of assets, leading to a rise in the long-term real rate of interest. If this is so, a policy of trying to stabilise the real interest rate at its base level, different from its new long-run equilibrium level after the fiscal expansion, will necessarily generate instability. In the LBS model this problem does not arise, since the long-run real interest rate is tied down by the world level: this is because the model incorporates uncovered interest parity and thereby perfect substitutability between domestic and foreign bonds. However, even in this model set-up the open-loop rule will generate instability if a shock at the world level causes the world real interest rate to change, and the domestic authorities attempt to stabilise the domestic real interest rate at its old base level.

A preferable approach is to try to model the government's actions by specifying a rule for the main policy instruments. If we think of a macro model in its most general form as a mapping from the known information set $X_t = x_0, \ldots, x_T, Y_t = y_0, \ldots, y_{t-1}$ onto the future endogenous variables $Y_{t+i}, i = 0, \ldots, T$ an expression for a general macromodel would be

$$\psi(y_t, X, Y) = 0 \qquad \ldots (1)$$

the solution to which can also be written as a function of current information and splitting the exogenous variables into n policy variables U, and the other exogenous variables X:

$$Y_{t+i} = \omega(X, Y), \quad i = 1, \ldots, T \qquad \ldots (2)$$

A policy rule might then be chosen to minimise any given cost function:

$$\min C = \sum_{i=0}^{T} (Y_{t+i} - \overline{Y}_{t+i})^2 \qquad \ldots (3)$$

where the optimal policy rule will be that which satisfies

$$\sum_{i=0}^{T} 2(Y - \overline{Y})\omega_{u_{jk}}(X, U) = 0, \quad j = 1, \ldots, n, k = 1, \ldots, T \qquad \ldots (4)$$

where

$$\omega_{u_{jk}}(X, U) = \frac{\partial \omega(X, U)}{\partial u_{jk}} \qquad \ldots (5)$$

The optimal control rule is therefore

$$u_{jk} = \phi(x_0, \ldots, x_T) \qquad \ldots (6)$$

If the function ϕ can be written down, then this forms a closed loop feedback, in that it would be possible to calculate the appropriate change in u_j for any change in x_t. This is only possible for linear models. For the non-linear case we have to solve the optimisation problem numerically and hence derive open loop trajectories for the policy instruments, i.e. a given value for each u_j in each t. If the future values of X change, then the optimisation problem has to be resolved and a new trajectory calculated.

It is clear from equation (6) that the fully optimal rule makes use of the entire state vector of the model, including all future values. This rule is therefore likely to be quite complex, but then the argument that interest rates should be used to achieve price stability is not in itself an argument for simplicity. However, the non-linearity of the real economy is likely to be particularly problematic. This would mean that the rule would have to be operated in an open loop manner by announcing a new profile for interest rates each month. While this might sound complicated, it seems hard not to believe that the intricacies of open loop optimal control could not be overcome, *if* the rule delivered what is promised. The key question is: Would it? And here there are two particular obstacles.

First, the function ϕ exploits the full information about the structure of the model. What tends to happen in practice on an empirical macro model is that the rule will exploit the dynamic characteristics of the system being controlled or else may find some facet of the model that does not truly reflect the real world. This might simply be some odd quirk in the model, an odd non-linearity, a corner solution or even an extreme assumption, such as rational expectations, which the optimal policy rule is able to exploit. Optimal policy rules therefore tend to be highly model specific, as is demonstrated by Bray *et al.* (1995). The optimal policy description may simply be erroneous or else be dependant upon the accuracy of the model specification, as was first identified in the Ball Report. In particular, it will be little help if there is uncertainty about either the underlying structure of the economy or at the very least the rate of dynamic adjustment in the economy. In general, policy conclusions stemming from specific elements of a model in which we have little faith should obviously be avoided.

The second problem, also identified by the Ball Report, related to the Lucas critique. Lucas (1976) was the first to raise doubts about the usefulness of macroeconomic models for policy-making when economic agents formed expectations that were forward looking. The mere announcement of a future change in policy could therefore alter agents' behaviour. The problem is that having changed agents' expectations and hence their behaviour, the incentive to carry through the announced policy might evaporate. Put formally, the presence of forward-looking expectations in the model will mean that the derivative of the model solution to future policy changes will not in general be zero, i.e.

$$\frac{\partial Y_t}{\partial u_{jt+i}} \neq 0 \qquad \qquad \dots (7)$$

This means that a policy for period $t + i$ will be optimal for the current period t in which it is derived but may no longer be optimal when the future period $t + i$ actually arrives. This is a time inconsistent policy.

As Kydland and Prescott (1977) point out, this raises serious problems regarding the credibility of the optimal policy in the eyes of the private sector because there may be an incentive to renege on any preannounced policy. They regard the time inconsistency property as a fundamental problem in the use of optimal control methods for macroeconomic policy design. In the concluding paragraphs of this seminal paper, Kydland and Prescott argue that instead of attempting to select a policy optimally,

> it is preferable that selected rules be simple and easily understood, so that it is obvious when a policy maker deviates from the policy. There should be institutional arrangements which make it a difficult and time-consuming process to change the policy rules in all but emergency situations.

To some extent some developments in the literature have attempted to circumnavigate this problem. Barro and Gordon (1983) examine whether reputational considerations can restore credibility for policy-makers and hence avoid the inferior outcome of the time consistency constraint. They assume that policy-makers suffer a loss of reputation if they renege on their earlier commitments. With this 'punishment' mechanism in place, Barro and Gordon show that credible and sustainable policies superior to the time consistent policy can exist.

This seems to ignore the main message in Kydland and Prescott, in that *building* credibility will require some process of monitoring the authorities' actions. This is going to be difficult if the optimal control rule is very complex. Of course in reality, as we have discussed above, there is not going to be a (feedback) 'rule'; rather, since the economy is non-linear, there is going to be a stated open loop trajectory for all the policy instruments. This would have to be updated with each new piece of economic data. Monitoring the authorities' actions would therefore consist of everyone having access to the same model and data sources that the authorities were using to calculate the optimal policy. While this might prove costly[4] and would not be particularly easy to communicate in the media, for example, it is not completely out of the question. Ultimately, therefore, it again comes down to the pertinence of the model.

The main objection to the use of optimal control in practical policy formulation therefore lies in the uncertainty over the true structure of the economy. It seems unlikely that economists will reach a consensus as to the true model of the economy that could be used for open loop optimal control. Moreover, even if a consensus were reached there would still be some uncertainty attached to the model in the form of estimated parameters, and stochastic error terms, reflecting uncertainty as to the nature of exogenous shocks that might perturb the economy. This sort of uncertainty is clearly going to be more problematic in a non-linear environment where the expected outcome and the deterministic solution are going to diverge.

One possible solution to this problem is to optimise across a number of different models (see, for example, Becker *et al.* (1986) and Hall and Henry (1988)). This approach recognises that we are uncertain as to which of a range of models may truly represent the real world and so optimisation is carried out subject to a range of models weighted together. This approach is useful when we are faced with a small range of discrete alternatives but is not a practicable way of dealing with general uncertainty. It does not, for example, allow for the stochastic terms in a single non-linear model.

An alternative would be to optimise the parameters across a wide range of shocks. Hall and Stephenson (1989) calculate optimal control solutions for non-linear models in a stochastic framework. They demonstrate that the non-linearities in a model are an important source of divergence between the deterministic optimal trajectory and the expected value of that trajectory. This is clearly going to be an important aspect of inflation control where we typically think of it being much harder to secure reductions in inflation at low levels (of inflation) and where the costs of falling prices may be substantial.

Optimising the expected value of the objective function enables use to tackle uncertainty over the model structure. However, this does not allow the optimal policy to be weighted towards a less risky calculation. Rustem (1993) outlines an algorithm that allows the calculation of robust optimal policies, i.e. policies that penalise the uncertainty of the final outcome so that more certain outcomes are favoured. This algorithm does not, however, make allowance for the effect of non-linearity on the stochastic nature of the model. This, and the earlier Hall and Stephenson work are brought together in Becker, Hall and Rustem (1994), who analyse robust optimal control rules on the National Institute model. They show that the robust decision performs better than the simple deterministic decision and that increased robustness makes the policy more risk averse, as one would expect. Such a conclusion obviously also stresses the importance of non-linearities in the model. This essentially is another reason for wanting to act early on interest rates.

There are therefore techniques that we could use to look for robust policy rules, i.e. rules that perform tolerably well to a variety of different shocks, and to uncertainty about the structure of the economy. This does not mean that we should expect it to be possible to design policies that are robust across entirely different models, or assumptions about the economy. At the end of the day the policy prescriptions of a monetarist are likely to be very different to the views of a Keynesian. Equally, it seems unlikely that a rule derived under rational expectations will prove robust to an alternative expectations hypothesis. But this is not as nihilistic a conclusion as it seems. Empirical testing should at the very least be able to distinguish between these sorts of polar cases. What is required is for the authorities to adopt some reasonable model of an economy and devote suitable resources to such a project. In so far as there are still uncertainties surrounding any model of the economy, techniques are available to construct rules that allow for this.

Fully optimal rules therefore are always likely to be a complex, rather technocratic means of conducting economic policy. This seems somewhat at odds with the concept of rules that are simple and easy to interpret. In a different vein, it is often argued that more simple rules that abstract from the fully optimal solution are in fact robust to uncertainty because they focus on very specific dynamic questions; for example, in this instance, the determination of inflation. It is to the analysis of this claim that we now turn.

9.3 SIMPLE FEEDBACK RULES

The weakness of the fully optimal solution tends to come from its dependence on the full state vector. An alternative would therefore be to design rules that exploit only the information that we believe to be useful and to de-emphasise the less reliable elements of the model's structure. Thus simple feedback rules are generally a restricted form of the full optimal control solution which limit the amount of information drawn from the structure of the model to those areas that are of special relevance to the policy question at hand (see, for example, Vines, Maciejowski and Meade (1983), Currie and Levine (1985), Taylor (1985) and Edison, Miller and Williamson (1988)). By implicitly excluding much of the model, simple rules are supposedly robust to uncertainty. Furthermore, if articulated publicly, they meet Kydland and Prescott's criteria of being simple and easy to interpret, and therefore useful when it comes to monitoring the authorities.

Simple feedback rules were developed in the engineering literature and later applied to economic systems. Phillips (1954, 1957) discusses the relative merits of proportional, integral, and derivative control. Proportional control, for example, is where interest rates are set in proportion to how far inflation is above the government's target, i.e.

$$i_t = \beta_2(\Pi_t - \Pi_t^{\text{base}}) \qquad \ldots (8)$$

where i is the nominal short-term interest rate and Π is the rate of inflation.

Blake and Westaway (1994) point out that a proportional rule with respect to inflation will leave the price level indeterminate and hence will not adequately close a macro model. In the language of the 1950s, this is because a 'complete error correction is not obtained' with such a rule 'since the correcting action continues only because the error exists' (Phillips (1954, p. 298)). Figure 9.1 shows the percentage differences from base, for inflation and interest rates when the LBS model (described in Allen, Hall and Nixon (1994)) is perturbed with interest rates determined by a proportionate rule of this sort. We see that this rule fails to stabilise inflation, even after 25 years. Once inflation begins to come down, so do interest rates, thus easing pressure on prices. The simultaneous movement of interest rates and inflation in this type of rule means that, rather like a cat chasing its tail, inflation can never be entirely squeezed out.

Integral control, on the other hand is where the policy instrument is adjusted in some proportion to the *sum* of the targets differences from its base or desired values:

$$i_t = \beta_3 \sum_{t=0}^{n} \Pi_t - \Pi_t^{\text{base}} \qquad \ldots (9)$$

Taking first differences this is equivalent to

$$\Delta i = \beta_3(\Pi_t - \Pi_t^{\text{base}}) \qquad \ldots (10)$$

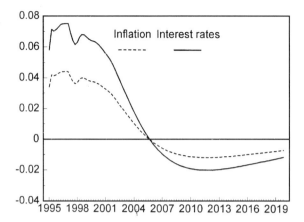

Figure 9.1 Proportional control in response to an inflationary shock

where the change in interest rates is given by the difference of inflation from base each period. This is equivalent to proportional control of the price level.

Technically, an integral control rule may be sufficient to ensure model closure. But this is true of only a limited class of models. Blake and Westaway (1994), for example, argue that an integral control rule is a sufficient condition for model closure and does stabilise inflation on the model at the National Institute of Economic and Social Research (NIESR). But this result seems to be conditional on their assumption of rational expectations. The LBS model uses a learning algorithm for expectations (see Hall and Garratt (1992a,b)) which is still forward looking and avoids systematic errors but does not require the extreme informational assumptions of rational expectations. This model is not stabilised by integral control.

The effect of integral control on the LBS model is shown in Figure 9.2. This rule is unstable, with large, explosive oscillations building up. An extensive grid search has shown that there is no value of β_3 that stabilises inflation on the LBS model. Thus integral control has the potential to induce large cyclical fluctuations depending on the correction lag in the system. This is because interest rates rise all the time inflation is above base, and will themselves be at their peak once inflation is back to base. This causes inflation to overshoot. In this particular case, using an annual definition of inflation and since inflation is a lagging indicator anyway, the correction lag is large enough to rule out any stable integral rule. What is interesting, as Phillips pointed out, is that if, for example, the authorities continuously strengthen their 'corrective action' the longer inflation remains above target, then they would be applying integral control.

In common with much of the previous research conducted in this area,[5] we find that both proportional and integral control are required to target inflation and adequately close the monetary side of the model. Finally, the performance

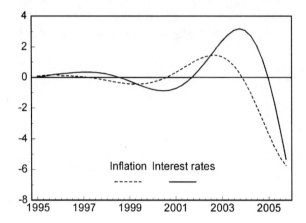

Figure 9.2 Integral control in response to an inflationary shock

of the final rule can be further enhanced by the inclusion of derivative control, where interest rates are set according to the rate at which inflation is accelerating. This gives

$$i_t = \beta_1(\Delta\Pi_t - \Delta\Pi_t^{base}) \qquad \dots (11)$$

In some sense this gives the rule an element of forward lookingness because once inflation begins to decelerate, the derivative part of the rule begins to prompt an early reduction in interest rates. Combining equations (8), (10) and (11) gives us the full closed loop feedback rule that includes elements of proportional, integral and derivative control:

$$\Delta i = \beta_1\Delta^2\pi + \beta_2\Delta\pi + \beta_3(\pi - \pi_{base}) \qquad \dots (12)$$

where i is the nominal interest rate and π is the annual rate of inflation.

The β coefficients can then be determined optimally to minimise any given objective function. For example, the deviation of inflation from a particular target is an obvious choice for the objective function but we might also wish to penalise sharp movements in the instrument or changes in inflation, to reduce instability. Figure 9.3 therefore shows the deviations of inflation from base following an inflationary shock when a feedback rule of this type, containing elements of proportional, derivative and integral control. Two simulations are shown, both have the same form as the rule above but in one case lagged inflation is targeted, while in the other current dated inflation is used. The parameters of both rules are chosen optimally to minimise deviations in inflation from base, and weighted changes in inflation, to try to reduce the cyclical response.

Both rules achieve the objective of controlling inflation but the rule that exploits the information in the model by using current dated information performs much better. Using only lagged information, inflation rises and then oscillates

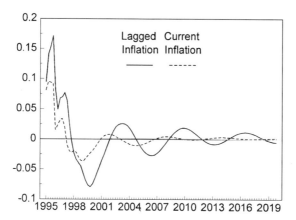

Figure 9.3

strongly and really only stabilises after about 15 years. Using current dated inflation based on the models forecast allows a much more stable rule: inflation
initially rises by only half as much and is easily fully stabilised within five years.

This provides a useful insight into the operation of inflation-targeting regimes.
There are clearly benefits from changing interest rates sooner rather than later.
Delaying an interest rate rise merely allows the inflationary pressure to build up
further, which means that the eventual policy response has to be larger and is
likely to induce strong cycles into the economy. The logical extension of this
is to try to target future, expected inflation. There is now a growing body of
literature that suggests that this is how inflation-targeting regimes are operated
in practice (see, for example, Leiderman and Svensson (1995)).

The issue of forecasting inflation is the subject of the final section, but from a
modelling point of view we can borrow from the rational expectations literature
and set up an interest rate rule of the following form:

$$i = \alpha i_{t-1} + (1 - \alpha)i_{t+1} + \beta_1 \Delta^2 \pi + \beta_2 \Delta \pi + \beta_3 (\pi - \pi_{\text{base}}) \qquad \dots (13)$$

If $\alpha = 0$, then repeated substituting for the future level of interest rates i_{t+1}, will
yield an equation for interest rates in period t that is essentially the sum of all
future deviations of inflation from target:

$$i_t = \sum_{t=1}^{\infty} \theta_i (\pi - \pi_{\text{base}})_{t+i} \qquad \dots (14)$$

where the parameter θ will be some combination of the $\beta_i's$. The parameter α
will act to weight future inflation as a geometric progression. If $\alpha = 1$, then the
rule collapses to the backward-looking equation (12). If α is less than one but
towards one, say 0.75 for example, then interest rates will be set on the basis of a

weighted sum of future deviations of inflation from target, where the immediate future is given more weight. This decreases until $\alpha = 0$, at which point all future deviations of inflation up to infinity are given equal weight. Thus for $1 > \alpha > 0$ the rule will take the form

$$i_t = \sum_{t=1}^{\infty}(1 - \alpha)^i \theta_i (\pi - \pi_{\text{base}})_{t+i} + \alpha i_{t-1} \qquad \ldots (15)$$

α therefore is a weight in a geometric progression.

We can solve our macro-model using this 'forward-looking' rule to target future inflation. Figures 9.4 and 9.5 therefore compare the operation of the previous current period inflation target with the forward-looking rule. This time α and β are optimised against the same objective function as before. The initial hike in interest rates is larger than before but this pre-emptive move is much more effective in preventing inflation from building up and eliminates the tendency for the model to cycle.[6] The forward looking rule is therefore preferred.

We are therefore able to model the current policy regime fairly accurately by using simple feedback rules. Indeed, this is now widespread practice on many of the macro models in the United Kingdom (see Church *et al.* (1995)). Might simple feedback rules therefore be used in the real world? The key question therefore is: How might they perform in practice, given that we are uncertain as to the true structure of the economy and about the nature of shocks? In particular, is it possible to design a rule that is robust to these types of uncertainty?

The simple feedback rules discussed here are not generally optimal rules (although their parameters may sometimes be chosen using an optimal control technique). This means that the use of a simple rule must inevitably lead to a loss of economic performance. The claim of robustness, which is often made, has no strong theoretical foundation. What is needed to actually implement these

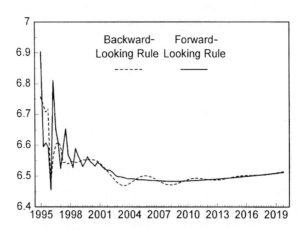

Figure 9.4   Interest rates under the two rules

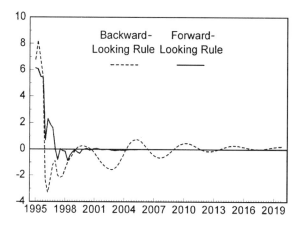

Figure 9.5 Deviations of inflation from target under two different rules

rules as real monetary policies is that they perform tolerably well whatever the shock that hits the economy and whatever we think the structure of the economy might be.

Unfortunately, much of the empirical evidence points in the opposite direction. This is borne out by our own experience on the LBS model. Typically, to target inflation we have to reoptimise the parameters of our feedback rule depending on what shock we are analysing. For example, Currie and Levine (1985) compare simple feedback rules against a variety of shocks in a small semi-empirical model of the United Kingdom. They find that the performance of the rules varies considerably depending on whether the shock is a monetary shock, to the exchange rate for example, or a real shock. Gawthrop and Vines (1989) explicitly set out to investigate whether a simple feedback rule performs better than an optimal rule when implemented on different models to which they were designed. They show that the simple rule is not 'in general more robust than the optimal rule'.

We would argue that the forward-looking 'feedward' rules shown here may be able to overcome this lack of robustness in simple rules. What really makes simple rules unsatisfactory is their inability to respond to information about where the shock may be coming from. The authorities' response may need to be different depending on whether inflation is generated because of excess aggregate demand or a one-off exchange rate shock. These sort of factors could, however, be taken into account when constructing a forecast of future inflation. Forward-looking rules should therefore be much more robust.

A number of observations therefore come out of our analysis at this stage. While we do not know what objective function most closely mimics the authorities' behaviour, we have a fair idea that large jumps in interest rates are to be avoided. In these simulations we have used an objective function that minimises deviations of inflation from target and also penalises large movements in interest rates. Thus the rules we have described here give a broad feel for how interest rates might be raised in response to an inflationary shock. Moreover, we are able to characterise how high interest rates might have to go depending on the severity of the shock and the swiftness of the authorities' response.

In particular we show that there are clear advantages to responding early and to targeting future expected inflation. This is likely to minimise the oscillations set up in the economy and to reduce the size of the overall policy response. Delaying an interest rate rise simply means that interest rates have to be pushed up further later and the eventual loss in output is greater. Indeed, this point is recognised explicitly by the Bank of England in the United Kingdom. The Bank produces a quarterly 'inflation projection' which it defines as an intermediate target offering advance warning of 'inflationary pressures, which then serve as a guidepost for monetary policy decisions' (Haldane (1995, p. 250)).

We would argue that one of the main weaknesses (of many) of this regime is that it places too much weight on the discretionary interpretation of a wide range of indicators in formulating a forecast of inflation. Without an explicit model of the inflation process, the temptation must always be there to take risks with inflation in the light of conflicting signals from a number of indicators. A possible way out of this would be to formulate an explicit composite indicator to forecast inflation and to publish quantified judgemental over-rides. The main problem with indicators is that their relationship with the economy usually changes over time, which, for example, is the main objection to using a specific indicator like the money supply to forecast inflation. This could be overcome by the use of a more sophisticated system as suggested by Garratt and Hall (1993) or Stock and Watson (1989, 1991). This would have the advantage of monitoring a wide range of indicators of inflation in a systematic way. This could readily be published and used to inform public debate about the appropriate tightness of the monetary stance. While it would not be 'tying the authorities' hands', it would certainly be nailing their feet to the ground.

It is important to realise the generality of this sort of framework. If, for example, one is an ardent monetarist, who argues that governments should target the money supply in order to control inflation, then the reason for doing so is that the money supply is a good predictor of inflation. Thus, if your model was that the money supply caused inflation, targeting future inflation, predicted on the basis of today's observed money supply figures, would be identically equivalent to targeting the money supply itself.[7] It really comes down to what model one uses to generate forecasts of inflation. Nominal GDP targets are frequently advocated as a preferred alternative to inflation targets (see, for example, McCallum (1988)). Nominal GDP targets work better than current-period inflation targets because inflation is a lagging indicator of the economy. GDP targets, on the other hand, contain information on the real economy, which acts as a partial indicator of inflation. However, both nominal GDP targets and monetary targets are both encompassed by a regime that targets *future* expected inflation.

9.4 CONCLUSION: BUILDING A STRENGTHENED MONETARY REGIME

Increasingly, in Western economies there is a trend towards using short-term interest rates to target a preannounced level of inflation; New Zealand, Canada and the United Kingdom have all announced specific targets for inflation. Despite the success of the central banks in those countries in attaining their inflation goals in the short term, Ammer and Freeman (1994) note that long-term bond yields suggest that inflation expectations for these countries persistently tend to exceed the stated targets. Inflation targeting regimes therefore seem to lack credibility. We believe this has much to do with the fact that monetary policy is operated in such regimes with large amounts of discretion over the both the interpretation of a range of economic indicators and the size of actual interest rate movements that are required to achieve a stated target. In this chapter we have considered whether optimal control theory might enable us to model this type of inflation targeting regime empirically and also whether control rules might be of practical use in the real economy. An implication being that if a specific rule could be announced and followed, this would significantly improve the credibility of such regimes.

In particular, we have made the distinction between optimal control rules that draw on the full information set and more limited simple rules. Optimal rules tend to be very complicated and would almost certainly have to be operated in an open loop manner because of the non-linearity of the economy. However, their main drawback is that such rules typically tend to be model specific. Policy recommendations in which we have little faith should obviously be avoided. Simple rules, on the other hand, have the attraction of being easy to understand and therefore easy to communicate both to the policy-makers and to the private sector. They are therefore easy to monitor. We doubt, however, the claim that these rules are robust to large degrees of uncertainty. Put another way, we find that such rules indicate that the authorities' response to a shock typically has to be shock specific, which is clearly an argument for discretion. Finally, where such regimes are implemented we show that it is advantageous to target expected inflation in the future. Our analysis therefore led us to a number of conclusions as to how these type of regimes might be strengthened and hence their credibility enhanced.

First, we would advocate the use of an explicit indicator for forecasting inflation. This removes one source of the authorities' discretion and could be combined with a simple feedback rule that states how interest rates would change. This would remove the second source of the authorities' discretion and would effectively combine the best features of fully optimal control and simple rules. This is because a suitably constructed indicator would focus on the information that was relevant for inflation. Much of the intrinsic complexity of the optimal control solution could therefore be shifted into the indicator. Interest rates could therefore be set by a simpler rule that was easy to monitor.

Optimal control has often been rejected in the past because of the difficulty in handling uncertainty. We have argued that techniques do exist for the construction of control rules that are robust to various levels of uncertainty, both about the nature of the economy and the nature of shocks that may hit the economy. However, for such techniques to work we need to come to some agreement as to the true nature of the economy. Some degree of discretionary override is always going to be required in practice. This is not to say that inflation regimes in general could not be significantly strengthened by greater openness, both in the forecasting of inflation and in the setting of interest rates in response to that forecast.

9.5 ENDNOTES

1. During the 1990s a number of countries have adopted a monetary framework centred on explicit inflation targets. Such a framework was first adopted in New Zealand in 1990, under the Policy Targets Agreement. This followed the 1989 Reserve Bank of New Zealand Act, which established a statutory commitment to price stability. Canada followed in February 1991 by introducing inflation reduction targets. Since then inflation targets have been adopted in Israel in December 1991, in the United Kingdom in October 1992, in Sweden and Finland in the early part of 1993, in Mexico in September 1994 and in Spain in November of the same year. Australia has also moved to an explicit target gradually over time, while it is clear that a number of countries, most notably the United States, Germany and France, conduct monetary policy along very similar lines without explicitly stating their inflation objective in public.
2. Haldane (1995) describes how 'the central bank's model-based extrapolation provides the starting point' for its inflation projection (p. 253).
3. The chapter concentrates on formulating rules for monetary policy but fiscal policy also needs to be considered for full model closure. At the moment this tends to be modelled separately, although using the same technology (see, for example, Smith and Wallis (1994)). But it is not clear how this ties in with monetary policy. Government borrowing is likely to increase in a recession. Implementing a rule that raises taxes when the PSBR increases would tend to exacerbate the downturn; this would clearly work in the opposite direction to any monetary rule that was targeting inflation.
4. Although perhaps not so costly — most of the finance houses in the city, for example, already have more than adequately qualified personnel. All that would be needed is the model.
5. A by no means exhaustive list, covering a representative sample of the work on large-scale macroeconomic models in the United Kingdom, would include Westaway (1986), Hall and Henry (1988), Budd et al. (1989) and Weale et al. (1989).
6. The erratic dynamic path taken by interest rates reflects the dynamic properties of our model. This illustrates one of the points we make above, in that any optimisation exercise carried out on a macro model will seek to exploit full dynamic behaviour and particular specification of the model. This is not therefore a property we would expect to see reflected in the real world.
7. This point seems lost on some commentators who condemn the current regime because it depends on forecasts but postulate using the money supply because it does not (see, for example, Wood (1994)).

—— 10 ——
The Stability of Expectational Equilibria in the LBS Model

ANTHONY GARRATT AND STEPHEN HALL

10.1 INTRODUCTION

The standard way of closing a macroeconomic model in which variables depend in part on the values of expected future variables, is to assume rational expectations (RE). However, the use of the RE assumption has increasingly been criticised as presupposing too much information and sophistication on the part of agents. In response to this criticism a less stringent approach has been suggested, which involves adopting an alternative expectations mechanism in the form of adaptive learning rules. Expectations rules, or the perceived laws of motion of future variables, are conditioned on current and past information as with RE, but the relationship between the expectations variable and the information set evolves recursively as a result of expectation errors that are incorporated into statistical or econometric procedures that update coefficients. In adopting this approach we have moved to a class of models which, whilst not containing full information, are able to adapt and in effect to 'learn' about the economic environment. We can define this alternative as weak rationality, which retains the attractive feature of avoiding systematic errors on the part of agents, whilst representing a small generalisation of the usual notion of weak rationality (e.g. Feige and Pearce (1976)) in which agents are assumed to use only a univariate model to form their expectations.

Sargent (1993) interprets the introduction of adaptive learning or boundedly rational expectations into economic models as a redressing of the balance between agents of the model who previously have had full information and

Macroeconomic Modelling in a Changing World. Edited by C. Allen and S. Hall
© 1997 John Wiley & Sons Ltd

econometricians who face estimation and inference problems that agents in the model have somehow solved. By excluding rational behaviour, agents are now more like the econometricians who estimate and adapt as they learn about probability distributions which, under RE, they are assumed to already know.

A range of issues arise when adaptive learning rules are used for expectations formation. For example, how can RE be attained if, as with adaptive learning, they do not start with RE? Or, in the case of multiple RE solutions, which one will learning mechanisms choose? The answers to questions of this sort are closely related to issues of expectational or E-stability as defined by Evans (1989) and Evans and Honkapohja (1990, 1992a,b,c, 1994), which relate RE solutions to fixed points of mappings between the actual and perceived law of motions or the expectations rule of the system. Hence sets of conditions exist that allow us to define solutions as E-stable and to make distinctions between weak and strong E-stability (see Section 10.2). An important related issue is the convergence of learning coefficients that change over time. Marcet and Sargent (1989a,b,c) show that results from Ljung (1977), giving the convergence conditions for recursive stochastic algorithms, can be used to determine convergence for a general class of multivariate linear models when learning occurs. However, thus far the learning literature has produced no general answers to these types of questions and the specific model in which adaptive learning operates is a key factor in determining outcomes.

The effect of the introduction of adaptive learning on the dynamics of key model variables is also of interest. The main difference between models that include learning as opposed to RE is to change the jump variables into being variables that change more gradually as agents learn about their environment. The dynamic paths will also differ according to the form of the learning rule adopted. Hence any policy recommendation, in the face of a shock, may well depend on the learning process in operation. E-stability may be achieved in a variety of cases, but the movement of key variables could be significantly different, particularly in the short run. Evans and Honkapohja (1993a,b) document interesting examples where adaptive learning in models that exhibit multiple equilibria can enable a more active role for economic policy in the face of productivity shocks. In these examples endogenous fluctuations occur and the dynamics of the main model variables are significantly altered.

In this chapter we seek to examine some of these issues when we introduce adaptive learning into the large non-linear dynamic macro model of the London Business School (LBS). Expectations are of the future values of endogenous variables, in this case the exchange rate, where the model includes lagged endogenous variables. The emphasis is to quantify the empirical effects of learning on output and inflation, and to investigate the sensitivity of model outcomes under adaptive expectations formation. In this exercise we examine the effects, under an exogenous oil price shock, on the existence of a solution and, where a solution exists, the actual outcomes for inflation and output, both in terms of the dynamic paths and the long-run or end-period values. We address these issues in two cases. The first, described in Section 10.3, looks at the effects of varying the expectations rule or law of motion of the system. This amounts to an examination of the E-stability properties of the LBS macro model. The second, described in Section 10.4, then examines one particular expectations rule and the effect of altering the conditions of the learning algorithm adopted; specifically, we look at a range of hyperparameters. We view this as an examination of the effects of the speed of learning on the properties of the system (for an example of the importance of this type of effect, see Evans and Honkopohja (1993a) where the convergence of the delta parameter to zero or a constant value appears to be an important factor).

In Section 10.2 we provide a general description of how adaptive learning is implemented in a large macroeconometric model. A general model structure is defined and a description of the Kalman Filter stochastic updating algorithm used when agents learn is outlined (Appendix 1 relates this to the Marcet and Sargent (1989a,b) algorithms). Section 10.3 reports the exercise which compares the outcomes from the same simulation when different expectations mechanisms are in operation. Section 10.4 examines the sensitivity of the simulation exercise to different values of the hyperparameters under one specific learning rule. This takes the form of first establishing the range of hyperparameters that allows for a solution and then examining the effects of varying the hyperparameters within the regions of stability. Section 10.5 offers some conclusions.

10.2 EXPECTATIONS, LEARNING AND NON-LINEAR MODELS

Much early empirical work on expectations centred around attempts to provide direct measures of agents' expectations, e.g. Katona (1951, 1958), Tobin (1959) or Eisner (1965), and the thrust of much of this research was towards a psychological understanding of individual expectations formation. Direct measures of expectations were undoubtedly useful in forming economic forecasts. However, this approach was limited by two inherent problems. First, gathering direct measures of expectations was very expensive and the data rapidly became outdated. Secondly, and perhaps even more important, direct measures of expectations gave little insight into how expectations would change as policy changed. Thus, although the importance of expectations to economic policy was stressed by the economic theorists, direct measures of expectations helped little in determining what the correct economic policy should be. The breakthrough that allowed a more general approach to expectations modelling came with the realisation that expectations could be treated as an unobservable component. This implied that expectations could be substituted by their determinants once an explicit rule for expectations formation was assumed. One early example of this treatment was the specification of the adaptive expectations hypothesis by Cagan

(1956) and Nerlove (1958): this was an important departure because it allowed the treatment of expectations to be made explicit for the first time in an empirical setting. Empirical work incorporating expectations was given an important boost by the work on the expectations augmented Phillips curve (Friedman (1968)) and the empirical models that implemented such ideas (Lucas and Rapping (1969)). If we define $(_{t-1}x_t^e)$ as the expectation of the value of x in period t formed in period $t - 1$ then the adaptive expectations hypothesis states that

$$(_{t-1}x_t^e - {}_{t-2}x_{t-1}^e) = \Phi(x_{t-1} - {}_{t-2}x_{t-1}^e), \quad 0 < \Phi < 1 \qquad \ldots (1)$$

That is to say, an individual holds a series of expectations for the variable x and at each point in time the expectation for the future is revised in a proportional way with the most recently observed error. By simply rearranging (1) we obtain:

$$(_{t-1}x_t^e) = \Phi x_{t-1} + (1 - \Phi)_{t-2}x_{t-1}^e \qquad \ldots (2)$$

and of course by successively substituting out for the lagged expectation we obtain:

$$(_{t-1}x_t^e) = \Phi x_{t-1} + \Phi(1 - \Phi)x_{t-2} + \Phi(1 - \Phi)_{t-1}^2 x_{t-3} \ldots \qquad \ldots (3)$$

and so we may model the unobservable expectation purely in terms of past observations of x. This seems intuitively appealing because it says that our expectations of the future are a simple extrapolation of the past. It is, however, easy to construct examples where this rule makes consistent and growing mistakes. Consider the case when x grows at a constant 10% rate. The adaptive expectations model would always underestimate the level of x and it would do so by an increasing absolute amount over time. It is of course possible to generalise the adaptive expectations model to overcome this specific problem by producing an extrapolative rule that would cope with growing variables, or any other specific form of time-series behaviour. There have been many such suggestions for such schemes; for example, Flemming (1976) and Pesaran (1987) define a broad class of expectations mechanisms that make use of past information as extrapolative expectations. But as a general statement all fixed parameter extrapolative rules are liable to perform poorly in one circumstance or another. For example, if a rule is chosen that copes well with the stationary behaviour in x, then that rule will generally not cope if the behaviour in x changes to become non-stationary. Any fixed parameter rule will therefore be likely to perform badly in the face of a change in the regime generating x.

These developments lead quite quickly and naturally to the suggestion of rational expectations (RE). While there had been some early precursors to the proposal of RE (e.g. Grunberg and Modigliani (1954)), Muth (1961) is widely regarded as the founder of this approach. However, RE was not widely adopted for more than a decade after Muth's work was published. Indeed, far from being viewed as a criticism of the adaptive expectations approach, the main perception throughout the 1960s of Muth's work was primarily that it justified adaptive expectations as rational under certain conditions. It was only some 10–15 years later that it began to be appreciated how restrictive these special conditions were and that an alternative empirical approach was needed.

The Lucas critique (Lucas (1976)) was one of the main arguments for implementing full RE. Essentially this emphasised the idea that policy regimes and particular policy rules will affect the reduced-form solution for all the endogenous variables in a model. If agents are rational, even if only in the weak sense that they will not make systematic errors, then agents' expectations rules will change as the policy rule changes. Hence any model that either uses fixed parameter extrapolative rules or, even worse, does not explicitly model expectations at all, will not be structurally stable across regime changes and will not be a suitable vehicle for policy analysis. Muth (1961) introduced the notion of a rational expectation to be 'Essentially the same as the prediction of the relevant economic theory'. In many formal contexts this is taken to mean the conditional expectation of the relevant stochastic system of equations, although Hall (1988) argues that in the case of non-linear systems the mathematical expectation may not always be a good measure of an agent's expectation. In the full, or strong, form of the RE hypothesis it is assumed that the economic agent has complete knowledge of the economic system about which he needs to form expectations. This knowledge includes both the functional form, the parameters of the system and any exogenous process that is entering the system. Under this extreme assumption about the degree of information available to an agent, the optimal expectations formation mechanism becomes the model's own prediction of what will take place. By construction there is always an extrapolative rule that is equivalent to the RE, but the advantage of the RE approach is that it can cope with regime changes and other structural shifts automatically whereas the extrapolative model would have to be continually respecified. The main disadvantage of the RE approach is the extreme assumption required about the information available to the economic agent.

A rapid explosion occurred in theoretical work incorporating RE, and RE became linked very closely with the new-classical approach to macroeconomics. Some main contributions in this area were Walters (1971), Lucas (1972a,b, 1973, 1975), Sargent (1973, 1976), Sargent and Wallace (1973, 1975, 1976), Barro (1976, 1977) and Kydland and Prescott (1977). The perceived connection between classical economics and RE became very strong at this time to the extent that many saw the two approaches as largely synonymous.

RE was soon applied to the large macro models; Fair (1979) is in many ways the natural departure point for our account. This model was the first sizeable model to be solved under model consistent expectations and so it was the first time a modeller had been faced with the new technical problems that this assumption posed. However, the Fair model has been isolated amongst US domestic models as the only one to adopt RE as a regular tool of solution. The main focus of development switched from the United States to the United Kingdom with the publication in 1980 of the first results from the Liverpool model (see Minford *et al.* (1984)). From this point on subsequent developments in solution techniques and the analysis of non linear models with rational expectations happened mainly in the United Kingdom. Holly and Corker (1984) reported on the introduction of model-consistent expectations into the exchange rate and financial sector of the London Business School model. Hall and Henry (1985, 1986) reported on the introduction of RE into both the exchange rate sector and the real side of the National Institute model. Westaway and Whittaker (1986) discussed the introduction of RE into H.M. Treasury's model. The late 1980s saw the spread of RE more widely: Murphy (1989) introduced expectations effects into an Australian model and Lahti and Viren (1989) report on the introduction of RE into a model of the Finnish economy. Masson *et al.* (1988) discussed the first introduction of RE into an international model, the IMF MULTIMOD, and Gurney (1990) introduced RE into the global econometric model (GEM). A large amount of work then began in order to understand fully the implications of these changes for the models; surveys of some of this work may be found in Fair (1984), Hall and Henry (1988), Fisher *et al.* (1988, 1989) and Fisher (1990).

An alternative approach to making this extreme assumption would be to assume that agents' expectations are on average correct but not make any specific assumption about how agents arrive at these expectations: we define this as weak rationality. The notion that agents do not make consistent predictable mistakes is an appealing one but, as noted above, it is not a property that any fixed parameter expectations rule will generally have. We must therefore move to a class of models which, while not containing full information, are able to adapt to regime changes and in effect to 'learn' about the economic environment.

The issue of learning is important in the context of the RE assumption where, in particular, the question of how agents come to know the true model is simply not addressed. As a consequence, learning has received increasing attention in the theoretical literature over the last decade. Learning can be modelled on the basis of a number of assumptions about the underlying knowledge that agents possess. The earlier theoretical literature that used rational learning models is the most demanding in terms of informational requirements, for example Friedman (1975), Townsend (1978, 1983), Bray (1983), Bray and Kreps (1984) or Frydman (1982). The assumption made in this literature is that agents know the true structure of the model but that some of the parameters of the system are unknown. Because the true structural equations are known, the agents' learning problem is essentially one of estimating the parameters of the system. As long as a consistent estimation procedure is used we would expect the system to converge to a full rational expectations equilibrium (REE), and indeed most of the theoretical investigation of small analytical models have shown this to be the case. However, rational learning models still make very stringent assumptions about the degree of knowledge that agents have of the structure of the system. Agents are still assumed to process all available information in an optimal fashion and the degree of sophistication on the part of economic agents is still considerable. The only departure from the strong form of RE is that agents are not assumed to have full information and so they are likely to make mistakes in the short run although they may well not make systematic errors over an extended period and hence the learning model may fulfil the criteria for weak RE.

A slightly weaker informational assumption gives rise to the boundedly rational learning models. Here the general assumption is that agents use some 'reasonable' rule of learning to form expectations and that the form of the rule remains constant over time. In fact choosing a rule that all agents regard as reasonable is rather difficult and almost always the choice has been the reduced form of the whole system. See, for example, DeCanio (1979), Radner (1982), and Bray and Savin (1986). Thus it is assumed that agents know the reduced form of the whole system as it would exist under RE but again do not know some or all of the parameters. The move to bounded rationality in this form may seem to be a rather small one and yet it has important consequences for the behaviour of the system. The reason for this is that even in the absence of regime changes the reduced form of the model is a combination of the stable structural equations and the changing parameters of the expectations rule, so that it is time-varying. The boundedly rational agent is usually assumed to be attempting to parameterise a stable reduced-form system and so is actually trying to estimate a misspecified model. Under this assumption Bray and Savin (1986) are able to show that, for a simple cobweb model, the model sometimes converges to the RE equilibrium and sometimes cycles or diverges from the RE equilibrium.

When we consider more realistic models, and in particular when we allow for the Lucas critique, a further important complication is that the behavioural equations may themselves be undergoing structural changes. So even if the learning process is able to converge on the true model it may be, in effect, chasing a moving target and so it may not converge to a stable set of parameters.

The behaviour of the parameters in the learning rule gives an important insight into the form of equilibria which may emerge from the system. Evans (1989) and Evans and Honkapohja (1990, 1992a,b,c, 1994) introduce the concept of E-stability, defining a set of conditions for stability across a range of linear and non-linear models which include the adaptive learning rule. Marcet and Sargent (1988) summarise the main results. The concept of learning is characterised as a mapping of the parameters of the agents' expectations rule. A fixed point of that mapping is then a situation where the parameters of the expectations rule cease changing. So, suppose an agent has a rule which is a linear function of a set of parameters D and the learning process (assumed to be some form of least squares learning) is represented by a mapping S, such that $D_{t+1} = S(D_t)$, so that the learning process produces a sequence of parameters of the expectations rule. Hence the concept of E-stability is defined in terms of the mapping S of the perceived law of motion (the expectations rules) to the actual laws of motion, where a solution is said to be E-stable if the differential equation above is locally asymptotically stable. A fixed point of the mapping is represented by convergence of this sequence to some fixed value; this point is sometimes referred to as an expectations equilibrium or an E-equilibrium. Marcet and Sargent (1989a) demonstrate that this fixed point is also a full rational expectations equilibrium. Furthermore, Evans (1983, 1985, 1986), Woodford (1990) and Marcet and Sargent (1989a,b) demonstrate that the least squares learning procedure actually rules out many of the undesirable rational equilibria which can arise in conventional rational expectations equilibria. When a fixed point of the mapping is found, then we not only have an RE solution but we also have one that is not dependent on an arbitrary terminal condition.

E-stability conditions can resolve or at least aid the problem of choosing a solution where a multiplicity of solutions exist (see Evans (1986)). For example, in the case where two solutions exist it may be possible to classify one as not satisfying the criteria for E-stability thereby identifying the other solution as the form to be adopted. The degree to which the use of adaptive learning schemes aids the choice of an appropriate equilibrium, where multiple equilibria are possible, depends on the form of the learning scheme adopted. It may be the case that all solutions satisfy E-stability criteria and therefore the choice is not narrowed. In addition, Evans (1989) and Evans and Honkapohja (1990, 1992a,b,c, 1994) make a distinction between weak and strong E-stability. For example, take the case where the solution to a structural model, which has multiple equilibria, is classified as having an AR(1) representation. For the case where the perceived law of motion is an AR(1) process this may imply that one of, say, two possible solutions is unstable thereby aiding selection. If this result can be shown to hold where the perceived law of motion is overparameterised (e.g. an AR(4) or more general ARIMA model where E-stability still holds), then the solution is said to be strongly E-stable. Hence a variation on the perceived law of motion around an AR(1) still enables the learning model to converge to an E-stable solution. We return to this distinction in Section 10.3.

10.2.1 Model Consistent Learning

Below we outline the framework adopted in this work which involves the combination of a large non-linear macro model and adaptive learning. Let a non-linear macro model which incorporates expectations be described by the following set of n structural equations:

$$Y_{it} = F_i(Y, X, Y^e_{t,t+1}), \quad i = 1, \ldots, n, t = 1, \ldots, T \qquad \ldots (4)$$

where Y is a vector of current and lagged values of the n endogenous variables, X is a vector of exogenous variables over all time periods and $Y^e_{t,t+1}$ is the expectation based on information available at time t of Y in period $t + 1$;[1] Y_{it} represents the specific endogenous variable that appears only in lagged form on the right-hand side of the equations.

In our application we assume that agents, at time t, have the perceived law of motion or expectations rule of the following form:

$$Y^e_{t,t+1} = D_t Z + e_{1t}, \quad \text{where } e_{1t} \text{ is } \sim N(0, W) \qquad \ldots (5)$$

which they use to form the current period's expectations of next period's value of Y, or by leading the equation and then forming expectations with a longer lead time. The vector Z is the information set which can consist of a subset of the matrices Y and X over all current and lagged time periods and D is a time-varying matrix of parameters which agents possess, which evolves according to following process:

$$D_t = D_{t-1} + e_{2t}, \quad \text{where } e_{2t} \text{ is } \sim N(0, Q) \qquad \ldots (6)$$

The change in the learning parameters is therefore determined by the value of the Q matrix, the hyperparameters of the state equation, where the coefficient on the lagged D term is always set equal to one. Having specified the mechanism that governs the evolution of these parameters through time it is possible to make the whole learning apparatus operational.

10.2.2 Method of Updating

In adaptive learning schemes we assume that agents utilise a standard statistical or econometric procedure for estimating the expectations rule or the perceived law of motion of the system. The assumption is that some element of the rule is not known with certainty. This element of uncertainty is usually taken to be the parameters of the rule and the basic idea is that through time the economic agent will use the specified statistical method to increase his knowledge about the true value of these parameters.[2] The forecasts needed in decision-making are then computed from the estimated law of motion. Agents are therefore boundedly rational in that the economic agents use models that are misspecified while they are learning, i.e. outside the rational expectations equilibrium.

The statistical framework we adopt in this application for the updating of the learning parameters is the Kalman Filter. Equation (5), the perceived law of motion, is the measurement equation and equation (6) is an AR(1) representation of the states of the system. The W and Q matrices are the hyperparameters of the system. Below, in equations (7)–(10), we define the recursive stochastic algorithm that determines the change in the learning parameters. The updating of the parameters is governed by the combination of the prediction and updating equations, which can be shown to be of the same form as those in Marcet and Sargent (1989a,b) (see Appendix 1) and therefore their theorem regarding convergence can be applied.

Prediction equations:[3]

$$\hat{D}_{t/t-1} = \hat{D}_{t-1} \qquad \ldots (7)$$

$$P_{t/t-1} = P_{t-1} + Q \qquad \qquad \ldots (8)$$

Updating equations:

$$\hat{D}_t = \hat{D}_{t/t-1} + P_{t/t-1}Z_t(Y_t - Z'_t\hat{D}_{t/t-1})/(Z'_tP_{t/t-1}Z_t + W) \qquad \ldots (9)$$

$$P_t = P_{t/t-1} - P_{t/t-1}Z_tZ'_tP_{t/t-1}/(Z'_tP_{t/t-1}Z_t + W) \qquad \ldots (10)$$

The solution sequence combines the learning algorithm described in equations (7)–(10) above with equations (4)–(6) in the following way. Assuming that we know D_{t-1} we can solve equation (6) for the expected value of D_t, which is simply the Kalman Filter prediction equations for D, equation (7). Given D_t we can solve equation (5) for the expected value of $Y^e_{t,t+1}$, and therefore we can solve equation (4) for Y_t. The matrix Q (the covariance matrix of the errors in the equations governing the evolution of the parameters, or in Kalman Filter terms the state equation error terms) used in the prediction equation (8) is computed when estimating the expectations rule by time-varying parameter methods. The same estimation also provides us with the starting value for the matrix P_{t-1} (the uncertainty of the parameters or state variables). We can therefore use the Kalman Filter prediction equation for P to derive an estimate of $P_{t/t-1}$. Having solved the complete model, equation (4), for Y_t we can then define $V_t = Z'_tD_{t/t-1} - Y_t = Y^e_t - Y_t$, i.e. the error that occurs between the expectation of the vector Y_t derived from the learning model and the model's final solution for Y_t. We then use the Kalman Filter updating equations, equations (9) and (10), to derive revised estimates of P_t and D_t. Hence the updating evolves according to the observed errors between the whole model's solution and the original expectations model forecast. The process can then be repeated for the next period, starting from the new updated estimates of D_t to predict D_{t+1}, and so on. In this way the learning model will adjust its own parameters to cope with any change in structure or regime of the whole model.[4]

This approach to the treatment of expectations has been adopted as the main modelling technique for expectations in the LBS model of the UK economy (Hall and Garratt (1992a,b, 1995)). The most important aspect of this is the exchange rate sector of the model. Hall (1987) derives an equation for the log of the real exchange rate which has the following general form:

$$E_t = \alpha_0 + \alpha_1 E^e_{t+1} + \alpha_2 E_{t-1} + \alpha_3 r_t + \alpha_4 r_{t-1} + \alpha_5 T_t + \alpha_6 T_{t-1} \qquad \ldots (11)$$

where E_t is the log of the real sterling/deutschmark exchange rate, r_t is the real interest rate differential between UK short-term rates and German short rates (both proxied here using the *ex post* definition for the three-month bank base rate for the United Kingdom and a 60-day interbank deposit rate for Germany) and T is the log of the ratio of exports to imports which is a measure of the real trade balance. This can be thought of as a proxy for a risk premium term reflecting imperfect substitutability between domestic and foreign assets. This equation may be derived in several ways which will not be repeated here. Hall (1987) uses a capital stock model with government intervention. Currie and Hall (1989) use a model that characterises capital markets as exhibiting both stock and flow elements in equilibrium. It is worth noting that Fisher *et al.* (1991) in an encompassing exercise of a range of exchange rate models found a preferred model which is clearly nested within this framework. At a pragmatic level it may also be thought of as a general encompassing model of a wide range of models; for example, if $\alpha_0 = \alpha_2 = \alpha_4 = \alpha_5 = \alpha_6 = 0$ and $\alpha_3 = \alpha_1 = 1$, then the model reduces to the open arbitrage model.

The estimation was carried out over the period 1973Q1–1989Q3. The term in the expected exchange rate was estimated using the Wickens (1982) errors-in-variables technique. The Wickens technique is an application of the rational expectations hypothesis which allows us to use actual lead data as a measure of expected future variables. The out-turns are then taken to be an estimate of expectations, where the data are subject to a white noise measurement error. The model is estimated by a system estimation technique (either three-stage least squares (3SLS) or full information maximum likelihood (FIML)), where an equation is specified for each of the expectations terms. These equations are generally an unrestricted reduced form of the model. Specifying these reduced-form equations for expectations corrects for the bias produced by the measurement error and the Wickens estimates are shown to be consistent. Because the expectations equations do not exploit the structure of the model this technique will not generally be fully efficient.

The equation reported below represents the outcome of the specification search and is a restricted form of the general equation. We do not report the expected exchange rate equation because this equation, within the Wickens framework, has no structural significance. The interest differential equation is an attempt to avoid problems of endogeneity and therefore simultaneous equation bias, highlighted by Hacche and Townsend (1981). This takes the form of two lagged dependent variables and the exchange rate. The stationarity properties of the variables to be used in the estimation exercise were checked but are not reported here to save space. The preferred structural exchange rate equation takes the following form:

$$E_t = \underset{(0.34)}{0.0329} + \underset{(3.42)}{0.675E_{t+1}^e} + \underset{(1.55)}{0.299E_{t-1}} + \underset{(0.57)}{0.352r_t} \qquad \dots (12)$$

Estimation: 3SLS, 1973Q1–1989Q3

S.E. $= 0.03265$, $R^2 = 0.93$, DW $= 2.44$

Box–Pierce, $(1) = 3.81$, $(2) = 4.78$, $(4) = 5.07$, $(8) = 8.59$.

('t'-statistics in parentheses)

The trade balance terms were almost always insignificant or, if significant, incorrectly signed, where both the UK and the German trade balance or current balance to GDP ratios were used. The interest rate term is correctly signed; the coefficients on the forward and backward exchange rate terms sum to one, with the emphasis on the forward term. In the long run the above equation is exactly equal to the uncovered interest parity (UIP) condition. In the learning exercise we imposed the following restrictions:

$$E_t = 0.7E_{t+1}^e + 0.3E_{t-1} + r_t \qquad \ldots (13)$$

The joint quasi-likelihood test of this restriction accepts the null, $\chi^2(3) = 7.5$ (critical value = 7.8). In the restricted form of the estimated equation, the first-order moving average process, which is apparent in the unrestricted equation errors, now becomes insignificant.

The equation we use to form our expectation rule has the following formulation:

$$E_{t+1}^e = \gamma_{0t} + \gamma_{1t}E_{t-1} + \gamma_{2t}r_{t-1} + \gamma_{3t}INF_{t-1}^{uk} + \gamma_{4t}T_{t-1}^{uk} + \gamma_{5t}PO_{t-1} \qquad \ldots (14)$$

where INF is the annual rate of producer price inflation and PO is the price of north sea oil.

We would justify it on the grounds that it contains the main factors that influence the structural determination of the exchange rate and so it is a reasonably restricted information set. Note that all information is dated $t - 1$ when this equation is used to forecast E_{t+1}, i.e. the information set does not include current information. We adopt this assumption partly to be conservative, the availability of current dated information is always open to question, and because the implication of using information which includes the current exchange rate term in an exercise of this type would be close to assuming that the exchange rate would be determined by itself. The time-varying parameters are then assumed to be generated as in (6). This allows us to apply the Kalman Filter to estimate the time-varying parameters of this model. Hall and Garratt (1995) then present a set of simulations that demonstrate that this estimated rule performs reasonably well, in the sense that the model converges fairly quickly to an RE solution under this learning process with broadly sensible simulation properties.

10.3 EFFECTS OF VARYING THE EXPECTATIONS RULE

In the empirical applications of this approach (Hall and Garratt (1995), Barrell *et al.* (1993)) the law of motion or expectations rule is an estimated equation. The form of econometric specification will, in combination with the whole model, contribute to the stability properties and dynamics of the system. However, the precise specification of the estimated expectations rule will to some extent always contain a degree of arbitrariness and for any given exercise there are a number of expectations rules we might have implemented. This raises the question of how this choice may affect the uniqueness and stability of the equilibrium, if it is attained, and also the dynamic paths of the model variables when converging toward an equilibrium. In this section we report on work that investigates the effects of varying the expectations rule on the results of a simple application to the LBS model. This amounts to investigating whether or not the system is weakly or strongly E-stable.

In the first instance we sought to investigate a wide range of alternative expectations rules to that used in the main version of the model given above (equation (11)). This entailed both nested and non-nested versions of equation (11). In the non-nested case our main concern was to include variables that were clearly endogenous to the system but need not necessarily bear any relation to the exchange rate via theory. The *ad hoc* nature of this approach was deliberate, in that if the model produced a solution under these conditions then clearly the stability properties of the model are very robust and the more likely that the learning rule, whatever rule is adopted, makes little difference.

We examined two versions of non-nested expectations rules for the exchange rate. The first specification related the expected exchange rate to real money supply growth (M4), the PSBR as a percentage of GDP, and GDP growth. The second rule uses real wage growth and investment as explanatory variables. For both rules no solution was found when the LBS model was subjected to a range of oil price increases (10% through to 200%). Hence simply producing results in this exercise requires some degree of relevant expectations formation. The second set of alternative expectation equations were all nested versions of equation (8). In the first instance this entailed dropping the stochastic intercept term, whilst retaining all the other variables in equation (8). This amounts to a reparameter-isation of the ARIMA form which bears a closer relation to a levels form of the equation (see the next section for more details). No solution was found in all instances (i.e. the range of oil price shocks) and the presence of a stochastic intercept term is clearly important for any solution to exist. Hence we proceed to the final set of alternative expectations rules, which form the basis of the rest of the section where we examine restricted versions of equation (11), all of which include the stochastic intercept term. These are as follows:

Rule 1 — Hall and Garratt (1995, equation (14)).
Rule 2 — time-varying intercept (γ_{1t}).
Rule 3 — time-varying intercept and $E(\gamma_{1t}, \gamma_{2t})$.
Rule 4 — time-varying intercept, E and PO ($\gamma_{1t}, \gamma_{2t}, \gamma_{6t}$).
Rule 5 — time-varying intercept, E and IF ($\gamma_{1t}, \gamma_{2t}, \gamma_{4t}$).

All the expectations rules examined are estimated over the same data period as equation (8) (1970Q1–1989Q1) and the associated hyperparameters and starting values of the learning parameters are different in each case.

10.3.1 Learning Results

Before we describe the output and inflation results we first need to establish whether or not we have attained an equilibrium, i.e. an RE or E-stable equi-librium. For simple models which include learning mechanisms it is usually straightforward to compute whether or not there exists a stable E-equilibrium. For example, this may well involve computing the eigenvalues of 2 × 2, were the model of a very simple form. However, in this application, given that we are dealing with a large-scale, non-linear macro model, we could only locally approximate the eigenvalues of what would be a very large matrix determining the E-stability properties. We therefore choose not to compute these properties but instead focus on the evolution of the learning parameters, as stated in the differential equation described in Section 10.2. If the rate of change in the learning parameters becomes a constant (as a deviation from a baseline number), then we regard this as evidence in favour of an RE equilibrium or E-stable equilibrium. If this is the case, then by virtue of the learning algorithm outlined above the expectations error term is zero and the system is no longer learning and can be said to have converged.

Table 10.1 reports the annual percentage change (from a baseline) in the learning coefficient associated with the exchange rate variable for each of the variants of the rules (with the exception of Rule 2 where we use the stochastic intercept).

The result is one of convergence to an RE E-stable equilibrium for four of the five rules, where the exception is Rule 4 (in the table, Rule 3 may appear relatively unstable but it is clearly oscillating towards a solution value, whereas Rule 4 is trending away and the other coefficients in that rule are highly unstable). Either the percentage change from base has settled at a constant, or by the end period they are sufficiently low in value and volatility. The qualification in this particular application is the relatively small number of periods over which we solve the model. Simulation exercises that involve learning, e.g. Fuhrer and Hooker (1993), with small calibrated models generally use a much large number

Table 10.1 Learning parameter for the exchange rate variable; outcomes as a result of a 100% increase in the oil price

	Rule 1	Rule 2*	Rule 3[†]		Rule 4	Rule 5
1990	−3.51	0.16	0.58	0.14	−16.7	10.7
1991	−9.47	1.21	4.37	1.14	−125.6	43.37
1992	−10.3	2.96	11.89	2.8	−149.5	0.42
1993	−10.0	5.74	18.22	5.59	−193.8	−10.83
1994	−10.0	7.63	18.14	7.55	−238.0	−17.82
1995	−10.0	6.66	13.63	6.56	−257.7	−19.92
1996	−10.1	5.16	7.3	5.02	−262.7	−23.23
1997	−10.1	3.70	2.78	3.53	−260.3	−23.85
1998	−10.1	2.55	−0.27	2.35	−259.3	−24.2
1999	−10.1	2.24	−0.99	2.08	−259.7	−24.2
2000	−10.1	3.02	1.98	2.95	−259.5	−24.2

Percentage deviations from base.
*Stochastic intercept learning coefficient.
[†]Second column is the stochastic intercept coefficient, for Rule 3 used in Section 10.4.

of periods. Hence we are examining what would be considered a very early period in most comparable exercises and we would argue that the stability of these coefficients are more pronounced than they first may seem. A possible exception to the general conclusion is Rule 3, which exhibits very large changes in the exchange rate coefficient. The resulting output and inflation profiles that arise when this expectations rule is operating, under the oil price shock, would suggest that this is in fact an outlier.

10.3.2 Economic Effects

In this subsection we report the output and inflation responses of the LBS model, when subject to an oil price increase, where in each case a different learning rule is used to form expectations of the exchange rate. The effects of varying the expectations rule on the output responses (as a percentage difference from base) to the oil price shock are plotted in Figure 10.1. The most noticeable feature of Figure 10.1 is the similarity of the percentage fall in output of approximately 3% less than the base by the end period, as a result of the simulation in four out of the five rules. The exception to this result is Rule 4, where the change in output is 4.5 percentage points below base by the end period and where the trajectory, on casual inspection, looks set to continue changing. For the examples plotted in Figure 10.1, the criteria for convergence (expectation errors tending to zero and constant movement of the time-varying parameters) are more closely satisfied by the four rules that by the end period show the same change in

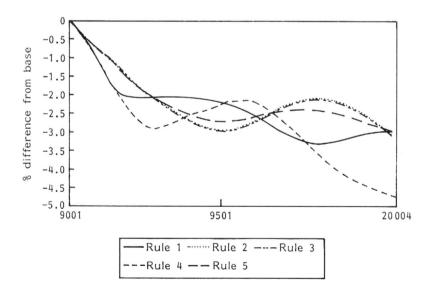

Figure 10.1 Comparison of learning rules; % change in GDP from 100% oil shock

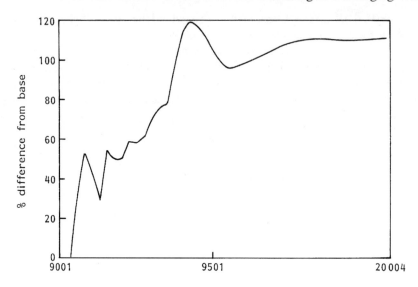

Figure 10.2 Oil learning coefficient; 100% oil price shock — rule 1

output than for the outlier Rule 4. Note that Table 10.1, column three, shows very large percentage movements from base of the learning parameter associated with the exchange rate variable in Rule 4. Hence we might tentatively conclude that where convergence does occur the same end-period value for output results from a range of information sets used in forming expectations. We interpret the results on output as the main evidence in favour of a strong rather than weak E-stability of the equation (13) expectations rule. Figure 10.2 plots a typical example of the movement of the learning parameters where convergence has been achieved. The period of learning is approximately five years with significant movements ceasing after 1995 (a similar timing is apparent in the movement of output in Figure 10.1).

Whilst it is the case that the long-run or end-point values of output look similar, the dynamic paths under different rules are significantly different. Rule 1 implies an output loss of approximately 2% in the first two years, which then stays flat at this level until 1995 when it moves downwards to the end-point level of 3% below the base level. In contrast, Rules 2, 3 and 5 have an output loss of around 1.5% after two years taking a further one to one and half years to reach the output loss implied of 2% below base. In the more medium term the implied output loss using Rules 2, 3 and 5 is greater, 3% versus 2%, and the path toward the similar end point oscillates significantly. In 1998 the percentage losses in output implied by Rules 2, 3 and 5 are around 1% higher than the path implied by Rule 1. We therefore conclude that the expectations rule, which shows signs of strong E-stability, nonetheless makes a significant difference to the size and timing of the movements in output in response to an oil price shock, and consequently will affect the policy recommendation.

The evidence regarding strong versus weak E-stability is less convincing when we examine the responses of inflation. Figure 10.3 plots the inflation responses to an oil price shock under the expectations rules 1–5. Unlike output, the trajectories for inflation differ both in terms of their dynamic paths and end-point or long-run values. Four of the five rules (the same four that exhibited stability in their output responses) show a positive inflation response but, despite being similar for three of the four rules up to the medium term, they differ significantly by the end period. For example, in the baseline case, Rule 1, we have an end-period response of 0% difference from base compared with 5%–6% for Rule 5, with Rules 2 and 3 lying between the two.

The dynamic paths differ, showing greater oscillation for Rules 2 and 3 compared with a more gradual and less volatile move toward the end period for Rule 5. Rule 1 oscillates by a small movement around zero. The short-run differences are less pronounced and, for approximately the first 16 quarters, the inflation paths for Rules 2, 3 and 5 are identical, although some 3–4 percentage points above the Rule 1 inflation path. However, at this point the inflation paths move apart and Rules 2 and 3 (which are virtually identical) move towards zero and then back up to its end value in cyclical movements, whilst Rule 5 continues at around 5%. Hence the medium-term inflation responses to an oil price shock is effected by the choice of expectations rule and therefore any policy recommendation regarding future target inflation may be required to take this into account.

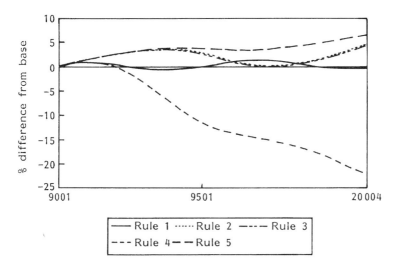

Figure 10.3 Comparison of learning rules; inflation after a 100% oil shock

As with the output responses there is a major discrepancy between the Rule 4 inflation path and end value and the other four rules. For Rule 4 the end-period inflation is −20% compared with a relatively low and positive response for the remaining four rules. This lends further evidence suggesting that in the case of Rule 4 convergence has not been achieved within the time span of the simulation exercise.

The overall conclusions on the effects of varying the expectations rules, Rules 1–5, are: (i) a reasonable degree of robustness is shown in terms of the similarity of the end-value output responses of the different rules; (ii) significant differences are exhibited in the end-value inflation responses of the different rules; and (iii) the dynamic paths of both output and inflation differ significantly when alternative expectations rules are used. We conclude that there is some evidence in support of strong as opposed to weak E-stability of the expectations rule, but that the choice of expectations rule nonetheless matters because it makes a significant difference to the dynamic output and inflation responses when an exogenous (oil price) shock hits the economy, as represented by the LBS macroeconometric model. The most noticeable exception to this is Rule 4, which clearly does not respond in the same way for output and inflation.

10.4 EFFECTS OF VARYING THE HYPERPARAMETERS

In the previous section we described the effect of varying the learning rule on the output and inflation responses of the LBS model to a 100% increase in the price of oil. The results, in the case where a solution to the oil price shock existed, appeared to be sensitive to the size of the hyperparameters for the time-varying (learning) coefficients and the related variance — covariance matrix (the Q and P matrices respectively defined in Subsection 10.2.2). The combination of these two matrices with the hyperparameters of the measurement equation, the matrix W, conditional on a given expectations error term (see equation (6)), determine the size of the change in the learning parameters.[5] Alternatively, we could state that the speed at which agents learn will depend on the values of the hyperparameters of the expectations rule and its associated coefficients. We would expect that generally very low hyperparameter values would be associated with very slow learning and, at least in some cases, this would give rise to behaviour like the simple adaptive expectations model, and an RE solution would not emerge. If the hyperparameters become too large, then the learning process may become unstable because the parameters will tend to over-react to any error and might give rise to explosive model properties. So we might expect to find three regions with only the intermediate one giving rise to stable learning behaviour which converges on a RE equilibria.

We can illustrate the extent of the sensitivity of the results to the values of the hyperparameters by making small changes in the value of the hyperparameters associated with one of the rules in the previous section. Rule 4 appears to be close to being unstable in that the parameters oscillate quite dramatically before converging. If we then increase the size of the hyperparameters of this rule we would expect to reach a point where convergence ceases to occur. Figures 10.4 and 10.5 plot the movement in the time-varying parameter associated with the oil price variable for Rule 4 and the associated expectations error, respectively, when the LBS model is subjected to a smaller oil price shock of only 10% but the hyperparameters are increased sufficiently to prevent convergence. The first six periods of the simulation solve both the expectations error and therefore the change in the learning coefficient, but become explosive in period 7 causing no solution to be found. Similar pictures can be shown for Rule 5, where again a relatively small change in hyperparameters can cause no solution to be found. Generally it is the case that for all the rules tried in the previous section there exists a range of hyperparameters such that a solution does not exist. Therefore in this section we seek to investigate this sensitivity in more detail, using a range of values for the hyperparameters of the learning coefficients, whilst keeping the expectations rule fixed.[6]

For simplicity and ease of interpretation we focus on Rule 3 of the previous section. Hence the structure of the expectations rule and associated hyperparameters are the following:

$$E^e_{t,t+1} = \gamma_{1t} + \gamma_{2t}E_{t-1} + e_t, \quad \text{where } e_t \text{ is } \sim N(0, W) \qquad \ldots (15a)$$

$$\gamma_{it} = \gamma_{it-1} + \varepsilon_{it}, \quad i = 1, 2, \quad \text{where } \varepsilon_{it} \text{ is } \sim N(0, Q) \quad \ldots (15b)$$

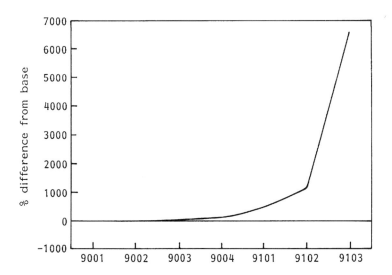

Figure 10.4 Oil learning coefficient — modified rule; 10% oil price shock

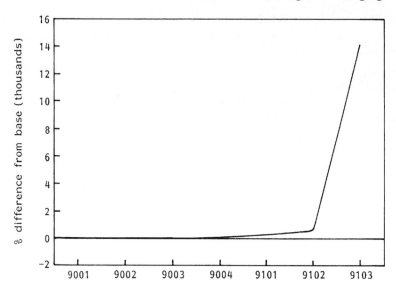

Figure 10.5   Expectations error — modified rule; 10% oil price shock

where the hyperparameters are given by:

$$W = [hyp3]; \quad \text{normalised to one;} \quad Q = \begin{bmatrix} hyp1 & 0 \\ 0 & hyp2 \end{bmatrix} \qquad \dots (16)$$

The variables that comprise Rule 3, or alternatively the information set it contains, are: a stochastic intercept term and the lagged exchange rate. Hence we have two state equations, one for each of the time-varying parameters and one measurement equation, requiring three hyperparameters in total. The first, *hyp1*, refers to the stochastic intercept term, and the second, *hyp2*, refers to the lagged exchange rate. The third hyperparameter, *hyp3*, refers to the measurement equation error term which in all cases below we normalise at one.

When examining the hyperparameters we are concerned primarily with their relative size. Hence we define ratios of the hyperparameters where the first and main ratio of interest is that of the two state equation hyperparameters, *hyp1:hyp2* (Ratio 1). Ratio 1 measures the relative size of the variances associated with the rates of change in the two learning parameters (note that equations (3) and (4) describe the time-varying parameters as random walks with unit coefficients). The lower the value of Ratio 1 the closer are the rates of change in the learning parameters. The second ratio of interest is *hyp1:hyp3* (Ratio 2). The value of Ratio 2 determines the allocation of the expectational errors between the expectations equation and the process determining the evolution of the learning parameters. The lower the value of Ratio 2 the greater is the proportion of the error term being allocated to the expectations equation and therefore the slower will be the change in the learning parameters. In the example below we adjust Ratios 1 and 2 to take account of the size of starting value for the learning parameters.[7] In all that follows references to Ratios 1 and 2 are with respect to the adjusted ratios.

10.4.1 Identifying Stable and Unstable Regions

In the first instance we seek to establish a range of values for the hyperparameters which enables us to solve the model. We therefore simulate the LBS macro model, where the perturbations range from a 10% to a 200% increase in the price of oil. The range of oil price increase enables us to identify regions in terms of the values of Ratio 1 and Ratio 2, where, say, all or no shocks solve and intermediate regions where, say, a 10% increase in the price of oil solves but a 50% increase does not. Where the intermediate region exists, we interpret the area as being where a stable region switches to an unstable region.

The starting point is the estimated version of Rule 3. The value of Ratio 1 is 1:18 (i.e. 2500:110 for the *hyp1:hyp2* unadjusted ratio) and therefore Ratio 2 is approximately 42:1. For these values we can produce a solution for the full range (10%–200%) of oil price shocks. We then establish an extreme position by setting $hyp1 = hyp2 = 0$, where in this instance we set the covariance matrix of the estimated learning parameters to zero. This represents the case where no learning occurs. The model solved for the full range of oil price shocks. Hence the learning mechanism is not required to produce a solution to the model.[8] We then proceeded with a range of combinations of $hyp1$, $hyp2$ and $hyp3$ defining a variety of the two ratios.

Figure 10.6 plots the results of the outcomes of the combinations of hyperparameters, i.e. whether or not a solution to the oil price shocks was achieved, defining stable and unstable regions in terms of the value of the two ratios. Ratio 1 is plotted on the x-axis and shows an increase in value as we move away from the origin, and Ratio 2 increases as we move up the y-axis. It is the case that reasonably well-defined regions of stability and instability exist. In terms of the two ratios the unstable region where no solution exists is defined, where Ratio 1 is less than 1:38 and Ratio 2 is greater than 3.2:1. A stable region above (RHS of Figure 10.5) the value of 1:38 for Ratio 1 exists for all values of Ratio 2. The values 1:38 and 8:1 for Ratios 1 and 2, respectively, represent the areas where stable and unstable regions cross. The cross-over from the stable to the unstable region is blurred and is defined as an area rather than a single line. In this region the 10% and, in some cases, the 50% oil price shocks solve but not the 100% and 200% oil price increases.

The interpretation we give to these two regions is that for the case where the hyperparameters of the state equations are close to one another (below 1:38 for Ratio 1) and in addition if the variance of the error terms of the state equations becomes large relative to the variability in the error term of the measurement equation (Ratio 2), then the implied speed of change for the learning coefficients

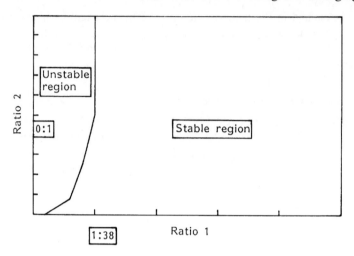

Figure 10.6 Stable (RHS) and unstable (LHS) regions

is too fast and the solution becomes unstable (as illustrated in Figures 10.4 and 10.5). This ceases to be a problem when one learning parameter moves much more slowly relative to the other, which is the case when Ratio 1 goes above 1:38. Note that a stable region exists close to the example of where no learning occurs. We interpret this as resulting from the fact that a large proportion of the expectations error term is taken up by the measurement equation, implying a slow rate of change for the learning parameters.

We have established three distinct regions, defined in terms of Ratio 1 and Ratio 2 (see Figure 10.6), which display particular features with respect to the solution of the model under learning. The first region is where the model converges under either no learning or very slow learning. Agents do not learn as a consequence of the hyperparameters and variance — covariance matrix of the learning coefficients being set to zero, causing the learning coefficients not to change over time, effectively imposing adaptive expectations. Allowing the hyperparameters, in the form of Ratios 1 and 2, to take on low values allows small movements in the learning coefficients such that learning occurs very slowly. In Figure 10.6 the first region starts at the origin where no learning occurs and then, as slow learning is allowed, extends along the horizontal (Ratio 1) axis, where as we move farther away from the origin the area increases to include areas defined higher up on the vertical (Ratio 2) axis. The second area is where the learning takes place, but the values of the ratios of hyperparameters are such that no solution exists. In Figure 10.6 this region is the region to the left of the bold line. Finally, the third region defines the region where learning takes place and a solution exists. We define this loosely as the E-stable region or area of E-equilibria, although it may well be the case that not all solutions found within this large area are E-stable or that they even exist. In terms of Figure 10.6 the third region is defined in terms of anywhere, provided Ratio 1 is greater than 1:38 (to the right in Figure 10.6).

An alternative interpretation of equations (15) would be to rewrite them in the following way:

$$E^e_{t,t+1} = E^e_{t-1,t} + \gamma_{2t}\Delta E_{t-1} + (\Delta e_t + \varepsilon_{1t}) \qquad \dots (17)$$

where the first component of equation (16), representing the stochastic intercept, is substituted into equations (15). The resulting equation is then subtracted from equation (15a) and rearranged under the assumption that $\gamma_{2t} = \gamma_{2t-1}$. Equation (17) is correct only if this assumption holds, which is the case when $\varepsilon_{2t} = 0$ which amounts to stating that $hyp2 = 0$. If this is the case, then $\gamma_{2t} = \gamma_2$ and agents do not learn. Equation (17) states that the expected change in the exchange rate depends on a proportion γ_2 of the lagged exchange rate change, where the value of $\gamma_2 = 0.0014$. Given the size of the coefficient, the expected change is in fact very small and therefore the response of expectations to model outcomes will be very slow. If, however, $\varepsilon_{2t} \neq 0$, then we cannot write equation (17) as $\Delta(\gamma_{2t}E_{t-1}) \neq \gamma_{2t}\Delta E_{t-1}$. However, if we think of equation (17) as an approximation, then we can view this as a random walk with drift, but where the drift is time-varying. Hence the implication is that the variability in the change term determines whether or not we have a solution, where the variability relates to the size of the hyperparameter, $hyp2$. If the variability of the growth factor is high relative to the levels term, then no solution exists. But because this term's variability decreases, a solution is more easily achieved.[9] The size of the changes in the learning coefficients during the course of the simulation varies according to the size of Ratio 1. The larger the value of Ratio 1, the larger is the implied variability and therefore the larger are the changes and the actual values of the growth term and hence the implied drift causes the exchange rate and the solution to be unstable.

10.4.2 Exogenous Oil Price Shock in the Stable Regions

Having identified two of three regions as exhibiting stability under adaptive learning, we now, in each of the regions, investigate the effects of different hyperparameter size on the output and inflation responses under an oil price increase of 100%. Figures 10.7, 10.8 and 10.9 plot a set of the results from a 100% increase in the oil price focusing on output, inflation and the learning parameter attached to the exchange rate term in the learning rule, respectively. Five cases are plotted in each diagram where the cases Hyp A through to Hyp E are in order of magnitude of Ratio 1. Hence the value of Ratio 1 for Hyp A is the estimated case of 1:18 (42:1 for Ratio 2), Hyp B is 1:27 (8:1 for Ratio 2), Hyp C is 1:38 (6:1 for Ratio 2) and Hyp D is 1:49 (2.6:1 for Ratio 2). The first four represent a range of values located in the third E-stable region. The fifth case, Hyp E, represents the first region where no learning occurs, as a result of setting $hyp1$, $hyp2$ and the covariance matrix of the estimated time-varying parameters P_t to zero.

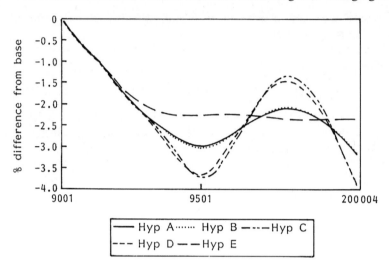

Figure 10.7 Comparison of different hyperparameters; % change in GDP after a 100% oil price shock

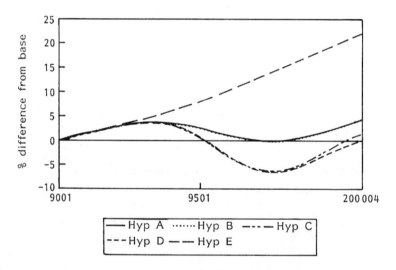

Figure 10.8 Comparison of different hyperparameters; % change in prices after a 100% oil price shock

Three distinct groups are apparent upon inspection of the graphs. The first, comprising Hyp E, is the case where no learning occurs and, as Figure 10.7 shows, after a period of approximately four years has reached a long-run level of output some 2% below the base level. Hence we have a strongly stable process for output where no learning occurs. Figure 10.8, which plots the effects of the oil price increase on inflation under no learning, presents a completely different impression. The effect of the oil price shock is to generate a non-stationary inflation process. Hence the effect of learning, as highlighted by the subsequent results of the two groups, is to induce stationarity into inflation at the expense of greater volatility in the output path. For example, introducing learning induces greater volatility into the movement of output, up to 1.5% points lower in 1995, then approximately the same order of magnitude higher in 1998, compared with case Hyp E. The second group, Hyp A and Hyp B (where case Hyp A is the same as Rule 3 in Figure 10.1) shows that increasing Ratio 1 from 1:18 to 1:27 makes little difference to the output and inflation responses of the model. However, the third group, Hyp C and Hyp D, show that the move of the ratio from 1:27 to 1:38 (Hyp B to Hyp C) is significant in terms of the path of output but that the move down in Ratio 1 to 1:49 (Hyp C to Hyp D) has little or no effect on output. The inflation response of moving from the second to the third group is to induce stationarity, as before, but where the cyclical movements are of a higher order of magnitude compared with the previous case. Hence Ratio 1 clearly matters for the time path of the variables of the model. The general pattern appears to be related to the size of Ratio 1. The larger is Ratio 1, i.e. the more to the right of the stable region, the smaller is the size of the oscillations and the slower is the effect of learning. However, as the ratio approaches the boundary, heading toward the unstable region, the larger are the oscillations. The output response is clearly more volatile the larger the value of Ratio 1.

There is far less variation of the output and inflation responses to changes in Ratio 2 compared with those where Ratio 1 is altered. For example, there is no discernible difference in output and inflation (and the movement of the learning parameters) where the value for Ratio 2 is 42:1 and 8:1. A difference does occur, however, when the ratio falls to 6:1, but the change thereafter, when moving from 6:1 to 2.6:1, for example, is again very small. The results are thus more sensitive to the value of Ratio 1. Faster learning, achieved through higher ratios of the learning coefficients hyperparameters (Ratio 1) will induce greater volatility in the output response.

The movement in the learning parameter plotted in Figure 10.9 serves to highlight the effect of the hyperparameters on the speed of learning and hence the dynamic path of output and inflation. All three groups have a similar response for the first two years of the simulation but at this point the third group's speed of learning or rate of change in the learning parameter accelerates, showing extremely high volatility. It is approximately this period when the instabilities causing no solution were found in a variety of other cases (see Figures 10.4 and 10.5).

The long-run or end values for both output and inflation are significantly different across the three groups, defining different hyperparameters. The no-learning case achieves stability in terms of output of 2% below base, whilst the

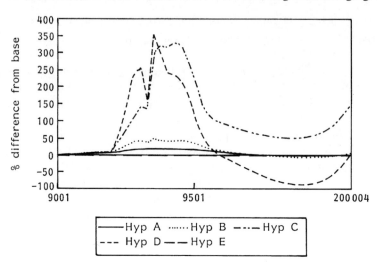

Figure 10.9 Comparison of different hyperparameters; exchange rate learning parameter, 100% oil price shock

end values for the other two groups are 3% and 4% below base and do not look to have achieved any form of stability. By way of contrast, the end value of inflation for the case of no learning is clearly non-stationary, compared with the stationary responses for inflation from the other two groups of 0% and 5%, respectively. It is possible that the long run or equilibrium has yet to be reached, but the implication is that the size of the hyperparameters matter far more for the end-value outcomes than does the variation in the expectations rule investigated in the previous section.

Overall we conclude that varying the hyperparameters (i) alters the end-value or long-run properties, particularly output, and also inflation. (ii) That the dynamic paths for both output and inflation are significantly different according to the size of the hyperparameters. Greater oscillations occur as Ratio 1 decreases in size, i.e. as we move toward the unstable region. (iii) That the overall stability, weak versus strong E-stability, appears to be more sensitive to the value of the hyperparameters than to a restricted version of the expectations rule in equation (8).

10.5 CONCLUSION

In this chapter we have investigated the variability of the dynamic paths and end-value responses of output and inflation of the LBS macroeconometric model under adaptive learning in the foreign exchange market. The need to learn results from an exogenous increase in the price of oil where the variants on output and inflation result from different assumptions concerning (i) the information set and (ii) the speed of learning. The first part took the form of varying the law of motion or expectations rule which agents use; hence the information set available to agents is altered. This amounts to a test of whether or not the solutions obtained are weakly or strongly E-stable. The second emphasis was to assess the effects of changing the hyperparameters associated with the time-varying learning coefficients, whilst keeping the expectations rule constant. The interpretation given to this part of the exercise was of the rate of change of the learning parameters or the speed of learning.

The first type of expectations rule introduced two sets of unrelated/ad hoc endogenous variables as the information set. No solution was found and hence we conclude that the choice of rule matters in so much that any arbitrary combination will not ensure stability. We then proceeded by examining the estimated expectations rule in Hall and Garratt (1995) and four restricted versions of it. The broad conclusions are: (i) a reasonable degree of robustness is shown in terms of the similarity of the end-value output responses of the different rules; (ii) significant differences are exhibited in the end-value inflation responses of the different rules; and (iii) the dynamic paths of both output and inflation differ significantly when alternative expectations rules are used. The similarity of the output responses in the case of the nested rules provides some evidence in support of strong as opposed to weak E-stability of the expectations rule, equation (8). The choice of expectations rule is important because it affects the dynamics of the output and inflation responses when an exogenous (oil price) shock hits the economy.

By varying the hyperparameters for a simple expectations rule containing a stochastic intercept term and the lagged exchange rate, we establish three regions with varying stability properties. The first is where a solution exists but no or very slow learning exists. The second and third regions allows learning to occur, one where the ratio of hyperparameters causes no solution to exist, the other defining an area where stable, in some cases E-stable, equilibria exist. We interpret the existence of stable and unstable regions as areas where the rate of change in the learning parameters is either sufficiently slow or too fast for a solution to exist. If it is the case that the hyperparameters of the state equations are approximately equal to one another and if the state equation hyperparameters become large relative to the hyperparameter of the error term of the measurement equation, then the implied speed of change in the learning coefficients is too fast and the solution becomes unstable. We then examined the two regions where solutions are possible. We found that both the dynamic paths and the end values of output and inflation are significantly affected by the values of the hyperparameters. Ratio 1, $hyp\ 1:hyp\ 2$, is the more important ratio; the smaller is this ratio the smaller is the size of the oscillations in output and inflation and the slower is the speed of learning.

Overall we conclude that the dynamic and end-value responses of output and inflation are more sensitive to the values of the hyperparameters than to the variation in the expectations rules examined.

10.6 ENDNOTES

1. A more general expectations term can be included which allows for expectations further into the future. In this exercise we only deal with expectations one period ahead.
2. The underlying parameters are assumed to be constant over time.
3. If the Q matrix is set to zero, then the Kalman filter algorithm described in equations (4)–(7) become the familiar recursive least squares described in Harvey (1981, pp. 53). In our case Q is an estimated matrix, where we restrict the off-diagonal elements to be zero but allow the elements on the diagonal to differ from one another. This amounts to weighted recursive least squares where the weights on each parameter are allowed to vary.
4. Convergence is possible because we operate in a deterministic world; see Appendix 1 and Bullard (1992).
5. For example, if both the hyperparameter and the variance and related covariances of a particular variable are set to zero, then the parameter ceases to vary over time.
6. In all that follows the starting value of the covariance matrix of the learning parameters (the P matrix) is the estimated value of Rule 3.
7. This involves square rooting the hyperparameters, dividing by the starting value and then comparing the ratios. In this example the starting value for the intercept term is 1.2 and for the lagged exchange rate 0.014.
8. The implication of this finding is that the introduction of adaptive learning can in fact destabilise the model.
9. The starting values for the two coefficients were the same in all cases.

APPENDIX 1

In this appendix we first define the general approach of Marcet and Sargent (1989b) and then show how this can rewritten, using Bullard (1992), to take the form of the Kalman Filter learning algorithm.

The state of the economy at time t is characterised by the values of the elements of a $k \times 1$ vector z_t. Agents observe a portion of the elements of z_t, and a portion of the elements of z_t are important to present decisions affecting future utility so that future values of these variables should be predicted. Let $z_{1t} = e_1 z_t$ be a $k_1 \times 1$ subvector of z_t, where the subscript 1 indicates that future values of these variables must be predicted and e_1 is a matrix that selects from z_t. Let $z_{2t} = e_2 z_t$ be a $k_2 \times 1$ subvector of z_t, where the subscript 2 indicates that these are variables agents use to predict z_{1t}. Because agents must make forecasts of the variables they care about:

$$z_{1t} = f(z_{2t-1}) \qquad \ldots (A1)$$

where $f(\cdot)$ is the forecast function. This assumes a lagged information structure, but contemporaneous information can be incorporated. The form of the law of motion or expectations rule is dependant on the forecast function $f(\cdot)$ used by agents. Marcet and Sargent (1989a,b) analyse

$$z_{1t} = \beta_t z_{2t-1} + \eta_t \qquad \ldots (A2)$$

where β_t is a $k_1 \times k_2$ matrix of parameters, and η_t is a $k_1 \times 1$ vector of noise such that $E\eta_t = 0$ and $E\eta_t \eta_t' = H$. The actual law of motion is therefore given by

$$\begin{bmatrix} z_{1t} \\ z_{1t}^c \end{bmatrix} = \begin{bmatrix} T_{11}(\beta_t) & T_{12}(\beta_t) \\ T_{21}(\beta_t) & T_{22}(\beta_t) \end{bmatrix} \begin{bmatrix} z_{2t-1}^c \\ z_{2t-1}^c \end{bmatrix} + \begin{bmatrix} V_1(\beta_t) \\ V_2(\beta_t) \end{bmatrix} u_t \qquad \ldots (A3)$$

where $T_{11}(\cdot)$ is $k \times (k_1 - k_2)$, $T_{12}(\cdot)$ is $k_1 \times k_2$, $[T_{21}(\beta_t)T_{22}(\beta_t)]$ is $(k - k_1) \times k$, $V_1(\cdot)$ is $k_1 \times m$, $V_2(\cdot)$ is $(k - k_1) \times m$, and u_t is an $m \times 1$ vector of white noise such that $Eu_t u_t' = U$, $\forall t$, where the superscript c indicates the complement and for simplification we set $T_{11}(\beta_t) = 0$. Equation (A3) can be written more concisely as

$$z_t = T(\beta_t)z_{t-1} + V(\beta_t)u_t \qquad \ldots (A4)$$

The partitioned operators T and V are of conformable dimensions, determined by the economic model being analysed. The learning algorithm is any method used to update the coefficients of the time-varying matrix β_t, or, in the notation used in the main text, D_t. Marcet and Sargent (1989a,b) assume agents use ordinary least squares, which using Ljung and Söderström (1983) can be written in the following form:

$$\bar{\beta}_t' = \beta_{t-1}' + (\alpha_t/t)R_t^{-1}\{z_{2t-2}z_{2t-2}'[T_{12}(\beta_{t-1})' - \beta_{t-1}'] + z_{2t-2}u_{t-1}'V_1(\beta_{t-1})'\} \qquad \ldots (A5a)$$

$$\bar{R}_t = R_{t-1} + (\alpha_t/t)[z_{2t-2}z_{2t-2}' - R_{t-1}/\alpha_t] \qquad \ldots (A5b)$$

where $R_t = [1/(t-1)]\sum_{j=2}^{t}\alpha_j z_{2j-2}z_{2j-2}'$ is a $k \times k$ matrix and $\{\alpha_t\}_{t=0}^{\infty}$ is a positive sequence. The α_t sequence can be set to weight observations appropriately; this formula is a version of weighted least squares. The algorithm in equations (A5a) and (A5b) can be combined with a projection facility to create a learning mechanism (our equations (4) and (5)). Using Bullard (1992), let us show how the algorithm above becomes a Kalman Filter.

If we ignore the projection facility and set the left-hand sides of equations (A5a) and (A5b) equal to β_t and R_t, respectively, then we can rewrite (A5a) and (A5b) in terms of a new matrix P_t. Since, $z_{1t-1}' = z_{2t-2}'T_{12}(\beta_{t-1})' + u_{t-1}'V(\beta_{t-1})'$, then

$$\beta_t' = \beta_{t-1}' + (\alpha_t/t)R_t^{-1}z_{2t-2}[z_{1t-1}' - z_{2t-2}'\beta_{t-1}'] \qquad \ldots (A6a)$$

$$R_t = R_{t-1} + (\alpha_t/t)[z_{2t-2}z_{2t-2}' - R_{t-1}/\alpha_t] \qquad \ldots (A6b)$$

We now define $P_t = (1/t)R_t^{-1}$, so that the algorithm becomes:

$$\beta_t' = \beta_{t-1}' + \alpha_t P_t z_{2t-2}[z_{1t-1}' - z_{2t-2}'\beta_{t-1}'] \qquad \ldots (A7a)$$

$$P_t^{-1} = P_{t-1}^{-1} + \alpha_t z_{2t-2}z_{2t-2}' \qquad \ldots (A7b)$$

Using the lemma $[W + XYZ]^{-1} = W^{-1} - W^{-1}X[ZW^{-1}X + Y^{-1}]^{-1}ZW^{-1}$ and by setting $W = P_{t-1}^{-1}$, $X = z_{2t-2}$, $Z = z_{2t-2}'$, the following algorithm can be developed:

$$\bar{\beta}_t' = \beta_{t-1}' + P_{t-1}z_{2t-2}f_{t-1}^{-1}[z_{1t-1}' - z_{2t-2}'\beta_{t-1}'] \qquad \ldots (A8a)$$

$$\bar{P}_t = P_{t-1} - P_{t-1}z_{2t-2}z_{2t-2}'P_{t-1}f_{t-1}^{-1} \qquad \ldots (A8b)$$

where the scalar $f_{t-1} = (1/\alpha_t) + z_{2t-2}'P_{t-1}z_{2t-2}$. Equations (A8a) and (A8b) are now directly interpretable as standard Kalman Filter updating equations, where the term in brackets in the first equation is the expectations error and the first part of the expression for f_t is set equal to W. The use of a single parameter α then imposes the restriction that all parameters change at an 'equal' rate on the Kalman updating equations. In the implementation above a general matrix is used here and so parameters may change at varying rates, in this sense the Kalman Filter applied here is more general than that used by Marcet and Sargent.

Bullard (1992) makes the point that if the underlying process which the learning algorithm is trying to approximate is itself time-varying, then the convergence results of Marcet and Sargent do not hold. However, this does not apply in our example because we are operating in a deterministic rather than stochastic environment and therefore the expectations error will tend to zero. Bullard (1992) uses a more general set-up where learning implies that the time-varying parameters of the underlying process allow the law of motion to evolve according to:

$$z'_{1t} = z'_{2t-1}\beta'_t + \eta'_t \qquad \ldots (A9a)$$

$$\beta'_{t+1} = \beta'_t + \omega_t \qquad \ldots (A9b)$$

where $E\eta_t = 0$ and $E\eta_t\eta'_t = H_t$ and $E\omega_t = 0$ and $E\omega_t\omega'_t = \Omega_t$. When the matrix $\Omega_t = 0$, then the resulting algorithm becomes (A7a) and (A7b), but when it is non-zero, then the convergence conditions do not hold. In our notation Ω_t is equal to the matrix Q, which is non-zero. However, in our case, we operate in a deterministic environment which sets $H_t = 0$ and therefore the algorithm will converge as the expectations error term goes to zero.

───── 11 ─────
Modelling the Effects of Changing Military Expenditure

HONG BAI, STEPHEN HALL, JAMES NIXON AND RON SMITH

11.1 INTRODUCTION

Although it has been posed repeatedly, the question 'What are the economic effects of reduced military spending?' is not well defined; the only answer can be: 'It depends'. In particular, it depends on the macroeconomic policy that is concurrent with the cut in military spending; the microeconomic flexibility of the economies concerned; and the time-horizon, since long-run and short-run effects are likely to be different. UNIDIR (1993) discusses the general issues involved in disarmament. In this chapter we will be concerned with the macro-economic aspects, trying to quantify the range of short- and long-run responses that may follow cuts in military expenditure under different macroeconomic policy regimes.

It is impossible to examine the effect of a cut in military spending, *ceteris paribus*; other things must change. If military expenditure is cut, then by iden-tity either other government spending, taxation or the deficit must change. If the deficit changes, the government budget constraint implies that government finance, the issue of money or bonds, must also change and this implies some interest rate response, a monetary policy adjustment. Changes in national debt or interest rates change government interest payments, a component of government expenditure, feeding back on the deficit, monetary policy and financing. Certain patterns of financing, e.g. an exploding deficit, may not be sustainable, because

---

Macroeconomic Modelling in a Changing World. Edited by C. Allen and S. Hall

the ability of the government to meet its interest obligations becomes suspect. Thus the assumptions that are made about government fiscal, monetary and financial behaviour play a central role in the specification of any simulation of the effects of changing military spending.

It should be noted that econometric estimates of the effect of military spending (e.g. Dunne and Smith (1990) who examine the effect on unemployment) that do not include measures of fiscal and monetary policy explicitly are not providing a measure of the *ceteris paribus* effect, but of the *mutatis mutandis* effect, with policy being adjusted as it was on average. To examine the sensitivity of the impact of changes in military spending to different macroeconomic policies, it is necessary to use a full model of the economy, which allows explicitly for policy adjustments.

The term 'Peace Dividend', which has been widely adopted in discussing the effects of lower military expenditure, is perhaps unfortunate. It gives the impression of an identifiable sum of money, a cheque through the post, which is available to be spent. In reality, one cannot identify where the money went because the budgetary consequences of reduced military expenditure are never transparent, either *ex ante* or *ex post*. What is involved in an *ex post* analysis is a comparison of the observed trajectory in which military expenditure fell, with a speculative counter-factual in which there was some specified mix of fiscal policy (government expenditures, taxes and deficits) and monetary policy (interest rate adjustments). This different policy mix would have effects on output, employment, etc. and these would feed back onto government revenues and expenditures, further complicating the comparison. Similarly, in an *ex ante* forecasting exercise some associated policy stance has to be specified. Thus in either case the question arises as to what extent the subsequent economic adjustment is a product of the cut in military spending or a product of the associated macroeconomic policies.

It is interesting that people rarely make the mistake of thinking that there is a unique answer to the corresponding question: 'What are the economic effects of increased military spending?' When this question is posed, for instance by Keynes asking 'How to pay for the war', it is recognised that different financing regimes will have different economic consequences and the policy question is then how best to finance the increase. Keynes begins his essay: 'This is a discussion of how best to reconcile the demands of war and the claims of private consumption.' Similarly, the financing of both the Vietnam War and the Reagan military build-up, and their implications for the international monetary system, have been a topic of heated debate about how the military demands could best have been reconciled with other objectives.

Another historical example will illustrate the importance of the concurrent policy. During the First World War both Britain and the United States incurred very heavy military expenditures, peaking at 45% and 13% of GDP, respectively. With demobilisation, the United States had a transitory increase in unemployment, but by 1923 it was back to low levels, 2.4%, and unemployment during the 1920s was very similar to that before the war. In contrast, British unemployment levels stayed high throughout the whole of the 1920s. This is not explained by the higher level of British military spending; both Britain and the United States maintained fairly full employment after the Second World War, despite higher shares of military spending in output than during the First World War. The explanation for the high British unemployment was the post-war monetary and fiscal policy stance, which was designed to return Britain to gold at the pre-war rate of exchange. This required massive deflation. Central government moved from a deficit of over £1 billion during the war, to a surplus of £50 million in 1920. Despite this substantial deflationary shock, nominal interest rates were increased. The bank rate was 5% from April 1917 to November 1919, then went up to 6% and was further raised to 7% in April 1920, staying there to April 1921, when interest rates started to come down very slowly. The Retail Price Index (RPI) went from 100 in 1914 to 276 in 1920 as a result of war-time inflation, then deflation drove it back down to 203 in 1921 and 180 in 1922 (all November figures). The combination of high nominal rates and negative inflation implied real rates of interest as high as 25% during the early 1920s, depressing output and employment. The nominal exchange rate appreciated from 3.7 $/£ in 1920 to 4.5 in 1923, and despite the deflation, the real exchange rate probably remained over-valued. The mass unemployment was thus a consequence of the fiscal and monetary policy rather than demobilisation. This historical example has of course some similarities with the Conservative Government's more recent attempts to defend an over-valued ERM parity, while cutting military spending.

The rest of the chapter is organised as follows. Section 11.2 examines the recent evolution of UK military expenditure. Section 11.3 discusses the specification of policy responses. Section 11.4 presents the simulation results and Section 11.5 examines their interpretation.

11.2 THE EVOLUTION OF UK DEFENCE EXPENDITURE

Traditionally, the United Kingdom has spent a rather larger share of its GDP on defence than other European countries, though less on average than the United States. This higher share gave it a total military expenditure of the same order of magnitude as France and Germany, though both of those had cheap conscript armies and rather different force structures. From a low of 4.3% of GDP in 1978–79, military expenditure increased rapidly in the early 1980s as Mrs Thatcher implemented the pledge given to NATO by the previous Labour Government to increase military spending by 3% a year in real terms. Military spending peaked in 1984–85 at almost £27 billion in 1992–93 prices, about 5.2% of GDP; see Table 11.1. From this peak it was cut back quite sharply, falling to 10% by 1989–90. While the real budget was being cut, the share of equipment in

Table 11.1 The UK defence budget: history and forecasts

Financial year	1984–85	1989–90	1993–94	1996–97
Defence budget as % of GDP	5.16	3.95	3.67	2.90
Budget 1992–93 prices:				
Total expenditure	26 670	24 767	22 601	19 440
Personnel	9319	9665	9499	7834
Equipment	12 209	10 186	8759	7718
Other expenditure	5143	4916	4343	3888
Share of equipment	46	41	39	40
Aggregate:				
UK unemployment rate (Q4)	10.9	5.9	10	9
Defence employment ('000):				
Armed forces	336	315	262	229
Civil servants	207	172	142	118
Industry	670	575	395	320
Total	1213	1062	799	667
Changes				
Budget		−1902	−2167	−3161
Employment		−151	−263	−132

the budget, which had been at an historical high in 1984–85, also fell sharply, so the real cut in the equipment budget was 20% by 1989–90. Because equipment is the marginal category it tends to fluctuate more than the total budget, doing particularly well in good times and particularly badly in bad times.

These cuts were associated with estimated falls in total defence employment of about 150 000 jobs, about 100 000 of them being in the defence industry. It should be emphasised that these official estimates of defence industry employment have a large margin of error. Between the 1993 and 1994 editions of *Defence Statistics* the estimate of total defence industry employment in 1991–92 was cut from 560 to 515. The cuts over the period 1985–90 provoked very little comment, since over this period the economy was growing quite rapidly and the unemployment rate was falling from 11% to 6%. In addition, a large proportion of defence jobs are located in the Southern part of the country, which was booming. The cuts in military spending also helped to allow the Conservative Government to reduce tax rates. The standard rate of income tax fell from 30% in 1985 to 25% in 1990, while the highest rate fell from 60% to 40%.

Following the fall of the Berlin Wall, the UK Ministry of Defence conducted a major review of defence policy entitled *Options for Change*. The results of the review were announced in July 1990 and were followed in August by the Iraqi invasion of Kuwait. The United Kingdom has been unfortunate in the timing of its Defence Reviews, the previous one by John Nott in 1981 was quickly followed by the Falklands/Malvinas War. However, despite the Gulf War, *Options for Change* resulted in a further cut of 10% in the total defence budget between 1989–90 and

1993–94. The impact on employment was larger, and some 250 000 defence jobs were lost. Members of the armed services were made redundant and the defence industry cut employment sharply as it tried to restructure. Even before the end of the Cold War there had been massive excess capacity in the industry. The political impact of these cuts was increased because the economy was going into a long recession over this period, with measured unemployment rising from 6% to over 10%. The latest government projection, given in the 1994 cost-cutting exercise, the Defence Cost Study entitled *Front Line First*, is that the share of defence will fall to 2.9% in GDP in 1996–97. This represents a further real fall of almost 10% and a loss, on our estimates, of another 120 000 defence jobs. This loss of jobs will continue to generate political repercussions, since unemployment seems likely to fall rather slowly over this period. For instance, there has been repeated expressions of Parliamentary concern over the closure of Swan Hunter, the Tyneside warship builder.

Of course, gross reductions in defence employment do not necessarily transmit into net increases in unemployment; this will depend on the state of the labour market and the availability of alternative jobs. This is clear from previous UK simulations, e.g. Dunne and Smith (1984) and Barker, Dunne and Smith (1991), which used the Cambridge Econometrics model. They indicated that the effects on total unemployment of cuts in military expenditure, balanced by increases in other government consumption and investment, were rather small, tending, if anything, to reduce unemployment. However, uncompensated cuts in military expenditure, where the deficit was sharply reduced, were strongly deflationary, as might be expected given the Keynesian macro structure of the model. The main focus of those simulations, given the highly disaggregated Cambridge Econometrics model, was on the industrial effects of the cuts in military expenditure. In fact, the compensated simulation was designed expressly to make the macro-policy effects as small as possible, by leaving the government deficit unchanged. Here we examine how different macro policies change the economic consequences of cuts in military spending.

11.3 SIMULATION DESIGN UNDER ALTERNATIVE FISCAL AND MONETARY POLICY RULES

The simulations are conducted on the recently re-estimated London Business School (LBS) model, see Allen, Hall and Nixon (1994). This has a relatively small transparent core of about 30 behavioural equations, a coherent supply side based on a system of factor demand functions, and models expectations (which primarily influence the exchange rate) through a learning process. The endogeneity of the exchange rate plays a central role in the simulations, as it has in recent British economic history. Like many models, the LBS model does not include military expenditure explicitly. However, it does distinguish between government spending on procurement and on direct employment (wages and salaries), since these have quite different labour market and thus wage and price effects. Something over half of military spending is procurement and the simulations will examine the differences between changes in government procurement and spending on direct employment.

In simulating the effect of cuts in military expenditure we have to specify the associated policy rules. On the fiscal side, the adjustment can be in other government expenditure, in taxation, in the deficit, or in a mix of all three. The simulations in Barker, Dunne and Smith indicated that the compositional effects of switching from military to compensating civil government consumption and investment were rather small at an aggregate level, so this is the least interesting from a macroeconomic point of view. In fact, in the LBS model such a switch would have no effect at all, given that total government expenditure and the procurement–employment spending mix did not change. Therefore, the simulations will focus on uncompensated cases where the deficit or taxation adjusts.

It is common in conducting simulations of this type to assume fixed, nominal interest rates but as the return to the Gold Standard in the 1920s indicated, this can be highly destabilising. Suppose military spending is cut, and the deficit reduced; this will tend to deflate the economy, reducing the rate of inflation and raising the real interest rate, which will tend to raise the real exchange rate. Higher real interest rates and exchange rate will further deflate the economy, and the process will continue explosively. Although this is a long-standing theoretical result, few traditional macro models exhibit this instability because the exchange rate is exogenous, real interest rate effects are rather small, and the government budget constraint and fiscal sustainability conditions are not imposed. For short-term forecasting of a year or so ahead, ignoring these feedbacks may not cause large errors. But large cuts in military spending will have medium- to long-term consequences, so it is important to allow for the longer term effects and the endogenous policy response.

While it is important to endogenise policy, it is not obvious how it should be done. Clearly, governments would not be passive in the face of the simulated economic events; they would respond and attempt to anticipate future developments. Thus inflexible rules, like fixed nominal interest rates, are completely implausible. However, it is not clear exactly what form a plausible response would take, since this is a matter of political objectives as well as economic constraints.

A minimal policy rule is to suppose that governments would try to keep real, rather than nominal, interest rates constant. This would ensure that any deflation is matched by a fall in the nominal rate, subject to non-negative nominal rates. Even here there is a potentially destabilising feedback through the exchange rate if uncovered interest parity holds, but this is more likely to be damped by other factors. However, should the real interest rate chosen not correspond to the new equilibrium real interest rate associated with lower military expenditure and the prevailing world real interest rate, this in itself could generate longer term instability.

A more plausible policy rule would respond to the simulated events through some sort of feedback rule intended to stabilise the economy. There are many such rules that could be adopted, and two that we consider are a monetary policy rule designed to stabilise inflation and a fiscal sustainability rule designed to keep the deficit (PSBR) as a share of GDP close to its historical track. The inflation rule broadly corresponds to current declaratory UK policy and involves interest rates responding to current and past inflation in an offsetting manner. The rule involves adjusting interest rates in accordance with proportional, integral and derivative (PID) feedback responses to the deviation of inflation from targets. Rules of this sort have been well known in economics since the work of Phillips (1954, 1957). Although the weights on the PID terms are derived from optimal control exercises, this is unlikely to be an optimal rule. Inflation is a lagging indicator and, as Phillips' work indicated, trying to stabilise a lagging indicator can induce oscillations. Nonetheless, this rule is simple enough to be politically feasible and does stabilise the economy over the medium term.

The final rule we examine is fiscal targeting, under which taxes are adjusted to keep the government deficit (PSBR) to GDP ratio as close to the historical or forecast base figure as possible over the whole simulation period. This is done using an optimal control regime to determine a single proportionate increase in all taxes rather than varying taxes from year to year. Thus the time profile of the simulated tax and expenditure changes can differ.

The base used runs from 1985 to 2013, so covering almost ten years of historical data. Two sets of simulations were run. One involves faster cuts in military expenditure than was actually observed, supposing that the government anticipated the end of the Cold War from 1985. The other involves keeping military expenditure at roughly its 1985 level. The first set of simulations involves examining a sustained reduction in (a) government procurement and (b) government spending on wages and salaries of £2bn a year from 1985, under (i) fixed nominal interest rates, (ii) fixed real rates, (iii) interest rates adjusted to stabilise inflation (inflation targeting) and (iv) inflation targeting plus taxation adjusted to keep the PSBR/GDP share close to its historical pattern (fiscal targeting).

The second set of simulations constructs a counterfactual analysis of what might have happened had military spending not been cut, had other government expenditure taken its historical values, had taxes been adjusted to keep the deficit roughly at its historical levels over the whole period, and had monetary policy been adjusted to target inflation. The higher military expenditure is simulated by adding a cumulating £500m p.a., from 1985 to 1995, to government expenditure, splitting the addition evenly between procurement and employment. From 1995 government consumption is £5bn above base. This is slightly smaller than the actual cuts in military spending shown in Table 11.1.

11.4 RESULTS

Table 11.2 presents the results for the change from base in employment for eight
simulations. These involve cutting either government spending on employment
or on procurement by £2bn in 1990 prices, under four scenarios about the policy
rules simultaneously adopted:
1. Fixed nominal interest rates.
2. Fixed real interest rates.
3. Inflation targeting.
4. Both inflation and fiscal targeting.
In reporting the results, we focus on the employment consequences because these
are the subject of most political controversy.

Scenario 1 is the equivalent of the post First World War response and shows
a very similar pattern. Cutting military spending and the deficit depresses prices

Table 11.2 Changes from base in employment as
a result of a £2bn cut

Under scenarios:
1. Fixed nominal interest rates
2. Fixed real interest rates
3. Inflation target
4. Inflation target + fiscal target

| | Cut in | |
	Wages and salaries	Procurement
1985		
1.	−535	−205
2.	−578	−189
3.	−569	−145
4.	−496	+5
1990		
1.	−1941	−1039
2.	−526	−305
3.	−493	−279
4.	−290	+134
1995		
1.	*	*
2.	−517	−237
3.	−631	−315
4.	−425	+108
2013		
1.	*	*
2.	−893	−257
3.	−415	−113
4.	−290	+144

*Failed to converge.

below base, raises real interest rates, and causes the real exchange rate to appreciate, which depress exports and investment, thus worsening deflation. At first this process is relatively slow; after five years of a cut in spending on employment, real interest rates and the real exchange rate are 5 percentage points above base. It then accelerates as expectations adjust and the shock is recognised as permanent. By year 7, real interest rates are 22% higher, the process explodes, and the model ceases to converge. On theoretical grounds one would expect the model to be unstable because of the open arbitrage condition; the difference in nominal interest rates between countries equals the change in the exchange rate. But this need not hold exactly because the model allows people to have mistaken expectations about the exchange rate in the short run while they are learning. However, in the medium term once they have learned, the condition starts to bind, the exchange rate adjusts, sending the economy off into an increasing slump. This is shown in Figure 11.1, which shows the percentage change in employment in the simulation from base, for both the procurement and the employment shocks.

As might be expected, if the cuts fall on procurement, then the employment impacts are much smaller: usually less than half the size of cuts in spending on wages and salaries. These differential employment effects feed back through the labour market, influencing wages and inflation, and interact with the policy rule to produce quite different dynamic responses to cuts in the two types of government expenditure. The reductions in employment are of the same order of magnitude as the reductions shown in Table 11.1 and are not large relative to the variation in employment over this period. It should be noted that the similarity in order of magnitude is largely coincidental. The figures in Table 11.1 are gross

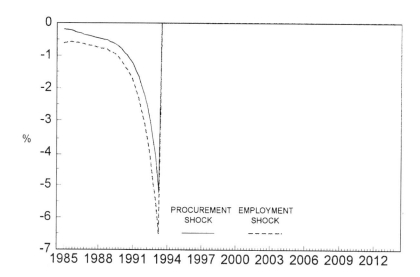

Figure 11.1 Fixed nominal interest rates

reductions in employment. The figures in Table 11.2 are the net effects measured in the simulation, i.e. after workers in the armed forces and defence industry have obtained other jobs, if they can, while the simulated effects in Table 11.2 also reflect the effects of the contractionary fiscal policy.

Under the fixed real rate rule the procurement shock causes employment to show a very long cycle (Figure 11.2), reaching a maximum three years after the shock began, falling to a minimum after 17 years and then rising again. For the spending on employment shock, there is a short cycle and then clear signs of explosive deflationary divergence. It seems likely that in the very long run, the fixed real rate rule is also unstable, since the open arbitrage condition is now essentially a unit root process.

The inflation rule is stable since it now adequately closes the model but introduces short cycles, peaking in 1994 for procurement and 1995 for spending on wages in salary. These oscillations are induced since the rule tries to stabilise the economy on the basis of a lagging indicator, namely inflation. Subsequently both seem to be returning monotonically, though rather slowly, to base (Figure 11.3). Again, the variations in employment are not large relative to variations over the historical period. In the first three scenarios the cut in military spending was reflected in a reduced government deficit to GDP ratio. Under scenario 4, taxes are now adjusted to keep the deficit close to its historical path, while at the same time using monetary policy to target inflation. For the employment shock, fiscal targeting reduces the contractionary effect and the reduction in employment is smaller than under the other scenarios. Cutting spending on procurement and cutting tax rates to meet fiscal targets causes employment to be higher than base throughout the whole of the simulation. Real GDP does fall slightly initially, but

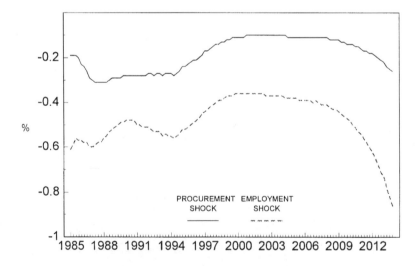

Figure 11.2 Fixed real interest rates

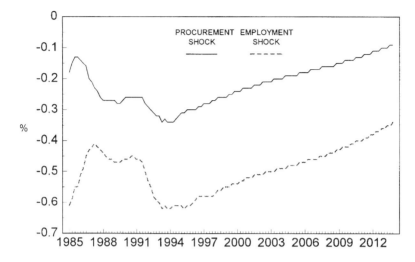

Figure 11.3 Inflation policy rule

because procurement has a low labour intensity relative to the other components of private GDP which increase, employment still rises (Figure 11.4).

The counterfactual simulation involves asking what would have happened had military spending been kept at its 1985 level; monetary policy had been used to target inflation and keep inflation at its historical (and forecast base) path; and taxes had been adjusted to keep future values of the deficit/GDP ratio at their

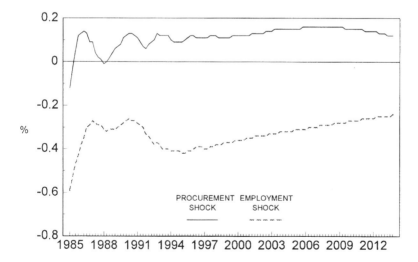

Figure 11.4 Inflation rule with fiscal solvency

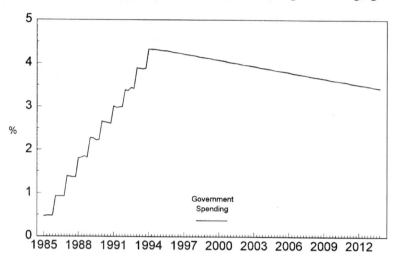

Figure 11.5   Counterfactual spending profile

historical (and forecast base) levels (Figure 11.5). Essentially the government looks forward and realises that without the cuts in military spending, taxes have to be higher over the whole period. At first, the higher taxes produced by the fiscal sustainability constraint outweigh the small increases in military expenditure relative to base, so the net effect is deflationary. Higher military expenditure and a fiscally conservative government is contractionary: producing lower employment and GDP over the first five years of the simulation. In the medium term, the expansionary effects of the higher military expenditure begin to dominate, with employment peaking about half a million higher after 15 years and then slowly declining. Real earnings match the profile of employment, being below base initially and above base subsequently. The balance of payments is rather better than in the base, since the higher government expenditure crowds out consumption and investment which have a higher import component. In 1995, government spending is 5% above base, consumption 0.69% below base and investment 0.34% below base.

To assess roughly the degree of non-linearity and path dependency, we can compare the counterfactual (no cuts) with the sum of the other two simulations (separate cuts in procurement and in employment spending) in 1992 (Figure 11.6). In this year the counterfactual involved procurement and spending on wages and salaries each being £2bn above base, so the shock is equal and opposite to the sum of the other two simulations. The dynamic path of the shock was different, steadily rising from 1985 in the counterfactual, as compared with the constant £2bn cuts from 1985. Under fixed real rates the employment differences from base were 866 and −820; under the inflation rule 750 and −885; and under inflation plus fiscal targeting 246 and −271 (all in thousands). The

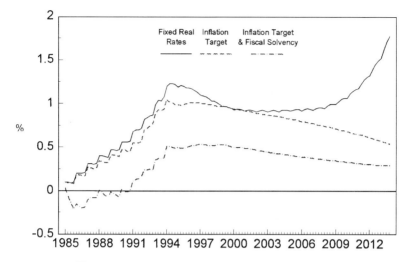

Figure 11.6 Counterfactual under different policies

largest difference is associated with the inflation rule, but this seems to come from the different oscillatory pattern induced by the different dynamics of the shocks. By the end of the simulation the counterfactual increase at +659 is almost the same as the scaled cuts, −663. Thus there do not seem to be any substantial non-linearities associated with the relatively small upward and downward shocks simulated.

11.5 INTERPRETATION

While at first sight some of these results may seem counter-intuitive — cuts in military spending can result in higher employment, not making the cuts can result in lower employment — they should not be unexpected. Cuts in military spending concentrated on procurement, matched by cuts in taxes and expansion in more labour-intensive forms of spending, will raise employment. Cuts in labour-intensive spending on wages and salaries which are used to reduce the deficit will reduce employment. This simply illustrates the point that the effects of cutting military spending will differ greatly depending on the concomitant macro policy. Were a macro policy designed to try to ensure that nothing much was different, then nothing much would be different. The initial simulations were intentionally contractionary: the reduction in military expenditure was used to reduce the government deficit, but the contractionary effects were not very large if accompanied by a sensible monetary policy.

One other feature is that most of the effects were rather small; less than half a million in a work force of about 28 million. The fact that the effects are small is partly a result of the structure of the model, partly a result of the structure of the counterfactual, and partly a result of the fact that we are not measuring the most important factors associated with the reduction of military spending. In this section we will discuss each of these three issues in a little more detail.

The first issue is that the structure of the model is such that changes in the composition of GDP (like cuts in military spending) have very little effect on the level of GDP and thus the level of employment. Given the neoclassical supply side of the model, the level of GDP (and the level of employment) are independently determined and are not very sensitive to changes in the composition of GDP. This is in sharp contrast to traditional Keynesian models, where additions to components of GDP do raise GDP permanently, through demand-side effects, to which it was assumed that supply would adjust. In fact, both extreme assumptions — the perfectly elastic supply of the Keynesian models and the perfectly inelastic supply of the neoclassical models — are implausible. The composition of demand, in particular the share devoted to investment, is almost certain to influence supply and potential output. If the cut in military expenditure has an effect on investment, as has been widely argued, then it will have an effect on the growth rate and on the long-run level of GDP.

Smith (1980) presents econometric evidence which suggests that there is a negative effect of the share of military expenditure on the share of investment in OECD countries. Subsequent work has tended to confirm that association. In particular, Findlay and Parker (1992) show that in the United States increases in military spending raise interest rates by more than increases in other forms of government spending, providing a possible transmission mechanism between military spending and investment. Despite the recent interest in endogenous growth, such effects of investment on the underlying rate of growth are absent from most macro models, including the LBS model; thus the change in military expenditure has no effect on long-run supply; the model returns to its trend equilibrium level of output, given stabilising policy. Endogenising the trend in long-run supply is a path for future research.

The second issue is that the counter-factual was designed to keep the government deficit and the inflation rate at their historical levels and it is not clear that this is would have been historically feasible. In particular it involved raising taxes to pay for the higher military expenditure. But given the narrowness of the Conservative victory in 1992, higher taxes could easily have lost them the election. But had taxes not been raised, the deficit and interest rates would have been higher, and it is unlikely that the government would have been willing to join the ERM at the exchange rate they did. Membership of the ERM was a central (though politically controversial) part of their policy, and it is not clear what strategy they would have adopted in its absence. Thus, these rather small fiscal and monetary changes to accommodate higher military spending could have had momentous political consequences if they had caused the Labour Party to win the 1992 election. In fact, one might argue that the main economic effect of cutting military expenditure in the United Kingdom is that it allowed the Conservative Government to stay in power longer than it otherwise would.

The third issue is that by focusing on the level of GDP and employment these calculations ignore the main benefits of the Peace Dividend: greater security with the end of the Cold War and the ability to use resources previously devoted to military preparations for other civilian uses. To judge these effects requires a social welfare function that includes security and civilian consumption, rather than an implicit social welfare that merely adds military to other spending or judges any policy by its employment consequences. Measuring social welfare and security is inevitably difficult, but we should not ignore the most important element of the Peace Dividend because of measurement difficulties.

Of course, it may be premature to count the positive security consequences. To return to our historical example, when Keynes wrote his great polemic, 'The economic consequences of the peace', after the end of the First World War, he rightly paid almost no attention to the economic effects of reduced military spending, though the reductions then were of an order of magnitude greater than any we will see now. What he was concerned about was the economic effects of the new security order, particularly the reparations imposed on the losers, economic effects he thought likely to provoke another war. Pessimists might fear that his conclusions could be applied to the peace that followed the Cold War. The peace 'includes no provision for the economic rehabilitation of Europe — nothing to make the defeated Central Empires into good neighbours, nothing to stabilise the new states of Europe, nothing to reclaim Russia; nor does it promote in any way a compact of economic solidarity amongst the allies themselves' (Keynes (1919, 1971, p. 143)).

—————— 12 ——————
Modelling Economies in Transition
—— STEPHEN HALL AND JOHN O'SULLIVAN ——

12.1 INTRODUCTION

The Eastern European economies are going through a time of fundamental structural change. Traditional tools of economic analyses and econometric model-building rest to a large extent on the precept that the structure of the economy is stable and thus on the notion that the future will be similar to the past. This assumption is almost certainly inappropriate in the case of the Eastern European economies at the present time, and for some time to come. The purpose of this chapter is to investigate the effects of structural change on the process of building econometric models and to explore how this process should depart from standard practice when the structural change is a significant factor. We will illustrate this methodology by estimating a model of the Polish Foreign Exchange market and by building a small but complete model of the Romanian economy and demonstrating how it adapts to structural change and how its forecasting is remarkably improved by recognising the underlying economic volatility.

The structure of the chapter is as follows. In Section 12.2 the process of model reduction is explored for the case of a general data-generation process which is time varying. Section 12.3 outlines how in general the Kalman Filter may be used to model the resulting estimating equations. Section 12.4 details the way specific information about the timing or form of the structural change may be incorporated within the framework of Section 12.3. Section 12.5 gives a simple example of structural change modelling procedures applied to the relationship between black market and official exchange rates in Poland. Section 12.6 details the specific way the Kalman Filter can be used in a complete macro model. Section 12.7 gives an example using the Romanian economy and illustrates the forecasting performance of the model. Section 12.8 draws some general conclusions.

Macroeconomic Modelling in a Changing World. Edited by C. Allen and S. Hall
© 1997 John Wiley & Sons Ltd

12.2 MODEL REDUCTION WHEN THE STRUCTURE IS UNDERGOING CHANGE

The framework we use to approach this problem is that associated with Sargan and Hendry in many papers and which is summarised in Hendry, Pagan and Sargan (1984); a simple account may be found in Hall, Cuthbertson and Taylor (1992, Chapter 4). The framework begins by setting out a completely general statement of the world, the data-generation process (DGP) and thereby clearly specifying the steps that are necessary to go from this general statement to a model which may be estimated and used for policy analysis. If all the steps are valid, then the result is a valid model. The use of this framework is however mainly that by clearly specifying the steps that we are implicitly taking when we formulate a model we can see how the model's structure should change in the light of varying assumptions about the nature of the DGP. So, let x_t be a vector of observations on all variables in period t, and let $X_{t-1} = (x_{t-1}, \cdots, x_0)$. Then the joint probability of the sample x_t, the DGP, may be stated as

$$\prod_{t=1}^{t} D_t(x_t|X_{t-1}; \alpha_t) \qquad \qquad \dots (1)$$

where α_t is a vector of unknown parameters. This statement of the DGP is slightly more general than that usually presented because there are time subscripts on both the parameter α and on the general functional form D. These are implicit in the normal discussion but are made explicit here for clarity. The process of econometric model-building consists of simplifying this very general statement of the world to the point at which it becomes feasible to use the model in practical analyses. This process of simplification is termed *model reduction* and consists principally of the following four steps.

1. Marginalise the DGP. The full DGP contains far more variables than we are normally interested in, or can possibly deal with. We therefore reduce this set by selecting a set of 'variables of interest' and relegate all the rest of the variables to the set which are of no interest to the issue at hand.

2. Conditioning assumptions. Given the choice of variables of interest we must now select a subset of these variables to be treated as endogenous (Y_t); these variables are then conditioned on the remaining exogenous variables (Z_t). For valid estimation the Z_t variables should be at least weakly exogenous.

3. Selection of a functional form. The DGP is a completely general functional specification, and before any estimation can be undertaken a specific functional form must be assumed. In many cases this is either a linear or log-linear specification.

4. Estimation. The final stage involves assigning values to the unknown parameters of the system; this is the process of econometric estimation.

Given the general DGP in (1) it is possible to represent the first two stages in the model reduction process by the following factorisation, where the function B represents what one might usually refer to as the structural equations of interest:

$$D_t(x_t|X_{t-1}; \alpha_t) = A_t(W_t|X_t; \alpha_t)B_t(Y_t|Y_{t-1}, Z_t; \alpha_t)C_t(Z_t|Y_{t-1}, Z_{t-1}; \alpha_t) \quad \ldots (2)$$

The first component, A, specifies the determination of W, the variables of no interest as a function of all the variables. The second term, B, gives the determination of the endogenous variables of interest as a function of lagged endogenous variables and all exogenous variables of interest. The final term, C, gives the determination of the exogenous variables as a function of lagged exogenous and endogenous variables.

These steps are all crucial in the formulation of an adequate model. If the marginalisation is incorrect, then this implies that some important variable has been relegated to the set of variables of no interest. This is then the classic error which gives rise to omitted variable bias. If the conditioning assumptions are incorrect, then we have falsely assumed that an endogenous variable is exogenous and so we generate the problem of simultaneous equation bias at the estimation stage and we may also be seriously misled about the nature of causality within the system.

Now when we consider the question of structural change we need to ask how this whole process of model reduction is affected by the changing structure.

1a. Marginalisation and structural change. There exists a marginalisation that is sufficiently general that it is correct. In the limit this may be achieved simply by retaining the full set X_t. In practice it may mean thinking about both the regimes before and after the change and ensuring that all the variables from both regimes are included. The fact that there is structural change taking place does not in any way change the relevance of the marginalisation step.

2a. Conditioning assumption. Here again there will always be a sufficiently large set of variables which, when treated as endogenous, produce a valid conditioning. In the limit if we treat all variables as potentially endogenous, then the conditioning must be valid. In practice we may want to consider all known regimes and formulate a joint set of endogenous variables consisting of the variables that are endogenous in any D_t.

3a. Functional form. In principle a general encompassing functional form can always be specified. This will only generally be possible in practice when theory provides a very precise specification as to the correct functional form both before and after the structural change. If we make the conventional assumption that an adequate local approximation is a linear or log-linear model both before and after the change, then the encompassing model is simply a combination of linear functional forms and so a linear encompassing model is a reasonable assumption.

4a. Estimation. It is this area that is most decisively affected by the presence of structural change. If either the α_t parameters are known to change or we are moving between two regimes with stable structural parameters, then the encompassing model will exhibit changing parameters at some point.

So, while the broad steps of model reduction remain valid under structural change the detailed specification of each step needs to be broadened slightly and in particular the notion of constant parameters is seen to be invalid.

A simple example might clarify this. Consider an economy moving from a command determination of output to a market-based one. Under the command system production plans are announced, and while there may be some systematic departure from these plans they are the principal determinant of production. So

$$P_i^c = \alpha P_i^* \qquad \qquad \ldots (3)$$

where P_i is the production of each individual firm and P^* is the planned level of production. We allow α to differ from unity to allow for systematic over- or under-production. Now we assume that the system is moving towards a market system where each individual firm would produce according to a reduced-form solution to the market system. For simplicity we assume that the market solution will have the following simple form:

$$P_j^m = \beta_1 Y + \beta_2 RC \qquad \qquad \ldots (4)$$

where Y is disposable income and RC is the relative unit cost of production to sales prices. Total production under either regime would simply be the sum of production across all firms, so under the full command system

$$P = \sum_{i=1}^{n} P_i^c \qquad \qquad \ldots (5)$$

and under the full market system

$$P = \sum_{j=1}^{n} P_j^m \qquad \qquad \ldots (6)$$

If the regime changed in a completely discrete way, then the nesting model would simply be

$$P = \delta \sum_{i=1}^{n} P_i^c + (1 - \delta) \sum_{j=1}^{n} P_j^m \qquad \qquad \ldots (7)$$

where δ would shift from zero to one in a completely discrete fashion. It would be easy to model this change simply by splitting the sample. However, a more realistic form of change would be to allow the units of production to move individually from one system to the other, so that each unit would change discretely but that they would not all change together. Total production would still be the sum of production in each firm but now it would sum together the individual types of firms

$$P = \sum_{i \in C} P_i^c + \sum_{j \in m} P_j^m \qquad \ldots (8)$$

and so

$$P = \alpha \left(\sum_{i \in c} \frac{P_i^c}{P} \right) P^* + \sum_{j \in m} (\beta_1 Y + \beta_2 RC) \qquad \ldots (9)$$

When production is fully command determined the coefficient on P^* would have the full value of α and there would be no effect from the market sections. When production is fully market driven the coefficient on Y would be $N\beta_1$ and the coefficient on RC would be $N\beta_2$. As the determination of production moves from the command-based system to the market-based system the coefficient on P^* would fall to zero and the coefficients on Y and RC would rise from zero to their full values. In other words, both sets of coefficients would follow non-stationary processes during the change period because the full encompassing model parameters would change gradually from one set of parameters to the other.

This illustrates the points made above, namely that structural change causes the need for a more general marginalisation and conditioning but the main problem raised comes at the estimation stage when the parameters of the encompassing model will be time varying in general. So the argument is that confronting structural change correctly will in general call for the estimation of models with time-varying structural parameters. The next section turns to this question.

12.3 TIME-VARYING PARAMETER ESTIMATION

In this section a standard state–space formulation of the time-varying parameter model is presented, with the appropriate Kalman Filter equations for the univariate case, following Harvey (1987). Let

$$y_t = \delta' z_t + \varepsilon_t \qquad \ldots (10)$$

be the measurement equation, where y_t is a measured variable, z_t is the state vector of unobserved variables, δ is a vector of parameters and $\varepsilon_t \sim \text{NID}\,(0, \Gamma_t)$. The state equation is then given as

$$z_t = \Psi z_{t-1} + \psi_t \qquad \ldots (11)$$

where Ψ are parameters and $\psi \sim \text{NID}\,(0, Q_t)$. Q_t is sometimes referred to as the hyperparameters.

The appropriate Kalman Filter prediction equations are then given by defining z_t^* as the best estimate of z_t based on information up to t, and P_t as the covariance matrix of the estimate z_t^*, and stating

$$z_{t|t-1}^* = \Psi z_{t-1}^* \qquad \ldots (12)$$

and

$$P_{t|t-1} = \Psi P_{t-1} \Psi' + Q_t \qquad \ldots (13)$$

Once the current observation on y_t becomes available we can update these estimates using the following equations:

$$z_t^* = z_{t|t-1}^* + P_{t|t-1}\delta(y_t - \delta'z_{t|t-1}^*)/(\delta'P_{t|t-1}\delta + \Gamma_t) \qquad \ldots (14)$$

and

$$P_t = P_{t|t-1} - P_{t|t-1}\delta\delta'P_{t|t-1}/(\delta'P_{t|t-1}\delta + \Gamma_t) \qquad \ldots (15)$$

Equations (12)–(15) then jointly represent the Kalman Filter equations.

If we then define the one-step-ahead prediction errors as

$$v_t = y_t - \delta'z_{t|t-1}^*$$

the concentrated log-likelihood function can be shown to be proportional to

$$\log(l) = \Sigma \log(f_t) + N \log(\Sigma v_t^2/Nf_t) \qquad \ldots (16)$$

where $f_t = \alpha'P_{t|t-1}\alpha + \Gamma_t$ and $N = T - k$, where k is the number of periods needed to derive estimates of the state vector. That is to say, the likelihood function can be expressed as a function of the one-step-ahead prediction errors, suitably weighted.

Equipped with these formulae, we can estimate time-varying parameter models such as (9) directly. We do this by first specifying δ as a vector of known variables (in the case of (9), P^*, Y and RC) and z_t as a vector of time-varying parameters (α, β_i, $i = 1, 2$). If Ψ is assumed to be a constant identity matrix, then additionally we have specified the form of the time variation within our model: each of the stochastic parameters follows a random walk. Finally, Q_t is specified as a diagonal matrix, the elements of which are to be estimated using maximum likelihood given the form of the likelihood function outlined. Given this specification, the assumptions outlined, and the likelihood function defined above, we can estimate time-varying models with a wide range of forms.

12.4 USING EXTRA INFORMATION

As a general rule much econometric modelling comprises making a trade-off between incorporating as much prior information as possible, so as to achieve efficient parameter estimates, and specifying a sufficiently general model, so that an inadvertent misspecification will not yield badly biased results. This trade-off is even more crucial when dealing with time-varying parameter models because a very general specification can often lead to identification problems and can certainly give poorly determined coefficients. So it is important to build into the estimated model as much information about the form and timing of the structural change as possible. This section shows how the Kalman Filter may be adapted to allow for specific knowledge of the timing of the changes.

12.4.1 Knowledge About the Timing of a Change

Perhaps the most diffuse form of knowledge we might have is simply to know the rough timing of the structural change. This might be in terms of an estimate of the time the change began and an estimate of when it was completed. This can be easily built into a model such as (10) or (11) by imposing a time-varying weighting pattern on the covariance terms of the state equation (10), Q_t. So, in an example such as the encompassing model (9), if we believed that over an initial period only plans mattered, then we could use initial parameter estimates of zero for the coefficients on Y and RC, with their respective elements in both the Q matrix and the P matrix set to zero. The coefficient on P^* would then be set to an arbitrary value with a zero element in the Q matrix and a very large (in principle, infinite) element in the P matrix. This set-up would then in effect perform a recursive ordinary least squares (OLS) estimation on the P^* parameter while fixing the other parameters at zero. When the time came for the structural change to begin, this would be allowed by raising the value of the diagonal element of the Q matrix and allowing all the coefficients to change. When the structural change is complete the Q matrix should return to zero.

12.4.2 Knowledge About the Speed of Change

If we have slightly more knowledge about the timing of the change, then we can do rather better than to simply control the speed of variation of the parameters. Suppose we have an indicator variable W_t, which is scaled between zero and one, that measures the degree of structural change. Then we can incorporate this information into the estimation in the following way. Let the measurement equation be

$$P_t = W_t S_{1t} + (1 - W_t) S_{2t} + e_t \qquad \ldots (17)$$

and the state equations be

$$S_{1t} = \alpha P^* + v_{1t} \qquad \ldots (18)$$

$$S_{2t} = \beta_1 Y + \beta_2 RC + v_{2t} \qquad \ldots (19)$$

In this case because we have a good measure of the rate of change between the two regimes we are able to specifically use this information to govern the rate of change of the overall parameters.

12.4.3 Modelling Change as a Switching System

Switching models have been popular in work on Eastern Europe for some years and these models may also be addressed within the state–space framework. Let the measurement equation be

$$Y_t = \beta_t X_t + e_t \qquad \ldots (20)$$

and the state equations be

$$\beta_t = \phi_1 \beta_{t-1} + \phi_2 \beta_1 + \phi_3 \beta_2 + v_t$$
$$\phi_2 = (1 - \phi_3) \qquad \ldots (21)$$
$$\phi_3 = (1 \text{ if } \gamma'Z > 0, \text{ else } 0 \text{ if } \gamma'Z \le 0)$$

If $\phi_1 = 0$, then the model will tend to switch discretely between the two sets of parameters, with only a random error. However, if $1 > \phi_1 > 0$, then the switching will occur gradually but smoothly between the two sets of parameters. While this type of switching model has traditionally been used to model disequilibrium in markets that switch between demand and supply constraints, obviously it can also be used to model structural change.

12.4.4 Knowledge About the Rate of Change of a Parameter

In the above analyses the parameters have always been assumed to follow a random walk process. This has the disadvantage that the forecast from the model will always be that structural change has ceased. If we have an idea as to the general speed or form of parameter change, then we can build this into the state equations in the following way.

Let the measurement equation be

$$Y_t = \beta_t X_t + e_t \qquad \ldots (22)$$

and the state equations be

$$\beta_t = \beta_{t-1} + \phi z_t + v_t \qquad \ldots (23)$$

Here the variable z will have a cumulative effect on the state variable and so as long as z is forecast to be non-zero, the parameter will be forecast to continue to change. We can use this form to build a wide range of assumptions into the model about the form and timing of the change simply by giving z a particular weighting pattern. At times of rapid change z would be large, while at times of slower change z would be small. Note that this state equation is still stochastic so we are allowing for the possibility that there is more going on in determining the parameter than simply our knowledge of z.

We can of course make z a part of the state vector and then possibly even include extra information about how z changes. This would be done by setting up the following simple state system:

$$\beta_t = \beta_{t-1} + \phi z_t + v_t$$
$$z_t = z_{t-1} + \zeta w_t + \varepsilon_t \qquad \ldots (24)$$

where now w is the extra information about the way z evolves over time.

These two forms of the model may be particularly useful in a forecasting context where we have a strong belief that structural change will continue during the time of the forecast. Equation (24) is particularly useful because it gives us an estimated basis for assessing the likely rate of future structural change.

12.5 AN EXAMPLE USING THE POLISH FOREIGN EXCHANGE MARKET

In this section an illustration of the time-varying models discussed above will be presented based around an analysis of the relationship between the official and black market exchange rates in Poland over the period 1976–91. Poland is a particularly good example for this purpose because it is now well along the transition path to a market economy and so we are able to illustrate the power of these techniques to capture the whole process. The behaviour of foreign exchange markets is also an apt area of study because it is an area of very obvious structural change with a move from an initial regime in the early 1970s of a fixed non-convertible currency to full convertibility by the early 1990s.[1]

Figure 12.1 shows the time path for the logarithm of both the official exchange rate against the dollar and the unofficial black market rate. During the late 1970s the official rate was fixed and not convertible. The shortage of domestic goods meant that many goods could only be purchased with hard currencies and so there was a large demand for illegal currency exchange. This led to a black market

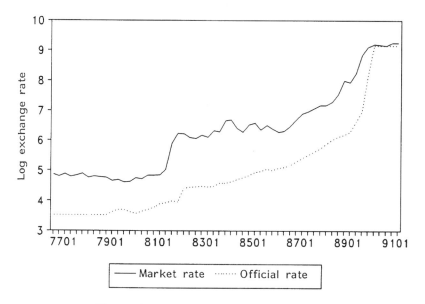

Figure 12.1 Official and market rates: Poland

rate that was well in excess of twice the official rate. The model we have in mind is a very simple one of a continuously switching regime. At one extreme, when a currency is fully convertible there is no incentive for a black market rate to operate at anything other than the official rate; one side of the trade could always do better by trading on the official market. The other extreme is when a currency is not convertible and is completely unresponsive to domestic/foreign price differentials. Under this condition the black market rate will be a function of the demand for illicit hard currency, which in turn will be a function of the price differential between domestic prices and hard currency prices. So we may postulate the following simple model for the determination of the black market exchange rate:

$$E^b = A_{1t}(P - P^*) + A_{2t}E^0 \qquad \qquad \ldots (25)$$

where E^b is the log of the black market exchange rate, E^0 is the log of the official rate, P and P^* are the logs of the domestic and US price level, and A_i are time-varying parameters. Under full convertibility we would expect $A_2 = 1$ and $A_1 = 0$, while under non-convertibility we would expect $A_1 > 0$ and A_2 could be almost anything. So as we move from the mid-1970s to the early 1990s we would expect to see systematic changes in these parameters as the system moves from one regime to the other. This is clearly a situation that is closely analogous to (9) and the parameters may be estimated directly by the procedure outlined in Section 12.3.

The time path for the estimates of these two parameters is shown in Figure 12.2. A_2 is estimated to have been above unity in the late 1970s. This simply reflects the fact that the official rate was well below the market rate while the effect of the price differential was estimated to be almost exactly unity. The price differential effect fell fairly smoothly over the whole period until it became effectively zero at the time of convertibility in the early 1990s. The coefficient on the official rate also fell slowly so that it became almost exactly unity by the end of the period.

The timing of the changes is of some interest. Most commentators on Poland would confirm that structural change had been proceeding through much of the 1980s and this is illustrated through the steady decline in the parameter on the price differential. There was an obvious increase in the rate of change in the parameter from around 1982, which again conforms well with most commentators' views about institutional changes. The final dramatic change is seen to have taken place in early 1990 when convertibility was established. So the model picks up rather more than simply the fact of convertibility, which did not happen until the end of the period: it also detects the progressive move in the official rate towards being more responsive to fundamental market forces.

As a final formal point it is possible to report an analysis of the properties of the one-step-ahead residuals. These are not serially correlated (Box–Pierce, $(1) = 1.2$, $(2) = 2.4$, $(8) = 13.3$, $(16) = 16.7$) although there is evidence of

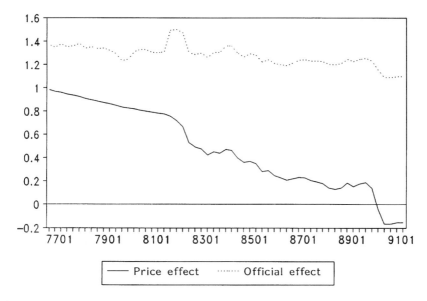

Figure 12.2 Time-varying parameters: Poland

excess kurtosis (Berra–Jarque (2) = 90.1) which seems to be due mainly to the sudden fixing of the convertible exchange rate in the early 1990s.

12.6 KALMAN FILTERS IN A FULL MACRO MODEL

The general form of the Kalman Filter given above is conventionally thought of as an estimation technique, but it can also be thought of as an integral part of a structural economic model. An obvious example of this is the work on learning undertaken by Garratt and Hall (1992), where the Kalman Filter is introduced into a large econometric model as a way of forming expectations. In this example an explicit expectations rule is set up and agents are viewed as having to learn about the parameters of this rule. The learning takes place within the model through the use of a Kalman Filter which changes the values of the perceived parameters in the light of observed expectations errors.

In this case we will be undertaking much the same exercise, but we will be using the Kalman Filter in a rather different and novel way. In particular, we will set up a general equation structure which will allow the parameters of an equation to change in the light of a structural change subject to an invariant underlying long-run structure. This means that the basic long-run simulation and policy properties of the model may be held unchanged, while the dynamics of the model will be allowed to respond to structural change to produce a well-fitting, time-series representation of the recent data which it is able to forecast well.

The basic structure we will be proposing is a variant of the conventional error correction model (ECM), i.e. each equation will have the following underlying form:

$$\Delta Y_t = \sum_{i=1}^{k} (\gamma_{0i} \Delta Y_{t-i} + \gamma_i' X_{t-i}) + \alpha(Y_{t-1} + \beta' X_{t-1}) \qquad \ldots (26)$$

where y is the dependent variable and X is a vector of independent (although not necessarily exogenous in a full model context) variables. The last term in this equation is the error correction term (ECT) which is closely related to the cointegrating vectors of the system (see Cuthbertson, Hall and Taylor (1991), and it is this term that provides the long-run solution to the model. The dynamics capture the short-run, time-series property of the data. It would of course be quite easy to allow the Kalman Filter to simply change all the parameters of the system, but this would then mean that it would be very hard to give the model any meaningful economic interpretation because we could not even be sure that the sign of the long-run effects would remain sensible. So we want a model formulation that allows us to fix the long-run properties of the model but also allows the dynamics to change in a flexible way. We also want to be able to control the updating of coefficients so that where data are available on a variable, updating takes place, and where there are no data, the parameters are held constant. The following general equation structure achieves these objectives:

$$ECT = (Y_{t-1} + \beta' X_{t-1}) \qquad \ldots (27)$$

$$\Delta \hat{Y}_t = \sum_{i=1}^{k} (\gamma_{0it} \Delta Y_{t-i} + \gamma_{it}' \Delta X_{t-i}) + \alpha_t ECT \qquad \ldots (28)$$

$$\hat{Y}_t = Y_{t-1} + \Delta \hat{Y}_t \qquad \ldots (29)$$

$$\text{if no data } Y_t^* = \hat{Y}_t, \text{ else } Y_t^* = \text{data} \qquad \ldots (30)$$

$$v_{t-1} = Y_{t-1}^* - \hat{Y}_{t-1} \qquad \ldots (31)$$

The first thing to note is that in this formulation all the parameters of equation (28) have t subscripts, i.e. they are now time-varying. The error correction term is constructed in (27) and does not have time-varying parameters so that the long-run solution to (28) will be invariant to the changing parameters. Equation (29) simply constructs the forecast of (28) for the level of Y. Equation (30) sets up a variable Y^* which is either equal to actual data or to the forecast of the model (28). Finally, (31) defines v, the prediction error used in the Kalman Filter, as the difference between Y^* and the forecast value of Y from (28). Note that when Y^* is set to actual data, a forecast error will be observed and the Kalman Filter will change the parameters in the light of that error, but when Y^* is set to the forecast of Y, then $v = 0$ by construction and so the Kalman Filter will cease changing the parameters.

This structure allows us to run the model over an historical data period. Setting Y^* to its historical values, the parameters will then change in the light of the model's forecast error. At the end of the available data period we can then begin an *ex ante* forecast by setting Y^* to its forecast values; the parameters will then cease changing but will remain at their latest values. We can, of course, set Y^* to its forecast value at any point over the historical period simply by switching in the first part of (14). This then allows us to see how the model would have performed in a forecasting context if it had been used in a real forecast, starting at various points over the historical data period.

12.7 AN EXAMPLE USING ROMANIA

As an example of this modelling strategy we have chosen to implement a simple aggregate model of the Romanian economy. We have chosen this economy for two reasons. First, structural change in Romania has been more recent and dramatic than in the case of many of the more developed Eastern European economies such as Poland or Hungary, where conventional modelling techniques might be argued to be adequate. Secondly, data are available on Romania from the IMF for a fairly long period; this is not the case for many of the other states in rapid transition such as Bulgaria or the new CIS states. So Romania offers us both a real challenge in terms of extreme and rapid change and an historical period long enough to begin to demonstrate the potential of our technique.

The dynamic specification of each ECM has been kept quite simple for two reasons. First, we do not believe the data can support a complex dynamic structure because the structural change would tend to give us spuriously complex dynamic specifications if we used conventional modelling techniques. Secondly, the time-varying parameters also imply the presence of quite complex dynamic properties in the model because the time varying parameter model can be given a complex ARIMA representation. The error correction terms have also been specified in a very simple form so that most of the main GDP aggregates are given a simple proportional relationship with GDP. This is partly because the data are not detailed enough to allow us to use a range of concepts in the conventional way (e.g. disposable income in the consumption function). We would stress, however, that we are not assuming that each component of GDP has an unchanging proportional relationship because the equilibrium proportion which a component has of GDP will be a function of the constant of the full ECM, and this is time-varying.

Figures 12.3–12.5 illustrate how the properties of the model change over time. We have data for Romania from 1982Q1 up to 1990Q1. We then run the model beginning in 1983Q1 (to allow for the required lags in the model) with all the

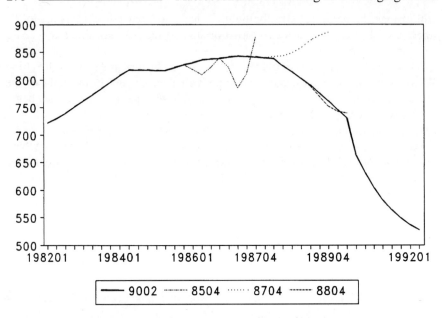

Figure 12.3   Forecast for output: different starting points

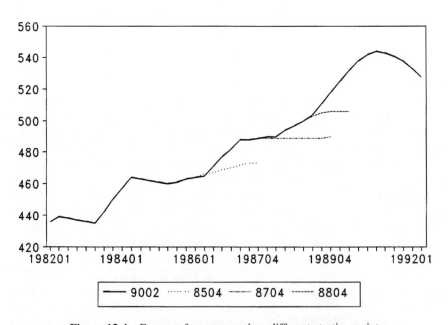

Figure 12.4   Forecast for consumption: different starting points

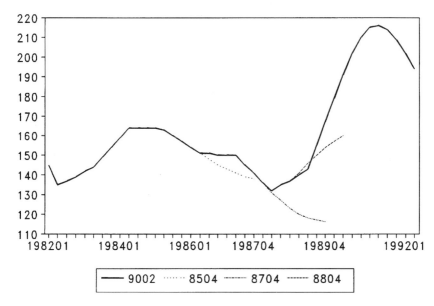

Figure 12.5 Forecast for imports: different starting points

Y^* terms set equal to their data values. Under these conditions the Kalman Filter will change the parameters as the economy changes. We then stop this process at four points (1985Q4, 1987Q4, 1988Q4 and 1990Q2) by setting Y^* to its forecast value and then proceed to forecast with the model conditional on the most recent set of parameter values. The model has no exogenous variables so this then forms a true *ex ante* forecast, as if we had been forecasting at the time. We can then see how the model's time-series forecasts respond to the changing behaviour of the data. Figure 12.3 gives the results for total GDP. We can see that Romania grew fairly steadily up to the beginning of 1988 when a sharp recession began. The forecast for GDP starting in 1985 has only about two years of data against which to calibrate its parameters, and so it is not surprising that its profile is a little erratic, but it does suggest a reasonable picture of past events. The forecast beginning at the end of 1987 is interesting because this is just before the main structural break in the data. This forecast projects a fairly smooth continuation of the growth that was observed over the previous five years, and would certainly have appeared to have been a reasonable forecast at the time. But of course we now know that there was a sharp change in the economic environment just ahead and so it is interesting to see how quickly the model can adjust to this change. The forecast beginning only four quarters later is completely different in that it tracks the fall in output up to the early 1990s when the data end almost perfectly. So the model has, over just three or four quarters, adjusted to the structural change and produced a completely different forecast of GDP which fully allowed for the structural change in early 1988. The forecast beginning in 1992 shows a continuation in the fall in GDP over the next two years. At the time of writing we have been unable to obtain actual data for this period and so this is a true forecast which can be evaluated at a later date.

Figures 12.4 and 12.5 show similar pictures for consumption and imports, where the model adjusts its forecast quite rapidly to match changes in the economy. The forecast for imports in particular changes very rapidly as the structural change hits the economy in 1988. The final forecast, beginning in 1990, also emphasises an important aspect of this model: it is not simply a set of univariate forecasting equations, it also has an underlying structure. The initial 1988–90 period was characterised by a fall in output, a rise in imports, but a growth in consumption. Clearly, this is unsustainable because consumption and imports cannot grow indefinitely if total GDP is falling. The underlying structure of the economy then brings these back into line in the forecast starting in 1990 and consumption is projected to fall, contrary to its recent trend, and imports are also projected to fall. Both of these effects come from the system's properties as a whole, which exist in the ECTs of each equation.

12.8 CONCLUSIONS

This chapter has explored the consequences of structural change in the data-generation process for forecasting and modelling. It proposed a modelling strategy that rests on a whole model approach which allows for time-varying parameters in the dynamic structure of each equation while imposing a coherent long-run solution to the model. This strategy has been illustrated by constructing a small model of the Romanian economy and demonstrating how its forecasting ability changes over time as the structure of the economy changes.

We would not argue that this is a first-best approach to econometric modelling. In an ideal world we would want an extensive run of data on many variables so that we could explicitly model and investigate the form of structural change taking place. In practice, however, many economies in transition are not only subject to economic change but also provide very little detailed reliable information on this change. Only the broadest aggregates are available and often then only for short periods on consistent data definitions. Best practice is simply not an option. We do argue that using the available data in the most flexible and efficient way is preferable to using wholly artificial models or even abandoning the formal modelling approach completely.

12.9 ENDNOTE

1. The data for this example have been kindly provided by Wojciech Charemza. Further analysis of the data and a discussion of some of the background economic developments in Poland may be found in Charemza (1992).

12.10 DATA SOURCES

Key to variable index

1. All series listed are for Romania apart from USP, the US GDP deflator.
2. All National Accounts Series (RMY, RMC, RMG, RMM, RMX, RMI, RMS, $RMBI$) are in constant (1985) prices. These series were created from the annual current price series listed in the IMF's International Financial Statistics (IFS). They were deflated using the GDP deflator (RMP).

Series code line no.	Description	IFS
RMX	Exports	90c
RMG	Government consumption	91f
RMI	Gross fixed capital formation	93e
RMS	Stockbuilding	93i
RMC	Consumption	96f
RMM	Imports	98c
RMY	GDP 1985 prices	99b
RMP	GDP deflator	99p

3. The quarterly series are linear interpolations of these annual constant price series, so that the annual figure becomes the second quarter figure (i.e. the number for 1990 becomes 199002).
4. $RMBI$, the balancing item, is the difference between constant price GDP series, and the figure derived by summing the components of GDP in constant prices (i.e. $RMC + RMG + RMX + RMI + RMS - RMM$).
5. $RMM1$, the money supply, is a linear interpolation of the annual series in IFS.
6. The source for $RMRX$, the \$/Lei exchange rate, is datastream (code $RMI.AE$).
7. All other series in the model are log transformations of the raw series described above.

APPENDIX 1: ROMANIAN MODEL MANUAL (CENTRE FOR ECONOMIC FORECASTING)

A description and equation listing

PREFACE

This is a complete listing of the equations in the Romanian model in the computer readable form used by the London Business School's economic modelling software.

Definitions of Operators

+ addition
− subtraction
∗ multiplication
/ division
ALOG(X) natural logarithm of variable X
X(−i) ith period lag of variable X
X∗∗i raise the value of X to power i.
exp(X) take the exponential of X
∗K indicates an equation with time varying parameters to be updated by the Kalman Filter
∗V indicates the equation generating the prediction error for the previous ∗K equation
∗CV indicates the covariance matrix of the time varying parameters (P_0)
∗Q indicates the hyperparameters for the Kalman Filter (Q)

ROMANIAN MODEL

First Kalman Filter equation (consumption)

```
*     LCY = ALOG(RMC) − ALOG(RMY)
*K    DLRMC# = a3 + a1 *DLRMC(−1) + a2*LCY(−1)
*V    VV = ALOG(RMC(−1)) − ALOG(RMC#(−1))
*CV   10
*     0 1 0
*     0 0 0
*Q    1 1 0
*     RMC# = RMC(−1)*EXP(DLRMC#)
*     RMC = RMC#
*     DLRMC = ALOG(RMC) − ALOG(RMC(−1))
```

Second Kalman Filter equation (government consumption)

```
*     LGY = ALOG(RMG) − ALOG(RMY)
*K    DLRMG# = a6 + a4 * DLRMG(−1) + a5 * LGY(−1)
*V    VV = ALOG(RMG(−1)) − ALOG(RMG#(−1))
*CV   10
*     0 1 0
*     0 0 0
*Q    1 1 0
*     RMG# = RMG(−1)*EXP(DLRMG#)
*     RMG = RMG#
*     DLRMG = ALOG(RMG) − ALOG(RMG(−1))
```

Third Kalman Filter equation (imports)

```
*     LMY = ALOG(RMM) − ALOG(RMY)
*K    DLRMM# = a9 + a7*DLRMM(−1) + a8*LMY(−1)
*V    VV = ALOG(RMM(−1)) − ALOG(RMM#(−1))
*CV   10
*     0 1 0
*     0 0 0
```

```
*Q    1 1 0
*     RMM# = RMM(-1)*EXP(DLRMM#)
*     RMM = RMM#
*     DLRMM = ALOG(RMM) - ALOG(RMM(-1))
```

Fourth Kalman Filter equation (exports)

```
*     LXY = ALOG(RMX) - ALOG(RMY)
*K    DLRMX# = a12 + a10*DLRMX(-1) + a11*LXY(-1)
*V    VV = ALOG(RMX(-1)) - ALOG(RMX#(-1))
*CV   10
*     0 1 0
*     0 0 0
*Q    1 1 0
*     RMX# = RMX(-1)*EXP(DLRMX#)
*     RMX = RMX#
*     DLRMX = ALOG(RMX) - ALOG(RMX(-1))
```

Fifth Kalman Filter equation (investment)

```
*     LIY = ALOG(RMI) - ALOG(RMY)
*K    DLRMI# = a15 + a13*DLRMI(-1) + a14*LIY(-1)
*V    VV = ALOG(RMI(-1)) - ALOG(RMI#(-1))
*CV   10
*     0 1 0
*     0 0 0
*Q    1 1 0
*     RMI# = RMI(-1)*EXP(DLRMI#)
*     RMI = RMI#
*     DLRMI = ALOG(RMI) - ALOG(RMI(-1))
```

Sixth Kalman Filter equation (stockbuilding)

```
*ADD  RMSY = RMS - (RMY - RMY(-1))
*K      DRMS# = a19 + a16*DRMS(-1) + a17*DRMS(-2) + a18*RMSY(-1)
*V      VV = RMS(-1) - RMS#(-1)
*CV    0
*     0 1
*     0 0 1
*     0 0 0 0
*Q    0 .01 .01 0
*ADD  RMS# = RMS(-1) + DRMS#
*ADD  RMS = RMS#
*ADD  DRMS = RMS - RMS(-1)
```

Seventh Kalman Filter equation (prices)

```
*     LPM = ALOG(RMP) - ALOG(RMM1)
*K    DLRMP# = a22 + a20*DLRMP(-1) + a21*LPM(-1)
*V    VV = ALOG(RMP(-1)) - ALOG(RMP#(-1))
*CV   10
*     0 1 0
*     0 0 0
*Q    1 1 0
```

```
*    RMP# = RMP(-1)*EXP(DLRMP#)
*    RMP = RMP#
*    DLRMP = ALOG(RMP) - ALOG(RMP(-1))
```

Eighth Kalman Filter equation (money)

```
*K    LRMM1# = a24 + a23*LRMM1(-1)
*V    VV = ALOG(RMM1(-1)) - ALOG(RMM1#(-1))
*CV   10
*     0 1 0
*Q    1 1
*     RMM1# = EXP(LRMM1#)
*     RMM1 = RMM1#
*     LRMM1 = ALOG(RMM1)
```

Balancing item

```
*    RMBI = RMBI(-1)
```

GDP

```
*    RMY = RMC + RMG + RMX + RMI + RMS + RMBI - RMM
```

Exchange rate

```
*    RMRX = RMRX(-1)
*    LRMRX = ALOG(RMP) - ALOG(USP) + 2.7929
*    USP = USP(-1)*(USP(-1)/USP(-2))
```

&&

References

Abel, A.B. (1988) Consumption and investment. NBER Working Paper, No. 2580.

Abel, A.B. and Blanchard, O.J. (1986) The present value of profits and cyclical movements in investment. *Econometrica* **54** (2) 249-73.

Allen, C.B. (1993) An empirical model of pricing, market share, and market conduct. LBS, mimeo.

Allen, C.B. (1994) A supply side model of the UK Economy: an application of non-linear cointegration. LBS Discussion paper.

Allen, C.B. and Robertson, D. (1990) Recovering the aggregate production function: supplyside modelling of three industralized economies. LBS Centre for Economic Forecasting Discussion Paper No. 28-90.

Allen, C.B. and Urga, G. (1995) Derivation and estimation of interrelated factor demands from a dynamic cost function. London Business School, Centre for Economic Forecasting Discussion Paper, No. 10-95.

Allen, C.B. and Whitley, J. (1994) Modelling bilateral trade. In S.G. Hall (ed.), *Applied Economic Forecasting Techniques*. Harvester Wheatsheaf, New York.

Allen, C., Hall, S.G. and Nixon, J. (1994) The new London Business School model of the UK economy. LBS CEF Discussion Paper DP 18-94.

Allen, R.G.D. (1938) *Mathematical Analysis for Economists*. Macmillan, London.

Ammer, J. and Freeman, R. (1994) Inflation targetting in the 1990's. The experiences of New Zealand, Canada and UK. Board of Governors of the Federal Reserve System, International Finance Discussion Paper No. 473, June.

Anderson, G.J. and Mizon, G. (1984) Parameter constancy tests: old and new. Discussion Paper in Economics and Econometrics No. 83-25, University of Southampton.

Anderson, G.J. and Blundell, R.W. (1982) Estimation and hypothesis testing in dynamic singular equation systems. *Econometrica* **50**, 1559-71.

Anderson, P.A. (1979) Rational expectations forecasts from non-rational models. *Journal of Monetary Economics* **5**, 67-80.

Anderton, R. (1992) U.K. exports of manufactures: testing for the effects of non-price competitiveness using stochastic trends and profitability measures. *The Manchester School* **LX**, 23-40.

Anderton, R., Pesaran, B. and Wren-Lewis, S. (1992) Imports, output and the demand for manufactures. *Oxford Economic Papers* **44**, 175-88.

Andrews, D.W.K. (1991) Heteroskedasticity and autocorrelation consistent covariance matrix estimation. *Econometrica* **59**, 817-58.

Andrews, D.W.K. (1993) Tests for parameter instability and structural change with unknown change point. *Econometrica* **61** (4) 821-56.

Andrews, D.W.K. and Fair, R.C. (1988) Inference in nonlinear models with structural change. *Review of Economic Studies* **55**, 615-40.

Arrow, K.J. (1974) The measurement of real value added. In P.David and M.Reder (eds), *Nations and Households in Economic Growth: Essays in* Honor of Moses Abromovitz. Academic Press, New York.

Arrow, K.J., Chenery, H.B., Minhas, B.S. and Solow, R.M. (1961) Capital-labor substitution and economic efficiency. *Review of Economics and Statistics* **43**, 225-50.

Atkinson, A.B. and Stiglitz, J.E. (1980) *Lectures on Public Economics*. McGraw-Hill, Maidenhead.

Banerjee, A. and Urga, G. (1995a) Looking for structural breaks in co-integrated systems. D.P. 18-95, Centre for Economic Forecasting, London Business School, June.

Banerjee, A. and Urga, G. (1995b) Modelling U.K. trade: an exercise in sequential structural break procedures. D.P. 24-95, Centre for Economic Forecasting, London Business School, July.

Banerjee, A., Lumsdaine, R.L. and Stock, J.H. (1992) Recursive and sequential tests of the unit-root and trend-break hypothesis: theory and international evidence. *Journal of Business and Economic Statistics* **10** (3) 250-71.

Banerjee, A., Dolado, J.J., Galbraith, J.W. and Hendry, D.F. (1993) *Cointegration, Error Correction, and the Econometric Analysis of Non-Stationary Data*. Oxford University Press, Oxford.

Bank of England (1985) The housing finance market: recent growth in perspective. *Bank of England Quarterly Bulletin*, **March**, 80-91.

Bank of England (1989) The housing market. *Bank of England Quarterly Bulletin*, **February**, 66-77.

Bank of England (1991) Housing finance — an international perspective. *Bank of England Quarterly Bulletin*, **February**, 56-66.

Bank of England (1992) Housing policy and finance. *Bank of England Quarterly Bulletin*, **May**, 173-9.

Barker, T., Dunne, J.P. and Smith, R.P. (1991) Measuring the Peace Dividend in the UK. *Journal of Peace Research* **28**, (4) 345-58.

Barnett, W.A. (1983) New indices of money supply and the flexible Laurent system. *Journal of Business and Economic Statistics* **1**, 7-23.

Barnett, W.A. (1985) The Miniflex-Laurent Translog flexible functional form. *Journal of Econometrics* **30**, 34-44.

Barnett, W.A. and Lee, Y.W. (1985) The global properties of the Miniflex Laurent, Generalized Leontief, and Translog functional forms. *Journal of Econometrics* **30**, 3-31.

Barr, D.G. and Cuthbertson, K. (1990) Modelling the flow of funds with an application to the demand for liquid assets by the UK personal sector. In S.G.B. Henry and K.D. Patterson (eds), *Economic Modelling at the Bank of England*. Chapman and Hall, London.

Barr, D.G. and Cuthbertson, K. (1991) Neo-classical consumer demand theory and the demand for money. *Economic Journal* **101**, 855-76.

Barrell, R., Caporale, G.M., Garratt, A. and Hall, S.G. (1992) Learning about monetary union: an analysis of boundedly rational learning in European labour markets. Paper presented at the ESRC Macromodelling Conference, Warwick.

Barrell, R., Caporale, G.M., Garratt, A. and Hall, S.G. (1993) Learning about monetary union: an analysis of boundedly rational learning in European labour markets. In S.G. Hall (ed), *Applied Economic Forecasting Techniques*. Simon and Schuster, New York.

Barro, R.J. (1976) Rational expectations and the role of monetary policy. *Journal of Monetary Economics* **2**, 1-33.

Barro, R.J. (1977) Unanticipated monetary growth and unemployment in the United States. *American Economic Review* **67**, 101-15.

Barro, R.J. and Gordon, D.A. (1983) Rules, discretion and reputation in a model of monetary policy. *Journal of Monetary Economics* **22**, 101–21.

Baumol, W.J. (1967) Macroeconomics of unbalanced growth: the anatomy of the urban crisis. *American Economic Review* **57** (3), 415–25.

Baumol, W.J. and Fischer, D. (1978) The cost minimizing number of firms and the determination of industry structure. *Quarterly Journal of Economics* **92**, 439–67.

Becker, R.G., Dwolatzky, B., Karakitsos, E. and Rustem, B. (1986) The simultaneous use of rival models in policy optimisation. *The Economic Journal* **96**, 425–48.

Bean, C.R. (1989) Capital shortage. *Economic Policy* **8**, 11–53.

Bean, C.R. (1994) European unemployment: a survey. *Journal of Economic Literature* **32**, 573–619.

Becker, R., Hall, S.G. and Rustem, B. (1994) Robust optimal decisions with stochastic nonlinear economic systems. *Journal of Economic Dynamics and Control* **18** (1), 125–48.

Bergson, A. (1936) Real income, expenditure proportionality, and Frisch's 'New methods of measuring efficiency'. *Review of Economic Studies* **4**, 33–52.

Berndt, E.R. and Christensen, L.R. (1973a) The internal structure of functional relationships: separability, substitution, and aggregation. *Review of Economic Studies* **40**, 402–10.

Berndt, E.R. and Christensen, L.R. (1973b) The translog function and the substitution of equipment, structures and labor in US manufacturing. *Journal of Econometrics* **18**, 235–52.

Berndt, E.R. and Wood, D.O. (1975) Technology, prices and the derived demand for energy. *Review of Economics and Statistics* **57**, 259–68.

Bernstein, J.I. and Mohnen, P. (1991) Price–cost margins, exports and productivity growth. NBER Working Paper No. 3584.

Bewley, R.A. (1979) The direct estimation of the equilibrium response in a linear dynamic model. *Economic Letters* **3**, 357–62.

Bewley, R. and Elliott, G. (1991) Accounting for non-stationarity in demand systems. In R. Bewley and T.V. Hoa (eds), *Contributions to Consumer Demand and Econometrics*. Macmillan, London.

Blackorby, C. and Russell, R.R. (1989) Will the real elasticity of substitution please stand up? (A comparison of the Allen/Uzawa and Morishima elasticities). *American Economic Review* **79**, 882–8.

Blackorby, C., Primont, D. and Russell, R.R. (1978) *Duality, Separability, and Functional Form*. North-Holland, Amsterdam.

Blake, A.P., and Pain, N. (1994) Investigating structural changes in U.K. export performance: the role of innovation and direct investment. *National Institute Economic Review*, **September 1994**.

Blake, A.P. and Westaway, P. (1994) Targeting inflation with nominal interest rates. National Institute of Economic and Social Research, Discussion Paper, No. 70.

Blanchard, O.J. (1985) Debts, deficits, and finite horizons. *Journal of Political Economy* **93**, 1045–76.

Blanchard, O. (1989) A traditional interpretation of macroeconomic fluctuations. Mimeo, MIT Dept of Economics, MIT, Boston.

Blanchard, O.J. and Kiyotaki, N. (1987) Monopolistic competition and the effects of aggregate demand. *American Economic Review* **77**, 647–66.

Blanchard, O.J. and Summers, L.H. (1986) Hysteresis and the European unemployment problem. *NBER Macroeconomics Annual* **1**, 15–89.

Blanchard, O.J., Rhee, C. and Summers, L.H. (1993) The stock market, profit, and investment. *Quarterly Journal of Economics* **108** (1), 115–36.

Blundell, R., Bond, S., Devereux, M. and Schiantarelli, F. (1992) Investment and Tobin's *Q*. *Journal of Econometrics* **51**, 233–57.

Bodkin, R.G., Klein, L.R. and Marwah, K. (1991) *A History of Macroeconometric Model Building*. Edward Elgar, Aldershot, England

Bollerslev, T. (1986) Generalised autoregressive conditional heteroskedasticity. *Journal of Econometrics* **31** (3), 307–28.

Bray, M.M. (1983) Convergence to rational expectations equilibrium. In R. Frydman and E.S. Phelps (eds), *Industrial Forecasting and Aggregate Outcomes*. Cambridge University Press, Cambridge.

Bray, M.M. and Kreps, C. (1984) Rational learning and rational expectation. Mimeo, Cambridge University.

Bray, M.M. and Savin, N.E. (1986) Rational expectations equilibria, learning and model specification. *Econometrica* **54**, 1129–60.

Bray, J., Hall, S., Kuleshov, A., Nixon, J. and Westaway, P. (1995) The interfaces between policy makers, markets and modellers. *The Economic Journal* **105** (431), 989–1000.

Brown, R.L., Durbin, J. and Evans, J.M. (1975) Techniques for testing the constancy of regression relationships over time. *Journal of the Royal Statistical Society, Series B* **37**, 149–92.

Brown, R.S. and Christensen, L.R. (1981) Estimating elasticities of substitution in a model of partial static equilibrium: an application to US agriculture 1947 to 1974. In E.R. Berndt and B.C. Field (eds), *Modelling and Measuring Natural Resource Substitution*. MIT Press, Cambridge, MA.

Brown, R.S. and Christensen, L.R. (1982) Estimating elasticities of substitution in a model of partial static equilibrium. In E.R. Berndt and B.C. Field (eds), *Modelling and Measuring Natural Resource Substitution*. MIT Press, Cambridge, MA.

Bruno, M. and Sachs, J.D. (1985) *The Economics of Worldwide Stagflation*. Basil Blackwell, Oxford.

Buchanan, J.M. and Tullock, G. (1962) *The Calculus of Consent*. University of Michigan Press, Ann Arbor.

Budd, A., Christodoulakis, N., Holly, S. and Levine, P. (1989) Stabilisation policy in Britain. In A. Britton (ed.), *Policy Making with Macroeconomic Models*. Gower, Aldershot.

Budd, A., Dicks, G., Holly, S., Keating, G. and Robinson, B. (1984) The London Business School econometric model of the UK. *Economic Modelling* **1**, (4).

Bullard, J. (1992) Time-varying parameters and nonconvergence to rational expectations under least squares learning. *Economics Letters* **40**, 159–66.

Burgess, D.F. (1974) A cost minimization approach to import demand functions. *Review of Economics and Statistics* **56**, 234–55.

Cagan, P. (1956) The monetary dynamics of hyper-inflation. In M. Friedman (ed.), *Studies in the Quantity Theory of Money*. Chicago University Press, Chicago.

Callen, T.S. and Henry, S.G.B. (1989) Stockbuilding and liquidity: some empirical evidence for the manufacturing sector. Bank of England Discussion Paper, No. 38.

Callen, T.S., Hall, S.G. and Henry, S.G.B. (1990) Manufacturing stocks: expectations, risk and co-integration. *Economic Journal* **100** (402), 756–73.

Calvo, G.A. (1979) Quasi-Walrasian models of unemployment. *American Economic Review* **69**, 102–8.

Campbell, J.Y. and Deaton, A. (1989) Why is consumption so smooth? *Review of Economic Studies* **56**, 357–74.

Campbell, J.Y. and Mankiw, N.G. (1989) Consumption, income, and interest rates: reinterpreting the time series evidence. NBER Working Paper, No. 2924.

Campbell, J.Y. and Mankiw, N.G. (1991) The response of consumption to income. *European Economic Review* **35**, 723–67.

Campos, J., Ericsson, N.R. and Hendry, D.F. (1993) Cointegration tests in the presence of structural breaks. International Finance Discussion Paper No. 440, Board of Governors of the Federal Reserve System, Washington, D.C.

Caves, D.W. and Christensen, L.R. (1980) Global properties of flexible functional forms. *American Economic Review* **70**, 422–32.

Chambers, M. (1991) The estimation of long-run equilibria subject to linear restrictions: an application to consumer demand. Essex University Discussion Paper No. 386.

Charemza, W.W. (1992) Formation and dynamics of foreign exchange rates in Eastern and Western Europe. University of Leicester Discussion Papers in European Economic Studies.

Chirinko, R.S. (1993) Business fixed investment spending: modeling strategies, empirical results, and policy implications. *Journal of Economic Literature* **31**, 1875–1911.

Chow, G.C. (1975) *Analysis and Control of Dynamic Economic Systems*. John Wiley and Sons, New York.

Christensen, L.R., Jorgenson, D.W. and Lau, L.J. (1971) Conjugate duality and the transcendental logarithmic production function. *Econometrica* **39**, 225–6.

Christensen, L.R., Jorgenson, D.W. and Lau, L.J. (1973) Transcendental logarithmic production frontiers. *Review of Economics and Statistics* **55**, 28–45.

Church, K.B., Mitchell, P.N., Smith, P.N. and Wallis, R.F. (1995) Comparative properties of models of the UK economy. *National Institute Economic Review* **153**, August.

Cobb, C.W. and Douglas, P.H. (1928) A theory of production. *American Economic Review* **18**, 139–65.

Confederation of British Industry (1988) *The Competitive Advantage*. Report of the CBI Public Expenditure Task Force, October.

Coulton, B. and Cromb, R. (1994) The UK NAIRU. Government Economic Service Working Paper No. 124, September.

Courakis, A.S. (1988) Modelling portfolio selection. *Economic Journal* **98**, 619–42.

Crowder, M.J. (1976) Maximum likelihood estimation for dependent observations. *Journal of the Royal Statistical Society, Series B* **38** (1), 45–53.

Cumby, R.E., Huizinga, J. and Obstfeld, M. (1983) Two-step two-stage least squares estimation in models with rational expectations. *Journal of Econometrics* **21**, 333–55.

Currie, D.A. and Levine, P. (1985) Simple macroeconomic policy rules in an open economy. *The Economic Journal* **85**, 60–70.

Currie, D.A. and Hall, S.G. (1989) A stock-flow model of the determination of the UK effective exchange rate. In R. Macdonald, and M.P. Taylor (eds), *Exchange Rates and Open Economy Macroeconomics*. Basil Blackwell, Oxford.

Currie, D.A. and Hall, S.G. (1993) Consistent expectations and learning in large scale macroeconometric models. In S. Honkapohja and M. Ingberg (eds), *Macroeconomic Modelling and Policy Implications*. North-Holland, Amsterdam.

Cuthbertson, K. (1991) The encompassing implications of feedforward versus feedback mechanisms: a reply to Hendry. *Oxford Economic Papers* **43**, 344–50.

Cuthbertson, K., Hall, S.G. and Taylor, M.P. (1991) *Applied Econometric Techniques*. Philip Allen, London.

Darby, J. and Ireland, J. (1993) Consumption, forward looking behaviour and financial deregulation. University of Strathclyde, presented to ESRC Macroeconomic Modelling Bureau Conference, Warwick, July.

Darby, J. and Wren-Lewis, S. (1993) Is there a cointegrating vector for UK wages? *Journal of Economic Studies* **20** (1/2).

Davidson, J. and Hall, S.G. (1991) Cointegration in recursive systems. *Economic Journal* **101**, (405), 239–52.

Davidson, J., Hendry, D.F., Srba, F. and Yeo, S. (1978) Econometric modelling of the aggregate time series relationship between consumers expenditure and income in the United Kingdom. *Economic Journal* **88**, 661-92.

Davidson, R. and MacKinnon, J.G. (1993) *Estimation and Inference in Econometrics.* Oxford University Press, New York.

Deaton, A.S. (1987) Life-cycle models of consumption: is the evidence consistent with the theory? In T.F. Bewley (ed.), *Advances in Econometrics, Fifth World Congress*, pp. 121-48, Vol. 2. Cambridge University Press, Cambridge and New York.

DeCanio, S.J. (1979) Rational expectations and learning from experience. *Quarterly Journal of Economics* **93**, 47-57.

Denny, M. and Fuss, M. (1977) The use of approximation analysis to test for separability and the existence of consistent aggregates. *American Economic Review* **67**, 404-17.

Dickey, D.A. and Fuller, W.A. (1981) Likelihood ratio tests for autoregressive time series with a unit root. *Econometrica* **49**, 1057-72.

Dickey, D.A. and Pantula, S.G. (1987) Determining the order of differencing in autoregressive processes. *Journal of Business and Economic Statistics* **5**, (4), 455-61.

Diewert, W.E. (1971) An application of the Shepherd duality theorem: a Generalized Leontief production function. *Journal of Political Economy* **79**, 481-507.

Diewert, W.E. (1974) Applications of duality theory. In M.D. Intriligator and D.A. Kendrick (eds), *Frontiers of Quantitative Economics*, Vol. 2. North-Holland, Amsterdam.

Diewert, W.E. and Morrison, C.J. (1988) Export supply and import demand functions: a production approach. In R.C. Feenstra (ed.), *Empirical Methods in International Trade.* MIT Press, Cambridge, MA.

Diewert, W.E. and Wales, T.J. (1987) Flexible functional forms and global curvature conditions. *Econometrica* **55**, 43-68.

Diewert, W.E. and Wales, T.J. (1988) Normalized quadratic systems of consumer demand systems. *Journal of Business and Economic Statistics* **6**, 303-12.

Dinenis, E. and Holly, S. (1989) Trade, prices, and supply in the UK economy. Centre for Economic Forecasting Discussion Paper, No. 9.

Dinenis, E., Holly, S., Levine, P. and Smith, P. (1989) The London Business School model of the UK economy. *Economic Modelling* **6** (3).

Dixit, A.K. and Stiglitz, J. (1977) Monopolistic competition and optimum product variety. *American Economic Review* **67**, 297-308.

Douglas, P.H. (1948) Are there laws of production? *American Economic Review* **38**, 1-41.

Downs, A. (1956) *An Economic Theory of Democracy.* Harper & Row, New York.

Downs, A. (1967) *Inside Bureaucracy.* Little, Brown & Co, Boston.

Dunne, J.P. and Smith, R.P. (1984) The economic consequences of reduced military expenditure. *Cambridge Journal of Economics*, **8** (3), 297-310.

Dunne, J.P. and Smith, R.P. (1990) Military expenditure and unemployment in the OECD. *Defence Economics* **1** (1), 57-74.

Edison, H., Miller, M. and Williamson, J. (1988) On evaluating and extending the target zone proposal. *Journal of Policy Modelling* **9**, 199-224.

Eisner, R. (1965) Realization of investment anticipations. In J.S. Duesenberry, G. Fromm, L.R. Klein, and E. Kuh, (eds), *The Brookings Quarterly Model of the United States.* Rand McNally and North-Holland, Chicago.

Engle, R.F. (1982) Autoregressive conditional heteroskedasticity with estimates of the variance of UK inflation. *Econometrica* **55** (4), 987-1008.

Engle, R.F. and Granger, C.W.J. (1987) Co-integration and error correction representations, estimation and testing. *Econometrica* **55**, 251-76.

Engle, R.F. and Granger, C.W.J. (1991) *Long Run Economic Relationships.* Oxford University Press, Oxford.

Engle, R.F., Lilien, D. and Robins, R. (1987) Estimating time varying risk premia in the term structure: the ARCH-M model. *Econometrica* **55** (2), 391–407.

Ermini, L. and Granger, C.W.J. (1993) Some generalizations on the algebra of I(1) processes. *Journal of Econometrics* **58**, 369–84.

Evans, G.W. (1983) The stability of rational expectations in macroeconomic models. In R. Frydman and E.S. Phelps (eds), *Individual Forecasting and Aggregate Outcomes*. Cambridge University Press, Cambridge.

Evans, G.W. (1985) Expectational stability and the multiple equilibria problem in RE models. *Quarterly Journal of Economics* **100**, 1217–33.

Evans, G.W. (1986) Selection criteria for models with non-uniqueness. *Journal of Monetary Economics* **18**, 147–57

Evans, G.W. (1989) The fragility of sunspots and bubbles. *Journal of Monetary Economics* **23**, 297–317.

Evans, G.W. and Honkapohja, S. (1990) Learning, convergence and stability with multiple rational expectations equilibria. STICERD Discussion Paper TE/90/212, LSE.

Evans, G.W. and Honkapohja, S. (1992a) On the robustness of bubbles in linear RE models. *International Economic Review* **33**, 1–14.

Evans, G.W. and Honkapohja, S. (1992b) Local convergence of recursive learning to steady states and cycles in stochastic nonlinear models. STICERD Discussion Paper TE/92/236, LSE.

Evans, G.W. and Honkapohja, S. (1992c) On the local stability of sunspot equilibria under adaptive learning rules. STICERD Discussion Paper TE/92/236, LSE. Forthcoming in *Journal of Economic Theory*.

Evans, G.W. and Honkapohja, S. (1993a) Adaptive forecasts, hysteresis, and endogenous fluctuations. *Federal Reserve Bank of San Francisco Economic Review* **1**, 3–13.

Evans, G.W. and Honkapohja, S. (1993b) Learning and economic fluctuations: using fiscal policy to steer expectations. *European Economic Review* **37**, 595–602.

Evans, G.W. and Honkapohja, S. (1994) Adaptive learning and expectational stability: an introduction. In A. Kirman and M. Salmon (eds), *Learning and Rationality in Economics*. Basil Blackwell, Oxford.

Fair, R.C. (1979) An analysis of a macro-econometric model with rational expectations in the bond and stock markets. *American Economic Review* **69**, 539–52.

Fair, R.C. (1984) *Specification, Estimation and Analysis of Macroeconometric Models*. Harvard University Press, Harvard.

Favero, C. and Hendry, D.F. (1992) Testing the Lucas critique, a review. *Econometric Reviews* **11**, 265–306.

Feige, E.L. and Pearce, D. (1976) Economically rational expectations: are innovations in the rate of inflation independent of innovations in measures of monetary and fiscal policy? *Journal of Political Economy* **84**, 499–522.

Findlay, D.W. and Parker, D. (1992) Military spending and interest rates. *Defence Economics* **3**, 195–210.

Fisher, P.G. (1990) Simulation and control techniques for nonlinear rational expectations. ESRC Macroeconomic Modelling Bureau, mimeo.

Fisher P.G. and Hughes-Hallett, A.J. (1988) An efficient strategy for solving linear and non-linear rational expectations models. *Journal of Economic Dynamics and Control* **12**, 635–57.

Fisher, P.G., Holly, S. and Hughes-Hallett, A.J. (1985) Efficient solution techniques for dynamic nonlinear rational expectations models. *Journal of Economic Dynamics and Control* **10**, 139–45.

Fisher, P.G., Tanner, S.K., Turner, D.S. and Wallis, K.F. (1991) Econometric evaluation of the exchange rate in models of the UK economy. *Economic Journal* **100** (403), 1230–44.

Fisher, P.G., Tanner, S.K., Turner, D.S., Wallis, K.F. and Whitley, J.D. (1988) Comparative properties of models of the UK economy. *National Institute Economic Review* **125**, 69–88.

Fisher, P.G., Tanner, S.K., Turner, D.S., Wallis, K.F. and Whitley, J.D. (1989) Comparative properties of models of the UK economy. *National Economic Review* **129**, 69–88.

Flemming, J.S. (1976) *Inflation*. Oxford University Press, Oxford.

Friedman, B.M. (1975) Rational expectations are really adaptive after all. Howard Institute of Economic Research Discussion Paper No. 430.

Friedman, M. (1968) The role of monetary policy. *American Economic Review* **53**, 381–84.

Frydman, R. (1982) Towards an understanding of market processes, individual expectations: learning and convergence to rational expectations equilibrium. *American Economic Review* **72**, 652–68.

Fuhrer, J.C. and Hooker, M.A. (1993) Learning about monetary regime shifts in an overlapping wage contract model. *Journal of Economic Dynamic and Control* **17**, 531–53.

Fuss, M., McFadden, D. and Mundlak, Y. (1978) Survey of functional forms in economic analysis of production In M. Fuss and D. McFadden, *Production Economics: A Dual Approach to Theory and Applications*, Vol. 1, pp. 219–68.

Gallant, A.R. (1987) *Nonlinear Statistical Models*. John Wiley and Sons, New York.

Garratt, A. and Hall, S.G. (1992) Model consistent learning: the Sterling Deutschemark rate in the London Business School model. LBS Discussion Paper No. 92–02.

Garratt, A. and Hall, S.G. (1993) A proposed framework for monetary policy. London Business School, Centre for Economic Forecasting, Discussion Paper, No. 9–93.

Gawthrop, P. and Vines, D. (1989) The robustness of simple policy rules compared with optimal policy rules: and example. In *Dynamic Modelling and Control of National Economies*, Vol. 2 International Federation of Automatic Control.

Ghysels, E. and Hall, A.D. (1990) A test for the structural stability of Euler condition parameters estimated via the Generalized Method of Moments estimator. *International Economic Review* **31**, 355–64.

Gonzalo, J. (1994) Five alternative methods of estimating long-run equilibrium relationships. *Journal of Econometrics* **60**, 203–33.

Gorman, W.M. (1959) Separable utility and aggregation. *Econometrica* **27**, 469–81.

Granger, C.W.J. (1983) Co-integrated variables and error correction models. UCSD Discussion paper.

Granger, C.W.J. (1986) Developments in the study of cointegrated economic variables. *Oxford Bulletin of Economics and Statistics* **48**, 213–28.

Granger, C.W.J. (1993) Modelling non-linear relationships between long-memory variables. Paper given at Econometric Society European Meeting, Uppsala, August.

Granger, C.W.J. and Hallman, J. (1988) The algebra of I(1). Finance and Economics Discussion Series, Division of Research and Statistics, Federal Reserve Board.

Granger, C.W.J. and Hallman, J. (1991) Nonlinear transformations of integrated time series. *Journal of Time Series* **12**, 207–24.

Granger, C.W.J. and Newbold, P. (1976) Forecasting transformed series. *Journal of the Royal Statistical Society, Series B* **38**, 189–203.

Granger, C.W.J. and Terasvirta, T. (1993) *Modelling Nonlinear Economic Relationships*. Oxford University Press, Oxford.

Granger, C.W.J. and Weiss, A.A. (1983) Time series analysis of error correcting models. In S. Karlin, T. Amemiya and L.A. Goodman, (eds), *Studies in Econometrics, Time Series and Multivariate Statistics*. Academic Press, New York.

Gregory, A.W., Pagan, A.R. and Smith, G.W. (1993) Estimating linear quadratic models with integrated processes. In P.C.B. Phillips (ed.), *Models, Methods, and Applications of Econometrics: Essays in Honour of A.R. Bergstrom* Blackwell, Cambridge, MA.

Griliches, Z. and Ringstad, V. (1971) *Economies of Scale and the Form of the Production Function*, North-Holland, Amsterdam.

Grinols, E.L. (1988) Comment on export supply and import demand functions. In R.C. Feenstra (ed.), *Empirical Methods in International Trade*. MIT Press, Cambridge, MA.

Grunberg, E. and Modigliani, F. (1954) The predictability of social events. *Journal of Political Economy* **62**, 465-78.

Gurney, A. (1990) Fiscal policy simulations using forward-looking exchange rates in GEM. *National Institute Economic Review* **131**, 47-50.

Gurney, A., Henry, S.G.B. and Pesaran, B. (1989) The exchange rate and external trade. In A. Britton (ed.), *Policy Making With Macroeconomic Models*. Gower, Aldershot.

Hacche, G. and Townsend, J. (1981) Exchange rates and monetary policy, modelling Sterling's effective exchange rate 1972-1980. *Oxford Economic Papers* **33**, 201-47.

Haldane, A. (1995) Inflation targets. *Bank of England Quarterly Bulletin* **35** (3), 250-59.

Hall, R.E. (1978) Stochastic implications of the life cycle-permanent income hypothesis: theory and evidence. *Journal of Political Economy* **86**, 971-87.

Hall, R.E. and Mishkin, F.S. (1982) The sensitivity of consumption to transitory income: estimates from panel data on households. *Econometrica* **50**, 461-81.

Hall, S.G. (1985) On the solution of large economic models with rational expectations. *Bulletin of Economic Research* **37**, 157-61.

Hall, S.G. (1986) An application of the Granger and Engle two-step estimation procedure to United Kingdom aggregate wage data. *Oxford Bulletin of Economics and Statistics* **48** (3), 229-40.

Hall, S.G. (1986b) An investigation of time inconsistency and optimal policy formulation in the presence of rational expectations. *Journal of Economic Dynamics and Control* **10**, 323-26.

Hall, S.G. (1987) A forward looking model of the exchange rate. *Journal of Applied Econometrics* **2**, 47-60.

Hall, S.G. (1988) Rationality and Siegel's paradox: the importance of coherency in expectations. *Applied Economics* **20** (11), 1533-40.

Hall, S.G. (1992) Modelling the Sterling effective exchange rate using expectations and learning. The Manchester School.

Hall, S.G. and Brooks, S.J. (1985) The use of prior regressions in the estimation of error correction models. *Economic Letters* **20**, 33-7.

Hall, S.G. and Garratt, A. (1992a) Model consistent learning: the Sterling Deutschmark rate in the London Business School model. LBS-CEF Discussion Paper No. 92-02.

Hall, S.G. and Garratt, A. (1992b) Expectations and learning in economic models. *Economic Outlook* **16** (5), 52-3.

Hall, S.G. and Garratt, A. (1995) Model consistent learning: The Sterling Deutschmark rate in the London Business School model. *Economic Modelling* **12**, 87-96.

Hall, S.G. and Henry, S.G.B. (1985) Rational expectations in an econometric model. NIESR Model 8. *National Institute Economic Review* **114**, 58-68.

Hall, S.G. and Henry, S.G.B. (1986) A dynamic econometric model of the UK with rational expectations. *Journal of Economic Dynamics and Control* **10**, 219-33.

Hall, S.G. and Henry, S.G.B. (1988) *Macroeconomic Modelling*. North-Holland, Amsterdam.

Hall, S.G. and Stephenson, M. (1989) Optimal control of stochastic non-linear models. In S.G.B. Henry and K. Patterson (eds), *Economic Modelling at the Bank of England*. Chapman and Hall, London.

Hall, S.G. and Symanski (1994) Modifying the rational expectations assumption in a large world model. CEF Discussion Paper No. 10-94, London Business School, London.

Hall, S.G., Cuthbertson, K. and Taylor, M.P. (1992) *Applied Econometric Techniques*. University of Michigan Press, Ann Arbor.

Hall, S.G., Henry, S.G.B. and Wren-Lewis, S. (1986) Manufacturing stocks and forward-looking expectations in the UK. *Economica* **53**, 447–65.

Hall, S.G., Urga, G. and Whitley, J. (1995) Structural change and economic behaviour: the case of UK exports. D.P. XX–95, Centre for Economic Forecasting, London Business School, November.

Hamilton, J.D. (1994) *Time Series Analysis*. Princeton University Press, Princeton.

Hanoch, G. (1975) Production and demand models with direct or indirect implicit additivity. *Econometrica* **43** (3), 395–420.

Hansen, B.E. (1992) Tests for parameter instability in regressions with I(1) variables. *Journal of Business and Economic Statistics* **10**, 321–35.

Hansen, L.P. (1982) Large sample properties of generalized method of moments estimators. *Econometrica* **50**, 1029–54.

Hansen, L.P. (1985) A method for calculating bounds on the asymptotic covariance matrices of generalized method of moments estimators. *Journal of Econometrics* **30**, 203–38.

Hansen, L.P. and Sargent, T.J. (1980) Formulating and estimating dynamic linear rational expectations models. *Journal of Economic Dynamics and Control* **2**, 7–46.

Harvey, A.C. (1981) *The Econometric Analysis of Time Series*. Philip Allan, Deddington, Oxfordshire.

Harvey, A.C. (1987) Applications of the Kalman Filter in econometrics. In T.F. Bewley (ed.), *Advances in Econometrics: Fifth World Congress*, Vol. 1. Econometric Society Monograph No. 13. Cambridge University Press, Cambridge.

Hatanaka, M. (1975) On the global identification of the dynamic simultaneous equation model with stationary disturbances. *International Economic Review* **16**, 545–54.

Hayashi, F. (1982a) The permanent income hypothesis: estimation and testing by instrumental variables. *Journal of Political Economy* **90**, 895–916.

Hayashi, F. (1982) Tobin's marginal Q and average Q: a neoclassical interpretation. *Econometrica* **40** (1), 213–24.

Hayashi, F. and Sims, C.W. (1983) Nearly efficient estimation of time series models with predetermined, but not exogenous instruments. *Econometrica* **51**, 783–98.

Heady, E.O. and Dillon, J.L. (1961) *Agricultural Production Functions*. Iowa State University Press, Ames, IA.

Helliwell, J., Sturm, P. Jarrett, P. and Salou, G. (1985) Aggregate supply in Interlink: model specification and empirical results. Working Paper 26, OECD, Paris.

Hendry, D.F. (1988) The encompassing implications of feedback versus feedforward mechanisms in econometrics. *Oxford Economic Papers* **40**, 132–49.

Hendry, D.F. and Mizon, G.E. (1993) Evaluating dynamic econometric models by encompassing the VAR. In P.C.B Phillips (ed.), *Models, Methods and Applications of Econometrics*, Basil Blackwell, Oxford.

Hendry, D.F. and von Ungern-Sternberg, T. (1981) Liquidity and inflation effects on consumers' expenditure. In A.S. Deaton (ed.), *Essays in Theory and Measurement of Consumers' Behaviour*, 237–60. Cambridge University Press, Cambridge.

Hendry, D.F., Pagan, A.R. and Sargan, J.D. (1984) Dynamic specification. In Z. Griliches and M.D. Intriligator (eds), *Handbook of Econometrics*. North-Holland, Amsterdam.

Henry, S.G.B and Wren-Lewis, S. (1984) The aggregate labour market in the UK: some experiments with rational expectations models. In P. Malgrange and P. Meut (eds), *Contemporary Macroeconomic Modelling*. Basil Blackwell, Oxford.

H.M. Treasury (1993) *Financial Statement and Budget Report 1994–95*. HMSO, London.

Holly, S. and Corker, R. (1984) Optimal feedback and feedforward stabilisation of exchange rates, money, prices and output under rational expectations. In A.J. Hughes Hallett (ed.) *Applied Decision Analysis and Economic Behaviour*. Martinus Nijhoff, Dordrecht.

Holly, S. and Smith, P. (1989) Interrelated factor demands for manufacturing. *European Economic Review* **33**, 111-26.

Holly, S. and Wade, K. (1991) U.K. exports and manufactures: the role of supply side factors. *Scottish Journal of Political Economy* **38**, 1-18.

Holly, S. and Zarrop, M.B. (1979) Calculating optimal economic policies when expectations are rational. *European Economic Review* **20**, 23-40.

Holly, S. and Zarrop, M.B. (1983) Calculating optimal economic policies when expectations are rational. *European Economic Review* **20**, 23-40.

Houthakker, H.S. (1965) Self-dual preferences. *Econometrica* **33**, 797-801.

Jenkinson, T.J. (1988) The NAIRU: Statistical fact or theoretical straitjacket? In R. Cross (ed.), *Unemployment, Hysteresis and the National Rate Hypothesis*. Basil Blackwell, Oxford.

Johansen, S. (1988) Statistical analysis of cointegrating vectors. *Journal of Economic Dynamics and Control* **12**, 231-54.

Johansen, S. (1991) Estimation and hypothesis testing of cointegration vectors in gaussian vector autoregressive models. *Econometrica* **59**, 1551-80.

Johansen, S. (1992) Identifying restrictions of linear equations. Preprint, Institute of Mathematical Statistics, University of Copenhagen.

Johansen, S. (1993) Identifying restrictions of linear equations. Preprint, Institute of Mathematical Statistics.

Johansen, S. and Juselius, K. (1990) Maximum likelihood estimation and inference on cointegration. *Oxford Bulletin of Economics and Statistics* **54**, 225-55.

Jones, R.W. (1965) The structure of simple general equilibrium models. *Journal of Political Economy* **73**, 557-72.

Jorgenson, D.W. (1986) Econometric methods for modelling producer behaviour. In Z. Griliches and M.D. Intriligator (eds), *Handbook of Econometrics*, Vol. 3. North-Holland, Amsterdam.

Jorgenson, D.W. and Fraumeni, B.M. (1981) Relative prices and technical change. In E.R. Berndt and B.C. Field (eds), *Modelling and Measuring Natural Resource Substitution*. MIT Press, Cambridge, MA.

Jorgenson, D.W., Gollop, F.M. and Fraumeni, B.M. (1987) *Productivity and US Economic Growth*. Harvard University Press, Cambridge, MA.

Joyce, M.A.S. (1990) The determination of average earnings in Great Britain. Bank of England Discussion Paper, December, No. 53.

Katona, G. (1951) *Psychological Analysis of Economic Behaviour*. McGraw-Hill, New York.

Katona, G. (1958) Business expectations in the framework of psychological economics (towards a theory of expectations). In M.J. Bowman (ed.), *Expectations, Uncertainty and Business Behaviour*. Social Science Research Council, New York.

Keating, G. (1985) The financial sector of the London Business School model. In D. Currie (ed.), *Advances in Monetary Economics*. Croom Helm, London.

Keynes, J.M. (1971, first published 1919) The economic consequences of the peace. *Collected Writings of J.M. Keynes*, Vol. II. Macmillan, London.

Kiviet, J.F. and Phillips, G.D.A. (1992) Exact similar tests for unit roots and cointegration. *Oxford Bulletin of Economics and Statistics* **54**, 349-68.

Klein, L.R. (1950) *Economic Fluctuations in the United States, 1921-1941*. John Wiley and Sons, New York.

Kmenta, J. (1967) On estimation of the CES production function. *International Economic Review* **8**, 180-93 (with discussion).

Kocherlakota, N.R. (1990) On tests of the representative consumer asset pricing models. *Journal of Monetary Economics* **26**, 285-304.

Kohli, U. (1978) A GNP function and the derived demand for imports and supply of exports. *Canadian Journal of Economics* **11**, 167–82.

Kohli, U. (1990) Price and quantity elasticities in US foreign trade. *Economics Letters* **33**, 277–81.

Kohli, U. (1991) *Technology, Duality, and Foreign Trade*. Harvester, London.

Kohli, U. (1993) A symmetric normalized quadratic GNP function and the US demand for imports and supply of exports. *International Economic Review* **34**, 243–55.

Kydland, F.E. and Prescott, E.C. (1977) Rules rather than discretion: the inconsistency of optimal plans. *Journal of Political Economy* **85**, 473–91.

Lahti, A. and Viren, M. (1989) The Finnish rational expectations QMED model: estimation, dynamic properties and policy results. Bank of Finland Discussion Paper No. 23/89.

Landesmann, M. and Snell, A. (1989) The consequences of Mrs Thatcher for U.K. manufacturing exports. *Economic Journal* **99**, 1–27.

Lau, L.J. (1974) Applications of duality theory: comments. In M.D. Intriligator and D.A. Kendrick (eds). *Frontiers of Quantitative Economics*, Vol. 2. North-Holland, Amsterdam.

Lau, L.J. (1978) Testing and imposing monotonicity, convexity, and quasi-convexity constraints. In M. Fuss and D. McFadden (eds), *Production Economics: A Dual Approach to Theory and Application*, Vol. 1, pp. 409–53. North-Holland, Amsterdam.

Lau, L.J. (1986) Functional forms in econometric model building. In Z. Griliches and M.D. Intriligator (eds), *Handbook of Econometrics*, Vol. III. Elsevier, Amsterdam.

Lau, L.J. (1969) Duality and the structure of utility functions. *Journal of Economic Theory* **1** (4), 374–96.

Layard, R. and Nickell, S. (1985) Unemployment, real wages and aggregate demand in Europe, Japan and the United States. *Carnegie Rochester Conference Series on Public Policy* **23**, 143–202.

Layard, R. and Nickell, S.J. (1986) Unemployment in Britain. *Economica* **53**, S121–69.

Layard, R., Nickell, S.J. and Jackman, R. (1991) *Unemployment: Macroeconomic Performance and the Labour Market*. Oxford University Press, Oxford.

Leiderman, L. and Svensson, L.E.O. (1995) *Inflation Targets*. Centre for Economic Policy Research, London.

Leontief, W. (1965) The economic impact — industrial and regional — of an arms cut. *Review of Economics and Statistics* **3**, 48.

LeRoy, S.F. (1989) Efficient capital markets and martingales. *Journal of Economic Literature* **27** (4), 1583–1621.

Lindbeck, A. and Snower, D.J. (1989) *The Insider–Outsider Theory of Employment and Unemployment*. MIT Press, Cambridge, MA.

Lipton, D., Poterba, J., Sachs, J. and Summers, L. (1982) Multiple shooting in rational expectations models. *Econometrica* **50**, 1329–33.

Litterman, R. (1986) Forecasting with Bayesian vector autoregressions — five years of experience. *Journal of Business and Economic Statistics* **4** (1), 25–38.

Ljung, L. (1977) Analysis of recursive stochastic algorithms. *IEEE Transactions of Automatic Control* **AC-22**, 551–7.

Ljung, L. and Söderström, T. (1983) *The Theory and Practice of Recursive Identification*. MIT Press, Boston, MA.

London Business School Quarterly Econometric Model of the U.K. Economy, Centre for Economic Forecasting, February 1995.

Lucas, R.E., Jr (1972a) Econometric testing of the natural rate hypothesis. In O. Eckstein (ed.), *Econometrics of Price Determination*. Federal Reserve System, Board of Governors, Washington DC.

Lucas, R.E., Jr (1972b) Expectations and the neutrality of money. *Journal of Economic Theory* **4**, 103–24.

Lucas, R.E., Jr (1973) Some international evidence on output inflation trade-offs. *American Economic Review* **65**, 326–34.

Lucas, R.E., Jr (1975) An equilibrium model of the business cycle. *Journal of Political Economy* **83**, 1113–44.

Lucas, R.E., Jr (1976) Econometric policy evaluation: a critique. In K. Bruner and A.H. Meltzer (eds), *The Phillips Curve and Labour Markets.* North-Holland, Amsterdam.

Lucas, R.E., Jr and Rapping, L. (1969) Real wages, employment and inflation. *Journal of Political Economy* **77**, 721–54.

Lynde, C. and Richmond, J. (1993) Public capital and long-run costs in UK manufacturing. *Economic Journal* **103**, 880–93.

Mabey, N. and Nixon, J. (1995) Are environmental taxes a free lunch?: Issues in modelling the macroeconomic effects of carbon taxes. London Business School, Centre for Economic Forecasting Discussion Paper, forthcoming.

Machin, S. (1994) Changes in the relative demand for skills in the UK labour market. In A. Booth and D. Snower (eds), *The Skills Gap and Economic Activity*, forthcoming.

Marcet, A. and Sargent, T.J. (1988) The fate of systems with adaptive expectations. *American Economic Review* 168–71.

Marcet, A. and Sargent, T.J. (1989a) Convergence of least-squares learning in environment with hidden state variables and private information. *Journal of Political Economy* **97** (6), 1306–22.

Marcet, A. and Sargent, T.J. (1989b) Convergence of least squares learning mechanisms in self referential linear stochastic models. *Journal of Economic Theory* **48**, 337–68.

Marcet, A. and Sargent, T.J. (1989c) Least squares learning and the dynamics of hyperinflation. In W.A. Barnett, J. Geweke and K. Shell (eds), *Economic Complexity, Chaos, Sunspots, Bubbles and Nonlinearity.* Cambridge University Press, Cambridge.

Masson, P.R., Symanski, S., Haas, R. and Dooley, M. (1988) Multimod: a multi region econometric model. Working Paper No. 88/23, IMF, Washington DC.

McCallum, B.T. (1988) Robustness properties of a rule for monetary policy. *Carnegie Rochester Conference Series* **29**, 173–202.

McFadden, D. (1963) Constant elasticity of substitution production functions. *Review of Economic Studies* **10**, 73–83.

McFadden, D. (1978) The general linear profit function. In M. Fuss and D. McFadden (eds), *Production Economics: A Dual Approach to Theory and Application*, Vol. 1, pp. 269–86. North-Holland, Amsterdam.

McKibbin, W.J. (1994) Dynamic adjustment to regional integration: Europe 1992 and NAFTA. *Journal of the Japanese and International Economies*, **December**.

McKibbin, W.J. and Sachs, J. (1991) *Global Linkages: Macroeconomic Interdependence and Cooperation in the World Economy.* The Brooking Institute, Washington, DC.

Miles, D.K. (1992) Housing markets, consumption and financial liberalisation in the major economies. *European Economic Review* **36**, 1093–1136.

Minford, A.P.L., Marwaha, S., Mathews, K. and Sprague, A. (1984) The Liverpool macroeconomic model of the United Kingdom. *Economic Modelling* **1**, 24–62.

Morrison, C.J. (1986) Structural models of dynamic factor demands with nonstatic expectations: an empirical assessment of alternative expectations specifications. *International Economic Review* **27** (2), 365–86.

Morrison, C.J. (1988) Quasi-fixed inputs in U.S. and Japanese manufacturing: a generalized Leontief cost function approach. *Review of Economics and Statistics* **70**, 275–87.

Muellbauer, J. (1994) The assessment: consumer expenditure. *Oxford Review of Economic Policy* **10** (2), 1–41.

Muellbauer, J. and Murphy, A. (1991) Measuring financial liberalisation and modelling mortgage stocks and equity withdrawal. Nuffield College, Oxford, mimeo.

Murphy, C.W. (1989) The macroeconomics of a macroeconomic model. Australian National University, mimeo.

Muth, J.F. (1961) Rational expectations and the theory of price movements. *Econometrica* **29** (6).

Nerlove, M. (1958) Adaptive expectations and cobweb phenomena. *Quarterly Journal of Economics* **72**, 227–40.

Nerlove, M. (1963) Returns to scale in electricity supply. In C.F. Christ (ed.), *Measurement in Economics*. Stanford University Press, Stanford, CA.

Newell, A. and Symons, J. (1986) The Phillips curve is a real wage equation. London School of Economics, Centre for Labour Economics Discussion Paper, No. 246, July.

Nickell, S. (1993) Unemployment revisited. *Journal of Economic Studies* **20** (1/2).

Nickell, S. and Bell, B. (1994) Unemployment across the OECD and the collapse in demand for the unskilled. Institute of Economics and Statistics, University of Oxford, mimeo.

Nordhaus, W.D. (1975) The political business cycle. *Review of Economic Studies* **42**.

Osterwald-Lenum, M. (1992) Quantiles of the asymptotic distribution of the maximum likelihood cointegration rank test statistics. *Oxford Bulletin of Economics and Statistics* **54**, 461–72.

Owen, C. and Wren-Lewis, S. (1993) Variety, quality and U.K. manufacturing exports. Discussion Paper 14, ICMM, The University of Strathclyde.

Pagan, A.R. (1984) Model evaluation by variable addition. In D.F. Hendry and K.F. Wallis (eds), *Econometrics and Quantitative Economics*. Basil Blackwell, Oxford.

Peacock, A.T. and Wiseman, J. (1961) *The Growth of Public Expenditures in the United Kingdom*. Oxford University Press, London.

Peeters, M. (1994) *Time-to-Build and Interrelated Investments and Labour Demand Under Rational Expectations*. NWO, Maastricht, Netherlands.

Pencavel, J. (1985) Wages and employment under trade unionism: microeconomic models and macroeconomic applications. *Scandinavian Journal of Economics* **87** (2).

Pesaran, M.H. (1987) *The Limits of Rational Expectations*. Basil Blackwell, Oxford.

Pesaran, M.H. and Evans, R.A. (1984) Inflation, capital gains and UK personal savings: 1951–1981. *Economic Journal* **94**, 237–57.

Pesaran, M.H. and Shin, Y. (1994) Long run structural modelling. DAE Cambridge, mimeo.

Phelps, E.S. (1967) Phillips curves, expectations of inflation and optimal unemployment over time. *Economica* **34** (3), 254–81.

Phelps, E.S. (1976) Money wage dynamics and labour market equilibrium. *Journal of Political Economy* **76** (2), 678–711.

Phelps, E.S. (1994) *Structural Slumps*. Harvard University Press.

Phillips, A.W. (1954) Stabilization policy in a closed economy. *Economic Journal* **64**, 290–323.

Phillips, A.W. (1957) Stabilization policy and the time form of lagged responses. *Economic Journal* **67**, 265–77.

Phillips, P.C.B. (1991) Optimal inference in cointegrated systems. *Econometrica* **59**, 283–306.

Pindyck, R.S. and Rotemberg, J.J. (1983a) Dynamic factor demands and the effects of energy price shocks. *American Economic Review* **73** (5), 1066–79.

Pindyck, R.S. and Rotemberg, J.J. (1983b) Dynamic factor demands under rational expectations, *Scandinavian Journal of Economics* **85** (2), 223–38.

Pollak, R.A., Sickles, R.C. and Wales, T.J. (1984) The CES/Translog: specification and estimation of a new cost function. *Review of Economics and Statistics* **66**, 602–7.

Powell, A.A. and Gruen, F.H.G. (1968) The constant elasticity of transformation frontier and linear supply system. *International Economic Review* **9** (3), 315-28.

Radner, R. (1982) Equilibrium under uncertainty. In K.J. Arrow and M.D. Intriligator (eds), *Handbook of Mathematical Economics*, Vol 2. North - Holland, Amsterdam.

Reimers, H.E. (1991) Comparisons of tests for multivariate cointegration. Discussion Paper No. 58, Christian-Albrechts University, Kiel.

Robertson, D. and Wickens, M. (1994) VAR modelling. In S.G. Hall (ed.), *Applied Economic Forecasting Techniques*. Harvester Wheatsheaf, London.

Rustem, B. (1993) Stochastic and robust control of nonlinear economic systems. *European Journal of Operations Research* **23**, 75-89.

Samuelson, P.A. (1965) Using full duality to show that simultananeously additive direct and indirect utilities implies unitary price elasticity of demand. *Econometrica* **33**, 781-96.

Sargan, S.D. (1971) Production functions. In R. Layard (ed.), *Qualified Man Power and Economic Performance*. Allan Lane, London.

Sargent, T.J. (1973) Rational expectations, the real rate of interest and the natural rate of unemployment. *Brookings Papers on Economic Activity* **2**, 429-72.

Sargent, T.J. (1976) The observational equivalence of natural and unnatural rate theories of unemployment. *Journal of Political Economy* **84** (3), 631-40.

Sargent, T.J. (1976) A classical macroeconomic model of the United States. *Journal of Political Economy* **84**, 207-37.

Sargent, T.J. (1978) Estimation of dynamic labour demand schedules under rational expectations. *Journal of Political Economy* **86**, 1009-44.

Sargent, T.J. (1987) *Macroeconomic Theory*, 2nd edition. Academic Press, Orlando, FL.

Sargent, T.J. (1993) *Bounded Rationality in Macroeconomics*. Oxford University Press, Oxford.

Sargent, T.J. and Wallace, N. (1973) Rational expectations and the dynamics of hyperinflation. *International Economic Review* **14**, 328-50.

Sargent, T.J. and Wallace, N. (1975) Rational expectations, the optimal monetary instrument and the optimal money supply rule. *Journal of Political Economy* **83**, 241-54.

Sargent, T.J. and Wallace, N. (1976) Rational expectations and the theory of economic policy. *Journal of Monetary Economics* **2**, 169-83.

Sato, K. (1967) A two level constant elasticity of substitution production function. *Review of Economic Studies* **34**, 201-18.

Schweppe, F. (1965) Evaluation of likelihood functions for Gaussian signals. *IEEE Transactions on Information Theory* **11** (1), 61-70.

Sedgley, N. and Smith, J. (1994) An analysis of U.K. imports using multivariate cointegration. *Oxford Bulletin of Economics and Statistics* **56** (2), 135-50.

Sefton, J. and Wright, S. (1994) The Phillips curve in empirical macro-models of the world economy. National Institute of Economic and Social Research Discussion Paper, No. 64.

Sentance, A. (1994) Consuming passion. *New Economy* **1** (4), 226-30.

Sentance, A.W.J. and Nixon, J. (1994) Paving the way to tax cuts. *Economic Outlook*, **December**.

Shephard, R.W. (1970) *Theory of Cost and Production Functions*. Princeton University Press, Princeton, NJ.

Sims, C. (1980) Macroeconomics and reality. *Econometrica* **48**, 1-48.

Smith, P.N. and Wallis, K.F. (1994) Policy simulations and long-run sustainability in forward looking macroeconometric models. ESRC Macromodelling Bureau Discussion Paper No. 34, University of Warwick.

Smith, R.J. (1992) Non-nested tests for competing models estimated by Generalized Method of Moments. *Econometrica* **60** (4), 973-80.

Smith, R.P. (1980) Military expenditure and investment. *Journal of Comparative Economics* **4**, 19–32.

Solow, R.M. (1956) The production function and the theory of capital. *Review of Economic Studies* **23**, 101–8.

Stock, J.H. and Watson, M.W. (1989) New indexes of leading and coincident economic indicators. *National Bureau of Economic Research Macroeconomics Annual*, pp. 351–94.

Stock, J.H. and Watson, M.W. (1991) A probability model of coincident economic indicators. In K. Lahiri and G.H. Moore (eds), *Leading Economic Indicators: New Approaches and Forecasting Records*, pp. 63–85. Cambridge University Press, New York.

Strotz, R.H. (1957) The utility tree — a correction and future appraisal. *Econometrica* 27, 482–8.

Tauchen, G. (1986) Statistical properties of generalized method of moments estimators of structural parameters obtained from financial market data. *Journal of Business and Economic Statistics* **4**, 397–416.

Taylor, J.B. (1979) Estimation and control of macroeconomic models with rational expectations. *Econometrica* **47**, 1267–86.

Taylor, J.B. (1985) International coordination in the design of macroeconomic policy rules. *European Economic Review* **28**, 53–82.

Theil, H. (1977) The independent inputs of production. *Econometrica* **45**, 1303–27.

Tinbergen, J. (1937) *An Econometric Approach to Business Cycle Problems*. Hermann et Compagnie, Editeurs, Paris.

Tobin, J. (1959) On the predictive value of consumers' intentions. *Review of Economics and Statistics*, **February**.

Townsend, R.M. (1978) Market anticipation, rational expectation and Bayesian analysis. *International Economic Review* **19**, 481–94.

Townsend, R.M. (1983) Forecasting the forecast of others. *Journal of Political Economy* **91**, 546–88.

Turner, D.S. and Rauffet, S. (1994) The effect of the wedge and productivity on the NAIRU in five major OECD economies. ESRC Macroeconomic Modelling Bureau, Discussion Paper, No. 38.

UNIDIR (1993) *Economic Aspects of Disarmament: Disarmament as an Investment Process*. United Nations Institute for Disarmament Research, New York.

Uzawa, H. (1962) Production functions with constant elasticities of substitution. *Review of Economic Studies* **9**, 291–9.

Vines, D., Maciejowski, J.M. and Meade, J.E. (1983) *Stagflation*, Vol. 2, *Demand Management*. George Allen and Unwin, London.

Virley, S. and Hirst, M. (1995) Public finances and the cycle. HM Treasury Occasional Paper No. 4, September.

Wagner, A. (1890) *Finanzweissenschaft*, 3rd edition. Leipzig.

Wales, T.J. (1977) On the flexibility of functional forms. *Journal of Econometrics* **43**, 183–93.

Wallis, K.F., Fisher, P.G., Longbottom, J.A., Turner, D.S. and Whitley, J.D. (1987) *Models of the UK Economy: A Fourth Review by the ESRC Macroeconomic Modelling Bureau*. Oxford University Press, London.

Walters, A.A. (1971) Consistent expectations, distributed lags and the quantity theory. *Economic Journal* **81**, 273–81.

Weale, M., Blake, A., Christodoulakis, N., Meade, J. and Vines, D. (1989) *Macroeconomic Policy: Inflation, Wealth and the Exchange Rate*. Unwin Hyman, London.

Westaway, P. (1986) Some experiments with simple feedback rules on the Treasury model. *Journal of Economic Dynamics and Control* **10**.

Westaway, P. and Whittaker, R. (1986) Consistent expectations in the Treasury model. Government Economic Services Working Paper No. 87.

Wickens, M.R. (1982) The efficient estimation of econometric models with rational expectations. *Review of Economic Studies* **49**, 55–67.

Wickens, M.R. (1993) Rational expectations and integrated variables. In P.C.B. Phillips (ed.), *Models, Methods, and Applications of Econometrics: Essays in Honour of A.R. Bergstrom* Blackwells, Cambridge, MA.

Wickens, M.R. and Breusch, T.S. (1988) Dynamic specification, the long run, and the estimation of transformed regression models. *Economic Journal* **98**, 189–205.

Wiley, D.E., Schmidt, W.H. and Bramble, W.J. (1973) Studies of a class of covariance structure models. *Journal of American Statistical Association* **68**, 317–23.

Willenbockel, D. (1994) *Applied General Economic Modelling; Imperfect Competition and European Integration.* John Wiley and Sons, Chichester.

Wood, A. (1994) *North–South Trade, Employment and Inequality: Changing Fortunes in a Skill Driven World.* Clarendon Press, Oxford.

Wood, G.E. (1994) A time to act or to bide your time? *Economic Affairs* **15** (1).

Woodford, M. (1990) Learning to believe in sunspots. *Econometrica* **58**, 277–308.

Wren-Lewis, S. (1988) Supply, liquidity and credit: a new version of the Institute's domestic macroeconometric model. *National Institute Economic Review* **128**.

Wren-Lewis, S. (1992a) Between the short run and the long run: vintages and the NAIRU. In C. Hargreaves (ed.), *Macroeconomic Modelling of the Long Run.* Edward Elgar, Aldershot.

Wren-Lewis, S. (1992b) Between the medium and the long run: vintages and the NAIRU. In C. Hargreaves (ed.), *Macroeconomic Modelling of the Long Run.* Edward Elgar, Aldershot.

Young, G. (1988) The small supply model. H.M. Treasury Working Paper.

Index

Index compiled by Geoffrey Jones